Reading Programs for Young Adults

Reading Programs for Young Adults

Complete Plans for 50
Theme-Related Units
for Public, Middle School
and High School Libraries

MARTHA SEIF SIMPSON

McFarland & Company, Inc., Publishers
Jefferson, North Carolina, and London

Cover by Jackie Urbanovic.

British Library Cataloguing-in-Publication data are available

Library of Congress Cataloguing-in-Publication Data

Simpson, Martha Seif, 1954–
    Reading programs for young adults : complete plans for 50 theme-
related units for public, middle school and high school libraries /
Martha Seif Simpson.
      p. cm.
    Includes bibliographical references (p.) and index.
    ISBN 0-7864-0357-8 (sewn softcover : 50# alkaline paper) ∞
    1. Young adults' libraries—Activity programs—United States.
2. Middle school libraries—Activity programs—United States.
3. High school libraries—Activity programs—United States.
4. Teenagers—United States—Books and reading.   5. Reading
promotion—United States. I. Title.
Z718.5.S56 1997
027.62'6—dc21   97-1499
                                          CIP

Manufactured in the United States of America

*McFarland & Company, Inc., Publishers
  Box 611, Jefferson, North Carolina 28640*

For my brother, Joel Seif;
his wife, Joan; and their sons,
Mark, Philip, and Jeremy

Table of Contents

Acknowledgments

I would like to thank the following librarians who reviewed sample units and offered comments: Debby Adams, Anne Campbell, Doina C. Lucas, Amy Tranzillo, Bobbie Borne, Kim Flynn, Mary M. Tiebout, Bonnie Lalor, Jane Ash, Laurie Averill.

Thanks also to Linda Waddle at YALSA for providing information regarding YA services in public libraries.

And a very special thank you to Barbara Blosveren, Assistant Director Youth Services who works with me at Stratford Library Association in Stratford, Connecticut, for her help and encouragement. Barbara established our Young Adult Department in 1990, and it has since achieved national recognition, including the ECONO-CLAD Reading or Literature Program Award in 1994. In 1997, the Young Adult Department's Youth Review Board was selected by YALSA as a winner in the Excellence in Library Service to Young Adults Competition. Barbara and the rest of the Young Adult staff have proven that teens really can connect with libraries, if they are only given the chance.

Introduction

What are young adults reading for fun these days? Unfortunately, not much. Aside from horror novels and titles by a few popular authors, many in the 12–18 age group don't spend much time with books. There are several possible reasons for this. Maybe they prefer to do other things—participate in sports, play video games, hang out with friends—all of which seem more important than reading. Maybe they think they do enough reading for school. Or perhaps it's just not "cool" to be seen reading a book. Or, just maybe, the fault for the decline of reading among young adults lies with us—the public and school librarians who have failed to reach out to this important but neglected age group.

Compare library services for children to those provided for young adults. Librarians and teachers spend a lot of energy creating displays, contests, story hours, read-alongs, and other activities to help young children learn to read, and to encourage them to exercise this skill as much as possible. Most public libraries design elaborate summer reading clubs to ensure that children in the primary grades will maintain their reading habits when school is not in session. For these kids, reading is fun, and libraries are sources of entertainment.

But what do we do for the young people who have outgrown the children's summer reading program? In many libraries, the sad truth is that we do very little. During the school year, teens are sent to the library to research an assignment or find a book for a report. They learn to associate libraries and reading with work, not enjoyment. And when school is dismissed for the day or let out for the summer, precious few public libraries schedule activities or provide services of any kind for teenagers. According to a recent survey conducted by the National Center for Education Statistics, one in every four patrons who enters a public library is a young adult. Yet only a scant 11 percent of these institutions employ a young adult specialist, and just 30 percent provide training for staff members who deal with the public in serving the needs of teen patrons. A library that goes to great lengths to generate reading enthusiasm among toddlers and grade-schoolers will often do nothing at all for its young adult patrons. In fact, some library employees are openly hostile to teenagers. No wonder many of them don't like to read!

Clearly, we must take steps to rectify this situation. We need to make older students feel welcome in the library, and to give them something to do that will capture their interest; otherwise we may lose them entirely. That is why I have written this book. *Reading Programs for Young Adults* offers ideas for fifty units based on themes that will appeal to teens. Each one contains suggestions for displays, prizes, activities, games, book report forms and activity sheets, plus lists of books, films, magazines and computer software. As with my previous book, *Summer Reading Clubs*, the units can be adapted to suit the needs of your patrons, either in a school or public library setting. Whether your library already has an established YA department or is just beginning to offer services to teens, it can benefit from these programming ideas.

Theme-based reading programs are one way to attract young adults. Other activities proven to boost teen enthusiasm for libraries include book discussion groups and readers' advisory boards, teen volunteer programs and service projects, homework help centers, and the recruitment of young adults to help with the children's summer reading club. Several excellent resources available to Young Adult librarians can provide in-depth information on these and other useful topics. I have listed these titles in this book's bibliography.

As librarians and educators, we know that reading for recreation is just as important as reading for information. There is no reason why the fun should end once a youngster enters middle school. It is my hope that the units described in this book will be used by public, middle school, and high school librarians to develop programming that will draw teens into the library during their free time, encourage them to participate in activities tailored to their interests, and motivate them to read for their own enjoyment. Let's not close the book on the kids who have graduated from the children's reading clubs. Instead, let's offer them even greater incentives to check out the library.

General Guidelines
for Using This Book

The fifty units in *Reading Programs for Young Adults* are based on themes that appeal to teenagers. Each unit is presented in the following order:

1. Introduction—A "grabber" paragraph designed to spark patron interest, this may be reproduced in publicity materials.

2. Display Idea—An attractive book display will focus attention on the reading program. Suggestions are given for theme-related books and media which patrons can borrow from the library. Appropriate props can be used to dress up the display.

3. Sponsorship for Prizes—Give-aways are always an incentive. Try to encourage local businesses, companies and organizations to sponsor all or a part of your program. Ask a movie theater, museum, or other entertainment venue to donate free passes to events that correspond to the reading theme. Stores that sell books, music, or other items may be approached for donations. Be sure to acknowledge your sponsors in your publicity materials.

4. Program Game—The game can be as simple or as elaborate as you wish. You may want to include theme-related trivia on the game board, or add instructions in the spaces (for example, in the *Animal Tales* unit, "If you have a pet dog, advance two spaces"). A touch of humor will also make the game more appealing.

There are a few different ways to use the game as a means of encouraging participation in the program. The game can be posted on a bulletin board, with markers for each person to note his/her progress. Depending on your space, you can set up either a tabletop or a floor model of the game, and patrons can note their places on a record sheet. An alternative is to give each participant a drawing of the game on a sheet of paper to serve as a reading log, and let each one record his or her progress by marking the spaces. Patrons who complete the game may be awarded a prize or admission to a party.

Each game is designed to run on a point system. Points can be awarded for a number of things, and you may want to assign some achievements more points than others. Suggestions for earning points include a) attending a theme-related YA activity; b) participating in another scheduled YA activity or project; c) volunteering to work in the Children's Department or another area of the library; d) reading a required number of pages; e) reading a book and turning in a completed program form; f) turning in a completed activity sheet; or g) correctly answering a weekly trivia question or participating in a scavenger hunt.

5. Program Forms—Samples for four forms are given in each unit. Patrons can complete the forms to earn points in the program game. Most forms require the patron to read a fiction or nonfiction book, which may or may not be related to the unit theme. Some forms ask the patron to review a movie, compare magazine articles, or report on some activity. Use one or more of the suggested forms and adapt them as you see fit. You may want to assign more game points to some forms (for example, ones that require patrons to read a book) than others (such as movie review forms). Set up a box in the library for YAs to drop off their forms. Using the "honor system" will allow teens to feel more grown-up and responsible.

Because of time or staff limitations, you may decide to forego the program game and just use the forms. In that case, you should set a minimum number of books to read or forms to complete in order for a patron to qualify for a prize, party admission, or other reward. Whatever method you choose, make sure you set a realistic goal so that all participants will have a fair chance to complete the program requirements.

6. Program Activities—Ideas for ten theme-related activities are given for each unit. Types of activities include movies, guest speakers or performers, field trips, discussions and debates, arts and crafts projects, job fairs, dance parties, game shows, product demonstrations, cooking classes, outdoor events or projects, volunteer work, fashion shows, creative writing endeavors, model-building projects and talent shows.

Most activities are one-day events, but some may run for the duration of the program. Several, such as the fashion shows, can be sponsored by local retailers or companies that deal in products or services geared to teenagers. You may want to ask patrons to register in advance if space is limited or if you have to purchase materials. It is also a good idea to provide refreshment for every meeting—the promise of free nachos and soda will always boost attendance.

7. Curriculum Tie-ins—General suggestions are given for theme-related activities for English, Science, Social Studies, and Math classes. These can be adapted for various grade levels.

8. Activity Sheet Ideas—Topics are given for word search or crossword puzzles, word scrambles or cryptograms, and matching activities. You can hand out a different activity sheet each week and award game points for completed papers, or teens can just do them for fun. There are several software programs on the market, such as *Puzzle Power* by Centron Software Technologies, that can help you formulate these word puzzles.

Teens may also enjoy taking part in a weekly trivia contest. Pose a theme-related question each week and have patrons submit their written answers. At the end of the week, award a prize to the person whose correct answer is pulled in a random drawing. A weekly trivia contest will also motivate patrons to visit the library often.

Another fun idea is to hold a scavenger hunt. List several trivia questions on a sheet of paper and let teens look for the answers. Prizes can be awarded for participants who correctly answer all the questions. Teens can work in groups or alone. For each of these games, set aside a selection of reference materials in which patrons can look up the answers. This is a great way to teach research skills.

9. Suggested Resources—At the end of each unit is a list of materials that correspond to the program theme. These lists include related nonfiction and fiction reading as well as other media:

Reference and Nonfiction includes YA and adult titles for casual reading or for researching activity sheet, trivia contest, and scavenger hunt questions.

Fiction includes books that have appeared on recommended reading lists for young adults. Both current favorites and classic titles are represented.

Periodicals include magazines, journals, and newsletters. Many teens who resist books will read magazines, so it is worthwhile to subscribe to several popular titles.

Feature-Length Films include commercial as well as made-for-TV releases. The name of the video distributor, original production year, and rating (if applicable) are listed. It is always wise to preview a film before showing it to an audience.

Computer Software includes mostly CD-ROM titles, but a few are available in floppy disk form. These are likely to be very popular with your teen patrons.

Occasionally, other types of resources may appear in the lists. For example, the unit *The Classics Never Die* includes a list of classic literature, and *Raves for Radio Waves* includes sound recordings of popular shows from the Golden Age of Radio.

Some of the books appearing in these lists, especially the novels, are classics that have been reprinted many times. In most cases the resource list cites a recent edition, but many other editions are of course available. Use whatever version is readily available in your library.

Working with young adults is challenging. They can be restless and demanding; they become bored easily; and they are struggling to cope with many changes in their lives. At the very least, a library can provide them a safe haven. But with a bit of effort, we can also stimulate their imaginations, open their eyes to new options and opportunities, and instill in them a love for reading and an appreciation of libraries that may last the rest of their lives.

1
Explore the Ancient World

Millions of years ago, the first primates appeared on Earth. You can learn how these primitive humans evolved when you read books about prehistoric life, archeology, ancient civilizations, evolution, and other subjects that are available in the library. There are also novels and videos that tell stories of how early humans might have lived. You can make some fascinating discoveries when you Explore the Ancient World.

Display Idea

Set up a display of nonfiction books about ancient Earth, including information about early humans, prehistoric animals, evolution, and ancient civilizations, as well as novels set in prehistoric and ancient times. Add related videos and magazines. Pictures and replicas of fossils, primitive art and tools, and models of Earth's first inhabitants and cities can decorate the display.

Sponsorship for Prizes

1. Ask a bookstore to donate fiction and nonfiction about the ancient world.
2. Ask a historical museum to donate free passes or discounts for gift store items.
3. Ask a video rental store to donate certificates for free rentals of movies set in the prehistoric or ancient world.
4. Ask a travel agency or novelty store to donate posters of ancient world scenes, such as Egyptian pyramids.

Program Game

The game board can represent a timeline of the evolution of life on Earth. Starting at several million years B.C., mark off increments of time and label them with the names of life forms that inhabited the Earth at those times. Include animal life, early humans, and ancient civilizations, ending the timeline when you deem appropriate. Patrons can advance an increment along the timeline for each point earned. Points can be earned for completing the activities mentioned in the General Guidelines, and for:

1. Reading a novel set in ancient times and completing an Ancient World Fiction Book Review Form.
2. Reading a novel not related to the ancient world theme and completing a Fiction Book Review Form.

3. Reading a nonfiction book related to the ancient world theme and completing an Ancient World Nonfiction Book Review Form.

4. Reading a nonfiction book not related to the theme and completing a Nonfiction Book Review Form.

Program Forms

1. Ancient World Fiction Book Review Form
Title:
Author:
Publisher and date:
Brief summary of plot:
How was the ancient world setting important to the story?
Would you recommend this book to a friend? Why or why not?
2. Fiction Book Review Form
Title:
Author:
Publisher and date:
Brief summary of plot:
I would rate this book: "An important archeological discovery," "A priceless artifact," "A significant find," "Flawed," "An old, worthless relic."
3. Ancient World Nonfiction Book Review Form
Title:
Author:
Publisher and date:
Brief description of information:
What was the most interesting part of the book and why?
Would you like to find out more about this subject? Why or why not?
4. Nonfiction Book Review Form
Title:
Author:
Publisher and date:
Brief description of information:
I would rate this book: "The product of an advanced civilization," "Quite evolved," "Shows evidence of some intelligence," "Primitive," "Sub-human."

Program Activities

1. Old Movies. Show a film that is set in the prehistoric or ancient world, such as *The Land That Time Forgot*.

2. Art History. Early humans created many works of art and architecture during various periods in history. Teens can break into groups and select one example, such as Stone Age cave paintings found in France, or the Roman Colosseum. Each group can build a model or draw a replica of their chosen work to display in the library.

3. How They Lived. Invite an expert on ancient civilizations, archeology, or anthropology to speak to teens. The guest can bring slides, charts, and samples to illustrate the talk.

Topics of interest might include how early humans made tools, the beginnings of agriculture, or primitive musical instruments.

4. Evidence of the Past. If there is a historical museum in the area, plan to take a group of teens to view exhibits of the ancient world.

5. Hunters and Gatherers. Archeologists search for artifacts from Earth's past. Arrange an outdoor scavenger hunt in which teens can hunt for replicas of primitive tools (such as arrowheads and flints), bones (use chicken bones), fossils (imprint small shells in plaster of Paris), and food foraged by early humans (nuts and berries). Hide items in advance and give teens a list of things to find.

6. Old World Trivia. Host a trivia game in which teens can answer questions about the origins of Earth and humans. Categories can include Dinosaurs and Mammals, Stone Age People, Ancient Civilizations, Art and Artifacts, The Changing Earth, and Prehistoric Tools.

7. Scribes. Provide samples of ancient alphabets, symbols, and hieroglyphics used by early humans in various parts of the world. If possible, include notes about their meanings. Let teens copy these writing forms with calligraphy pens or paints.

8. Ancient Mysteries. There are many mysteries about prehistoric Earth and its early inhabitants. Provide books and articles that express theories on some of these mysteries: for example, why the dinosaurs became extinct, or how and why Stonehenge (or the pyramids or another ancient monument) was built. Include some books with unusual theories, such as *Chariots of the Gods*. Teens can discuss some of these ideas and express their opinions.

9. Primitive Workers. Introduce young adults to some careers related to the ancient world theme. Courses of study can include archeology, history, languages, architecture, geology, art history, genetics, anthropology, paleontology and biology, as well as work associated with museums. Provide information on these subjects and a list of colleges that offer degrees in them.

10. Artifacts of the 1990s. A thousand years from now, our towns and cities may be considered ancient civilizations. Ask teens to gather some contemporary objects that they think would be prime examples of historical artifacts from the United States to display in a mock museum exhibit. Teens can write a short caption for each "artifact" that explains its purpose to future generations of Earth's inhabitants.

Curriculum Ideas

1. English Literature/Composition. Students can read nonfiction and fiction about a specific prehistoric era or ancient civilization, such as the Ice Age or Ancient Egypt, then write an account of a week in the life of a person living during that time. In this fictional journal, include facts about the type of community in which the person might have lived, how food was obtained, the clothes worn, and the home or shelter.

2. Science. Just as humans evolved from early primates, modern animals also have primitive ancestors. Have students choose an animal, such as a horse, and look up its family roots. They should list previous variations of their animals, noting the changes that occurred along the way and when each type lived.

3. History/Geography. On a map of the world, have students mark where evidence of early humans (*Homo habilis, Homo erectus,* and Neanderthal) were found. Also have students indicate routes along which it is believed early humans traveled to populate other areas of the world. How did the Earth look in these prehistoric times? Students can draw maps to show how continental drift and the Ice Ages would have changed Earth's land features.

4. **Math.** In studying the distant past, we speak about Earth time in years B.C. Have students solve math problems involving B.C. time.

Activity Sheet Ideas

1. Word search and crossword puzzles of: a) prehistoric animals, b) tools and other useful objects, or c) plants and crops cultivated by early humans.

2. Word scrambles or cryptograms of: a) periods in history, b) titles of related books, or c) characteristics of primates and early humans.

3. Matching activities: match a) prehistoric life forms to the time period in which they lived, b) tribes or nations of people to where and when they lived, or c) ancient place names to what they are now called.

Suggested Resources

Reference and Nonfiction

Bailey, Jill, and Seddon, Tony. *The Young Oxford Book of the Prehistoric World.* Oxford University, 1995.

Bronowski, Jacob. *The Ascent of Man.* Little, 1974.

Builders of the Ancient World: Marvels of Engineering. National Geographic, 1986.

Caselli, Giovanni. *The First Civilizations.* Bedrick, 1985.

David, A. Rosalie. *The Egyptian Kingdoms.* Bedrick, 1988.

Gallant, Roy A. *Before the Sun Dies: The Story of Evolution.* Macmillan, 1989.

History of the Ancient and Medieval World. 12 vols. Marshall Cavendish, 1996.

Hodges, Henry. *Technology in the Ancient World.* Knopf, 1970.

The Human Dawn. Time-Life, 1990.

Lambert, David, and the Diagram Group. *The Field Guide to Early Man.* Facts on File, 1987.

Lauber, Patricia. *Tales Mummies Tell.* Harper, 1985.

Macaulay, David. *City: A Story of Roman Planning and Construction.* Houghton, 1974.

McIntosh, James. *The Practical Archaeologist.* Facts on File, 1988.

Malpass, Michael A. *Daily Life in the Inca Empire.* Greenwood, 1996.

Martell, Hazel Mary. *The Kingfisher Book of the Ancient World: From the Ice Age to the Fall of Rome.* Kingfisher, 1995.

Merriman, Nick. *Early Humans.* **Eyewitness Books** series. Knopf, 1989. (Also in series: *Prehistoric Life* and books on ancient civilizations.)

Mysteries of the Ancient World. National Geographic, 1985.

Oliphant, Margaret. *The Earliest Civilizations.* Facts on File, 1993.

Peters, David. *From the Beginning: The Story of Human Evolution.* Morrow, 1991.

Reader, John. *The Rise of Life.* Knopf, 1986.

Robbins, Lawrence H. *Stones, Bones, and Ancient Cities.* St. Martin's, 1990.

Sacks, David. *Encyclopedia of the Ancient Greek World.* Facts on File, 1995.

Saint-Blanquat, Henri de. *The First Settlements.* Silver Burdett, 1986.

Sasson, Jack M., ed. *Civilizations of the Ancient Near East.* 4 vols. Scribner, 1995.

Schwartz, Max. *Machines, Buildings, Weapons of Biblical Times.* Revell, 1990.

Splendors of the Past: Lost Cities of the Ancient World. National Geographic, 1981.

Tingay, Graham I.F., and Badcock, John. *These Were the Romans*. Dufour, 1989.
Von Daniken, Erich. *Chariots of the Gods? Unsolved Mysteries of the Past*. Putnam, 1970.
Warren, Peter. *The Aegean Civilizations*. Bedrick, 1989.
Westwood, Jennifer, ed. *The Atlas of Mysterious Places*. Weidenfeld & Nicolson, 1987.
White, Randall. *Dark Caves, Bright Visions: Life in Ice Age Europe*. Norton, 1986.
Whitehouse, Ruth, and Wilkins, John. *The Making of Civilization: History Discovered Through Archeology*. Knopf, 1986.

Fiction

Auel, Jean M. *The Clan of the Cave Bear*. Crown, 1980.
_____. *The Mammoth Hunters*. Crown, 1985.
_____. *The Plains of Passage*. Crown, 1990.
_____. *The Valley of Horses*. Crown, 1982.
Bradshaw, Gillian. *Horses of Heaven*. Doubleday, 1991.
_____. *Imperial Purple*. Houghton, 1988.
Brennan, J.H. *Shiva Accused: An Adventure of the Ice Age*. HarperCollins, 1991.
Carter, Dorothy Sharp. *His Majesty, Queen Hatshepsut*. Lippincott, 1987.
Davis, Lindsey. *Silver Pigs*. Crown, 1989.
Denzel, Justin. *Hunt for the Last Cat*. Philomel, 1991.
Golding, William. *The Inheritors*. Harcourt, 1963.
Graves, Robert. *I, Claudius*. Random, 1983.
Harrison, Sue. *Mother Earth, Father Sky*. Doubleday, 1990.
_____. *My Sister, the Moon*. Doubleday, 1992.
Kurten, Bjorn. *Dance of the Tiger: A Novel of the Ice Age*. Pantheon, 1980.
L'Engle, Madeleine. *An Acceptable Time*. Farrar, 1989.
_____. *Many Waters*. Farrar, 1986.
Levitin, Sonia. *Escape from Egypt*. Little, 1994.
Llwellyn, Morgan. *Druids*. Morrow, 1991.
Longyear, Barry B. *The Homecoming*. Walker, 1989.
Mackey, Mary. *The Horses at the Gate*. NAL, 1996
Mazer, Norma Fox. *Saturday, the Twelfth of October*. Dell, 1989.
Norton, Andre. *Shadow Hawk*. Ballantine, 1987.
Pryor, Bonnie. *Seth of the Lion People*. Morrow, 1988.
Rosny, J.H. *Quest for Fire*. Ballantine, 1982.
Sienkiewicz, Henryk. *Quo Vadis*. Amereon, 1981.
Speare, Elizabeth George. *The Bronze Bow*. Houghton, 1961.
Tempest, John. *Vision of the Hunter*. Harper, 1989.
Thomas, Elizabeth Marshall. *The Animal Wife*. Houghton, 1990.
Turnbull, Ann. *Maroo of the Winter Caves*. Clarion, 1984.
Walton, Evangeline. *The Sword Is Forged*. Ultramarine, 1983.
Wolf, Joan. *Daughter of the Red Deer*. Dutton, 1991.

Periodicals

Ancient History: Resources for Teachers. Macquarie Ancient History Association.
Archaeology. Archaeological Institute of America.

National Geographic. National Geographic Society.
Parabola. Society for the Study of Myth and Tradition.
Smithsonian. Smithsonian Associates.

Feature-Length Films

Caveman. MGM/UA, 1981. (PG)
A Funny Thing Happened on the Way to the Forum. CBS/Fox, 1966.
Land That Time Forgot. Vestron, 1975. (PG)
One Million BC. Rex Miller, 1940.
The Robe. CBS/Fox, 1953.
Sparticus. MCA/Universal, 1960. (PG-13)

Computer Software

Exploring Ancient Architecture. Medio Multimedia, 1993.
Exploring Ancient Cities. Sumaria, 1994.
Grolier Prehistoria: A Multimedia Who's Who of Prehistoric Life. Grolier Electronic Publishing, 1994.
Microsoft Ancient Lands. Microsoft, 1994.
The Story of Civilization. Compton's NewMedia, 1994.

2
Animal Tales

If you like animals, then you'll really go ape over the programs and materials you'll find at the library. We have magazines to satisfy the curious cat, nonfiction to make you as wise as an owl, novels to keep you as busy as a bee, and videos and CDs that are more fun than a barrel full of monkeys. Whether you want to learn how to care for a pet, look up facts about an endangered animal, or just curl up with a book about a furry friend, you'll discover some terrific Animal Tales at the library.

Display Idea

Provide a selection of novels featuring animals, as well as nonfiction books on pet care and endangered animals, animal identification guides, biographies of people who have worked with animals, information on careers dealing with animals, and other related works. Magazines and videos about animals, plus CDs by music groups named after animals, can also be featured. Pet care items and posters of animals will draw attention to the display.

Sponsorship for Prizes

1. Ask a bookstore to donate fiction and nonfiction books about animals.
2. Ask a local pet store to donate merchandise certificates.
3. Ask a local zoo or aquarium to donate free passes.
4. Ask a video rental store to donate free rental certificates for videos about animals.

Program Game

Design a game board that represents a natural animal habitat, such as a tropical rainforest, woodland, or marsh. Mark off squares with notes about wildlife that can be seen along the way. Patrons can advance one square for each point earned. Points can be earned for completing the activities mentioned in the General Guidelines, and for:

1. Reading a novel featuring one or more animals and completing an Animals Fiction Book Review Form.
2. Reading a novel not featuring animals and completing a Fiction Book Review Form.
3. Reading a nonfiction book related to the animals theme and completing an Animals Nonfiction Book Review Form.
4. Reading a nonfiction book not related to the animals theme and completing a Nonfiction Book Review Form.

Program Forms

1. Animals Fiction Book Review Form
Title:
Author:
Publisher and date:
Brief summary of plot:
Is an animal the main character in the story or a supporting character?
If supporting, what is its relationship to the main character?
If it is the main character, how does it relate to humans in the book?
2. Fiction Book Review Form
Title:
Author:
Publisher and date:
Brief summary of plot:
I would rate this book: "King of the beasts," "Top dog," "A cool cat," "A strange bird,"
"A slimy slug."
3. Animals Nonfiction Book Review Form
Title:
Author:
Publisher and date:
Brief description of information:
Name one interesting fact from this book:
Who would be most interested in reading this book?
4. Nonfiction Book Review Form
Title:
Author:
Publisher and date:
Brief description of information:
I would rate this book: "A blue ribbon in the county fair," "Second place," "An honor-
able mention," "Passed over by all the judges," "Refused admission to the competition."

Program Activities

1. **Animals on Film.** Show a movie that features animals, such as *Gorillas in the Mist*.
2. **Pet Project.** Encourage teens to bring in photos of their pets and to write a brief
description or true story about each one. Bind these into a looseleaf notebook or display them
in the library.
3. **Cartoon Critters.** Invite an artist or cartoonist to conduct a workshop on how to
draw animal figures. Provide sketch paper and pencils so that teens can follow the artist's
instructions. Perhaps one of your teen patrons has a talent for drawing and can lead this workshop.
4. **Live Animals.** Arrange to take a group of teens to a local zoo, aquarium, animal shelter, or veterinary hospital. Ask someone who works there to give a tour of the facility and
answer questions. Or, invite a traveling animal exhibit to come to the library.
5. **Animals at Risk.** Show teens a documentary film or slide show about one or more
endangered animals. Provide reading materials on animals that are at risk or extinct. If you

have some old nature magazines that are no longer needed, you can have teens cut out pictures of endangered animals for a display or bulletin board.

6. Big Game Hunting. Devise questions on animal topics for a game show program. Teens can answer questions in categories such as Animal Actors (what is the name of the dog on television's *Frasier*?), Animal Groups (a *flock* of birds, etc.), Indigenous Species (where do tigers live?), Endangered Animals (tell where they live), Strange But True Animal Facts (multiple choice), and Animal Puns and Clichés (familiar expressions).

7. Field Trip. Contact a member of the Audubon Society or another nature organization to lead a group of teens on a walk along a local nature trail or park. The naturalist can point out birds, insects, or signs of wildlife such as animal tracks. Participants can bring along field guides to help identify wildlife, and keep a log of what they see.

8. Rights vs. Research. The use of animals for medical research is a major controversy. Animal Rights activists argue that animal testing is cruel and unnecessary; scientists contend it is vital to their research. Invite speakers who represent both sides to debate this issue in front of a young adult audience. Or, teens can hold their own discussion about the merits of animal testing.

9. Beastly Jobs. Feature occupations involving working with animals in a career day program. Teens can find out about areas such as veterinary medicine, livestock breeding, wildlife management, marine biology, zoology, taxidermy, and entomology. Jobs such as zookeeper, game warden, pet store owner, and jockey can also be explored. Provide books and career information on these subjects for patrons to check out.

10. Dance Menagerie. Host a dance party for teens at the library featuring music by artists or groups named after animals, such as Counting Crows or Buddy Holly and the Crickets. You can also play songs that mention animals in the lyrics, or soundtrack music from movies about animals.

Curriculum Tie-Ins

1. English Literature/Composition. Many novels feature animals. Allow students to read an animal story of their choice. Have them fill in an information sheet about the main animal character in the book, noting the type of animal it is, its relationship to the main human characters, and other facts. Then have students rewrite a scene from the book, adopting another perspective; for example, if the story is told from the human owner's perspective, retell it from the animal's point of view. If it is told from an animal's perspective, choose a scene in which the animal relates to a human, and retell it from the human's perspective.

2. Science. Many wild animals have symbiotic relationships with other animals or plants. Several also depend upon a certain prey or can survive only in a specific habitat. Let students explore the unique living conditions of a variety of animals. Humans have destroyed the natural habitats of many animals. Discuss how this has affected the animal populations in those areas.

3. History/Geography. Certain animals are indigenous to specific parts of the world. For example, in nature, kangaroos are found only in Australia. Make a list of animals and have students locate on a world map where each one lives. You can also include extinct animals and ask students to note where they lived and why they became extinct.

4. Math. Have students draw up charts or graphs comparing various animal number facts, such as height, weight, speed, and population statistics.

Activity Sheet Ideas

1. Word search or crossword puzzles of: a) mythical and legendary beasts, b) extinct animals, or c) popular pets.

2. Word scrambles and cryptograms of: a) movies and TV shows that feature animals, b) names of zoos and aquariums, or c) people renowned for their work with animals.

3. Matching activities: match a) the common names for animals to their genus and species, b) sports teams to their animal mascots, or c) states to their state birds.

Suggested Resources

Reference and Nonfiction

Ackerman, Diane. *The Rarest of the Rare: Vanishing Animals, Timeless Worlds.* Random, 1995.

Alden, Peter. *Peterson First Guide to Mammals of North America.* Houghton, 1987.

Alderton, David. *A Birdkeeper's Guide to Pet Birds.* Tetra, 1987.

Audubon, John James. *The Birds of America.* Macmillan, 1985.

Banister, Keith, and Campbell, Andrew. *The Encyclopedia of Aquatic Life.* Facts on File, 1986.

Chrystie, Frances N., and Facklam, Margery. *Pets: A Comprehensive Handbook for Kids.* Little, 1995.

Curtis, Patricia. *All Wild Creatures Welcome: The Story of a Wildlife Rehabilitation Center.* Dutton, 1985.

De Laroche, Robert, and Labat, Jean-Michel. *The Secret Life of Cats.* Barron's, 1995.

Endangered Wildlife of the World. 11 vols. Marshall Cavendish, 1993.

Fogle, Bruce. *The Encyclopedia of the Dog.* Dorling Kindersley, 1995.

Freedman, Russell. *Animal Superstars: Biggest, Strongest, Fastest, Smartest.* Prentice, 1984.

Freeman, Robert B., and Freeman, Toni C. *Breeding and Showing Purebred Dogs.* Betterway, 1992.

Garisto, Leslie, and Streep, Peg. *The Best-Ever Book of Dog and Cat Names.* Holt, 1989.

Gravelle, Karen, and Squire, Anne. *Animal Talk.* Messner, 1988.

Jurmain, Suzanne. *Once Upon a Horse: A History of Horses and How They Shaped Our History.* Lothrop, 1989.

Lawlor, Elizabeth P. *Discover Nature at Sundown: Things to Know and Things to Do.* Stackpole, 1995.

Lee, Mary Price, and Lee, Richard S. *Opportunities in Animal and Pet Care Careers.* VGM, 1993.

McClung, Robert. *Lost Wild America: The Story of Our Extinct and Vanishing Wildlife.* Linnet, 1993.

Miller, Louise. *Careers for Animal Lovers and Other Zoological Types.* VGM, 1991.

Moore, Peter D., ed. *The Encyclopedia of Animal Ecology.* Facts on File, 1987.

Patent, Dorothy Hinshaw. *How Smart Are Animals?* Harcourt, 1990.

Rahn, Joan Elma. *Animals That Changed History.* Macmillan, 1986.

Remarkable Animals: A Unique Encyclopaedia of Wildlife Wonders. Guinness, 1987.

The Reader's Digest Illustrated Book of Dogs. Reader's Digest, 1989.

Scott, Peter W. *The Complete Aquarium.* Dorling Kindersley, 1995.

Sherry, Clifford J. *Animal Rights.* ABC-CLIO, 1995.

Stevens, Paul Drew. *Real Animal Heroes: True Stories of Courage, Devotion and Sacrifice.* NAL, 1990.

Thomson, Peggy. *Keepers and Creatures at the National Zoo*. Harper, 1988.
Tremain, Ruthven. *The Animals' Who's Who*. Scribner, 1982.
Walters, Mark Jerome. *The Dance of Life: Courtship in the Animal Kingdom*. Arbor, 1988.

Fiction

Ames, Mildred. *Who Will Speak for the Lamb?* Harper, 1989.
Avi. *Blue Heron*. Bradbury, 1992.
Bawden, Nina. *Henry*. Lothrop, 1988.
Buchanan, William J. *One Last Time*. Avon, 1992.
Burgess, Melvin. *The Cry of the Wolf*. Morrow, 1992.
Byars, Betsy. *Wanted: Mud Blossom*. Delacorte, 1991.
Clement, Aaron. *The Cold Moons*. Delacorte, 1989.
Curwood, James Oliver. *Baree: The Story of a Wolf-Dog*. Newmarket, 1990.
Donovan, John. *Family*. Harper, 1986.
Forman, James D. *Cry Havoc*. Scribner, 1988.
George, Jean Craighead. *There's an Owl in the Shower*. HarperCollins, 1995.
Haas, Jessie. *The Sixth Sense and Other Stories*. Greenwillow, 1988.
High, Linda Oatman. *Hound Heaven*. Holiday, 1995.
Holland, Isabelle. *The Unfrightened Dark*. Little, 1990.
Katz, Welwyn Wilton. *Whalesinger*. Macmillan, 1990.
Kilworth, Garry. *The Foxes of Firstdark*. Doubleday, 1989.
King, Stephen. *Cujo*. Viking, 1981.
Mayfield, Sue. *I Carried You on Eagle's Wings*. Lothrop, 1991.
Maynard, Meredy. *Dreamcatcher*. Polestar, 1995.
Mikaelsen, Ben. *Rescue Josh McGuire*. Hyperion, 1991.
Parnall, Peter. *Marsh Cat*. Macmillan, 1991.
Paulsen, Gary. *The Haymeadow*. Delacorte, 1992.
Peyton, K.M. *Darkling*. Delacorte, 1990.
Rawls, Wilson. *Where the Red Fern Grows*. Bantam, 1985.
Sherlock, Patti. *Some Fine Dog*. Holiday, 1992.
Smucker, Barbara. *Incredible Jumbo*. Viking, 1991.
Springer, Nancy. *Colt*. Dial, 1991.
Taylor, Theodore. *The Hostage*. Delacorte, 1988.
Wersba, Barbara. *The Farewell Kid*. Harper & Row, 1990.
Wilson, A.N. *Stray*. Orchard, 1989.

Periodicals

Animal Kingdom. New York Zoological Society.
The Animals' Agenda. Animal Rights Network.
Audubon. National Audubon Society.
Cat Fancy. Fancy Publications, Inc. (Also *Dog Fancy*.)
National Wildlife. National Wildlife Federation.

Feature-Length Films

Bless the Beasts and Children. Columbia Tristar, 1971. (PG)
Born Free. Columbia Tristar, 1966.

Black Beauty. Warner, 1994. (G)
The Day of the Dolphin. Sultan Entertainment, 1973. (PG)
Dunston Checks In. CBS/Fox, 1996. (PG)
Gorillas in the Mist. MCA/Universal, 1988. (PG-13)
White Fang 2. Walt Disney, 1994. (PG)

Computer Software

Animal Kingdom. MediaClips, 1993.
Beachman's International Threatened, Endangered, and Extinct Species. Zane, 1994.
Eyewitness Virtual Reality Bird. Dorling Kindersley Multimedia, 1996. (This series also
    features other animals.)
How Animals Move. Discovery Multimedia, 1995.
Mammals: A Multimedia Encyclopedia. National Geographic, 1993.
Microsoft Dangerous Creatures. Microsoft, 1994.

3
Check Out a Work of Art

Look around the library. You will see that art is everywhere: on posters, book jackets, covers of music CDs, and in framed pictures. There are books about famous works of art, artists, art history, art instruction, crafts, art museums and more. Have you ever judged a book by its cover? Chances are you formed your first opinion of a book based on whether you liked the cover art. There are lots of "masterpieces" on the shelves of the library—so come in and Check Out a Work of Art.

Display Idea

Set up a display of nonfiction books about types and styles of art, biographies of artists, books about careers in art, art encyclopedias and dictionaries, how-to arts and crafts books, and books about famous museums and works of art. Add some art magazines and fiction involving an art plot. Decorate the display with some art supplies, and showcase samples of artwork by famous or local artisans.

Sponsorship for Prizes

1. Ask an art supply store to donate arts and crafts materials.
2. Ask a store to donate art prints or posters.
3. Ask a bookstore to donate how-to drawing, painting, or crafts books.
4. Ask a local art gallery, museum or crafts fair to donate free passes.

Program Game

Give participants a paint-by-number picture of a famous work of art. They can color or paint in one piece of the picture for each point earned. Points can be awarded for completing the activities mentioned in the General Guidelines, and for:

1. Reading a novel and completing a Fiction Book Review Form.
2. Reading a nonfiction art-related book and completing an Art Nonfiction Book Review Form.
3. Reading a nonfiction book not relating to art and completing a Nonfiction Book Review Form.
4. Researching a famous work of art in a magazine article or reference source and completing an Art Appreciation Form.

Program Forms

1. Fiction Book Review Form
Title:
Author:
Publisher and date:
Brief summary of plot:
I would rate this book: "A masterpiece!" "Made by a skilled craftsman," "Beauty is in the eye of the beholder," "A poor exhibit," "Unpallette-able."

2. Art Nonfiction Book Review Form
Title:
Author:
Publisher and date:
Brief description of information:
Why did you choose this book?
Did you like it? Why or why not?

3. Nonfiction Book Review Form
Title:
Author:
Publisher and date:
Brief description of information:
I would rate this book: "A blue-ribbon winner," "Exhibits great composition and style," "Has some nice lines," "Not a work of art," "Just a bunch of scribbles."

4. Art Appreciation Form
Name of artwork:
Name of artist or craftsman:
Date or period work was created:
Source use in research:
Brief summary of information given:
What is your opinion of this work of art?

Program Ideas

1. Art Film. Show a feature film about an artist, such as *The Agony and the Ecstasy*. After the screening, discuss the artist and his or her work.

2. Handmade Art. Schedule one or more workshops in which teens can experiment with painting, pottery, cartoon drawing, tie-dyeing, origami, embroidery, or other types of arts and crafts. Invite local artists and craftsmen to lead the session(s).

3. Art Appreciation. Invite an art expert to give a talk on various art forms and styles. The guest can explain art terms, discuss art techniques, relate anecdotes about famous artists and their creations, and inform patrons on how to evaluate works of art. Or, invite a local artist to speak about how he or she works.

4. Museum Visit. Take young adults on a field trip to tour an art gallery or museum. Arrange for a guide to be on hand to offer information and answer questions about the exhibits. Afterwards, ask teens what they liked best and why. Or, take teens to a craft show and have them offer opinions later on what interested them the most.

5. Art History. Present a slide show, video, or multimedia presentation of notable art forms and masterpieces throughout history. A soundtrack of music corresponding to each time period can add to the enjoyment of the show.

6. Jeop-Art-Y. Host a *Jeopardy*-type game show in which teens can give the questions to art-related answers. Categories may include: Renaissance Artists (who painted which picture), American Artists (same), What's My Style? (identify pictures of impressionistic, gothic, etc. works), Shady Colors (magenta is a shade of …), Caldecott Winners (match illustrator to book), Name That Craft (identify works such as needlepoint, quilting, etc.)

7. Technique Clinique. Supply patrons with a selection of art materials and let them explore different painting techniques. They can experiment with various brushes, paints, inks, types of paper, textures, and materials. Some techniques to try can include stencilling, spattering or airbrushing, painting with sponges, collage, or 3-D art. Encourage patrons to create their own techniques and styles.

8. Is It Art or Not? People's opinions are often divided over what constitutes a work of art. Show several art samples and ask teens for their views. Have them consider different styles such as cubism, avant-garde, caricature, cartoon, etc. Can graffiti, photography, cake decorating, calligraphy, jewelry-making and other handicrafts be considered "art"? What is "fine art"? Take a survey of patrons' responses to these samples.

9. An Artist's Life. Hold a career day that celebrates various art-related occupations. Set up booths with information on job opportunities for cartoonists, book illustrators, art historians, art teachers, craftsmen, graphic artists, art editors, art critics, fashion designers, museum curators, portrait artists, art restorers, etc. Prepare a list of vocational schools, colleges, art schools and other educational institutions that offer related majors. Have several books available on these subjects for patrons to check out.

10. Art Gallery. Invite teens to submit their own works of art to exhibit in the library. Label each item with the artist's name, grade/school or age, and title of the piece. Sponsor a public Gallery Opening and let the artists discuss their work.

Curriculum Tie-Ins

1. English Literature/Composition. Read some folktales about art, artists, or colors, such as *Liang and the Magic Paintbrush*. What phase of art do they explore, and how? Have students look at a painting and create their own stories about the characters or scenes depicted. Students should use their imaginations to write about what might have occurred before or after the moment captured in the picture.

2. Science. There are many types of paint—oils, acrylics, gouache, and tempera, to name a few. Look at the chemical compositions of some of these. What are some common ingredients? What are some properties of each type of paint? What natural substances did people use for paints in the past?

3. History/Geography. Tell students to choose a famous artist from the past and explore the world in which he or she lived. Where was the artist born, where did he or she grow up and create his or her most famous works? What historical events happened during the artist's lifetime? What effect did the artist have on the world?

4. Math. Many types of arts and crafts require careful measuring. Give students problems such as figuring out the amount of fabric needed to make a quilt with a specific pattern, measuring ingredients to mix a varnish or a particular shade of paint, or calculating how to center a picture in a mat and frame.

Activity Sheet Ideas

1. Word search or crossword puzzles of: a) styles of art, b) art or crafts materials, or c) related occupations.

2. Word scrambles or cryptograms of: a) famous artists, b) works of art, or c) art museums.

3. Matching activities: match a) famous works of art to the artists who created them, b) artists to the time or place in which they lived, or c) an art or craft to a material used in creating it.

Suggested Resources

Reference and Nonfiction

American Federation of Arts. *Who's Who in American Art*. Bowker, annual.

Artist's Market. Writer's Digest, annual.

Brommer, Gerald F. *Exploring Drawing*. Davis, 1988.

Burn, Barbara. *Masterpieces from the Metropolitan Museum of Art*. Bullfinch, 1993.

Cumming, Robert. *Annotated Art: The World's Greatest Paintings Explored and Explained*. Dorling Kindersley, 1995.

Cummings, Pat, ed. *Talking with Artists*. Bradbury, 1992.

Ehberts, Marjorie, and Gisler, Margaret. *Careers for Culture Lovers and Other Artsy Types*. VGM, 1991.

First Impressions series. Abrams.

Gatto, Joseph A., et al. *Exploring Visual Design*. Davis, 1987.

Gautier, Dick. *The Career Cartoonist: A Step-by-Step Guide to Presenting and Selling Your Artwork*. Putnam, 1992.

Gowing, Sir Lawrence, ed. *Biographical Dictionary of Artists*. Facts on File, 1995.

Grant, Daniel. *The Artist's Resource Handbook*. Allworth, 1994.

Greenberg, Jan. *The Painter's Eye: Learning to Look at Contemporary American Art*. Delacorte, 1991.

Hamberger, Alan S. *Art for All: How to Buy Fine Art for Under $300*. Wallace-Homestead, 1994.

Hammond, Lee. *How to Draw Lifelike Portraits from Photographs*. North Light, 1995.

Harrison, Hazel. *Watercolor School*. Reader's Digest, 1993.

Heslewood, Juliet. *The History of Western Painting: A Young Person's Guide*. Raintree/Steck-Vaughn, 1995.

Hutton-Jamieson, Iain. *Colored Pencil Drawing Techniques*. North Light, 1986.

Janson, H. W. *History of Art for Young People*. Abrams, 1987.

Kaplan, Andrew. *Careers for Artistic Types*. Millbrook, 1991.

Larbalestier, Simon. *The Art and Craft of Collage*. Chronicle, 1995. (Also others in series.)

Lehrman, Lew. *Being an Artist*. North Light, 1992.

McGill, Ormand. *Chalk Talks! The Magical Art of Drawing with Chalk*. Millbrook, 1995.

Ochoa, George, and Corey, Melinda. *The Timeline Book of the Arts*. Ballantine, 1995.

Opie, Mary-Jane. *Sculpture*. Dorling Kindersley, 1995.

Salman, Mark. *Opportunities in Visual Arts Careers*. VGM, 1993.

Sattler, Helen R. *Recipes for Art and Craft Materials*. Morrow, 1994.

Shaw, Robert. *America's Traditional Crafts*. Hugh Lauter Levin, 1993.

Smith, Ray. *An Introduction to Perspective*. Dorling Kindersley, 1995.

Fiction

Anderson, Mary. *The Unsinkable Molly Malone*. Harcourt, 1991.

Atwood, Margaret. *Cat's Eye*. Doubleday, 1989.

Brooke, William J. *A Brush with Magic: Based on a Traditional Chinese Story*. HarperCollins, 1993.

Cary, Joyce. *The Horse's Mouth*. Amereon, 1986.

Christian, Mary Blount. *Linc*. Macmillan, 1991.

Coker, Carolyn. *The Vines of Ferrara*. Dodd, 1986.

Cole, Brock. *Celine*. Farrar, 1989.

Cook, Robin. *Sphinx*. NAL, 1983.

Cormier, Robert. *Tunes for Bears to Dance To*. Delacorte, 1992.

Cross, Gillian. *Wolf*. Holiday, 1991.

Deaver, Julie Reece. *Chicago Blues*. HarperCollins, 1995.

Fleischman, Paul. *Graven Images*. HarperCollins, 1982.

Fox, Paula. *Western Wind: A Novel*. Orchard, 1993.

Gleeson, Libby. *I Am Susannah*. Holiday, 1989.

Gould, Marilyn. *Graffiti Wipeout*. Allied Crafts, 1992.

Green, Patricia Baird. *The Sabbath Garden*. Lodestar, 1993.

Haynes, Mary. *Catch the Sea*. Bradbury, 1989.

Highwater, Jamake. *I Wear the Morning Star*. Harper, 1986.

Levoy, Myron. *A Shadow Like a Leopard*. HarperCollins, 1994.

Llewellyn, Caroline. *The Masks of Rome*. Scribner, 1988.

MacLeod, Charlotte. *The Gladstone Bag*. Mysterious, 1990.

Madison, Winifred. *A Portrait of Myself: A Novel*. Random, 1979.

Oneal, Zibby. *In Summer Light*. Viking Kestrel, 1985.

Paulsen, Gary. *The Island*. Orchard, 1988.

_____. *The Monument*. Delacorte, 1991.

Plummer, Louise. *My Name Is Sus5an Smith, the 5 Is Silent*. Delacorte, 1991.

Potok, Chaim. *The Gift of Asher Lev*. Knopf, 1990.

Pullman, Philip. *The Broken Bridge*. Knopf, 1992.

Rabinowich, Ellen. *Underneath I'm Different*. Delacorte, 1983.

Shannon, Monica. *Dobry*. Puffin, 1993.

Periodicals

American Artist. Billboard Publications.

Art in America. Brandt Publications.

Artist's Magazine. F & W Publications.

ARTnews. ARTnews Associates.

Feature-Length Films

The Agony and the Ecstacy. CBS/Fox, 1965.

Moulin Rouge. MGM/UA, 1952.

The Portrait. Turner Home Entertainment, 1993.

Sunday in the Park with George. Warner, 1986.

The Train. MGM/UA, 1965.
Vincent and Theo. Ingram International, 1990.

Computer Software

Electronic Encyclopedia of Art. EBook Multimedia, 1990.
History Through Art: The Renaissance. Zane, 1994. (Also others in series.)
Microsoft Art Gallery: The Collection of the National Gallery, London. Microsoft, 1994.
Microsoft Fine Artist. Microsoft, 1994.
A Passion for Art: Renoir, Cezanne, Matisse and Dr. Barnes. Corbis, 1995.
Print Artist. Maxis, 1995.

4
Star-Crossed Books

What's your sign? Do you know what celebrities were born on your birthday? How do you cast a horoscope? Are you curious about the constellations? What's astrology all about, and how does it differ from astronomy? The answers to these questions and more can be found in the library. Whether you are searching for a scientific explanation or just want something fun to read, you'll discover the perfect Star-Crossed Books at the library.

Display Idea

Set up a selection of nonfiction books about astrology and astronomy; books of mythology and legends about the stars and planets; and some science fiction and fantasy with related themes. Display the signs of the zodiac, astrological charts, and pictures of the constellations. Post the horoscope from a local newspaper and update it daily.

Sponsorship for Prizes

1. Ask a novelty store to donate posters or other items showing zodiac signs.

2. Ask a magazine or stationery store to donate booklets of daily horoscope predictions.

3. Ask a bookstore to donate paperback books with related themes.

4. Ask a professional astrologer to donate a free consultation.

Program Game

Draw up a calendar of an astrological year, starting with Capricorn of the current year and ending with Sagittarius. Patrons will advance a certain number of days for each point they earn. Points can be earned for completing the activities mentioned in the General Guidelines, and for:

1. Reading a novel and completing a Fiction Book Review Form.

2. Reading a nonfiction book about astrology and completing an Astrological Opinion Form.

3. Reading a nonfiction book on any topic other than astrology, and completing a Nonfiction Book Review Form.

4. Reading horoscopes by two or more astrologers and completing a Horoscope Comparison Form.

Program Forms

1. Fiction Book Review Form
Title:
Author:
Publisher and date:
Brief summary of plot:
I would rate this book: "A constellation that lights up the heavens," "A brilliant star," "This planet shows signs of life," "Nebulous," "A black hole."

2. Astrological Opinion Form
Title:
Author:
Publisher and date:
Brief description of information:
What is the author's opinion of astrology?
After reading this book, what is your opinion of astrology?

3. Nonfiction Book Review Form
Title:
Author:
Publisher and date:
Brief description of information:
I would rate this book: "A strong sign with positive aspects," "A rising sun," "Aspects are in harmony," "The planets are in opposition," "Many negative aspects."

4. Horoscope Comparison Form
Name of first astrologer and frequency of horoscope:
Source:
Name of second astrologer and frequency of horoscope:
Source:
Compare the styles of these horoscopes:
Which do you like best, and why?

Program Activities

1. Personality Plus. Each constellation of the zodiac represents a story about gods, people, or creatures from Greek mythology. Have teens choose a character from these ancient stories and write a personal advertisement about him or her on one side of a note card. Write the name of the character on the other side. Divide participants into two teams and have them try to guess the name of each mythological character based on their personal ad.

2. Zodiac Shirt Shop. Tell teens to bring in their own plain white shirts or sweatshirts. Provide stencils of zodiac signs and symbols, dyes and brushes. Let patrons design their own zodiac shirts.

3. Star Charts. Invite an astrologer to conduct one or more workshops on how to draw an astrological chart. The guest can explain the terms used in forecasting a horoscope, tell about the influences of stars and planets, and give other basic information.

4. Star Search. Sponsor a night-time stargazing session. Invite an astronomer to bring along a telescope to help patrons locate various constellations, stars, and planets. If a field trip is not possible, present a film or slide show about the stars in the sky.

5. Your Lucky Number. Numerology is closely related to astrology. Begin a numerology program by explaining the symbolism or meanings of numbers 1–9, and some superstitions about numbers. Then have patrons calculate their own "magic numbers" according to their birthdates. Read the personality traits of numbers 1–9. Let teens discuss whether they think these descriptions are accurate. How do their numerology traits compare to their astrological readings?

6. What's Their Sign? Young adults can compete in teams as they try to guess the astrological signs of famous people in this game show program. Each question should contain a clue or a riddle that hints at the answer. For example: "When Mick Jagger sings, he opens his mouth wide and *roars* into the microphone." (Answer: Leo) Prepare four or five clues for each celebrity, in case participants cannot guess the answer right away.

7. More Fortunes. Palmistry and tarot readings are other forms of fortune-telling that are linked to astrology. Present a program on one or both of these topics. Compare the symbols on tarot cards to the signs of the zodiac and the planets. Look at a palm-reading chart in which fingers and hand features are named for the planets and assigned astrological qualities.

8. Your Horoscope: True or False? Give each participant a photocopy of his or her horoscope calendar for the current month or for the duration of this unit. At the completion of each day, have teens mark on their calendars whether or not the day's prediction was accurate. At the end of the month, ask them to review their calendars and decide if they think there is some degree of truth in astrological predictions.

9. Future Careers? Astrologers believe that a person's astrological sign can determine his or her career interests. Set up twelve tables, one for each sign of the zodiac. On each table, display books and other materials pertaining to jobs that are supposedly suited to people who are born under that sign. Teens can visit the table with career information for their sign. Then let them browse the other job tables. Have patrons fill out a questionnaire of their career interests, and tell whether or not they match their horoscope's predictions.

10. Zodiac Costume Party. Ask teens to make a list of famous people, from the past and present, who share their astrological sign. Then host a costume party in which people must dress and act like a person from their list. Teens can try to guess each other's identities.

Curriculum Tie-Ins

1. English Literature/Composition. Use program activities in conjunction with a unit on mythology or folklore. Students can read legends from various cultures relating to the signs of the zodiac. Have them make up stories about other constellations in the galaxy.

2. Science. Show students how astrology and astronomy are related. Study constellations, planets, the sun and the moon. Many myths were created to explain earthly phenomena, such as the changing seasons. Compare astrological and mythological reasoning to factual information in a unit on earth sciences.

3. History/Geography. Ancient Sumerians, Babylonians, Egyptians, Romans, Greeks, and Chinese all believed in the science of astrology. Study the historical origins and beliefs of these civilizations as they relate to astrology. Trace the spread of astrology on a timeline and a map of the world.

4. Math. In astrology, aspects are formed when a circle (360 degrees) is divided by certain numbers. Have students practice measuring angles and degrees of a circle. The number twelve is also significant in astrology, such as twelve signs of the zodiac. For fun, teach students some math tricks involving the number twelve.

Activity Sheet Ideas

1. Word search or crossword puzzles of: a) constellations, b) astronomy terms, or c) terms used in telling horoscopes.

2. Word scrambles or cryptograms of: a) astronomers from the past and present, b) names of popular astrologers, or c) popular phrases that have astrological references.

3. Matching activities: match a) astrological signs to their symbols, b) signs to their time or year, or c) stars to their constellations.

Suggested Resources

Reference and Nonfiction

Anderton, Bill. *Life Cycles: The Astrology of Inner Space and Its Application to the Rhythms of Life*. Llewellyn, 1990.

Ash, Lucy. *A Taste of Astrology*. Knopf, 1988.

Barton, Tamsyn. *Ancient Astrology*. Routledge, 1995.

Campion, Nicholas. *The Practical Astrologer*. Abrams, 1987.

Cosmic Connections. Time-Life, 1988.

Cowger, Barry D. *Family Dynamics and Astrology*. Envision, 1990.

Deocz, Hans, and Monte, Tom. *Numerology: Key to Your Inner Self*. Avery, 1994.

Dell, Pamela. *Hotscopes: Day-by-Day Horoscopes*. Western, annual. (Individual volumes for the various signs.)

Farley, Stacey J. *Astrology: Is Your Future in the Stars?* PPI, 1993.

Filbey, John. *Natal Charting: How to Master the Techniques of Birth Chart Construction*. Aquarian, 1984.

Friedman, Sylvia. *The Stars in Your Family: How Astrology Affects Relationships Between Parents and Children*. Hay, 1995.

Gibson, Paul. *How to Be Your Own Astrologer*. Astor, 1987.

Goodavage, Joseph F. *Write Your Own Horoscope*. NAL, 1990.

Goodman, Frederick. *Zodiac Signs*. Brian Trodd, 1990.

Goodman, Linda. *Linda Goodman's Love Signs: A New Approach to the Human Heart*. Harper-Perennial, 1992.

_____. *Linda Goodman's Sun Signs*. Taplinger, 1985.

Griffin, T. Wynne. *The Illustrated Guide to Astrology*. Mallard, 1990.

Hasbrouck, Muriel Bruce. *Tarot and Astrology: The Pursuit of Destiny*. Destiny, 1986.

Henbest, N. *The Night Sky*. EDC, 1993.

Holloway, Lee. *The Artful Astrologer: Aquarius*. Gramercy, 1993. (Also available for other signs.)

Jagendorf, M.A. *Stories and Lore of the Zodiac*, Vangard, 1977.

Lewis, James R. *The Astrology Encyclopedia*. Gale, 1994.

Li, Xiao M. *The Mending of the Sky and Other Chinese Myths*. Oyster River, 1989.

Magee, James E. *Your Place in the Cosmos, Vol. I: A Layman's Book of Astronomy and the Mythology of the Eighty-Eight Celestial Constellations and Registry*. Mosele, 1988.

Mayall, R. Newton, et al. *The Sky Observer's Guide*. Western, 1977.

McEvers, Joan. *Planets: The Astrological Tools*. Llewellyn, 1989.

McLeish, Kenneth. *The Shining Stars: Greek Legends of the Zodiac*. Cambridge University Press, 1981.

O'Neill, Terry, ed. *Opposing Viewpoints: Paranormal Phenomena*. Greenhaven, 1990.

Penfield, Marc Heeren. *An Astrological Who's Who*. Arcane, 1972.

Pottenger, Maritha. *Complete Horoscope Interpretation: Putting Together Your Planetary Profile*. ACS, 1986.

Reinstein, Reina J., and Reinstein, Mike. *Don't Blame Me, I'm a Gemini!: Astrology for Teenagers*. Barron's, 1996.

Ridpath, Ian. *Atlas of Stars and Planets*. Facts on File, 1993.

Royer, Mary P. *Opposing Viewpoints: Astrology*. Greenhaven, 1991.

Schwartz, Alvin. *Telling Fortunes: Love Magic, Dream Signs, and Other Ways to Learn the Future*. HarperCollins, 1990.

Stepko, Barbara. *'Scoping: A Teen's Star Guide to School, Friends, and of Course, Guys*. Avon, 1995.

Tester, S.J. *A History of Western Astrology*. Boydell, 1987.

Weiss, Ann E. *Seers and Scientists: Can the Future Be Predicted?* Harcourt, 1986.

Wyatt, Katharine, et al. *Children's Names and Horoscopes*. Granata, 1983.

Zodiac Charted Designs for Cross-Stitch, Needlepoint, and Other Techniques. Dover, 1985.

Zolar. *Zolar's Book of Astrology, Dreams, Numbers, and Lucky Days*. Prentice, 1990.

Fiction

Bova, Ben. *Orion Among the Stars*. Tor, 1995.

Ellis, Carol. *In Leo's Lair*. Bullseye, 1995.

_____. *Rage of Aquarius*. Bullseye, 1995.

Foxx, Aleister. *Harm's Way*. St. Martin's, 1992.

Goodwin, Marie D. *Where the Towers Pierce the Sky*. Four Winds, 1989.

Howe, Norma. *The Game of Life*. Crown, 1989.

Kamida, Vicki. *Never Love a Libra*. Bullseye, 1995.

Koeppel, Ruth. *Virgo's Vengeance*. Bullseye, 1996.

Platt, Kin. *Chloris and the Freaks: A Novel*. Bradbury, 1975.

Regan, Dian Curtis. *Monsters in the Attic*. Holt, 1995.

Sachs, Marilyn. *Circles*. Dutton, 1991.

Shusterman, Neal. *Scorpian Shards*. Tor, 1995.

Steiber, Ellen. *Pisces Drowning*. Bullseye, 1996.

_____. *The Thirteenth Sign*. Bullseye, 1996.

_____. *Twisted Taurus*. Bullseye, 1995.

Stewart, Mary. *Ludo and the Star Horse*. Morrow, 1975.

Thatcher, Julia. *Home to the Night*. J. Curley, 1976.

Periodicals

American Astrology. Starlog Group.

Astro Digest. JMT Publications, Inc.

Astrological Review. Astrologers' Guild of America.

Dell Horoscope. Dell Magazines.

Sky Calendar. Abrams Planetarium.

Welcome to Planet Earth. Great Bear Press.

Feature-Length Films

Eliza's Horoscope. Active, 1970.
The Fish That Saved Pittsburgh. Warner, 1979. (PG)
Local Hero. Warner, 1983. (PG)
When's Your Birthday? Nostalgia, 1937.

Computer Software

Amazing Universe III. Hopkins Technology, 1995.
Astro Navigator. ASCII Corp., 1996.
Astrology Source. Multicom, 1994.
Palmistry. Emerald Entertainment, 1994.
Time/Life Astrology. PMEP, 1994.
Virtual Tarot. Virtual Media Works, 1994.

5

Fun in the Sun

Surf's up! There's waves of fun waiting for you at the library. In addition to travel guides that list coastal resorts and books of beach sports and activities, you'll find novels and videos that are set on warm, sunny shores. You can also groove to some cool summer sounds on CD and tape. Let the library bring out the beachcomber in you as you find Fun in the Sun.

Display Idea

Novels that are set on the beach and nonfiction about beach activities, the shore, environment, travel information, and shore-related careers can be displayed along with CDs of surfer music and videos set on the beach. Add beach posters and props such as inflatable swim rings and a surf board to convey the fun mood.

Sponsorship for Prizes

1. Ask a clothing store to donate discount certificates for swimwear and accessories.

2. Ask a department or sports store to donate fun-in-the-sun items, such as sunglasses, suntan lotion, and beach balls.

3. Ask a tanning salon to donate certificates for tanning sessions.

4. Ask a bookstore to donate books about beach fun as well as magazine swimsuit issues.

Program Game

The game will resemble a walk along the shore. Draw footprints in the sand that stretch along the water's edge and that visit various concession stands nearby. Patrons can advance one footprint for each point earned. Points can be earned for completing the activities mentioned in the General Guidelines, and for:

1. Reading a novel that takes place on the beach or shore and completing a Beach Fiction Book Review Form.

2. Reading a novel that is not related to the beach/shore theme and completing a Fiction Book Review Form.

3. Reading a nonfiction book related to the beach and shore theme, and completing a Beach Nonfiction Book Review Form.

4. Reading a nonfiction book not related to the beach/shore theme and completing a Nonfiction Book Review Form.

31

Program Forms

1. Beach Fiction Book Review Form
Title:
Author:
Publisher and date:
Brief summary of plot:
Who was the most interesting character and why?
What was your favorite part of the book and why?
2. Fiction Book Review Form
Title:
Author:
Publisher and date:
Brief summary of plot:
I would rate this book: "Totally Awesome," "Rad," "OK," "Boring," "Bummer."
3. Beach Nonfiction Book Review Form
Title:
Author:
Publisher and date:
Brief description of information:
What interested you most about this book and why?
Would you read more books on this subject? Why or why not?
4. Nonfiction Book Review Form
Title:
Author:
Publisher and date:
Brief description of information:
I would rate this book: "A week at Club Med," "A long weekend at Daytona Beach," "A day at the municipal shore," "A couple of hours at a friend's backyard pool," "A run through the sprinkler."

Program Activities

1. **Frankie and Annette**. Treat teens to a marathon of beach movies from the 1960s, or show another movie set at the beach.

2. **Small Crafts**. Provide an assortment of shoreline items, such as colored sand, fishnet, beach glass, driftwood, small shells, and dried plants for teens to use in making craft projects. Patrons can create shell earrings, driftwood table centerpieces, sand art, 3-D collages, or other decorative items.

3. **Shoreline Life**. Ask someone who collects seashells to bring in samples and give a talk about identifying shoreline creatures. Show slides or videos about life in tidepools, on rocky and sandy shores, and in coastal waters. Discuss some environmental dangers to these plants and animals, and what teens can do to help.

4. **Beach Beautification**. Beaches, ponds, and other waterfront areas are popular recreational spots. Unfortunately, people who visit often leave behind a startling amount of litter. If you live near one of these places, organize teens to take part in a beach clean-up day. Bring garbage bags and pick up papers, cans and bottles, cigarette butts, and other trash during this community service program.

5. Sun Care. Most sun worshippers like to get a tan, but overexposure can be dangerous. Conduct a program of sun safety tips, including skin care and eye protection, how to avoid sunburn and sunstroke, and how to tell if you've had too much sun. Provide samples of tanning lotion and sunscreen, and let teens decide which type is best for them to use.

6. Life is a Beach. Contestants can show how much they know about the beach in this game show program. Questions can be in areas such as Beach Safety Rules (explain them), Identify the Beach Creature (from a photo or shell), Beach Talk (interpret sailing and surfing jargon), Name that Beach Song (from audio clues), Beach Babies (identify swimsuit models), and Beach Treats (identify foods sold at beach concessions, such as corn dogs)

7. Beach Togs. Arrange for a store that sells beach wear to lend clothes and accessories for a fashion show. Teens can model swimwear, cover-ups, shorts and tops, sandals, hats, sunglasses, and other items commonly worn at the beach.

8. Vacation Plans. Many people like to spend part or all of their vacations at the beach. Gather a variety of brochures and tourist guides from travel agencies that provide information on beach resorts, coastal getaways, and shoreline attractions. Let patrons browse these materials and discuss their ideas for the perfect beach vacation. Teens who have taken slides or photos of a trip to the shore can share their experiences.

9. Beach Bums. Many teens find summer employment at the beach. Invite local and municipal employers to talk to patrons about applying for summer jobs as lifeguards, vendors at concession stands, ice cream truck drivers, swimming or sailing instructors, etc. Teens can also learn about careers in shoreline conservation, oceanography, marine life research, oceanfront architecture, municipal or state beach management, and other related occupations. Provide information on colleges that offer degrees in the specialized areas.

10. Songs of Summer. Teens can wear their summer tops and shorts to a beach party at the library. Play surfer music and other tunes that have been popular during the summertime. Teach kids how to dance the Swim. Decorate the room with inflatable palm trees and floats, seashells, and other beach items. If there is room, let teens play volleyball. Provide iced tea and picnic foods, which partygoers can eat while sitting on beach blankets and towels.

Curriculum Ideas

1. English Literature/Composition. Have students read excerpts of novels that are set on a beach or shore. How are beaches usually perceived? (Examples: romantic, harsh, stormy.) What descriptions are given of shoreline habitats or creatures? Then read magazine articles and field guides that describe coastal areas. Students can write a composition, either fiction or nonfiction, that incorporates a description of a beach or shore.

2. Science. Shoreline environments are beautiful but delicate. Introduce an ecology unit wherein the class studies tidepool, coral reef, sand beach and rocky shore habitats. How do waves and weather affect coastlines and the plants and animals that live there? What are the effects of pollution and tourism? Students can construct dioramas of coastal habitats and identify the various forms of life there.

3. History/Geography. On a map of the world, locate some famous beaches and resort areas. What types of activities do each of these offer for vacationers? Coastlines are not always recreation sites. In times of war, many battles have been fought along waterfronts. Have students research some of these coastal confrontations and compare their notes to how those beaches are used in times of peace.

4. Math. Create problems based on facts about tides. The tide comes in and goes out twice a day, at intervals of 6 hours and 13 minutes. Have students create a tide chart giving high and low tides twice a day for one month, starting with high tide on the first day at 6:00 A.M.

Activity Sheet Ideas

1. Word search or crossword puzzles of: a) types of shells, b) plants, creatures, and objects found along the shore, or c) beach activities and sports.
2. Word scrambles or cryptograms of: a) lyrics from summertime songs, b) world-famous beaches, or c) brand names of products used by beachgoers.
3. Matching activities: match a) actors to the beach movie they were in, b) beach songs to the year they were popular, or c) popular beach resorts to their geographical locations.

Suggested Resources

Reference and Nonfiction

Adkins, Jan. *The Art and Industry of Sandcastles*. Walker, 1971.
Allen, Thomas P. *Treasures of the Tide*. NWF, 1990.
Amos, William Hopkins. *Atlantic and Gulf Coasts*. Knopf, 1985.
Arnosky, Jim. *Near the Sea: A Portfolio of Paintings*. Lothrop, 1990.
Bascom, Willard. *Waves and Beaches: The Dynamics of the Ocean Surface*. Anchor, 1980.
Canada's Incredible Coasts. National Geographic, 1991.
Carson, Rachel. *The Edge of the Sea*. Houghton, 1979.
Crump, Donald J., ed. *The World's Wild Shores*. National Geographic, 1990.
Evans, Jeremy. *The Complete Guide to Short Board Sailing*. International Marine, 1987.
Ferrell, Nancy Warren. *The U.S. Coast Guard*. Lerner, 1989.
Hecht, Jeff. *Shifting Shores: Rising Seas, Retreating Coastlines*. Macmillan, 1990.
Ketels, Hank, and McDowell, Jack. *Sports Illustrated Scuba Diving*. NAL, 1988.
Lee, Owen. *The Skin Diver's Bible*. Doubleday, 1986.
Lye, Keith. *Coasts*. Silver Burdett, 1988.
Maxwell, Gavin. *Ring of Bright Water*. Penguin, 1987.
Meinkoth, Norman A. *The Audubon Society Field Guide to North American Seashore Creatures*. Knopf, 1981.
Meyerson, A. Lee. *Seawater: A Delicate Balance*. Enslow, 1988.
Miller, Christina G., and Berry, Louise A. *Coastal Rescue: Preserving Our Seashores*. Macmillan, 1989.
The Ocean Realm. National Geographic, 1978.
Padget, Sheila. *Coastlines*. Bookwright, 1983.
Swanson, Diane. *Safari Beneath the Sea: The Wonder of the North Pacific Coast*. Sierra, 1994.
Tiner, Ralph W. *A Field Guide to Coastal Wetland Plants of the Northeastern United States*. University of Massachusetts Press, 1987.
Trefil, James. *Scientist at the Seashore*. Macmillan, 1987.
Vaz, Katherine, et al. *Swim Swim: A Complete Handbook for Fitness Swimmers*. Contemporary, 1986.

Wallace, Don. *Watersports Basics.* Prentice, 1985.

Winans, Chip, et al. *Boardsailing Made Easy: Teaching and Techniques.* Chip Winans, 1985.

Wolverton, Ruthe. *The National Seashores: The Complete Guide to America's Scenic Coastal Parks.* Woodbine, 1988.

Zim, Herbert S. *Seashores.* Western, 1955.

Fiction

Abe, Kobo. *The Woman in the Dunes.* Random, 1972.

Angell, Judie. *Don't Rent My Room.* Bantam, 1990.

Applegate, Katherine. *Swept Away.* HarperPaperback, 1995. (Also others in *Ocean City* series.)

Avi. *A Place Called Ugly.* Pantheon, 1981.

Beatty, Patricia. *Sarah and Me and the Lady from the Sea.* Morrow, 1989.

Benchley, Peter. *Jaws.* Bantam, 1991.

Bond, Nancy. *Another Shore.* McElderry, 1987.

Cargill, Linda. *The Surfer.* Scholastic, 1995.

Clarke, Judith. *Al Capsella Takes a Vacation.* Holt, 1992.

Crew, Linda. *Someday I'll Laugh About This.* Delacorte, 1990.

Cusick, Richie Tankersley. *The Lifeguard.* Scholastic, 1988.

Davidson, Nicole. *Demon's Beach.* Avon, 1992.

Gilden, Mel. *Which Way to the Beach?* HarperPaperback, 1992.

Haynes, Mary. *Catch the Sea.* Bradbury, 1989.

Hunter, Mollie. *A Stranger Came Ashore.* Harper, 1975.

Jones, Janice. *Secrets of a Summer Spy.* Bradbury, 1990.

Kehret, Peg. *Sisters, Long Ago.* Dutton, 1990.

Kimmel, Eric A. *One Good Tern Deserves Another.* Holiday, 1994.

McCorkle, Jill. *Ferris Beach.* Algonquin, 1990.

McCutcheon, Elsie. *Storm Bird.* Farrar, 1987.

McMahon, Sean. *The Light on Illancrone.* Poolbeg, 1990.

Maloney, Ray. *The Impact Zone.* Delacorte, 1986.

Murray, Marguerite. *Odin's Eye.* Macmillan, 1987.

O'Dell, Scott. *The Cruise of the Atlantic Star.* Houghton, 1973.

Perry, Carol J. *Going Overboard.* Willowisp, 1991.

Schwartz, Joel L. *Upchuck Summer.* Dell, 1982.

Schwemm, Diane. *Summer Love.* Bantam, 1995. (Also others in *Silver Beach* series.)

Sonnenmark, Laura A. *The Lie.* Scholastic, 1992.

Stine, R.L. *Beach Party.* Scholastic, 1990.

Westall, Robert. *Stormsearch.* Farrar, 1992.

Periodicals

Motor Boating and Sailing. Hearst Magazines.

Skin Diver. Petersen Publishing Co.

Surfer Magazine. Surfer Publishing, Inc.

Water Skier. Water Skier Association.

Feature-Length Films

Beach Blanket Bingo. HBO, 1965. (G) (Also other Frankie and Annette beach movies of the 1960s.)
Jaws. MCA/Universal, 1975. (PG)
One Crazy Summer. Warner, 1986. (PG)
Point Break. Fox Video, 1991. (R)
Ride the Wild Surf. Columbia Tristar, 1964.
Shag: The Movie. HBO, 1989. (PG)

Computer Software

The Beach! An Educational and Fun Look at Everything from A(ngel Wings) to Z(inc Oxide). Carole Marsh Family CD-ROMS, 1994.
Coral Kingdom. Sunburst, 1993.
Let's Play Beach Volleyball. Intellimedia Sports, 1994.
Oceans in Motion: Coastal Clips in QuickTime. Wayzata Technology, 1994.
Surf's Up! Pacific CD.
Who Killed Brett Penance? Creative Multimedia, 1994.

6
Cruisin' in the Library

What's your dream car? A souped-up Trans Am? A luxurious Caddy? A rugged ATV? A hot Corvette convertible? Whatever it is, you can learn all about it at the library. Parked on our shelves you'll find information on car repairs, consumer advice, auto racing, classic cars, and much more. Not into wheels? No problem. Our lot is full of books, videos, magazines and music to suit all interests. So don't drive yourself crazy looking for something to do. Head on down the highway and go Cruisin' in the Library.

Display Idea

Hang posters of hot cars and showcase model cars. Display magazines and nonfiction books about new and old cars, automotive repair, the automobile industry, consumer information, auto racing, and other related areas, as well as novels and videos that involve cars or driving in the plot. Include information about car safety and how to obtain a driver's license.

Sponsorship for Prizes

1. Ask a hobby store to donate car models or posters.
2. Ask a bookstore to donate fiction and nonfiction books about cars, and car magazines.
3. Ask a video arcade to donate tokens to use in racing car arcade games.
4. If there is an auto museum, auto show, or auto race arena in your area, ask for donations or free passes.

Program Game

On a map of Europe, mark the route of the Grand Prix automobile race. Patrons will advance one space along the route for each point earned. Points can be earned for completing the activities mentioned in the General Guidelines, and for:
1. Reading a novel and completing a Fiction Book Review Form.
2. Reading a nonfiction book about cars or driving, and completing a Car Nonfiction Book Review Form.
3. Reading a nonfiction book not relating to the car theme and completing a Nonfiction Book Review Form.
4. Reading a car magazine and completing a Car Magazine Review Form.

Program Forms

1. Fiction Book Review Form

Title:

Author:

Publisher and date:

Brief summary of plot:

I would rate this book: "A Grand Prix winner," "Fast and exciting," "Rides well," "Tends to stall at times," "Ready for the scrap heap."

2. Car Nonfiction Book Review Form

Title:

Author:

Publisher and date:

Brief description of information:

Did you find this book to be useful or interesting? Why or why not?

When would you most likely need to use this information?

3. Nonfiction Book Review Form

Title:

Author:

Publisher and date:

Brief description of information:

I would rate this book: "A fully equipped Rolls Royce," "A top-of-the-line luxury car," "A dependable family car," "A cheap second-hand car," "A lemon."

4. Car Magazine Review Form

Name and date of magazine:

Title of one feature article:

Brief summary of the article:

To whom would this magazine appeal and why?

Would you like to read more magazines of this type? Why or why not?

Program Activities

1. Cars on Film. Treat teens to famous car scenes from various movies, such as *Rebel Without a Cause*, *Back to the Future*, *American Graffiti*, and *Thelma and Louise*. Challenge viewers to guess the film from which each clip was taken.

2. All Washed Up. Encourage teen volunteers to participate in a car wash in order to raise funds for the library.

3. Car Care. Invite an auto mechanic to conduct an outdoor workshop on basic car care. Teens can gain hands-on experience in changing a tire; checking, draining, and changing the oil; replacing windshield wiper blades; and other simple car maintenance tasks.

4. Comparison Shopping. Before the program, go to various car dealerships and collect color brochures on all the new cars. Also get copies of the latest consumer magazines about cars. Allow teens to select brochures of the cars they think they would like to own. Next, ask them to name some features they would like in a car (such as a sun roof, good mileage, four-wheel drive, etc.) and have them record these on a checklist. Teens should then look through their car brochures and the consumer magazines, noting on their checklists the features available on their cars. After they have "shopped around," ask teens if they would prefer to own another car, or stick with their original choice.

5. **Stock Cars.** Racing radio-controlled model cars is a popular hobby. Invite some local enthusiasts to show their cars at a library program and talk to teens about how they can become involved in this activity.

6. **Driver Ed.** Have teens compete in a game show that tests how much they know about motor vehicle regulations. Questions can be about driving safely, understanding traffic signs, and "what would you do?" scenarios similar to what is covered in the driver education manual. Ask a driving instructor or Motor Vehicle Department employee to serve as game show host.

7. **Auto Racing.** Ask a race car driver to speak to teens about this sport. Slides, models, and other visual aids can be used to illustrate different types of races, race tracks, race cars, and safety equipment used in racing.

8. **Designs for the Future.** Cars in science fiction novels, TV shows, and movies often are embellished with technologically advanced features. Ask teens to name some fictional car improvements they have read about or seen in the movies. Then have them brainstorm features they would like to see in a car. Divide teens into groups and have each one develop a design for a car of the future. They should describe the physical appearance of the vehicle, as well as its capabilities, the type of fuel it would use, and other details. Encourage creativity.

9. **Automotive Careers.** Showcase various occupations involving cars. These jobs can include auto mechanic, driving instructor, Motor Vehicle Department employee, safety inspector, traffic officer, race car or limousine driver, auto insurance salesperson, plus all the people who design, manufacture, test drive, transport and sell new cars. Provide information on local trade schools that offer courses on servicing automobiles. Make a list of college degrees, such as chemistry, engineering, physics and marketing, that can be applied to jobs in the automobile industry.

10. **Car Hop.** Hold a dance for young adults, playing only music that has to do with cars or driving. Songs by groups with related names, such as the Cars or Crash Test Dummies, can also be used. Encourage teens to bring in their own car songs.

Curriculum Tie-Ins

1. **English Literature/Composition.** Have the class read a novel or some short stories about journeying in a car. Discuss the characteristics of a "road trip" story. Then tell students to write their own stories of this type.

2. **Science.** The inner workings of a car's electrical and chemical systems can be the basis of some science lessons. Discuss what happens when fuel burns, how the exhaust and cooling systems work, and other systems that involve electrical or chemical applications.

3. **History/Geography.** Students can draw a timeline of important events in the invention and development of the automobile. Note such facts as early attempts to create a "horseless carriage," the invention of the steam engine, the introduction of various successful (and unsuccessful) models of cars, factory openings, the creation of gasoline, and other improvements and major events in the automobile industry. Also indicate where in the world each of these developments occurred.

4. **Math.** Assign math problems that involve cars. For example: a) Figure out how long it would take cars at various speeds to travel a certain distance, how many seconds it would take cars at various speeds to come to a complete stop after braking; and what would be a safe distance to follow another car at various speeds; b) Convert driving distances from miles to kilometers; and c) Given the price of a new car, work out a payment plan to finance its purchase.

Activity Sheet Ideas

1. Word search or crossword puzzles of: a) car parts, b) racing terms, or c) gasoline brand names.

2. Word scrambles or cryptograms of: a) famous race car drivers, b) classic cars, or c) TV shows or movies about cars.

3. Matching activities: match a) car models to their manufacturers, b) car models to their trademark logos or insignias, or c) car manufacturers to the countries in which they are headquartered.

Suggested Resources

Reference and Nonfiction

Automotive Encyclopedia. Goodheart-Willcox, 1989.

Berliant, Adam. *The Used Car Reliability and Safety Guide*. Betterway, 1994.

Black, Naomi, and Smith, Mark. *America on Wheels: Tales and Trivia of the Automobile*. Morrow, 1986.

Consumer Guide editors. *Consumer Guide to Cars*. NAL, annual.

Doty, Dennis. *Model Car Building: Getting Started*. Tab, 1989.

Evans, Arthur N. *The Automobile*. Lerner, 1985.

Flammang, James. *The Great Book of Dream Cars*. Publications International, 1990.

Fox, Jack C. *The Illustrated History of the Indianapolis 500*. Carl Hungness, 1985.

Freeman, Kerry A., ed. *Chilton's Easy Car Care*. Chilton, 1985. Also other Chilton repair manuals.

Georgano, G.N., and Wright, Nicky. *The American Automobile: A Century, 1893–1993*. Smithmark, 1992.

Golenbock, Peter. *American Zoom: Stock Car Racing—from the Dirt Tracks to Daytona*. Macmillan, 1993.

Gunnell, John. *A Collector's Guide to Automobilia*. Krause, 1994.

Hensel, George. *Learn to Drive*. Warner, 1987.

Jacobs, David H., Jr. *How to Paint Your Car*. Motorbooks International, 1991.

Johnstone, Michael. *Cars*. Dorling Kindersley, 1994.

Knox, Jean McBee. *Drinking, Driving and Drugs*. Chelsea, 1988.

Knudson, Richard L. *Racing Yesterday's Cars*. Lerner, 1986.

Latham, Caroline, and Agresta, David. *Dodge Dynasty: The Car and the Family That Rocked Detroit*. Harcourt, 1989.

Lyons, Pete, et al. *Ferrari: The Man and His Machines*. Publications International, 1989.

Makower, Joel. *How to Buy a Used Car/How to Sell a Used Car*. Putnam, 1988.

May, George S., ed. *The Automobile Industry, 1920–1980*. Facts on File, 1989.

Nader, Ralph, and Ditlow, Clarence. *Lemon Book: Auto Rights*. Moyer Bell, 1990.

Neely, William, and McCormick, John S.F. *Five-Hundred-Five Automobile Questions Your Friends Can't Answer*. Walker, 1984.

New Car Buying Guide. Publications International, annual.

Nye, Doug. *Famous Racing Cars: Fifty of the Greatest, from Panhard to Williams-Honda*. Patrick Stevens, 1989.

Perry, Philip. *Opportunities in Automotive Services*. VGM, 1996.

Schultz, Morton, Jr. *Keep Your Car Running Practically Forever: An Easy Guide to Routine Care and Maintenance*. Consumer Reports, 1991.

Sclar, Deanna. *Auto Repair for Dummies*. McGraw Hill, 1988.

Swope, Mary, and Kerr, Walter H., eds. *American Classic: Car Poems for Collectors*. SCOP, 1986.

Weber, Robert M. *Opportunities in Automotive Service Careers*. VGM, 1989.

Fiction

Altman, Millys N. *Racing in Her Blood*. Harper, 1980.

Bennett, Jay. *Coverup*. Watts, 1991.

Brooks, Bruce. *Midnight Hour Encores*. Harper, 1986.

Bunting, Eve. *Such Nice Kids*. Houghton, 1990.

_____. *A Sudden Silence*. Harcourt, 1988.

Cooney, Caroline B. *Driver's Ed*. Delacorte, 1994.

Ellis, Ella Thorp. *Riptide*. Macmillan, 1973.

Estleman, Loren D. *Edsel*. Mysterious, 1995.

Faulkner, William. *The Reivers*. Random, 1962.

Grove, Vicki. *The Fastest Friend in the West*. Putnam, 1990.

Hobbs, Valerie. *How Far Would You Have Gotten If I Hadn't Called You Back?* Orchard, 1995.

Juster, Norton. *The Phantom Tollbooth*. Random, 1964.

Karl, Herb. *The Toom County Mud Race*. Delacorte, 1992.

King, Stephen. *Christine*. Viking, 1983.

McCracken, Mark. *A Winning Position*. Dell, 1982.

Mooser, Stephen. *The Hitchhiking Vampire*. Delacorte, 1989.

Paulsen, Gary. *The Car*. Harcourt, 1994.

Pinkwater, Daniel. *Borgel*. Macmillan, 1990.

Swallow, Pamela Curtis. *No Promises*. Putnam, 1989.

Taylor, Mildred. *The Gold Cadillac*. Dial, 1987.

Updike, John. *Rabbit, Run*. Knopf, 1960.

Van Leeuwen, Jean. *Seems Like This Road Goes on Forever*. Dial, 1979.

Watson, Harvey. *Bob War and Poke*. Houghton, 1991.

Wells, Rosemary. *The Man in the Woods*. Dial, 1984.

Wood, Phyllis Anderson. *A Five-Color Buick and a Blue-Eyed Cat*. Westminster, 1977.

Periodicals

Car and Driver. Ziff-Davis Publishing Co.

Car Craft. Petersen Publishing Co.

Four Wheeler Magazine. Penthouse International.

Hot Rod. Petersen Publishing Co.

Motor Trend. Petersen Publishing Co.

Road and Track. Diamandis Communications, Inc.

Feature-Length Films

Back to the Future. MCA/Universal, 1985. (PG)

Days of Thunder. Paramount, 1990. (PG-13)

Heart Like a Wheel. CBS/Fox, 1983. (PG)
License to Drive. CBS/Fox, 1988. (PG-13)
Smoky and the Bandit. MCA/Universal. (PG)
Those Daring Young Men in Their Jaunty Jalopies. Paramount, 1969. (G)
Tucker: The Man and His Dream. Paramount, 1988. (PG)

Computer Software

Auto Almanac. CE3, annual.
Auto Mania: The Ultimate Interactive Car Buying Guide. Creative Multimedia Corp., 1995.
Automap: The Intelligent Road Atlas. Software Marketing Corp., 1993.
Backroad Racers. Revell-Monogram, 1993.
NASCAR Racing. Papyrus Design Group, 1994.
World Circuit. Microprose Software, 1994.

7

Cartoon Cavalcade

What's faster than a speeding bullet, annoys old Mr. Wilson, eats spinach to get strong, lives in a Magic Kingdom in Florida, and says, "What's Up, Doc?" Cartoon characters, of course! The library has cartoon compilations, books on animation and political cartoons, videos based on comic book characters, and much more to draw you in. So take the Batmobile, a silver surfboard, a pizza-encrusted skateboard, or run like the Flash to the library, and join in the Cartoon Cavalcade.

Display Idea

Display graphic novels, comic strip compilations, and books about drawing cartoons. Spread out a few comic books along with nonfiction about animation, comic book art and collecting comics. Include animated videos and live-action movies based on comic book characters that would appeal to teens. Add T-shirts, action figures, and other objects that feature comic characters to create an eye-catching display.

Sponsorship Ideas

1. Ask a comic book dealer to donate comic books.

2. Ask a bookstore to donate compilations of comic strips, books on cartooning, and other related books.

3. Ask a clothing store to donate T-shirts, caps, or other items that feature characters from comic books or strips.

4. Ask a video rental store to donate free rental certificates for animated films or films based on cartoon characters.

Program Game

Post the pages of a popular comic book and number each panel. Patrons can start at the first panel and advance one panel for each point earned. Points can be earned for completing the activities mentioned in the General Guidelines, and for:

1. Reading a cartoon anthology or graphic novel and completing a Cartoon/Graphic Novel Review Form.

2. Reading a prose novel and completing a Fiction Book Review Form.

3. Reading a nonfiction book on a cartoon-related topic and completing a Cartoon Nonfiction Book Review Form.

4. Reading a nonfiction book not related to the cartoon theme and completing a Nonfiction Book Review Form.

Program Forms

1. Cartoon/Graphic Novel Review Form
Title:
Author:
Publisher and date:
If this is a graphic novel, give a brief summary of the story:
If this is a cartoon anthology, what character(s) or type of cartoon is featured?
What did you like best about this book?
Do you think this format suits the story better than prose? Why or why not?
2. Fiction Book Review Form
Title:
Author:
Publisher and date:
Brief summary of plot:
I would rate this book: "Yabba-dabba-doo!" (*Fred Flintstone*), "Cowabunga, dude!" (*Teenage Mutant Ninja Turtles*), "I yam what I yam" (*Popeye*), "Good grief!" (*Charlie Brown*), "Eat my shorts" (*Bart Simpson*).
3. Cartoon Nonfiction Book Review Form
Title:
Author:
Publisher and date:
Brief description of contents:
What did you like most about this book?
What did you learn about the cartoon/comics medium?
4. Nonfiction Book Review Form
Title:
Author:
Publisher and date:
Brief description of information:
I would rate this book: "Super comic—make it into a blockbuster movie," "Popular enough to put it on TV," "Sales of comic book are respectable," "Major publishers turned it down," "Worthless doodles."

Program Activities

1. Comics on Film. Show an animated movie that would appeal to teens, such as *Gargoyles*, or a live-action movie based on a comic book character, such as *Batman Forever*.
2. Art Class. Invite a local artist to conduct a cartooning workshop. Teens can learn the basics of drawing popular comic strip or comic book characters. Or, ask an artist to give a workshop on how to draw caricatures or political cartoons.
3. Comic$. Some comic books have become quite valuable to collectors. Ask an expert to talk to interested teens about the hobby of collecting comic books. The guest can discuss

which comics and artists to collect, how to store collectibles, the value of certain items, clubs and conventions, and collecting for investment.

4. Teen 'Tooners. You may have some artistic patrons who like to draw their own cartoon creations. Set aside an area for them to display examples of their artwork. You can also ask budding cartoonists to submit black and white comics. Compile these into a comic book which can be copied and given to teen patrons.

5. Animation Innovation. Present a program on the history of animation. Display books such as *Disney's Art of Animation,* and show films that give information about the animation process. In the past, each cell was drawn separately. Discuss how computers have revolutionized this process.

6. Cartoon Trivia. Test your patrons' knowledge of comic book trivia in a game show program. Teens can answer questions in categories such as Secret Identities of Superheroes (who does Clark Kent become?), Sidekicks (who is Batman's sidekick?), Team Members (to what team does the Human Torch belong?), Comics on Screen (who played Popeye in the movie?), Publishers (what company publishes *Casper*?), and Origins (how did Spiderman get his super powers?)

7. Comic Book Convention. Teens can come dressed as a character from a comic strip or book to a library-sponsored comic book convention. Provide several comic books, cartoon parody magazines, science fiction and horror magazines, and graphic novels for patrons to read. Show videos of TV cartoons. Ask vendors to display and sell comics and related items. Invite patrons to bring in their own items to display, trade, and sell.

8. Comics Controversy. At various times throughout history, most notably during the 1950s, comic books have been called subversive and dangerous. Provide articles and books in which critics have charged that comic books contribute to juvenile delinquency. Hold a discussion on this topic, or have teens role-play a scene in which comic book artists and publishers must defend their art to critics and censors. You may also want to include current TV cartoons, such as *Ren and Stimpy* and *Beavis and Butthead*, in your discussion.

9. Comical Lives. Provide information on careers associated with cartooning at a job fair for young adult patrons. Freelance jobs can include comic strip or comic book artist, political cartoonist, and caricature artist. There are also job opportunities in animation, syndicating features, publishing and marketing comic books, producing and distributing merchandise, voice acting (supplying voices for animated characters), and dealing comic collectibles. Supply materials for patrons to check out in these and related areas.

10. Tuneful 'Toons. Young adults can celebrate cartoons at a dance party where all the music played has been inspired by cartoon characters. Play songs recorded by the Archies, the Simpsons, Alvin and the Chipmunks, Beavis and Butthead, etc., as well as theme songs from TV cartoons and soundtrack music from comics-inspired movies such as *Dick Tracy*. It may be fun to let partygoers lip synch to some of these songs. Show videos of some classic cartoon music scenes, such as Disney's *The Sorcerer's Apprentice* or Bugs Bunny's version of *The Barber of Seville*.

Curriculum Tie-Ins

1. English Literature/Composition. Have students read some graphic novels, such as *Maus: A Survivor's Tale*, or adaptations of classic novels and plays. Discuss whether students think this is a valid form of literature. Also compare graphic novels to comic books. How are they similar? Different? Then have students choose a scene from a prose novel and describe how they would rewrite it as a graphic novel.

2. Science. Take a look at how several comic book superheroes gained their super powers. Many mutated when they were exposed to large doses of radiation or were immersed in a toxic substance. Students can draw up a chart of superheroes, the scientific event that altered them, and the changes that occurred. Then have students create a separate chart of real-life consequences of these accidents.

3. History/Geography. Look at popular comic strips and comic books, as well as political cartoons throughout American history, to see how they conveyed the political mood of the times. Students can relate comic book and strip references to specific events or eras. For example, Captain America was created by Marvel in 1941 in response to the Nazi takeover of Europe, and he also fought Communists in the 1950s during the Cold War in Russia.

4. Math. Have students conduct a poll to determine the most popular comic strip, cartoon character, comic book superhero, TV cartoon, comic strip artist, etc. Then students should chart the top ten responses in each category. Compare the results according to overall responses, girls versus boys, and teens versus adults.

Activity Sheet Ideas

1. Word search or crossword puzzles of: a) TV cartoon characters, b) comic book superheroes and villains, or c) comic strip characters.

2. Word scrambles or cryptograms of: a) comic book artists, b) animated feature films, or c) expressions made popular by comic characters.

3. Matching activities: match a) comic strip artists to the names of their comic strips, b) comic books to their publishers, or c) superheroes to their secret identities.

Suggested Resources

Reference and Nonfiction

Bendazzi, Giannalberto. *Cartoons: One Hundred Years of Cinema Animation.* Indiana University Press, 1994.

Callahan, Bob, ed. *The New Comics Anthology.* Collier, 1991.

Cawley, John, and Korkis, Jim. *How to Create Animation.* Pioneer, 1990.

The Editors of Comics Journal. *The Best Comics of the Decade.* Fantagraphics, 1990.

Gautier, Dick. *The Art of Caricature.* Putnam, 1985.

Glasbergen, Randy. *Getting Started Drawing and Selling Cartoons.* North Light, 1993.

Gonick, Larry. *The Cartoon History of the Universe II: Volumes 8–13: From the Springtime of China to the Fall of Rome, India Too!* Doubleday, 1994.

Goulart, Ron. *The Comic Book Reader's Companion: An A-to-Z Guide to Everyone's Favorite Art Form.* HarperPerennial, 1993.

_____. *The Encyclopedia of American Comics.* Facts on File, 1990.

Hart, Christopher. *How to Draw Comic Book Heroes and Villains.* Watson-Guptill, 1995.

Harvey, Robert C. *The Art of the Funnies: An Aesthetic History.* University Press of Mississippi, 1994.

Johnson, Rheta Grimsley. *Good Grief: The Story of Charles M. Schultz.* Pharos, 1989.

Jones, Chuck. *Chuck Amuck: The Life and Times of an Animated Cartoonist.* Farrar, 1989.

Kane, Bob, and Andrae, Tom. *Batman and Me.* Eclipse, 1989.

McCloud, Scott. *Understanding Comics: The Invisible Art.* Tundra, 1993.

McKenzie, Alan. *How to Draw and Sell Comic Strips*. North Light, 1987.

O'Sullivan, Judith. *The Great American Comic Strip: One Hundred Years of Cartoon Art*. Bulfinch, 1990.

Overstreet, Robert M. *Overstreet's Comic Book Price Guide*. Avon, 1995.

Owens, Thomas *Collecting Comic Books: A Young Person's Guide*. Millbrook, 1995.

Reed, Arthea J.S. *Comics to Classics*. International Reading Association, 1988.

Reidelbach, Maria. *Completely Mad: A History of the Comic Book and Magazine*. Little, 1991.

Rothschild, D. Aviva. *Graphic Novels: A Bibliographic Guide to Book-Length Comics*. Libraries Unlimited, 1995.

Rovin, Jeff. *The Encyclopedia of Superheroes*. Facts on File, 1985.

Simon, Joe, and Simon, Jim. *The Comic Book Makers*. Crestwood, 1990.

Solomon, Charles. *Enchanted Drawings: The History of Animation*. Knopf, 1989.

Staake, Bob. *The Complete Book of Caricature*. North Light, 1991.

Thomas, Bob. *Disney's Art of Animation: From Mickey Mouse to Beauty and the Beast*. Hyperion, 1991.

Tower, Samuel A. *Cartoons and Lampoons: The Art of Political Satire*. Messner, 1982.

Wiater, Stan, and Bissette, Stephen. *Comic Book Rebels: Conversations with the Creators of New Comics*. D.I. Fine, 1992.

Weiner, Stephen. *100 Graphic Novels for Public Libraries*. Kitchen Sink, 1996.

Graphic Novels

Alfred, Mike. *The Collected Madman Adventures*. Kitchen Sink, 1995. (Also *Madman: The Oddity Odyssey*.)

Avi, and Floca, Brian. *City of Light, City of Dark: A Comic Book Novel*. Orchard, 1993.

Busiek, Kurt. *Marvels*. Marvel, 1994.

Castelli, Alfredo, and Manara, Milo. *The Snowman*. Catalan Communications, 1990.

Chadwick, Paul. *The Complete Concrete*. Dark Horse Comics, 1994. (Also *Concrete: Fragile Creature*.)

Cruse, Howard. *Stuck Rubber Baby*. Paradox Press/DC Comics, 1995.

London, Jack, and Moser, Barry. *Call of the Wild*. Macmillan, 1994.

McCaffrey, Anne, et al. *Dragonflight*. Eclipse, 1991.

Mairowitz, David Zane, and Crumb, Robert. *Introducing Kafka*. Kitchen Sink, 1994.

Marder, Larry. *Larry Marder's Beanworld: Book One*. Beanworld, 1995.

Mason, Patrick, and Russell, P. Craig. *Wolfgang Amadeus Mozart's The Magic Flute*. Eclipse, 1990.

Mignola, Mike. *Hellboy: Seed of Destruction*. Dark Horse Comics, 1994.

Moore, Alan. *A Small Killing*. Dark Horse Comics, 1993.

Pekar, Harvey, and Brabner, Joyce. *Our Cancer Year*. Four Walls Eight Windows, 1994.

Pini, Wendy, and Pini, Richard. *The Complete Elfquest Graphic Novel*. Warp Graphics, various years.

Posey, Carl. *The Big Book of Weirdos*. Paradox Press/DC Comics, 1995.

Russell, P. Craig. *Fairy Tales of Oscar Wilde, Vol. 2*, NBM, 1992.

Sacco, Joe. *War Junkie: Illustrated Tales of Combat, Depression, and Rock 'n' Roll*. Fantagraphics.

Sakai, Stan. *Usagi Yojimbo*. Fantagraphics.

Schultz, Mark. *Dinosaur Shaman: Nine Tales from the Xenozoic Age*. Kitchen Sink, 1990.

Shelley, Mary Wollstonecraft, and Wrightson, Bennie. *Bennie Wrightson's Frankenstein: or, The Modern Prometheus*. Underwood Miller, 1995.

Sim, Dave. *Cerebus: Flight* (Mothers and Daughters, Book 1). Aardvark-Vanaheim, 1993.

Smith, Jeff. *The Complete Bone Adventures, Vol. 1–3*. Cartoon Books.

Spiegelman, Art. *Maus I: A Survivor's Tale*. Pantheon, 1992. (Also: *Maus II*)

Stradley, Randy. *Aliens vs. Predator*. Dark Horse Comics, 1991.
Talbot, Bryan. *The Tale of One Bad Rat (Books One Through Four)*. Dark Horse Comics.
Tamarkin, Jeff, and Schreiner, David. *Grateful Dead Comix*. Hyperion, 1992.
Taylan, Justin R. *No Place for a Picnic*. Wanpela, 1994.
Tolkien, J.R.R., and Wenzel, David. *The Hobbit; or, There and Back Again*. Eclipse, 1990.
Veitch, Tom, and Kennedy, Cam. *Star Wars: Dark Empire Collections*. Dark Horse Comics, 1995.

Fiction

Cheetham, Ann. *The Pit*. Holt, 1990.
Covington, Vicki. *Gathering Home*. Simon & Schuster, 1988.
Gilden, Mel. *Harry Newberry and the Raiders of the Red Drink*. Holt, 1989.
James, Mary. *Frankenlouse*. Scholastic, 1994.
Lee, Stan, ed. *The Ultimate Spider-Man*. Berkley, 1994.
O'Neil, Dennis. *Batman: Knightfall*. Bantam, 1994.
Say, Allen. *The Ink-Keeper's Apprentice*. Houghton, 1994.
Wolf, Gary. *Who Censored Roger Rabbit?* St. Martin's, 1981. (Also: *Who P-P-P-Plugged Roger Rabbit?*)

Periodicals

Animation Magazine. VSD Publications, Inc.
Comics Buyers Guide. Krause Publications, Inc.
Comics Interview. Comics Interview.
Comics Journal. Fantagraphics Books.
Comics Scene. Starlog Group.
Mad Magazine. E.C. Publications, Inc.

Feature-Length Films

Artists and Models. Paramount, 1955.
Batman Forever. Warner, 1995. (PG-13)
Fantasia. Walt Disney, 1940.
50 of the Greatest Cartoons. Starmaker Entertainment, 1990.
Dick Tracy. Touchstone, 1990. (PG)
Gargoyles, the Movie: The Heroes Awaken. Touchstone, 1994. (G)
Who Framed Roger Rabbit? Touchstone, 1986. (PG)

Computer Software

Beneath a Steel Sky. Virgin Interactive Entertainment, 1994.
The Cartoon History of the Universe. Putnam New Media, 1993.
Comic Book Confidential. Voyager Company, 1992.
Comic Creator. Putnam New Media, 1995.
ComicBase Encyclopedia of Comics. Human Computing, 1994.
Interactive Computer Based Comic ICBC. Multicom Info Systems, 1993.

8

Books for the Concerned Citizen

Do you know what's going on in this country? You can find the resources you need to learn about how the government works, current issues, elections, legislation and other national and local information at the library. There are books, magazines, newspapers and pamphlets to keep you informed, as well as novels, essays and editorials to help you form your own opinions. You can demonstrate your interest in the United States political process when you read Books for the Concerned Citizen.

Display Idea

Nonfiction books on topics such as human rights, citizenship, politics, elections and voting rights, democracy and other types of government, laws, and the lives of various politicians can be displayed along with related fiction. You can also include political magazines, essays, editorials, and speeches. Post reproductions of important government documents and add campaign memorabilia to the display.

Sponsorship for Prizes

1. Ask a bookstore to donate books on citizenship issues, politics, and other related topics.

2. If a local government building has a gift shop, ask them to donate souvenir items.

3. If there is an upcoming election in your area, contact the campaign headquarters for each party and ask them to donate bumper stickers, buttons, and other items.

4. Ask a magazine vendor to donate issues of political and current events magazines.

Program Game

For the game board, use a street map of Washington, D.C., that indicates the sites of the major federal government buildings. Draw a trail from the Washington Monument, past several landmarks, ending at the White House. Patrons can advance one space along the trail for each point earned. Points can be earned for completing the activities mentioned in the General Guidelines, and for:

1. Reading a novel related to the citizenship theme and completing a Citizenship Fiction Book Review Form.

2. Reading a novel not related to the theme and completing a Fiction Book Review Form.

3. Reading a nonfiction book related to the citizenship theme and completing a Citizenship Nonfiction Book Review Form.

4. Reading a nonfiction book not related to the theme and completing a Nonfiction Book Review Form.

Program Forms

1. Citizenship Fiction Book Review Form
Title:
Author:
Publisher and date:
Brief summary of plot:
How does this story comment on citizenship issues?
Do you think the story is true to life? Why or why not?
2. Fiction Book Review Form
Title:
Author:
Publisher and date:
Brief summary of plot:
I would rate this book: "Sweeps the polls," "Might win in a runoff," "A distant contender," "A poor campaigner," "Doesn't deserve a place on the ballot."
3. Citizenship Nonfiction Book Review Form
Title:
Author:
Publisher and date:
Brief description of information:
Did you find the information in the book to be interesting and valuable? Why or why not?
Would you like to read more on this topic? Why or why not?
4. Nonfiction Book Review Form
Title:
Author:
Publisher and date:
Brief description of information:
I would rate this book: "President," "Senator," "Governor," "Selectman," "Dog Catcher."

Program Activities

1. Screening Politics. Show a film that depicts or satirizes politics in the United States, such as *Tanner '88*.

2. Campaign Signs. Provide construction paper, markers, glue, and stencils for teens to create banners, flags, and posters for an upcoming election or political event. Or, teens can pretend that they are running for a political office and create a billboard or banner for their own campaigns.

3. Meet the Candidates. If there is an upcoming election in your community, invite some candidates to discuss their platforms with a group of teens. Provide patrons with information about the issues at hand so they can prepare appropriate questions to ask the candidates.

4. Official Visit. Arrange to take a group of teens on a tour of a government building, such as the state house or town hall. Make sure a guide is available to offer comments and answer questions.

5. The Right to Vote. Contact the registrar of voters in your community to arrange to have a voter registration drive at the library. Teens who are too young to vote can help out by making posters and writing articles to publicize the drive in their schools, and by encouraging their friends who are 18 and over to register.

6. Informed Citizens. Teens can show how much they know about political issues and government in this game show program. Categories of questions can include Famous Political Quotes, United States Presidents, Government Branches, Campaigns and Elections, Federal (or State) Laws, and Know Your Rights.

7. Pick a Cause. Many politicians and private citizens concerned about government issues have given impassioned speeches for their causes. Provide the texts for speeches by presidents and other elected officials, candidates, activists, human rights leaders, and others. Teens can choose one they like and read their interpretations of the speech to the group.

8. Teens Speak Out. Involve teens in a discussion related to the citizenship issues theme. Some ideas for possible topics are: "What does it mean to be a good citizen?" "Does democracy work?" "The biggest problem facing this country today is…" or "What would you do if you were president?" Give each person a chance to express an opinion, and try to have teens reach a consensus at the end of the discussion.

9. Political Careers. Various jobs in local, state, and federal government can be spotlighted in a theme-related careers program. Information on other work, such as political analyst, lobbyist, news reporter, speech writer, lawyer, and activist, can also be made available to patrons. Provide materials for teens to check out, as well as sources for gaining further career information.

10. Election. Hold a mock election, with teens running for various offices. You can sponsor a debate or political convention, complete with campaign slogans and posters, so that the candidates can state their views on issues that concern their voters. Teens can vote at the polls and tally the votes. Losers should give short concession speeches, and winners can give their acceptance speeches.

Curriculum Tie-Ins

1. English Literature/Composition. Assign several political essays and editorials, such as those written by Mark Twain, Henry David Thoreau, or William F. Buckley, for students to read and discuss in class. With what issue is the author concerned? What is the author's political point of view (liberal or conservative), and how is that reflected in the writing? After students have analyzed these pieces, have each choose a current political issue and write an essay or editorial that states his or her own opinion on the subject.

2. Science. One of the earliest computers was invented to tabulate election results. Show students how past and modern computers process votes. How has the use of computers affected elections in the United States?

3. History/Geography. The right to vote was not always granted to all United States citizens. Students can learn about how various groups (the poor, blacks, women, etc.) struggled for suffrage in this country. You may also want to teach a related unit on human rights and the fight for all people to gain equality. How do conditions in the United States compare to the political conditions in other countries?

4. Math. Have students conduct a public opinion poll on several current issues, or a political poll to determine how many people plan to vote for certain candidates in an upcoming election. Students can tally and chart the answers, make predictions, and calculate percentages based on a variety of demographics (age or sex of voter, etc.)

Activity Sheet Ideas

1. Word search or crossword puzzles of: a) political terms, b) government offices, or c) current issues.

2. Word scrambles or cryptograms of: a) quotes from political speeches, b) names of elected officials, or c) titles of major pieces of legislation.

3. Matching activities: match a) United States vice presidents to the presidents they served under, b) governors or senators to their states, or c) famous statesmen to quotes from their speeches.

Suggested Resources

Reference and Nonfiction

Aaseng, Nathan. *America's Third-Party Presidential Candidates*. Oliver, 1995.

Adler, Mortimer J. *We Hold These Truths: Understanding the Ideas and Ideals of the Constitution*. Macmillan, 1987.

Archer, Jules. *Winners and Losers: How Elections Work in America*. Harcourt, 1984.

_____. *You Can't Do That to Me! Famous Fights for Human Rights*. Macmillan, 1980.

Baum, Lawrence. *The Supreme Court*. Congressional Quarterly, 1988.

Baxter, Neale J. *Opportunities in Federal Government*. VGM, 1992.

_____. *Opportunities in State and Local Government*. VGM, 1993.

Brown, Jean, ed. *Preserving Intellectual Freedom: Fighting Censorship in Our Schools*. NCTE, 1994.

Buch, Julie S., ed. *Opposing Viewpoints: Civil Liberties*. Greenhaven, 1988.

Carrel, Annette. *It's the Law! A Young Person's Guide to Our Legal System*. Volcano, 1995.

Carter, Jimmy. *Talking Peace: A Vision for the Next Generation*. Dutton, 1995.

Davidson, Roger, and Oleszek, Walter J. *Congress and Its Members*. Congressional Quarterly, 1985.

Guggenheim, Martin, and Sussman, Alan. *The Rights of Young People*. Southern Illinois University Press, 1985.

Hakim, Joy. *All the People*. Oxford University Press, 1995.

Hentoff, Nat. *American Heroes: In and Out of School*. Delacorte, 1987.

_____. *The First Freedom: The Tumultuous History of Free Speech in America*. Delacorte, 1986.

Howell, John C. *Everyday Law for Everyone*. TAB, 1987.

Kronenwetter, Michael. *Are You a Liberal? Are You a Conservative?* Watts, 1984.

_____. *Protest!* Twenty-First Century, 1996.

Kuklin, Susan. *Irrepressible Spirit—Conversations with Human Rights Activists*. Putnam, 1996.

Langley, Winston E., and Fox, Vivian C., eds. *Women's Rights in the United States: A Documentary History*. Greenwood, 1994.

Lipset, Seymour Martin, ed. *The Encyclopedia of Democracy*. Congressional Quarterly, 1995.

Melder, Keith. *Hail to the Candidate: Presidential Campaigns from Banners to Broadcasts*. Smithsonian, 1992.

Modl, Tom. *Opposing Viewpoints: America's Elections*. Greenhaven, 1988.

Raber, Thomas R. *Election Night*. Lerner, 1988.

Relsche, Diana. *Electing a U. S. President*. Watts, 1992.

Samuels, Cynthia. *It's a Free Country! A Young Person's Guide to Politics and Elections*. Atheneum, 1988.

Sherrow, Victoria. *Image and Substance: The Media in U. S. Elections*. Millbrook, 1992.

Steele, James. *Freedom's River: The African-American Contribution to Democracy*. Watts, 1995.

Stevens, Doris. *Jailed for Freedom: American Women Win the Vote*. NewSage, 1995.

Wilson, Robert A., ed. *Character Above All: Ten Presidents from FDR to George Bush*. Simon & Schuster, 1996. (Also others in series.)

Zeinert, Karen. *Free Speech: From Newspapers to Music Lyrics*. Enslow, 1995.

Fiction

Avi. *Nothing but the Truth*. Orchard, 1991.

Buss, Fran Leeper. *Journey of the Sparrows*. Lodestar, 1991.

Cohen, Miriam. *Laura Leonora's First Amendment*. Lodestar, 1990.

Davis, Ossie. *Just Like Martin*. Simon & Schuster, 1992.

Drury, Allen. *Advise and Consent*. Doubleday, 1959.

Facklam, Margery. *The Trouble with Mothers*. Clarion, 1989.

Feinstein, John. *Running Mates*. Random, 1992.

First, Julia. *The Absolute, Ultimate End*. Watts, 1985.

Hentoff, Nat. *The Day They Came to Arrest the Book*. Dell, 1983.

Langton, Jane. *The Fragile Flag*. Harper, 1984.

Lehrer, Jim. *Short List*. Putnam, 1992.

Lipsyte, Robert. *Jock and Jill*. Harper, 1977.

Lucas, Cynthia K. *Center Stage Summer*. Square One, 1988.

Malmgren, Dallin. *The Ninth Issue*. Delacorte, 1989.

Miles, Betty. *Maudie and Me and the Dirty Book*. Knopf, 1980.

Moore, Yvette. *Freedom Songs*. Orchard, 1991.

Nixon, Joan Lowery. *A Candidate for Murder*. Macmillan, 1992.

O'Connor, Edwin. *The Last Hurrah*. Little, 1956.

Pfeffer, Susan Beth. *A Matter of Principle*. Delacorte, 1982.

Rand, Ayn. *Atlas Shrugged*. Random, 1957.

Ross, Rhea Beth. *The Bet's On, Lizzie Bingham!* Houghton, 1988.

Thompson, Julian. *The Trials of Molly Sheldon*. Holt, 1995.

Truman, Margaret. *Murder at the Kennedy Center*. Random, 1989.

VanOosting, James. *Electing J.J.* Farrar, 1990.

Vonnegut, Kurt. *Jailbird: A Novel*. Dell, 1979.

Walker, Alice. *Meridian*. Harcourt, 1976.

Warren, Robert Penn. *All the King's Men*. Buccaneer, 1981.

White, Ellen Emerson. *White House Autumn*. Avon, 1985.

Periodicals

Center Magazine. Center for the Study of Democratic Institutions.

Congressional Record. U.S. Government Printing Office.

Current History. Current History, Inc.
Newsletter on Intellectual Freedom. American Library Association.
Vital Speeches of the Day. The City News Publishing Co.

Feature-Length Films

An American President. Columbia Tristar, 1995. (PG-13)
Legend of Billie Jean. CBS/Fox, 1985. (PG-13)
The Long Walk Home. Live Home Video, 1989. (PG)
Mr. Smith Goes to Washington. Columbia Tristar, 1939.
Separate But Equal. Republic Pictures, 1991. (PG)
Tanner '88. HBO, 1988.

Computer Software

Capitol Hill. Mindscape, 1993.
Constitution Hall. Westwind Media, 1994.
Inside the White House. Bureau of Electronic Publishing, 1995.
Origins of the Constitution. Queue, 1992.
U.S. Civics/Citizenship on Disc. Quanta Press.
Vote America. Virtual Entertainment, 1996.

9

Life in the City

Almost half of the people on Earth live in a city. You can find out about the people, culture, tourist attractions, industries, problems, and other information about many cities at the library. Besides nonfiction, you can read lots of great novels and check out videos that are set in metro areas around the world. You don't have to be an urban dweller to enjoy Life in the City at the library.

Display Idea

Feature novels in which a city setting is an important part of the story. Nonfiction relating to cities, such as travel guides, poetry, and photo essays, should be included. Magazines about city life, plus videos set in cities and music by groups named after cities, can also be added to the display. Hang posters of the world's great cities by this area.

Sponsorship for Prizes

1. Ask a travel agency to donate posters, maps, and other tour books of major cities around the world.

2. Ask a video rental store to donate free rental certificates for films set in major cities.

3. Ask a clothing store to donate caps and T-shirts that have names of cities printed on them.

4. Ask a bookstore to donate novels set in cities or travel books featuring various cities.

Program Game

Use a political map of the United States, with several major cities identified, as the game board. Patrons can place a star on one city for each point earned. Points can be earned for completing the activities mentioned in the General Guidelines, and for:

1. Reading a novel related to the city theme and completing a City Fiction Book Review Form.

2. Reading a novel not related to the city theme and completing a Fiction Book Review Form.

3. Reading a nonfiction book about one or more cities and completing a City Nonfiction Book Review Form.

4. Reading a nonfiction book not related to the city theme and completing a Nonfiction Book Review Form.

Program Forms

1. City Fiction Book Review Form
Title:
Author:
Publisher and date:
Brief summary of plot:
Why is the city location important in the book?
Is (Are) the city (cities) depicted favorably or not? How?
2. Fiction Book Review Form
Title:
Author:
Publisher and date:
Brief summary of plot:
I would rate this book: "Ranked in the Top Ten of Best United States Cities," "A good place to live and work," "Many positive aspects, but has some big-city problems," "Not much opportunity in this city," "Poorly run, polluted, and crime-ridden."
3. City Nonfiction Book Review Form
Title:
Author:
Publisher and date:
Brief description of information:
Name one interesting fact from the book:
Which place mentioned in the book would you most like to visit and why?
4. Nonfiction Book Review Form
Title:
Author:
Publisher and date:
Brief description of information:
I would rate this book: "My kind of town!," "A nice place to visit," "May want to go there someday," "Doesn't interest me," "A place to avoid."

Program Activities

1. City View. Entertain patrons with a movie about life in a city, such as *Urban Cowboy*.

2. City Symbols. Teens can make craft items that relate to a specific city. Some suggestions: Make a clay Liberty Bell model to represent Philadelphia, a miniature Mardi Gras float for New Orleans, or a trolley car for San Francisco. Provide craft materials and pictures of objects which relate to specific cities for teens to use.

3. City Sights. Invite someone who has traveled or lived in an interesting city to speak to patrons, show slides or pictures, and display souvenirs. You may want to present a series of travelogues about several cities throughout this unit.

4. Urban Adventure. Teens can use actual city maps to invent a board game based on a local or famous city. The game may involve visiting popular tourist spots, shopping, building or using the transit system, or any other ideas patrons may have. Teens must decide on the object of the game, devise rules for playing, create any game pieces that are needed, and name their game. Later, they can have fun playing it. Or, teens can draw up plans for a video game about visiting or building a city, such as the *SimCity* computer games.

5. Food Fair. Some cities are famous for certain foods. Ask teens to help cook dishes such as Cincinnati 5-Way Chili, Boston Baked Beans, or New York's Coney Island Hot Dogs, to serve at a City Foods Buffet. Provide cookbooks so that teens can choose a recipe they want to prepare.

6. Metro-Game. Challenge young adults to compete in a game show program about cities. Categories can include Ancient Cities, Capitals, Tourist Spots, Famous Citizens, Which Is Bigger? and Claims to Fame.

7. Post It. Set aside a bulletin board or wall space to create a gallery of postcards depicting scenes from major cities. Encourage teens to bring in their postcards and write a brief caption for each one.

8. Metropolis. Ask teens to consider what an American city of the future might look like. As a group project, they can build a model space-age city of their own design. What would a futuristic city use as its primary energy source? Would overpopulation or pollution be a problem? What new types of communication systems would be in use? How would these factors affect building architecture, modes of transportation, and other physical features? Teens can use their imaginations to create their futuristic city out of various recycled materials.

9. On the Job. Spotlight city-related jobs in a career program. Include positions in municipal government, planning and zoning, architecture, education, libraries, news media, law enforcement, civil engineering, construction, sanitation, parks and recreation, the tourist industry and other areas. Provide books and career information on these jobs for patrons to read.

10. City Beat. Sponsor a dance for young adults at which all the music played is either by a group named after a city, such as Boston, or is a song that names one or more cities in its lyrics.

Curriculum Tie-Ins

1. English Literature/Composition. Provide several copies of Sunday newspapers from a number of large United States cities. Devise a survey form for students to complete that compares the writing styles, news formats, editorial pages, travel sections, and other features of these papers. Which newspaper is easier to read, provides the most information, has the best sports coverage? Then ask students to write news articles or editorials about current events in a local city.

2. Science. The causes and effects of environmental pollution, which is a crisis in many cities, can be studied. Have students choose a large city, anywhere in the world, and research the causes of the air and water pollution there. What industries or other factors contribute to the problem? How does this pollution affect the health of local humans and animals? What is being done to improve the quality of the environment?

3. History/Geography. Let each student choose a major city anywhere in the world to study. They can present their information in the form of a travel brochure which includes descriptions of major points of interest, historic sites, population statistics, weather information, language(s) spoken, currency used, best times to visit, and other news of interest to travelers. Pictures and maps of the city should also be included.

4. Math. Have students look up statistics pertaining to several cities, such as population, area, number of schools, birth/death rates, etc. Students can draw up charts or graphs to compare these statistics, or compare percentages (for example, percent of the population over age 65).

Activity Sheet Ideas

1. Word search or crossword puzzles of names of: a) cities, b) city government terms, or c) names of mayors from cities in your home state.

2. Word scrambles or cryptograms of: a) verses from songs about cities, b) tourist bureau slogans for cities, or c) major companies and industries in local cities.

3. Matching activities: match a) current city names to their names in earlier times, b) major celebrations and festivals to the city with which they are associated, or c) historical events to the cities in which they happened.

Suggested Resources

Reference and Nonfiction

Adoff, Arnold. *Street Music: City Poems*. HarperCollins, 1992.

Baxter, Neale J. *Opportunities in State and Local Government*. VGM, 1993.

Bettmann, Otto L. *The Good Old Days—They Were Terrible*. Random, 1974.

Brunvand, Jan Harold. *The Vanishing Hitchhiker: Urban Legends and Their Meanings*. Norton, 1981.

Cities of the World. 4 vols. Gale, 1997.

Cochrane, Jennifer. *Urban Ecology*. Watts, 1987.

Comes, Pilar, and Hernandez, Xavier. *Barmi: A Mediterranean City Through the Ages*. Houghton, 1990. (Also others in series.)

Fodor's...Europe's Great Cities. Fodor Travel Publications, 1990. (Also other Fodor Travel guides.)

Gay, Kathlyn. *Cities Under Stress*. Watts, 1985.

Hanmer, Trudy. *The Growth of Cities*. Watts, 1985.

Janeczko, Paul B. *Brickyard Summer*. Watts, 1989.

Jungreis, Abigail. *Know Your Hometown History: Projects and Activities*. Watts, 1992.

Krull, Kathleen. *City Within a City: How Kids Live in New York's China Town*. Lodestar, 1994.

_____. *The Other Side: How Kids Live in a California Latino Neighborhood*. Lodestar, 1994.

Larrick, Nancy, ed. *On City Streets: An Anthology of Poetry*. Evans, 1968.

Loewen, Nancy, and Stewart, Gail. *Great Cities of the U.S.* 8 vols. Rourke, 1989.

Macaulay, David. *Underground*. Houghton, 1976.

Mackay, Donald A. *The Building of Manhattan: How Manhattan Was Built Overground and Underground from the Dutch Settlers to the Skyscrapers*. HarperCollins, 1987.

Merriam, Eve. *The Inner City Mother Goose*. Simon & Schuster, 1996.

Murphy, Jim. *The Great Fire*. Scholastic, 1995.

Royston, Robert. *Cities*. Facts on File, 1985.

Shaffer, Carolyn, and Fielder, Erica. *City Safaris*. Sierra, 1987.

Urban Wilds. Time-Life, 1975.

Webb, Margot. *Coping with Street Gangs*. Rosen, 1990.

Wright, David. *A Multicultural Portrait of Life in the Cities*. Marshall Cavendish, 1993.

Yepsen, Roger. *City Trains: Moving Through America's Cities*. Macmillan, 1993.

Fiction

Alexander, Lloyd. *The Philadalphia Adventure*. Dutton, 1990.

Austin, Doris J., and Simmons, Martin, eds. *Streetlights: Illuminating Tales of the Urban Black Experience*. Viking Penguin, 1996.

Avi. *City of Light, City of Dark: A Comic Book Novel*. Orchard, 1993.

Bonham, Frank. *Durango Street*. Dutton, 1965.

Clark, Mary Higgins. *Loves Music, Loves to Dance*. Simon and Schuster, 1991.

Cohen, Daniel. *Southern Fried Rat and Other Gruesome Tales*. Evans, 1983.

Danziger, Paula. *Remember Me to Harold Square*. Delacorte, 1987. (Also *Thames Doesn't Rhyme with James*.)

Garland, Sherry. *Song of the Buffalo Boy*. Harcourt, 1992.

Gregory, Kristiana. *Earthquake at Dawn*. Harcourt, 1992.

Harris, Mark Jonathan. *Come the Morning*. Bradbury, 1989.

Herzig, Alison Cragin, and Mali, Jane Lawrence. *Sam and the Moon Queen*. Clarion, 1990.

Hicyilmaz, Gaye. *Against the Storm*. Little, 1992.

Holman, Felice. *Secret City, U.S.A.* Scribner, 1990. (Also *Slake's Limbo*.)

Hughes, Dean. *Family Pose*. Atheneum, 1989.

Keene, Carolyn. *The Picture of Guilt*. Pocket, 1994.

Likhanov, Albert. *Shadow Across the Sun*. Harper, 1983.

Littke, Lael. *Loydene in Love*. Harcourt, 1986.

Llewellyn, Caroline. *The Masks of Rome*. Scribner, 1988.

Lowry, Lois. *Taking Care of Terrific*. Houghton, 1983.

Mazer, Norma Fox. *Downtown*. Morrow, 1984.

Murphy, Pat. *The City, Not Long After*. Doubleday, 1989.

Myers, Walter Dean. *The Mouse Rap*. Harper, 1990.

Nelson, Theresa. *The Beggar's Ride*. Orchard, 1992.

Neville, Emily Cheney. *The China Year*. HarperCollins, 1991.

Paretsky, Sara. *Burn Marks*. Delacorte, 1990.

Peck, Richard. *Voices After Midnight*. Delacorte, 1989.

Petersen, P.J. *The Boll Weevil Express*. Dell, 1984.

Roberts, Willo Davis. *What Could Go Wrong?* Atheneum, 1989.

Shusterman, Neal. *Dissidents*. Little, 1989.

Smith, David Alexander, ed. *Future Boston: The History of a City 1990–2100*. Tor, 1995.

Periodicals

City Family (also available in Spanish as *La Familia de la Ciudad*). Box 748 Ansonia Station, New York, N.Y. 10023.

Journal of Urban History. Sage Publications.

New York. K-III Magazines. (Also other magazines about specific cities.)

Feature-Length Films

Earthquake. MCA/Universal, 1974. (PG)

Ferris Bueller's Day Off. Paramount, 1986. (PG-13)

Forget Paris. Columbia Tristar, 1995. (PG-13)
L.A. Story. Warner, 1991. (PG-13)
The Out-of-Towners. Paramount, 1983. (PG)
Streetwise. Starmaker Entertainment, 1985.
Urban Cowboy. Paramount, 1980. (PG)

Computer Software

Environmental Views Series: Cities and Settlements. Optilearn, 1995.
Frommer's A Guide to America's Most Travelled Cities. Prentice Hall/Simon and Schuster. (Also other Frommer titles.)
Great Cities of the World Vol. 1. InterOptica Publishing, 1991. (Also Vol. 2.)
SimCity 2000. Maxis, 1993. (Also other *Sim* games.)
Street Atlas USA. DeLorme Mapping Systems, 1993.

10
The Classics Never Die

The library is a real class act—and we can prove it! Browse the shelves to find classic works of art, poetry, drama, and prose. Listen to classical music on CD, or view a filmed version of a classic piece of literature. Of course, we have a wide selection of recently published novels, some of which are surely destined to become future classics. You are cordially invited to come in and enrich your life, because at the library, The Classics Never Die.

Display Idea

Fiction, poetry, and plays that are considered classic literature can be displayed along with books on mythology, great philosophers, important works of art and art history. Also include CDs of classical music, videos of classic literature, and related magazines. Prints of art masterpieces and posters depicting scenes from classic plays can be hung near the display.

Sponsorship for Prizes

1. Ask a local bookstore to donate classic works of literature.
2. Ask a music store to donate CDs or tapes of classical music.
3. Ask an art museum, theater, or concert hall to donate free passes.
4. Ask a stationery or art store to donate free calligraphy supplies.

Program Game

A reproduction of a classical building, such as the Colosseum in Rome, can serve as the game board. For each point earned, the patron can fill in a block of the building, until the entire building has been completed. Points can be earned for completing the activities mentioned in the General Guidelines, and for:

1. Reading a classic work of literature (play, poetry collection, or novel) and completing a Classic Literature Book Review Form.
2. Reading a fiction book not related to the classics theme and completing a Fiction Book Review Form.
3. Reading a nonfiction book not related to the classics theme and completing a Nonfiction Book Review Form.
4. Watching a live or video performance of a classic ballet, opera, play, or attending a concert of classical music, and completing a Classic Entertainment Review Form.

Program Forms

1. Classic Literature Book Review Form
Title:
Author or editor:
Publisher and date:
Brief summary of plot (or type of poetry):
Did you enjoy reading this? Why or why not?
Would you want to read other works by this author or of this style of literature? Why or why not?

2. Fiction Book Review Form
Title:
Author:
Publisher and date:
Brief summary of plot:
I would rate this book: "A class act—one of the all-time greats," "A leader in its class," "Some of it is pretty classy," "I'd classify it as non-essential," "A classic mistake to avoid."

3. Nonfiction Book Review Form
Title:
Author:
Publisher and date:
Brief description of information:
I would rate this book: "An outstanding work for its time," "Time well spent," "A timely work," "Will not stand the test of time," "A waste of time."

4. Classic Entertainment Review Form
Name of piece(s) performed:
Name of performance group:
Type of performance:
Did you enjoy this performance? Why or why not?
Would you want to view another entertainment of this type? Why or why not?

Program Activities

1. Classics on Film. Show a film version of a classic work of literature, or a classic black and white movie from the early days of film.

2. Form Letters. Once upon a time, literature was hand-written by skilled calligraphers. Conduct a workshop in which teens can learn basic calligraphy. They can letter a poster of a famous quotation or verses from a classic poem.

3. Classic Tunes. Show scenes from cartoons that make use of classical music, such as Bugs Bunny's version of *The Barber of Seville* or any part of Disney's *Fantasia*. Then play the entire piece of music for teens to enjoy. Sometimes commercials use classical music. Play a few musical selections and ask teens if they recognize the tune from a commercial they have seen.

4. Masterpieces. Arrange to take patrons to an art museum to see classic paintings, sculpture, tapestry, and other works of fine art. Or provide several books and reproductions of classic art for teens to view and discuss at the library.

5. An Evening of Culture. If a local music hall is producing an opera, ballet, or a program of classical music, sponsor a musical program appreciation trip. Before you go to an opera or ballet, review the plot of the story so teens will understand it when they view the performance.

6. Educated in the Classics. Use sound recordings, photographs and illustrations in this game show of classical trivia. Contestants must correctly identify the classic work depicted in the picture or musical selection that is played. Categories can include Classic Cars, Old-Fashioned Clothing Styles, Classical Music, Fine Art Masterpieces, Buildings That Have Stood the Test of Time, and Furniture Styles That Have Never Gone Out of Style.

7. Great Performances. Choose one or more classic plays and let teens read scenes for a reader's theater program. If a local theater company is performing a classic play, you may want to take a group to see it.

8. Once and Future Classics. Ask teens to think about plays and young adult novels that have been written within the last 30 years. Which ones do they think will withstand the test of time and be considered classic literature 100 years from now? What recent music might be future classics? Teens should give reasons for their choices. Compile a list of possibilities and have teens vote.

9. Classic Opportunities. Teens, especially those who are college-bound, can learn about careers involving classical pursuits at this library program. Courses of study can include music, art, philosophy, literature, dance, theater, film, archeology, ancient civilizations and history. Provide information on some colleges that specialize in these majors and books on notable people who have made a living in these fields.

10. Steppin' Out. Sponsor a classical dance party at the library. Teach young adults dances that were popular during the 1500s to 1800s, such as the minuet and the gavotte. You can also invite local dancers to perform a short scene from a ballet and to teach teens a few simple ballet positions.

Curriculum Tie-Ins

1. English Literature/Composition. The possibilities here are endless. You can teach units on classic plays, poetry, mythology, or prose. Your class can study the plots of famous ballets and operas. Or you can read the works of great philosophers. Students can write papers in which they critique a classic novel, plot a sequel to it, or write an alternate ending. Or, they can compose a story or poem in the style of a particular writer.

2. Science. Some philosophers, such as Aristotle, put forth theories on various scientific topics, including physics, astronomy, biology, and physiology. The class can compare some of these philosophic ponderings to what is now known about these sciences. Much of Greek, Roman, and Norse mythology was an attempt to explain events that occurred in the physical world. Students can compare some ancient myths to the scientific explanations for occurrences such as the seasons, volcanoes, lightning, and the rising and setting of the sun.

3. History/Geography. Again, there are many possibilities for classroom projects. Students can create a timeline of classical theater, literature, art, or music. They can study the world of some ancient philosophers, or a period of history, such as the Renaissance, when many classical masterpieces were created.

4. Math. This is a good time for a refresher course in Roman numerals. Go over the numbers that are represented by the various letters of the alphabet, and let students have fun working out math problems with Roman numerals. You can also demonstrate how ancient peoples used the abacus as the world's first computer.

Activity Sheet Ideas

1. Word search or crossword puzzles of: a) names of classical authors, philosophers, artists, or musicians, b) classic cars, or c) classic styles of dance.

2. Word scrambles or cryptograms of: a) verses from classical poetry, b) famous quotes from great philosophers, or c) lines from classic plays.

3. Matching activities: match a) classic works of art to the artists who created them, b) music to the composers, or c) literature to the authors.

Suggested Resources

Reference and Nonfiction

Boardman, John, et al., eds. *The Oxford History of the Classical World.* Oxford University, 1986.
Brown, John Russell. *Shakespeare and His Theatre.* Lothrop, 1982.
Downs, Robert B. *Books That Changed the World.* ALA, 1978.
Grant, Michael. *The Classical Greeks.* Macmillan, 1989.
Hamilton, Dorothy. *Mythology.* NAL, 1942.
Magill's Survey of American Literature. 8 vols. Marshall Cavendish, 1990.
Magill's Survey of World Literature. 8 vols. Marshall Cavendish, 1992.
Nigg, Joe. *Wonder Beasts: Tales and Lore of the Phoenix, the Griffin, the Unicorn, and the Dragon.* Libraries Unlimited, 1995.
Recommended Reading: 500 Classics Reviewed. Salem, 1995.
Ross, Stewart. *Shakespeare and Macbeth.* Viking, 1995.
Singleman, Jeffrey L. *Daily Life in Elizabethan England.* Greenwood, 1995.
Vickers, Michael. *The Roman World.* Bedrick, 1989.
Warry, John. *Warfare in the Classical World.* University of Oklahoma, 1995.

Classic Literature and Nonfiction

(Editions are suggestions only; many other editions are generally available.)

Aesop. *Aesop's Fables.* Morrow, 1988.
Alcott, Louisa May. *Little Women.* Knopf, 1988.
Aristotle. *Aristotle: On Man in the Universe.* Random, 1995.
Austin, Jane. *Pride and Prejudice.* Putnam, 1984.
Blackmore, R.D. *Lorna Doone.* Penguin, 1984.
Brontë, Charlotte. *Jane Eyre.* Airmont, 1964.
Brontë, Emily. *Wuthering Heights.* Signet, 1959.
Browning, Elizabeth Barrett. *Sonnets from the Portuguese and Other Love Poems.* Hanover, 1954.
Cervantes, Miguel de. *The Adventures of Don Quixote de la Mancha.* Dent, 1983.
Chaucer, Geoffrey. *The Canterbury Tales.* Random, 1965.
Coleridge, Samuel Taylor. *The Rime of the Ancient Mariner and Other Poems.* Dover, 1992.
Conrad, Joseph. *Lord Jim.* Buccaneer, 1982.
Cooper, James Fenimore. *The Last of the Mohicans.* Macmillan, 1986.
Crane, Stephen. *The Red Badge of Courage.* Random, 1980.
Defoe, Daniel. *Robinson Crusoe.* Macmillan, 1983.
Dickens, Charles. *A Tale of Two Cities.* Dodd, 1985.
Dickinson, Emily. *Emily Dickinson Poetry Collection.* DOVT, 1995.

Dumas, Alexandre. *The Count of Monte Cristo*. Putnam, 1984.
Eliot, George. *Silas Marner*. Bantam, 1983.
Eliot, T.S. *The Complete Poems and Plays*. Harcourt, 1962.
Euripides. *Medea and Other Plays*. Viking Penguin, 1963.
Fielding, Henry. *Tom Jones*. NAL, 1982.
Fitzgerald, F. Scott. *The Great Gatsby*. Simon and Schuster, 1995.
Flaubert, Gustave. *Madame Bovary*. Random, 1981.
Frost, Robert. *Collected Poems, Prose, and Plays*. Library of America, 1995.
Hardy, Thomas. *Far from the Madding Crowd*. NAL, 1961.
Hawthorne, Nathaniel. *The House of the Seven Gables*. Bantam, 1981.
Hemingway, Ernest. *The Old Man and the Sea*. Scribner, 1980.
Homer. *The Iliad*. Doubleday, 1989. (Also *The Odyssey*.)
Hugo, Victor. *Les Misérables*. Random, 1980.
Kipling, Rudyard. *Kim*. Dell, 1982.
Longfellow, Henry Wadsworth. *Evangeline: A Tale of Acadia*. Chelsea, 1995.
Maupassant, Guy, de. *Selected Short Stories*. Penguin, 1971.
Melville, Herman. *Moby Dick*. Random, 1982.
Molière. *Don Juan and Other Plays*. Oxford University Press, 1989.
Nye, Robert. *Beowulf: A New Telling*. Dell, 1982.
Plato. *Plato's Republic*. Norton, 1996.
Poe, Edgar Allan. *The Fall of the House of Usher and Other Tales*. NAL, 1960.
Sandberg, Carl. *The Complete Poems of Carl Sandberg*. Harcourt, 1970.
Scott, Sir Walter. *Ivanhoe*. Airmont, 1964.
Shakespeare, William. *The Complete Works of William Shakespeare*. W.J. Black, 1965.
Shelley, Mary Wollstonecraft. *Frankenstein*. Dell, 1964.
Sophocles. *Antigone, Oedipus the King, Electra*. Oxford University Press, 1994.
Steinbeck, John. *The Red Pony*. Viking Penguin, 1994.
Stevenson, Robert Louis. *Kidnapped*. Puffin, 1995.
Swift, Jonathan. *Gulliver's Travels*. Pocket, 1996.
Tolstoy, Leo. *Anna Karenina*. Random, 1978.
Twain. Mark. *The Adventures of Tom Sawyer*. Messner, 1982.
Verne, Jules. *A Journey to the Center of the Earth*. Dodd, 1984.
Virgil. *The Aeneid of Virgil*. Bantam, 1981.
Voltaire. *Candide*. Random, 1985.
Wilde, Oscar. *The Picture of Dorian Gray*. NAL, 1995.
Wyss, Johann. *The Swiss Family Robinson*. Viking Penguin, 1996.
(Also other works by these authors.)

Fiction

Alexander, Lloyd. *The Arkadians*. Dutton, 1995.
Coville, Bruce. *William Shakespeare's The Tempest*. Delacorte, 1994.
Dean, Pamela. *Tam Lin*. Tor, 1991.
Fleischman, Paul. *Dateline: Troy*. Candlewick, 1996.
Gilmore, Kate. *Enter Three Witches*. Houghton, 1990.
Godwin, Parke. *The Tower of Beowulf*. Morrow, 1995.
Grimes, Martha. *The Dirty Duck*. Dell, 1990.

Henderson, Jason. *The Spawn of Loki*. Baen, 1994.
Hoover, H.M. *The Dawn Palace: The Story of Medea*. Dutton, 1988.
Jones, Diana Wynne. *Eight Days of Luke*. Greenwillow, 1988.
Jones, Robin D. *No Shakespeare Allowed*. Macmillan, 1989.
Kay, Susan. *Phantom*. Delacorte, 1991.
Keaney, Brian. *No Need for Heroes*. Oxford University Press, 1989.
Lester, Julius. *Othello: A Novel*. Scholastic, 1995.
McKinley, Robin. *The Outlaws of Sherwood*. Greenwillow, 1988.
Melnikoff, Pamela. *Plots and Players: The Lopez Conspiracy*. Bedrick, 1988.
Nelson, Peter. *Deadly Games*. Archway, 1992.
Orgel, Doris. *The Princess and the God*. Orchard, 1996.
Silverberg, Robert. *Letters from Atlantis*. Simon and Schuster, 1990.
Sonnenmark, Laura A. *Something's Rotten in the State of Maryland*. Scholastic, 1990.
Voigt, Cynthia. *Orfe*. Atheneum, 1992.
Wrede, Patricia C. *Snow White and Rose Red*. T. Doherty, 1989.

Periodicals

Classical World. Classical Association of the Atlantic States.
Classics Illustrated. Berkley Publishing Group.
Shakespeare Quarterly. Folger Shakespeare Library.
Smithsonian. Smithsonian Associates.

Feature-Length Films

Little Women. Columbia Tristar, 1994. (PG)
Roxanne. Columbia Tristar, 1987. (PG)
Rudyard Kipling's The Jungle Book. Walt Disney, 1994. (PG)
Sense and Sensibility. Columbia Tristar, 1995. (PG)
Treasure Island. Turner Home Entertainment, 1989.
William Shakespear's Romeo and Juliet. Columbia Tristar, 1996.

Computer Software

Athena: Classical Mythology on CD-ROM. G.K. Hall, 1994.
Beowulf: Attack of Grendel. Terra Glyph, 1996.
Best Literature Workbook Ever! Queue, 1992.
Great Poetry Classics. Compton's NewMedia, 1993.
History of Music: The Classical Period. Zane, 1994.
Monarch Notes. Bureau of Electronic Publishing, 1992.
The Shakespeare Collection. Zane, 1995.

11
Log On at the Library

Computers have become prevalent in the modern industrialized world. Let the library help you learn more about how they work and what they can do. We have nonfiction books and magazines to help you learn computer skills and tell you about new software programs; CDs of computer music; novels with computer plots; and of course, computers! Whether you're interested in using computers to access information or to play computer games, we want you to Log On at the Library.

Display Idea

Line up nonfiction books and magazines on all aspects of computers, along with novels and videos that contain computer-related plots. Also include CDs of computer-generated music, computer printouts and accessories to dress up the display.

Sponsorship for Prizes

1. Ask a computer store to offer discount certificates for various items.
2. Ask a bookstore to donate computer manuals and other related books.
3. Ask a magazine store to donate copies of computer magazines.
4. Ask a computer consultant to donate time to teach a computer class or other services.

Program Game

Draw a flowchart for a computer program to act as the reading game. Each shape of the flowchart can direct the reader to perform an action. (See illustration on page 68.)

Participants can move through the flow chart, following these directions, with the points they earn. Points can be earned by completing the activities mentioned in the General Guidelines, and for:

1. Reading a novel with a computer plot and completing a Computer Fiction Book Review Form.

2. Reading a novel not related to the computer theme and completing a Fiction Book Review Form.

3. Reading a nonfiction book not related to the computer theme and completing a Nonfiction Book Review Form.

4. Reading a computer-related magazine or book and completing a Computer Nonfiction Information Form.

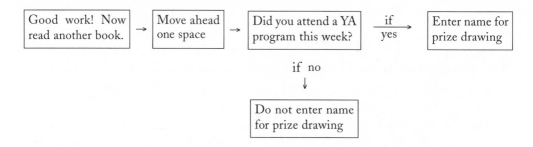

Program Forms

1. Computer Fiction Book Review Form
Title:
Author:
Publisher and date:
Brief description of plot:
How was (were) the computer(s) important to the plot?
Did you like this book? Why or why not?
2. Fiction Book Review Form
Title:
Author:
Publisher and date:
Brief summary of plot:
I would rate this book: "A hyper-text: save document," "User friendly: run program," "Has limited appeal: sort list," "A peripheral choice: store in auxiliary file," "Terminally dull: delete document."
3. Nonfiction Book Review Form
Title:
Author:
Publisher and date:
Brief description of information:
I would rate this book: "An excellent program with many applications," "A useful data-base," "Contains good, BASIC information," "Faulty logic," "This program is full of bugs."
4. Computer Nonfiction Information Form
Name of magazine or book:
Author (if book):
Publisher and date:
Do you think the information in this publication is useful? Why or why not?
To whom would this publication appeal?

Program Activities

1. Computer Screen. Show a movie with a computer theme, or in which a computer plays a major role, such as *The Net*.

2. Computer Artistry. There are several painting, graphics, and animation programs available for computers. Use one of these programs to demonstrate how to create computer-generated art. Perhaps you can sponsor an art contest in the library. Allow teens to sign up for computer time so that they can produce a work of art, or let them submit computer pictures they made at home. Put those entries in a display area and have all library patrons vote for their favorites.

3. Muzik. Many recording artists are experimenting with computer-generated music. Play samples of this type of music from CDs and computer or video games. If possible, install music software into a library computer and let students create their own tunes. Ask teens to compare computer-generated music to instrumental music. What are the pros and cons of each type?

4. Field Trip. If there is a science and technology museum nearby, schedule a day when you can take a group of teen patrons for a visit. Arrange for someone from the museum to speak to the group about the computer exhibits(s). In what other areas of the museum are computers in use?

5. Computer Games. Take a survey of teens to find out what their favorite computer games are in categories such as educational, adventures, simulations, strategy, etc. If your library has computer games, you can hold a tournament. Choose one game for the contest and hold qualifying rounds over a period of time. Players with the top scores can participate in the final round of games, which patrons can watch. Award a prize to the champion player.

6. Computer Whiz. Challenge teens to compete in a game show that tests their knowledge of computer trivia. Categories can include Early Computers (answer questions about computer history), Computer Speak (define terms), Computer Games (trivia about popular ones), New Technology (questions about new hardware, software, and applications), Movie and TV (how computers figure into some plots), and Surfing (knowledge of online data bases). You may occasionally want to throw in bonus questions in which a player must search a specific subject in the library's online catalog or in a multimedia encyclopedia.

7. Demos. Invite a computer store to set up some state-of-the-art computers and demonstrate the latest software. Teens can try them out and ask questions to determine what hardware and software they like best. Provide consumer and computer magazines to which patrons can refer.

8. Science Fiction. Computers figure prominently in the plots of many science fiction movies, TV shows, and novels. Conduct a session in which teens can discuss their favorite computers in fiction. How integral are computers to the plot? Are the computers solely mechanical, or do they have personalities? Teens can compile a list of recommended computer-related books and entertainment to distribute to patrons.

9. Nerds R Us. Profile computer-related occupations in this career program. Include jobs in computer design, programming, animation, instruction and consulting, repair, sales, manual writing, software development and engineering. Mention other jobs in which computers are used, such as librarian, writer, cashier, air traffic controller, secretary, receptionist, writer, pharmacist, etc. Provide information on colleges that offer computer majors.

10. Computer Literacy. Take advantage of this opportunity to familiarize young adult patrons with all the computers and programs that are available to them at the library. Conduct classes on how to search various data bases, and give an overview of which ones are most likely to help them find information they would need for current or upcoming school assignments.

Curriculum Tie-Ins

1. English Literature/Composition. Many terms from computer jargon have become part of our daily language. Ask students to list some of these terms, along with their computer-related definitions and their common meanings. Have students write short stories in which they use several examples of computer slang.

2. Science. Give students some basic information on how computers work. Compare early computers to modern technology. Discuss the jobs of various computer components and how they interact with software. Go over some programming basics and have students try to create their own simple computer programs.

3. History/Geography. Explore the history of computers with the class. When were the first computers invented, what did they look like, and what did they do? How has computer technology progressed, and what were some major developments along the way? In what parts of the world have there been major advancements? What computer technology is available in other countries?

3. Math. Computer language is based on a binary code. Explain this system to the class and have them convert binary codes into numbers and letters. How can computers use the binary code to read barcodes? Discuss ASCII and show students how it works as a shared electronic language.

Activity Sheet Ideas

1. Word search or crossword puzzles of: a) computer jargon, b) computer components, or c) computer companies (past and present).

2. Word scrambles or cryptograms of: a) software programs, b) computer-related science fiction novels, or c) computers from the past and present.

3. Matching activities: match a) scientists to their contributions in the development of computer technology, b) computer languages to their uses, or c) computer terms to their meanings.

Suggested Resources

Reference and Nonfiction

Adler, Bill, Jr., and Fraser, Kristy. *The Computer Support Directory: Voice, Fax, and Online Access Numbers.* McGraw, 1995.

Billings, Charlotte. *Supercomputers: Shaping the Future.* Facts on File, 1995.

Bishop, Ann. *Hello, Mr. Chips! Computer Jokes and Riddles.* Lodestar, 1982.

Borman, Jami Lynne. *Computer Dictionary for Kids...and Their Parents.* Barron's, 1995.

Boyd, Aaron. *Smart Money: The Story of Bill Gates.* Morgan Reynolds, 1995.

Bretschneider, Udo. *DOS for Beginners: "No Experience Required!"* Abacus, 1994.

Burns, Julie King. *Opportunities in Computer Systems.* VGM, 1996.

Constable, George, ed. **Understanding Computers** series. Time-Life, 1985.

Ehberts, Marjorie, and Gisler, Margaret. *Careers for Computer Buffs and Other Technological Types.* VGM, 1993.

Frazier, Doreen, et al. *Internet for Kids.* Sybex, 1995.

Hafner, Katie, and Markoff, John. *Cyberpunk: Outlaws and Hackers on the Computer Frontier.* Simon & Schuster, 1992.

Harmon, Charles, ed. *Using the Internet, Online Services, and CD-ROMs for Writing Research and Term Papers*. Neal-Schuman, 1995.
Hordeski, Michael F. *Repairing PCs: Beyond the Basics*. McGraw, 1995.
Judson, Karen. *Computer Crime: Phreaks, Spies and Salami Slicers*. Enslow, 1994.
Kanter, Elliott. *Opportunities in Computer Maintenance*. VGM, 1995.
Kettlekamp, Larry. *Computer Graphics: How It Works, What It Does*. Morrow, 1989.
Kling, Julie Lepick. *Opportunities in Computer Science*. VGM, 1991.
Knightmare. *Secrets of a Super Hacker*. Loompanics, 1994.
Olsen, Gary. *Getting Started in Computer Graphics*. North Light, 1993.
Pedersen, Ted, and Moss, Francis. *Internet for Kids: A Beginner's Guide to Surfing the Net*. Price Stern Sloan, 1995.
Rathbone, Andy. *Windows 95 for Dummies*. IDG Books, 1995. (Also others in series.)
Resumes for Computer Careers. VGM, 1996.
Salzman, Marian, and Pondiscio, Robert. *Kids On-line: 150 Ways for Kids to Surf the Net for Fun and Information*. Avon, 1995.
Shimomura, Tsutomu, and Markoff, John. *Takedown: The Pursuit and Capture of America's Most Wanted Computer Outlaw—By the Man Who Did It*. Hyperion, 1996.
Slater, Robert. *Portraits in Silicon*. MIT Press, 1987.
Turkle, Sherry. *Life on the Screen: Identity in the Age of the Internet*. Simon and Schuster, 1995.

Fiction

Card, Orson Scott. *The Memory of Earth*. Tor, 1992.
Crispin, A.C., and Marshall, Deborah A. *Starbridge Four: Serpent's Gift*. Ace, 1992.
Duane, Diane. *High Wizardry*. Delacorte, 1990.
Gerrold, David. *When H.A.R.L.I.E. Was One (Release 2.0)*. Bantam, 1988.
Gibson, William, and Bruce Sterling. *The Difference Engine*. Bantam, 1992.
Goldman, E.M. *The Night Room*. Viking, 1995.
Hambly, Barbara. *The Silent Tower*. Ballantine, 1988.
Heinlein, Robert A. *The Moon Is a Harsh Mistress*. Ace, 1987.
Herbert, Frank. *Destination: Void*. Ace, 1987.
Huff, Tanya. *Blood Price*. DAW, 1991.
Johnston, Norma. *The Dragon's Eye*. Four Winds, 1990.
Kennedy, William P. *The Toy Soldiers*. St. Martin's, 1988.
King, Buzz. *Silicon Songs*. Doubleday, 1990.
Knox, Bill. *The Interface Man*. Doubleday, 1990.
McCrumb, Sharyn. *Bimbos of the Death Sun*. TSR, 1988.
Mace, Elisabeth. *Under Siege*. Orchard, 1990.
Mazer, Harry. *City Light*. Scholastic, 1988.
Menick, Jim. *Lingo*. Carroll and Graf, 1991.
Nelson, Peter. *Deadly Games*. Archway, 1992.
Peck, Richard. *Lost in Cyberspace*. Dial, 1995. (Also: *The Great Interactive Dream Machine*.)
Pohl, Frederik. *Gateway*. Ballantine, 1987.
Pratchett, Terry. *Wings*. Delacorte, 1991.
Rendal, Justine. *A Very Personal Computer*. HarperCollins, 1995.
Rucker, Rudy. *Wetware*. Avon, 1988.
Ryan, Thomas J. *The Adolescence of P-1*. Baen, 1985.

Spinrad, Norman. *Little Heroes*. Bantam, 1992.
Strachan, Ian. *The Flawed Glass*. Little, Brown, 1990.
Vonnegut, Kurt, Jr. *Player Piano*. Delacorte, 1972.
Watkins, Graham. *Virus*. Carroll and Graf, 1995.
Wilhelm, Kate. *Smart House*. St. Martin's, 1989.

Periodicals

Compute! Compute! Publications, Inc.
Family and Home Office Computing. Scholastic, Inc.
InfoWorld. InfoWorld Publishing, Inc.
Macworld. PC World Communications, Inc.
PC Magazine. Ziff-Davis Publishing Co.
Personal Computing. VNU Business Publications, Inc.

Feature-Length Films

2001: A Space Odyssey. MGM/UA, 1968.
Electric Dreams. MGM/UA, 1984. (PG)
Hackers. MGM/UA, 1995. (PG-13)
The Net. Columbia Tristar, 1995. (PG-13)
Sneakers. MCA/Universal, 1992. (PG-13)
Wargames. CBS/Fox, 1983. (PG)

Computer Software

Computer Reference Library. Chestnut, 1993.
Computer Works: Your High Tech Tour Guide. Software Marketing Corp.
The Guided Tour of Multimedia. Graphic Zone, 1993.
How Computers Work. Time-Warner Interactive, 1993.
Learn to Do Word Processing. Allegro New Media, 1994. (Also others in series.)
Walking the World Wide Web. Ventana Communications, 1995.

(See Check Out a Work of Art and Whole Lotta Music Goin' On! units for additional titles.)

12
Psyched Up About Cycling

Attention all you bikers! If you like motorcycles, mopeds, dirt bikes, mountain bikes, or just plain leisure bicycles, there's a book for you at the library. Cycle maintenance, safety, tours, racing, and buying tips are some of the topics you can look up. Of course, there's a great variety of books, music, videos, and magazines to suit all interests, too. So whether you're a Harley fan who is born to be wild, or an easy rider strolling along on a bicycle built for two, you'll agree that the library is Psyched Up About Cycling!

Display Idea

Posters of all types of bicycles and motorcycles can surround a display of novels and nonfiction books on these topics. Also display related magazines and videos. Models of cycles and assorted gear can be added to the display for fun. (This program can be adapted to feature bicycles, motorized cycles, or both.)

Sponsorship for Prizes

1. Ask a bicycle store to donate discount coupons for bikes, bike service and accessories.
2. Ask a bookstore to donate books and magazines about bicycles and motorcycles.
3. Ask a sporting goods store to offer discount certificates for biker clothes and accessories.
4. Ask a T-shirt shop to donate shirts and iron-on transfers picturing cycles.

Program Game

Base the game board on a popular trail used for dirt bikes or another kind of cycle. Mark spaces along the trail with specific start and finish lines. Patrons can move a space along the trail for each point earned. Points can be earned for completing the activities mentioned in the General Guidelines, and for:

1. Reading a novel or nonfiction book about cycling and completing a Cycling Book Review Form.

2. Reading a novel not related to the cycling theme and completing a Fiction Book Review Form.

3. Reading a nonfiction book not related to the biking theme and completing a Nonfiction Book Review Form.

4. Reading a magazine about cycling or a related topic and completing a Cycling Magazine Information Form.

Program Forms

1. Cycling Book Review Form
Title:
Author:
Publisher and date:
Brief summary of plot or information:
What was the most interesting part of this book?
Would you recommend this book to other teens? Why or why not?

2. Fiction Book Review Form
Title:
Author:
Publisher and date:
Brief summary of plot:
I would rate this book: "A motocross-winning cycle," "A sturdy road-racer," "A good leisure motorcycle," "A temperamental moped," "A glorified scooter."

3. Nonfiction Book Review Form
Title:
Author:
Publisher and date:
Brief description of information:
I would rate this book: "A high-quality, rugged mountain bike," "A shiny new 3-speed bicycle," "A steady but simple one-speed bicycle," "A second-hand bike that barely runs," "A rusty old bike with flat tires."

4. Cycling Magazine Information Form
Name of magazine and date:
Brief summary of a feature article:
Who is the main audience for this magazine?
Did you enjoy reading it? Why or why not?

Program Activities

1. Reel Cycles. Show teens a movie in which bicycles or motorcycles are featured, such as *Breaking Away*.

2. Shirt Shop. Teens can bring in their own T-shirts for a craft program. Supply iron-on transfers of bikes and motorcycles, assorted letters, and an iron or pressing machine. Teens can choose a transfer and spell out their names or a short message on their shirts. For safety reasons, an adult should do the ironing.

3. Bike Care. Invite someone who repairs bikes to present a workshop on bicycle maintenance. Teens can bring in their bikes and learn how to fix a flat tire, replace a chain, adjust the handlebars, oil gears, and perform other simple repairs and upkeep chores.

4. Cycle Show-Offs. There may be a person or group in your area who performs bike, unicycle, or motorbike stunts. Take teen patrons on a field trip to see a performance, or invite the cyclist(s) to do an outdoor show near the library.

5. Hot Wheels. Many people like to race bikes and motorcycles. Present a slide show or video about cycle racing. Provide some books and magazines on the subject and discuss the history of the sport, popular races, records set, racing equipment, and other aspects of this sport.

6. **Spokes of Fortune.** Convert an old bicycle tire into a spinner to be used in a game show that tests players' knowledge of bike-related topics. Contestants can spin the tire to determine the number of points they will gain for correctly answering a question. Categories can include Biker Songs, Motorcycle Logos, Biking Safety, Cycle Types, Early Inventions, or Racing.

7. **Gearing Up.** Biking gear can be quite trendy. Ask a sporting goods store to sponsor a fashion show in which young adults can model various helmets, T-shirts, jackets, spandex shorts and pants, sneakers, gloves, and other clothing items and accessories. Play biker music to jazz up the show.

8. **Helmet or Not?** Many states have laws that require riders of bicycles and motorcycles to wear helmets. This is a very controversial topic among bikers. What are the laws in your state? Ask people who support both sides of the issue to present a debate about helmet laws, or let teens hold their own discussion. Members of the audience can ask questions and vote on whether they think these laws are good.

9. **Careers on Wheels.** Jobs involving various types of bikes and motorized cycles can be discussed during a special program. Supply information about careers in cycle design, manufacturing, repair, racing, and sales. Related jobs include designing and selling clothes and accessories for bikers, organizing and reporting on sports events, writing handbooks, and publishing related magazines. Provide a list of cycling organizations and have books on these topics available for patrons to check out.

10. **Take It for a Spin.** Arrange for a bicycle shop to bring several demonstration models to the library for a bike show. Teens can learn about special features and perhaps test-drive some bikes. Provide some consumer resources about cycles for patrons to read.

Curriculum Tie-Ins

1. **English Literature/Composition.** Do some free-association writing with the class. Tell students to write what they think of when they hear these words: biker, cyclist, mountain bike, unicycle, Harley, moped, 10-speed, racing, competition, *Easy Rider*. Students can compare their images to each others' papers.

2. **Science.** Discuss the long-term fitness benefits of riding a bicycle or mountain bike. Students can research aspects such as endurance training, muscle-strengthening, aerobics, heart rate, calories burned, and other related areas. Develop a training program using a stationary or moving bike for beginning and advanced exercising.

3. **History/Geography.** Have students create a visual history of the various types of cycles. They can search magazines, books, and online reference sources to find pictures of the earliest bicycles to the most recent models, and do the same for motorized cycles. What companies were/are famous for their cycles and where are they located? In which countries are bicycles used as a primary mode of transportation?

4. **Math.** Refer to the charts and formulas in *Mountain Bike Handbook* or another nonfiction source to devise cycling-related math problems. Students can calculate the perfect seat, tire, and handlebar height for males and females of various heights; pedal speed based on the gear size and number of rotations; etc.

Activity Sheet Ideas

1. Word search or crossword puzzles of: a) cycling terms, b) motorcycle parts, or c) biking accessories.

2. Word scramble or cryptograms of: a) name brands of bicycles or motorcycles, b) names of famous cyclists, or c) cycling organizations.

3. Matching activities: match a) cycling races to the state or country in which they occur, b) logos or trademarks to the bicycle or motorcycle to which they are associated, or c) bicycle racers to their Olympic or marathon wins.

Suggested Resources

Reference and Nonfiction

Alexander, Rod. *BMX Racing: A Step-by-Step Guide.* Troll, 1990.

Bennett, James. *The Complete Motorcycle Book: A Consumer's Guide.* Facts on File, 1995.

Berto, Frank J. *Bicycling Magazine's Complete Guide to Upgrading Your Bike.* Rodale, 1988.

Bicycling Magazine editors. *All-Terrain Bikes.* Rodale, 1985.

_____. *Fitness Through Cycling.* Rodale, 1985.

Buettner, Dan. *Sovietrek: A Journey by Bicycle Across Russia.* Lerner, 1994.

Coello, Dennis. *Touring on Two Wheels: The Bicycle Traveler's Handbook.* Lyons and Burford, 1988.

Cook, J. *Mountain Bikes.* EDC, 1990.

Cuthberton, Tom. *Anybody's Bike Book.* Ten Speed, 1990.

Davis, Don, and Carter, Dave. *Mountain Biking.* Human Kinetics, 1994.

Honig, Daniel. *How to Bike Better.* Ballantine, 1985.

Kent, J. *Racing Bikes.* EDC, 1990.

Lafferty, Peter, and Jefferis, David. *Superbikes: The History of Motorcycles.* Watts, 1990.

Langley, Jim. *The New Bike Book: How to Make the Best of Your New Bicycle.* Bicycle Books, 1990.

Lehrer, John. *The Complete Guide to Choosing a Performance Bicycle.* Running Press, 1988.

LeMond, Greg. *Greg LeMond's Pocket Guide to Bicycle Maintenance and Repair.* Putnam, 1990.

Martin, John. *The World's Fastest Motorcycles.* Capstone, 1994.

Nye, Peter. *The Cyclist's Sourcebook.* Perigee, 1991.

Osborn, Bob. *The Complete Book of BMX.* Harper, 1984.

Paulsen, Gary. *Track, Enduro, and Motocross—Unless You Fell Over.* Raintree, 1979.

Perry, David B. *Bike Cult: The Ultimate Guide to Human-Powered Vehicles.* Four Walls Eight Windows, 1995.

Pirsig, Robert M. *Zen and the Art of Motorcycle Maintenance: An Inquiry Into Values.* Morrow, 1974.

Purnell, Geoff. *Motorcycle Restorer's Workshop Companion: The Complete Guide to Techniques and Tools for Bike Restoration and Repair.* Patrick Stephens, 1992.

Scott. *Motorcycle Mania: Harley-Davidson: The Power, the Glory, the Legend Lives.* St. Martin's, 1995.

Seidl, Herman. *Mountain Bikes: Maintaining, Repairing, and Upgrading.* Sterling, 1991.

Thomson, H.E. *The Tour of the Forest Bike Race: A Guide to Bicycle Racing and the Tour de France.* Bicycle Books, 1990.

Tully, Brock. *Coming Together: A Ten Thousand Mile Bicycle Journey.* Simon and Schuster, 1991.

van der Plas, Robert. *Mountain Bike Handbook.* Sterling, 1992.

Venture Freestyle Biking. Boy Scouts of America, 1990.

Wagner, Herbert. *Harley-Davidson, 1930-1941: Revolutionary Motorcycles and Those Who Rode Them*. Schiffer, 1996.

Wilson, Hugo. *Encyclopedia of the Motorcycle*. Dorling Kindersley, 1995.

_____. *The Ultimate Motorcycle Book*. Dorling Kindersley, 1993.

Fiction

Abels, Harriette Sheffer. *Moto-cross Monkey*. Crestwood, 1981.

Bawden, Nina. *Granny the Pag*. Clarion, 1995.

Bibee, John. *The Magic Bicycle*. InterVarsity, 1983.

Covington, John P. *Motorcycle Racer*. Doubleday, 1973.

Cross, Gillian. *A Map of Nowhere*. Holiday, 1989.

Davis, Terry. *If Rock and Roll Were a Machine*. Delacorte, 1992.

Gauch, Patricia Lee. *Morelli's Game*. Putnam, 1981.

Gault, William Campbell. *Gasoline Cowboy*. Dutton, 1974.

Hardy, Jon. *Biker*. Oxford University Press, 1985.

Heck, B. Holland. *Golden Arrow*. Scribner, 1981.

Hewett, Joan. *Motorcycle on Patrol*. Houghton, 1990.

Howe, Fanny. *Race of the Radical*. Viking, 1985.

Lawrence, Mildred. *Inside the Gate*. Harcourt, 1968.

Mark, Jan. *Handles*. Macmillan, 1985.

Mooney, Thomas J., ed. *Gang on Wheels: And Other Stories of Motors and Chills*. Xerox Education, 1976.

Ogan, Margaret Nettles. *Donovan's Dusters*. Westminster, 1975.

Pascal, Francine. *The Hand-Me-Down Kid*. Viking, 1980.

Petersen, P.J. *Nobody Else Can Walk It for You*. Delacorte, 1982.

Phillips, Tony. *Full Throttle*. Ballantine, 1989.

Quin-Harkin, Janet. *Summer Heat*. Ballantine, 1990.

Russell, David A. *Superbike*. High Octane, 1993.

St. George, Mark. *The Wolfpack*. Proteus, 19

Soto, Gary. *Summer on Wheels*. Scholastic, 1995.

Wardlaw, Lee. *Corey's Fire*. Avon, 1990.

Westall, Robert. *Futuretrack5*. Greenwillow, 1984.

Wilson, Johnniece Marshall. *Oh, Brother*. Scholastic, 1988.

Periodicals

BMX Action. Wizard Publications, Inc.

Bicycling Magazine. Rodale Press.

Cycle. Ziff-Davis Publishing Co.

Cycle World. CBS Magazines.

Dirt Bike. Hi-Torque Publications, Inc.

Feature-Length Films

American Flyers. Warner, 1985. (PG-13)

Born to Ride. Warner, 1991. (PG)

Breaking Away. CBS/Fox, 1979. (PG)
Evel Knievel. MPI, 1972. (PG)
Pee Wee's Big Adventure. Warner, 1985. (PG)
The Wild One. Columbia Tristar, 1954.

Computer Software

Greg LeMond's Bicycle Adventure. Eden Interactive, 1993.
Maya Quest. MECC.
Mountain Biking. Media Mosiac, 1994.

13
Do You Wanna Dance?

Dancing is a popular pastime for people all over the world, and has been for centuries. Whether you prefer ballroom, classical, theatrical, modern, or street dancing, you can find out more about it at the library. We have books about all types of dance and choreography, plus biographies of dancers. Our videos include movies with famous dance sequences, and our CDs represent a variety of dance styles. So keep the library in mind next time someone asks: Do You Wanna Dance?

Display Idea

Fiction and nonfiction books on dance and movement can be displayed with videos on dance instruction and films with dance scenes. Arrange music CDs according to dance style (waltz, disco, hip-hop, etc.) Feature posters of local or famous dance companies, and related magazines.

Sponsorship for Prizes

1. Ask a local dance studio to donate free introductory lessons.
2. Ask a music store to donate tapes or CDs of dance music.
3. Ask a store that specializes in dance wear to donate merchandise certificates.
4. Ask a video store to donate certificates for free rentals of dance-related films.

Program Game

One or more dance charts, with numbered shoe prints to indicate the steps of the dance, can serve as the game board. Patrons can move ahead one shoe print for each point earned. Points can be earned for completing the activities mentioned in the General Guidelines, and for:

1. Reading a novel and completing a Fiction Book Review Form.
2. Reading a nonfiction book about dance, movement, or a related biography, and completing a Dance Nonfiction Book Review Form.
3. Reading a nonfiction book not relating to the dance theme and completing a Nonfiction Book Review Form.
4. Watching a movie, play, or dance performance and completing a Dance Performance Review Form.

Program Forms

1. Fiction Book Review Form
Title:
Author:
Publisher and date:
Brief summary of plot:
I would rate this book: "Get up on the floor and dance!," "Has a nice beat, and you can dance to it," "Toe-tappin' music," "Think I'll sit this one out," "Clear the dance floor!"

2. Nonfiction Dance Book Review Form.
Title:
Author:
Publisher and date:
Brief description of information:
Did you find this book to be instructive or interesting? Why or why not?
To whom would you recommend this book?

3. Nonfiction Book Review Form.
Title:
Author:
Publisher and date:
Brief description of information:
I would rate this book: "Tony Award-winning choreography," "A chorus line like the Rockettes," "Has some nice dance numbers," "Dancers are out of step with the music," "Take away their tap shoes."

4. Dance Performance Review Form
Name of performance:
Type of performance:
Where and when seen:
What was your opinion of this performance?
Would you like to see more of this type of dance? Why or why not?

Program Activities

1. Dance Screening. Show a movie about dancing, or one with several great dance sequences.

2. Marathon. Teens can participate in a dance marathon fund-raiser for the library. Dance teams should gather pledges for each half hour they stay on the dance floor. Schedule occasional breaks for dancers and play a variety of dance music. You may want to set a limit on the total number of hours for the marathon.

3. Stepping Out. Invite dance enthusiasts to conduct one or a series of dance workshops. Each dance session should have a theme, such as ballroom dancing, tap dance, square dancing, line dances, dances of the '60s, folk or ethnic dances.

4. On Stage. Sponsor a field trip to a ballet, a modern or ethnic dance company performance, or a musical play which features dancing. Beforehand, you could discuss with teens the style of dance or choreography they will be observing.

5. All That Jazz. All dance numbers in musical plays, movies, and even rock videos are choreographed. Show young adults some film clips of choreographed dance routines. Then place teens in groups and let them select a theatrical or popular song to choreograph themselves. Explain that even if some people think they can't dance, they can at least step to the beat of the music. Allow teens time to plan and rehearse their dances before performing for their peers.

6. Dance Buffs. Teens can compete in a game show of questions that involve dance themes. Categories can include Dance Crazes, Name That Dance Song (with sound clues to identify), Dance Movies, Famous Choreographers, Ethnic Dances, and Famous Dancers/Dance Teams.

7. Leotards, etc. Have teens put on a fashion show of dance clothing. Ask a dance wear shop to provide leotards and other apparel. A costume store or dance company may lend traditional dance costumes from other countries. Play background music that corresponds to each type of clothing being modeled.

8. Twinkle-Toes Awards. Let teens discuss which qualities they think a person should have to be considered a good dancer. Then have them come up with categories, such as Best Broadway Show Dancer, Best MTV Video Dancer, Most Athletic Dancer, and Best Splits. Additional categories can include Best Dance Music, Best Modern Dance Choreography, Most Innovative Prop Used in a Dance Number, etc. Teens can nominate and vote for their favorites in each category.

9. The Dance of Life. Provide information about careers in dance and related areas. Teens can learn about occupations such as dancer, choreographer, dance instructor, movement coach, dance theater or tour manager, dance critic, dance therapist, dance wear and costume designer, musician, composer, plus other jobs involved with putting on a dance performance for an audience. Provide lists of local and nationally renowned dance schools, dance companies, books about the dance business, and biographies of famous dancers for patrons to take out.

10. Everybody Dance. Patrons of all ages can join teens in an intergenerational dance at the library. Ask couples to do a "spotlight dance" of their choice at various times throughout the event. Make sure all age groups are represented. You can have volunteers fill out a dance card ahead of time, listing their choice of dance music and the type of dance they will be demonstrating.

Curriculum Tie-Ins

1. English Literature/Composition. Have students read the stories upon which some ballets are based and watch filmed scenes from these ballet performances. Then have each student choose a traditional or modern story, and write an essay on how it might be performed as a ballet or modern dance performance.

2. Science. Relate dancing to a lesson in physiology. Sample questions to consider: What are the ideal physical characteristics for a ballet dancer, and why? How can a ballerina stand on point? What are some good exercises for dancers, and why? Some African dances require dancers to move parts of their bodies to several different rhythms at once—how, physically, can this be done? What muscles are used for various dance positions?

3. History/Geography. Have students draw a timeline of the history of dance, from ancient times to the present. For each major development, indicate the century or decade, and where in the world it occurred. On a map of the world, note forms of dance that were/are popular in various countries to correspond with the timeline. Or, have each student choose one type of dance and trace its history.

4. Math. Many types of dance follow mathematical patterns. For example, a waltz pattern is 1-2-3 1-2-3, and a cha-cha pattern is 1-2 1-2-3. Play different types of dance music and have students chart their patterns.

Activity Sheet Ideas

1. Word search and crossword puzzles of: a) types of dance, b) dance steps, or c) other dance terms.
2. Word scrambles or cryptograms of: a) dance companies, b) classical ballets, or c) ceremonial dances.
3. Matching activities: match a) dancers to movies they made, b) choreographers to their Broadway shows, or c) famous dance partners (for example, match Fred Astaire to Ginger Rogers).

Suggested Resources

Reference and Nonfiction

Anderson, Jack. *Ballet and Modern Dance: A Concise History*. Princeton University Press, 1986.
Banes, Sally. *Terpsichore in Sneakers: Post-Modern Dance*. Wesleyan University Press, 1987.
Butterworth, Emma Macelik. *As the Waltz Was Ending*. Scholastic, 1985.
Casey, Betty. *International Folk Dancing U.S.A.*. Doubleday, 1981.
Clarke, Mary, and Crisp, Clement. *The Ballet Goer's Guide*. Knopf, 1981.
_____. *Dancer: Men in Dance*. Parkwest, 1987.
Cohen, Robert. *The Dance Workshop: A Guide to the Fundamentals of Movement*. Simon & Schuster, 1986.
DeMille, Agnes. *Dance to the Piper*. Da Capo, 1980. (Also *And Promenade Home*.)
Dunning, Jennifer. *"But First a School": The First Fifty Years of the School of American Ballet*. Viking, 1985.
Early, Barbara. *Finding the Best Dance Instruction*. Betterway, 1992.
Gordon, Suzanne. *Off Balance: The Real World of Ballet*. McGraw, 1983.
Greene, Hank. *Square and Folk Dancing: A Complete Guide for Students, Teachers and Callers*. Harper, 1984.
Gruen, John. *People Who Dance: 22 Dancers Tell Their Own Stories*. Princeton, 1988.
Haskins, James. *Black Dance in America: A History Through Its People*. Harper, 1990.
Hirschhorn, Clive. *Gene Kelly: A Wonderful Life*. G.K. Hall, 1985.
Holiday, Ron, et al. *Cat Dancers*. Pineapple, 1987.
Jackson, Ellen. *Dancing: A Guide for the Dancer You Can Be*. Danceway, 1983.
Kirkland, Gelsey, and Lawrence, Greg. *The Shape of Love*. Doubleday, 1990.
Kozodoy, Ruth. *Isadora Duncan*. Chelsea, 1988.
Kuklin, Susan. *Reaching for Dreams: A Ballet from Rehearsal to Opening Night*. Lothrop, 1987.
Long, Richard A. *The Black Tradition in American Dance*. Rizzoli, 1989.
Mueller, John E. *Astaire Dancing: The Musical Films*. Wings, 1991.
Robertson, Allen. *The Dance Handbook*. G.K. Hall, 1990.
Royal Academy of Dancing. *Ballet Class*. Arco, 1985.
Schlaich, Joan, and Dupont, Betty. *Dance: The Art of Production*. Dance Horizons, 1988.
Severson, Molly. *Performing Artists from Alvin Ailey to Julia Roberts*. Gale, 1995.

Speaker-Yuan. *Agnes de Mille*. Chelsea, 1990.
Taylor, Paul. *Private Domain: The Autobiography of Paul Taylor*. Knopf, 1987.
Thorpe, Edward. *Black Dance*. Overlook, 1990.
Watkins, Andrea. *Dancing Longer, Dancing Stronger: A Dancer's Guide to Improving Technique and Preventing Injury*. Princeton, 1990.

Fiction

Ames, Mildred. *The Dancing Madness*. Delacorte, 1980.
Asher, Sandy. *Just Like Jenny*. Delacorte, 1982.
Bennett, Cherie. *Did You Hear About Amber?* Puffin, 1993.
Betancourt, Jeanne. *Kate's Turn*. Scholastic, 1992.
Dean, Karen Strickler. *Maggie Adams, Dancer*. Avon, 1982.
Gerber, Merrill Joan. *Also Known as Sadzia! The Belly Dancer*. Harper, 1987.
Godden, Rumer. *Thursday's Children*. Dell, 1984.
Hall, Lynn. *Dagmar Schultz and the Green-Eyed Monster*. Scribner, 1991.
Hooks, William H. *A Flight of Dazzle Angels*. Macmillan, 1988.
Hurwin, Davida Wills. *A Time for Dancing*. Little, 1995.
Ibbotson, Eva. *A Company of Swans*. St. Martin's, 1985.
Landis, J.D. *The Sisters Impossible*. Bantam, 1981.
Littke, Lael. *Prom Dress*. Scholastic, 1989.
Pendergraft, Patricia. *Hear the Wind Blow*. Putnam, 1988.
Roberts, Nora. *Dance to the Piper*. Silhouette, 1988.
Ryan, Mary E. *I'd Rather Be Dancing*. Doubleday, 1989. (Also *Dance a Little Close*.)
_____. *Me, My Sister, and I*. Simon and Schuster, 1992.
Slepian, Jan. *Something Beyond Paradise*. Putnam, 1987.
Stewart, Edward. *Ballerina*. Dell, 1989.
Ure, Jean. *The Most Important Thing*. Morrow, 1986.
_____. *What If They Saw Me Now?* Delacorte, 1984. (Also *You Win Some, You Lose Some*.)
Voight, Cynthia. *Come a Stranger*. Macmillan, 1986.
Williams-Garcia, Rita. *Blue Tights*. Dutton, 1988.
Wolff, Ferida. *Pink Slippers, Bar Mitzvah Blues*. Jewish Publication Society, 1989.
Yep, Laurence. *Ribbons*. Putnam, 1996.
Zindel, Bonnie, and Zindel, Paul. *A Star for the Latecomer*. Harper, 1980.

Periodicals

American Dance Circle. Lloyd Shaw Foundation.
American Square Dance. Sanvorn Enterprises.
Dance Magazine. Ruder Publishing Co.
Dancing USA. Dot Publications.
IDEA Today. International Dance Exercise Association, Inc.

Feature-Length Films

Footloose. Paramount, 1984. (PG)
Saturday Night Fever. Paramount, 1977. (PG)

Stepping Out. Paramount, 1991. (PG)
That's Dancing! MGM/UA, 1985. (G)
The Turning Point. Fox, 1977. (PG)
White Nights. Columbia Tristar, 1985. (PG-13)
(Also various MGM musicals.)

Computer Software

Dance! Dance! Dance! MGE Communications, 1994.
Dance on Disc. Macmillan, 1992.
Virtual Variety Show. Scitron and Art.

14

A Cleaner, Greener Planet

Pollution, deforestation, and endangered animals are just a few of the many problems facing our environment. But there are things you can do to help solve these problems. You can look in a reference book to find addresses of environmental organizations and write to them. Check out a book or read a magazine to find out what the dangers are and what people are doing about them. Take part in activities that show you care about the world in which you live. You can work to make this A Cleaner, Greener Planet.

Display Idea

Fiction with environmental plots can be displayed with nonfiction books, biographies, and magazines that deal with ecology, nature, recycling, conservation, the environment, and other "green" issues. Buttons, stickers or literature from environmental organizations and CDs of nature music can also be included.

Sponsorship for Prizes

1. Ask a florist or nursery to donate small plants.
2. Ask a bookstore to donate books about nature or environmental matters.
3. Ask a department store to donate reusable items that reduce waste, such as thermos bottles and plastic sandwich containers.
4. Ask an organic food store to donate merchandise certificates.

Program Game

A blank page, representing a forest that has been clear-cut, should be given to each participant. For each point earned, place a sticker or stamp a picture of a tree on the page to represent the replanting of the forest. Points can be earned for completing the activities mentioned in the General Guidelines, and for:

1. Reading a novel or nonfiction book related to the environment theme and completing an Environment Book Review Form.
2. Reading a novel not related to the environmental theme and completing a Fiction Book Review Form.
3. Reading a nonfiction book not related to the environment theme and completing a Nonfiction Book Review Form.
4. Reading two magazine or reference articles on a single environmental topic and completing an Environmental Articles Information Form.

Program Forms

1. Environment Book Review Form
Title:
Author:
Publisher and date:
Brief description of environmental issue:
What was the most important thing you learned from reading this book?
Did this book encourage you to work towards protecting the environment? Why or why not?

2. Fiction Book Review Form
Title:
Author:
Publisher and date:
Brief summary of plot:
I would rate this book: "Great story; this book will be used many times," "Clear, concise writing, with no excess packaging," "Book will appeal to certain people; sort it correctly," "Plot was recycled from other books," "A waste of paper."

3. Nonfiction Book Review Form
Title:
Author:
Publisher and date:
Brief description of information:
I would rate this book: "A lush rainforest, with diverse plant and animal life," "A national forest preserved as a wildlife refuge," "A replanted forest to which animals are returning," "Half the forest has been cut down and wildlife is dying," "The soil is no longer able to support plant life."

4. Environmental Articles Information Form
Article #1:
Source and date:
Article #2:
Source and date:
What was the main topic of these articles?
Was the tone of the articles positive (constructive), negative (warning), or neutral?
What did you learn about the environment from reading these articles?

Program Activities

1. Nature Film. National Geographic and other companies produce various nature films. View a film about an endangered habitat or species. Afterward, teens can discuss their reactions to the film.

2. Recycled Crafts. There are several books on the market that explain ways of making arts and crafts projects out of recycled materials. Do one of these projects with your teenagers.

3. Waste Not. Invite a representative from a local recycling company or a municipal recycling employee to talk to teens on this topic. The guest can speak about why recycling is important, what items can be recycled and how, and what products can be made from recycled materials.

4. Clean-Up Day. Organize teens to clean up the area around the library (or another site) on a specified day. They can pick up litter, weed the garden, collect recyclables, or perform other jobs to beautify the area. You may want to conclude the day by having a tree-planting ceremony. Teens can read poems and brief stories to honor their tree.

5. Green Consumers. Ahead of time, purchase several food and non-food products which require a lot of excess packaging, such as tea bags, juice boxes, individual-size snack foods, single-use detergent boxes, etc. At the program, let teens examine these items and explain why they are over-packaged. Then discuss some alternatives, such as using thermos bottles instead of juice boxes. Let them describe what it means to be a "green consumer."

6. Teen Solutions. Young adults can participate in a game show in which teams are asked to solve various environmental dilemmas. The host will present a problem or issue, and each team has one minute to come up with a solution. The audience can vote for the answer they think is best. Questions can be about conserving resources, recycling materials, protecting endangered species, habitat loss, stopping pollution, and other relevant topics.

7. Poster Contest. Challenge teen patrons to design ecology-related posters and slogans. They can create their posters either at home or at the library. Display the posters and let them vote on their favorites in different categories such as Best Slogan, Best Collage, Best Recycling Poster, Best Endangered Species Poster, Best Environmental Safety Poster and Best Anti-Pollution Poster.

8. Issues Debate. Most state and local governments are involved in controversial issues concerning the environment. Choose one such issue, such as building a trash-to-energy plant, spending tax dollars to save an endangered species, or deciding whether to drain a swamp in order to develop the land. Invite speakers who support both sides of the issue to present a debate for young adult patrons. Afterwards, let teens ask questions, discuss their opinions, and decide which side of the argument they support.

9. Environmental Careers. Careers in conservation, ecology, nature, and other environmentally related fields can be discussed in a special career day program. Provide information for jobs in such fields as forest conservation, wildlife management, biology, oceanography, zoology, resource management, waste disposal, pollution control, air and water quality, and energy efficiency. Note colleges that offer majors in these areas and provide a list of organizations concerned with various environmental issues.

10. Eco-Rock. Several popular musicians and groups have recorded songs with environmental themes. Ask teens to bring in any such songs they own to play at an environmentally friendly party. Decorations can be made from recycled or recyclable materials. Use washable (or paper if you must—but not Styrofoam!) plates and cups. Buy refreshments in bulk to avoid excess packaging. Compost any fruit or vegetable scraps. Remind patrons to clean up after themselves—no littering allowed!

Curriculum Tie-Ins

1. English Literature/Composition. Have students read some fiction and nonfiction accounts of several endangered animals, and then choose one of them. They should write a fictional story from the point of view of their animal. How does it react to its situation? What happened to its habitat? Its family? Will it survive?

2. Science. Conduct a science fair in which all projects and experiments must involve an environmental theme. Sample topics: the cause and effects of a particular environmental disease, recycling projects, making environmentally safe cleaning products, inventing new pollution-control devices, and so forth.

3. History/Geography. Make a list of several recent disasters that have harmed the environment, such as the radiation leak at the Chernobyl Power Plant. Students can report on one of these events. They should note on a world map where the tragedy occurred, what happened, and how it affected the human, animal and plant life of the surrounding area.

4. Math. How much water do people waste every day? Students should keep a daily journal of their water use: how long they run tap water, how many times they flush the toilet, etc., and compare these numbers to a chart that estimates how much water is used in each instance. How can students cut down on water waste? You can also have students chart their daily use of electricity and look for ways to reduce waste.

Activity Sheet Ideas

1. Word search or crossword puzzles of: a) conservation terms, b) waste and recycling terms, or c) types of natural habitats.

2. Word scrambles or cryptograms of: a) environmental organizations, b) names of ecologists, or c) environmental issues.

3. Matching activities: match a) endangered species to their habitats, b) parts of the world to the environmental disaster that happened there, or c) products that cause pollution and waste to alternatives that are friendly to the environment.

Suggested Resources

Reference and Nonfiction

Basta, Nicholas. *The Environmental Career Guide: Job Opportunities with the Earth in Mind.* Wiley, 1991.

The Big Book for Our Planet. Dutton, 1993.

Buzzworm Magazine editors. *Earth Journal: Environmental Almanac and Resource Directory.* Buzzworm, annual.

Carson, Rachel. *Silent Spring.* Houghton, 1962.

The Curious Naturalist. National Geographic, 1991.

Dashefsky, H. Steven. *Environmental Literacy: The A-to-Z Guide.* Random, 1993.

The Dictionary of Nature. Dorling Kindersley, 1994.

Dolan, Edward F. *The American Wilderness and Its Future: Conservation Versus Use.* Watts, 1992.

Eco-Design. North Light, 1995

Endangered Wildlife of the World. 13 vols. Marshal Cavendish, 1993.

Environmental Reference series. Enslow.

Fanning, Odom. *Opportunities in Environmental Careers.* VGM, 1995.

Gardiner, Brian. *Energy Demands.* Gloucester, 1990.

Heifetz, Jeanne. *Green Groceries: A Mail-Order Guide to Organic Foods.* HarperPerennial, 1992.

Kinney, Jane, and Fasulo, Mike. *Careers for Environmental Types and Others Who Respect the Earth.* VGM, 1993.

Koebner, Linda. *Zoo Book: The Evolution of Wildlife Conservation Centers.* Forge, 1994.

Middleton, Nick. *Atlas of Environmental Issues.* Facts on File, 1989.

Miller, Louise. *Careers for Nature Lovers and Other Outdoor Types.* VGM, 1992.

Newton, David E. *Taking a Stand Against Environmental Pollution.* Watts, 1990.

Overview Series: Our Endangered Planet. Lucent.

Paehlke, Robert, ed. *Conservation and Environmentalism: An Encyclopedia.* Garland, 1995.

Petrikin, Jonathan S., ed. *Environmental Justice.* Greenhaven, 1995.

Pringle, Laurence. *Restoring Our Earth.* Enslow, 1987.

Rainis, Kenneth G. *Environmental Science Projects for Young Scientists.* Watts, 1995.

Rosenberg, Kenneth. *Wilderness Preservation: A Reference Handbook.* ABC-CLIO, 1994.

Sayre, April Pulley. **Exploring Earth's Biomes** series. Twenty-First Century, 1994.

Shore, William H., ed. *The Nature of Nature: New Essays from America's Finest Writers in Nature.* Harcourt, 1994.

Teitel, Martin. *Rain Forest in Your Kitchen: The Hidden Connection Between Extinction and Your Supermarket.* Island, 1992.

Thoreau, Henry David. *Walden.* Buccaneer, 1983.

Wille, Christopher M. *Opportunities in Forestry Careers.* VGM, 1992.

World Resources Institute. *The Information Please Environmental Almanac.* Houghton, annual.

Fiction

Barron, T.A. *The Ancient One.* Philomel, 1992.

Bond, Nancy. *The Voyage Begun.* Macmillan, 1981.

Brenner, Barbara. *The Falcon Sting.* Bradbury, 1988.

Card, Orson Scott. *Pastwatch: The Redemption of Christopher Columbus.* Tor, 1996.

Clarke, Arthur C. *The Ghost from the Grand Banks.* Bantam, 1990.

Collier, James Lincoln. *When the Stars Begin to Fall.* Delacorte, 1986.

Cussler, Clive. *Sahara.* Simon and Schuster, 1992.

Dekkers, Midas. *Arctic Adventure.* Watts, 1987.

Duane, Diane. *Deep Wizardry.* Delacorte, 1985.

George, Jean Craighead. *The Missing 'Gator of Gumbo Limbo.* HarperCollins, 1992.

_____. *On the Far Side of the Mountain.* Dutton, 1990.

Herzig, Alison Cragin. *Shadows on the Pond.* Little, 1985.

Hesse, Karen. *Phoenix Rising.* Holt, 1994.

Hobbs, Will. *Changes in Latitude.* Atheneum, 1988.

Hopper, Nancy J. *The Interrupted Education of Huey B.* Dutton, 1991.

Killingsworth, Monte. *Eli's Song.* Macmillan, 1991.

Kingsolver, Barbara. *Animal Dreams.* HarperCollins, 1990.

Klass, David. *California Blue.* Scholastic, 1994.

Llewellyn, Sam. *Deadeye.* Summit, 1991.

Macdonald, Caroline. *The Lake at the End of the World.* Dial, 1989.

Park, Ruth. *My Sister Sif.* Viking, 1991.

Pohl, Frederik. *Chernobyl: A Novel.* Bantam, 1987.

Sachs, Elizabeth-Ann. *Kiss Me, Janie Tannenbaum.* Atheneum, 1992.

Sargent, Sarah. *Seeds of Change.* Bradbury, 1989.

Shachtman, Tom. *Driftwhistler: A Story of Daniel au Fond.* Holt, 1991.

Silverberg, Robert. *The New Springtime.* Warner, 1990.

Streiber, Whitley. *Nature's End: The Consequences of the Twentieth Century*. Warner, 1987.
Taylor, Theodore. *Sniper*. Harcourt, 1989.
Tepper, Sheri S. *Beauty*. Doubleday, 1991.
Wittlinger, Ellen. *Noticing Paradise*. Houghton, 1995.
Wrightson, Patricia. *Moon Dark*. Macmillan, 1988.

Periodicals

Amicus Journal. National Resources Defense Council, Inc.
Buzzworm: The Environmental Journal. Buzzworm.
National Parks and Conservation Magazine. National Parks and Conservation Association.
The Nature Conservancy Magazine. The Nature Conservancy.
Sierra. Sierra Club.
Wilderness. Wilderness Society.

Feature-Length Films

Journey to Spirit Island. Academy Entertainment, 1992. (PG)
The Milagro Beanfield War. MCA/Universal, 1988. (R)
Mountain Man. Lucerne Media, 1977.
Silent Running. MCA/Universal, 1971. (G)
Star Trek 4: The Voyage Home. Paramount, 1986. (PG)
Whale for the Killing. CBS/Fox, 1981.

Computer Software

The Big Green Disc. Media Design Interactive, *1993*.
Environmental Views Series: Earth's Biomes. Optilearn, 1995. (Also others in series.)
The Eyewitness Encyclopedia of Nature. Dorling Kindersley Multimedia, 1995.
Focus on the Environment. EME Corp., 1995.
Learning About Our Environment. Queue, 1992.
SimLife. Maxis, 1992.

15
Find Fame at the Library

There are many famous people at the library. Just check out our biographies to read about celebrities and important figures from the past and present. We also have novels by renowned authors, videos starring famous and soon-to-be-famous actors, and magazines that feature stories on all the popular people of the day. You don't have to go to Hollywood to see the stars; you can Find Fame At The Library.

Display Idea

Celebrity biographies and fiction about people who become famous should be featured. Include videos about famous people and films in which actors received their "big break," plus magazines that report on the rich and famous. Posters of successful people can be hung near the display.

Sponsorship for Prizes

1. Ask a bookstore to donate biographies and related fiction.
2. Ask a novelty store to donate posters of celebrities.
3. Ask a magazine store to donate issues of gossip and entertainment magazines that profile people.
4. Ask a video rental store to donate free rental certificates for films featuring well-known actors or films about famous people.

Program Game

The game board can resemble a giant ladder or mountain, at the top of which is a large dressing room door with a star. Patrons start at the bottom and move a step up for each point earned. Points can be earned for completing the activities mentioned in the General Guidelines, and for:
1. Reading a novel about becoming famous or a related theme and completing a Fame Fiction Book Review Form.
2. Reading a novel not related to the fame theme and completing a Fiction Book Review Form.
3. Reading a nonfiction book other than a biography and completing a Nonfiction Book Review Form.
4. Reading a biography and completing a Biography Book Review Form.

Program Forms

1. Fame Fiction Book Review Form
Title:
Author:
Publisher and date:
Brief summary of plot:
How does the famous person in the story deal with being a celebrity?
Would you recommend this book to a friend? Why or why not?

2. Fiction Book Review Form
Title:
Author:
Publisher and date:
Brief summary of plot:
I would rate this book: "Legendary," "Well-known in its own time," "Achieved local fame," "Its 15 minutes of fame was up a long time ago," "Never heard of it."

3. Nonfiction Book Review Form
Title:
Author:
Publisher and date:
Brief description of information:
I would rate this book: "Star Quality," "Deserves respect," "Good showing," "Don't go out of your way for it," "Ignore it."

4. Biography Book Review Form
Title:
Author:
Publisher and date:
Brief description of information:
Did this biography present an interesting and true portrayal of the person's life?
Would you recommend this book to a friend? Why or why not?

Program Activities

1. Famous Flick. Show a movie that is based on the life of a famous person, or a movie about achieving fame, such as *Coal Miner's Daughter.*

2. Person of the Year. Ask teens to bring in 3" × 5" or 8" × 10" photographs of themselves. Provide construction paper in assorted colors to use as framing mats, and paper triangles to fit into the corners of the mats. Teens can mount their photos onto the background mat of their choice, then add two triangles in matching or contrasting colors, one in the top left corner and one in the bottom left corner. On the top one, teens can letter "Man of the Year," "Woman of the Century," "Superstar," or another laudatory phrase. On the bottom triangle they can letter their names. Provide lettering stencils, markers, glitter and glue, as well as some of *Time Magazine*'s "Man of the Year" covers for teens to use as models.

3. Famous Kids. Many children and teens have achieved fame as entertainers, athletes, or models. Others have become famous because they had famous parents, or because they were at the center of some controversy. Post pictures or news headlines of several famous youngsters. Number each one and challenge teens to identify the people in the photos and explain what happened to the children in the headlines. Encourage participants to use reference sources to find the answers, and award a prize to the winner.

4. Best of the Best. Take a poll of young adult patrons to find out who they most admire. Patrons can write the names of one male and one female from the past or present. Or, you can offer choices in categories such as athlete, entertainer, public figure, American, etc. Tabulate the answers and announce the results. Compare teens' answers to polls taken by *People Weekly* and other sources.

5. Your Big Break. Many plays and movies have been written about entertainers who are trying to break into the big time. Gather some soundtracks and scripts from vehicles such as *Dames at Sea*, *Applause*, *A Star Is Born* and *Fame*. You can play songs from these shows and let teens read scenes aloud.

6. Name That Fame. Young adults can take part in a game show about famous people. Contestants will have to identify the person after hearing a short description of his or her most memorable feat. Categories can include Literary Giants, Great Statesmen, Show Biz Legends, All-Star Athletes, Super Scientists, or Notorious Bad Guys.

7. Great Bios. Ask teens to bring in their favorite biographies to discuss with the group. Compile a list of these titles to distribute to patrons.

8. The Good Life? Is it really all that great to be famous? Ask teens to consider this question by having them list the advantages and disadvantages of being famous. What are some of the consequences of fame? Let teens consider the controversies surrounding some famous people, such as Michael Jackson or Princess Diana. Provide articles about how celebrities have dealt with their fame and let teens discuss this issue.

9. Whatever Happened to … ? Fame is often fleeting. Someone who is wildly popular today can fade from view tomorrow. Provide biographical reference sources and magazine articles (such as *People Weekly*'s "What Ever Happened to …?" issues). Ask teens to look up what happened to some people after their fame ended. Then list several currently famous people. Have teens speculate on what these stars will be doing in ten years. Will they still be famous?

10. Celebrity Bash. Teens can come to a costume party dressed as a famous person from the past or present, real or fictitious. They should act and speak in character during the party. People can try to guess each other's identities for prizes.

Curriculum Tie-Ins

1. English Literature/Composition. Ask students to consider: If they could be famous, what would they want to be famous for? Have them read magazine articles and interviews about famous people in several fields. Then tell students to write a fictitious magazine article about themselves as a famous person in whatever endeavor they choose.

2. Science. Assign each student a different scientist to research. Students must find out what this person did to become renowned is his or her field and write a description of that discovery, invention, theory, etc.

3. History/Geography. Many people achieved fame because they were the first person to accomplish, discover, or invent something. Provide a list of famous "first" people throughout history. Students can look up when and where the person lived, and what particular "first" was his or her claim to fame.

4. Math. Have students look at several current issues of various teen, gossip, and entertainment magazines. Tell them to record the name of each celebrity discussed or pictured.

Students can draw graphs to illustrate the number of articles devoted to each person. Then compare results: Who seems to be the most currently popular teen? Actor? International figure? (Think of several categories.)

Activity Sheet Ideas

1. Word search or crossword puzzles of: a) reasons for which a person may become famous, b) things a famous person may encounter, or c) people who work for or with celebrities.

2. Word scrambles or cryptograms of: a) gossip magazines and newspaper tabloids, b) names of teen idols, or c) quotes by or about famous people.

3. Matching activities: match a) names of celebrities to their reason for being famous, b) people to the titles of their biographies, or c) famous people to their photographs.

Suggested Resources

Reference, Nonfiction, and Biographies

Andronik, Catherine. *Prince of Humbugs: A Life of P.T. Barnum*. Atheneum, 1994.

Asimov, Isaac. *Asimov's Biographical Encyclopedia of Science and Technology*. Doubleday, 1982.

Barr, Roseanne. *Roseanne: My Life as a Woman*. Harper, 1989.

Brown, Peter, and Gaines, Steven. *The Love You Make: The Insider's Story of the Beatles*. NAL, 1983.

Claghorn, Charles E. *Popular Bands and Performers*. Scarecrow, 1995.

Crocker, Chris. *Great American Astronauts*. Watts, 1988.

Cross, Milton, and Ewen, David. *The Milton Cross New Encyclopedia of the Great Composers and Their Music*. Doubleday, 1989.

Davenport, Robert. *The Celebrity Birthday Book*. General Publishing Group, 1996.

Fradin, Dennis B. *Remarkable Children: Twenty Who Made History*. Little, 1987.

Freedman, Russell. *Eleanor Roosevelt: A Life of Discovery*. Clarion, 1993. (Also other biographies by this author.)

Green, Jonathon. *The Greatest Criminals of All Time: An Illustrated Compendium of More Than 600 Great Crooks*. Scarborough, 1982.

Harris, Laurie Lanzen, ed. *Biography Today: Profiles of People of Interest to Young Readers*. Omnigraphics.

Hohler, Robert T. *"I Touch the Future...": The Story of Christa McAuliffe*. Random, 1986.

Hoobler, Dorothy, and Hoobler, Thomas. *Cleopatra*. Chelsea, 1986.

Hook, Jason. *American Indian Warrior Chiefs: Tecumseh, Crazy Horse, Chief Joseph, Geronimo*. Firebird, 1990.

Hyndley, Kate. *The Voyage of the Beagle*. Bookwright, 1989.

Jackson, Michael. *Moonwalk*. Doubleday, 1988.

Jacobs, William Jay. *Great Lives: Human Rights*. Macmillan, 1990. (Also others in series.)

Jakoubek, Robert E. *Martin Luther King, Jr.* Chelsea, 1989.

Kerr, M.E. *Me Me Me Me Me: Not a Novel*. Harper, 1983.

Lash, Joseph P. *Helen Keller and Anne Sullivan*. Dell, 1990.

Leder, Jane. *Amelia Earhart*. Greenhaven, 1990.

LeVert, Suzanne. *The Doubleday Book of Famous Americans*. Doubleday, 1989.

Levine, Michael. *The Address Book No. 7: How to Reach Anyone Who Is Anyone*. Berkley, 1995.

McClung, Robert. *The True Adventures of Grizzly Adams*. Morrow, 1985.

Martin, Christopher. *Shakespeare*. Rourke, 1989.

Paletta, Lu Ann. *The World Almanac of First Ladies*. St. Martin's, 1990.

Parè, Michael A. *Sports Stars*. 2 vols. U-X-L, 1994.

Peary, Danny, ed. *Cult Baseball Players: The Greats, the Flakes, the Weird, and the Wonderful*. Simon & Schuster, 1990.

Rees, Dafydd, and Crampton, Luke *Encylopedia of Rock Stars*. DK, 1996.

Shiels, Barbara. *Winners: Women and the Nobel Prize*. Dillon, 1985.

Show Biz Kids: Quest for Success. E.T.C., 1995.

Thompson, Kenneth W. *Great American Presidents*. University Press of America, 1995.

Van Steenwyk, Elizabeth. *Levi Strauss: The Blue Jeans Man*. Walker, 1988.

Wilson, Derek. *The Circumnavigators*. Evans, 1989.

Zupp, Brad. *Success! Interviews with Performers about Fame, Fortune and Happiness*. Oasis, 1995.

Fiction

Avi. *The Man Who Was Poe*. Orchard, 1989.

Childress, Mark. *Tender*. Crown, 1990.

Collins, Max Allan. *Stolen Away: A Novel of the Lindbergh Kidnapping*. Bantam, 1991.

Colman, Hila. *Rich and Famous Like My Mom*. Crown, 1988.

Conford, Ellen. *You Never Can Tell*. Little, 1984.

Coonts, Stephen. *Under Siege*. Pocket, 1990.

Forster, Margaret. *Lady's Maid: A Novel of the Nineteenth Century*. Doubleday, 1991.

Gingher, Marianne. *Bobby Rex's Greatest Hit*. Macmillan, 1986.

Goodwin, Marie D. *Where the Towers Pierce the Sky*. Four Winds, 1989.

Greenberg, Martin H., ed. *Celebrity Vampires*. DAW, 1995.

Harris, Mark Jonathan. *Confessions of a Prime Time Kid*. Lothrop, 1985.

Kerr, M.E. *I'll Love You When You're More Like Me*. Harper, 1977.

_____. *The Son of Someone Famous*. Harper, 1974.

Kidd, Ronald. *Dunker*. Bantam, 1984.

Levy, Elizabeth. *All Shook Up*. Scholastic, 1986.

Levy, Marilyn. *Remember to Remember Me*. Fawcett, 1988.

Major, Kevin. *Dear Bruce Springsteen*. Delacorte, 1988.

Melnikoff, Pamela. *Plots and Players: The Lopez Conspiracy*. Bedrick, 1988.

Parker, Jackie. *Love Letters to My Fans*. Bantam, 1986.

Paterson, Katherine. *Come Sing, Jimmy Jo*. Dutton, 1985.

Pfeffer, Susan Beth. *Starring Peter and Leigh*. Delacorte, 1978.

Roosevelt, Elliott. *Murder in the Blue Room*. St. Martin's, 1990.

Seidler, Tor. *The Tar Pit*. Farrar, 1987.

Sherburne, Zoa. *The Girl Who Knew Tomorrow*. Morrow, 1970.

Smucker, Barbara. *Incredible Jumbo*. Viking, 1991.

Stolz, Mary. *Pangur Ban*. Harper, 1988.

Tyler, Anne. *A Slipping-Down Life*. Berkley, 1983.

West, Pamela E. *Yours Truly, Jack the Ripper*. St. Martin's, 1987.

Wojciechowska, Maia. *Shadow of a Bull*. Macmillan, 1973.
Yep, Laurence. *The Mark Twain Murders*. Macmillan, 1982.

Periodicals

16 Magazine. 16 Magazine.
People Weekly. Time.
Splice. Ira Friedman, Inc.
Star Hits. Pilot Communications, Inc.
Super Teen. Sterling's Magazines, Inc.
Wow. Pilot Communications, Inc.

Feature-Length Films

All About Eve. Fox, 1950.
Coal Miner's Daughter. MCA/Universal, 1980. (PG)
Come Back to the Five and Dime, Jimmy Dean, Jimmy Dean. Sultan Entertainment, 1982. (PG)
Fame. MGM/UA, 1980. (R)
A Star Is Born. Warner, 1954.

Computer Software

Cameron's People and Events. Cameron, 1994.
Famous Faces. Jasmine Multimedia Publishing, 1992.
Greatest Sports Legends. Compton's NewMedia, 1994.
Hollywood: The Bizarre. ScanRom Publications, 1993.
The Lifestyles of the Rich and Famous Cookbook. Compton's NewMedia.
People Behind the Holidays. National Geographic Society, 1994.

16

A Fantastic World

Dragons, sorcerers, and strange new worlds await you at the library. In the alternate reality of a fantasy novel, you can possess a magical talisman, become a wizard, battle monsters, and embark on a quest to save the kingdom. Anything is possible, and the library has a great selection of fantasy novels and films that will satisfy the wildest imagination. So if you're eager to experience the unusual, open the magic portals of a book and encounter A Fantastic World.

Display Idea

Display several fantasy novels, including individual and series titles, short story collections, books based on fantasy TV shows and ones that were made into movies, as well as related magazines. Post lists of books that have won Hugo and Nebula Awards, and hang posters of fantasy scenes. You can also add nonfiction books and magazines about the magical arts, unexplained phenomena, and other related topics.

Sponsorship for Prizes

1. Ask a video rental store to donate free movie rental certificates for fantasy movies.
2. Ask a bookstore to donate paperback copies of fantasy novels.
3. Ask a local movie theater to donate movie passes or posters of fantasy movies.
4. Ask a video arcade to donate free tokens for fantasy games or virtual reality rides.

Program Game

Provide an outline of a dragon's body. For every point earned, patrons can paste a scale onto the dragon, until the dragon is covered with scales. Points can be earned for completing the activities mentioned in the General Guidelines, and for:
1. Reading a fantasy novel and completing a Fantasy Fiction Book Review Form.
2. Reading a novel not related to the fantasy theme, and completing a Fiction Book Review Form.
3. Reading a nonfiction book and completing a Nonfiction Book Review Form.
4. Reading a fantasy genre magazine or short story collection and completing a Fantasy Stories Review Form.

Program Forms

1. Fantasy Fiction Book Review Form
Title:
Author:
Publisher and date:
Brief summary of plot:
Is the story believable? Why or why not?
What is your opinion of this book?

2. Fiction Book Review Form
Title:
Author:
Publisher and Date:
Brief summary of plot:
I would rate this book: "Fantas-tic," "It has a great spirit," "Successfully completed its quest," "It took an act of heroism to read this," "Feed it to the dragons."

3. Nonfiction Book Review Form
Title:
Author:
Publisher and date:
Brief description of information:
I would rate this book: "A wizardly work," "A clever bit of sorcery," "Has some magical moments," "The work of an incompetent troll," "Make it disappear."

4. Fantasy Stories Review Form
Title of magazine or story collection:
Author/editor:
Publisher and date:
Name and author of your favorite story:
Brief description of its plot:
Why is this your favorite story?
Would you want to read more of this form of literature? Why or why not?

Program Activities

1. Film Fantasy. Show a fantasy film, such as *The Princess Bride*. If it was based on a book, ask patrons to read the novel and then discuss it afterwards.

2. Dragon Tales. Dragons are a mainstay of fantasy novels, but each writer's vision of a dragon differs. Booktalk dragon stories by various authors. Ask patrons to read dragon stories and, as a group, draw up a chart to compare their features. You can also provide art materials and let patrons create their own dragons.

3. Wizard's Manual. Have patrons copy spells, charts and magical potions used by wizards and other conjurers in several fantasy novels. For each work of magic, note the name of the book, the author, the character who performed it, and the desired result. Collect these instructions and print them in a wizard's manual to distribute to patrons.

4. Kiddie Fantasies. Fantasy stories for young children often include talking animals and various make-believe elements. Suggest several fantasy picture books and let teens choose one or more to adapt into a puppet show format. Teens can write the script, draw the scenery, and design the puppets. Arrange for young adults to perform their puppet shows to children in an elementary school or public library.

5. **Create-a-Creature.** Supply theater make-up, rubber masks, wigs, and assortment of odd-looking accessories. Let teens use these materials to make themselves into fantastic creatures. Take photos of these characters to display in the library.

6. **The Quest.** Host a game show in which teens can answer trivia questions on fantasy topics. Categories may include Time Travelers, Magical Lands, Fantastic Films, Weird Creatures, Dragons, Wizards and Other Magical Folk.

7. **Supernatural TV Marathon.** A subgenre of fantasy is the supernatural. Some TV shows of the 1960s were popular examples of this form of story. Show teens several episodes of *The Twilight Zone*, *The Outer Limits*, or more recent series, such as *Tales of the Crypt*. How are these stories similar and different from other fantasies?

8. **Other Worlds.** Many tales of fantasy take place in a magical world of the author's own creation. Discuss some of these, such as J.R.R. Tolkien's Middle Earth or Ursula LeGuin's Earthsea. What is the terrain of these lands? What are its inhabitants like? What magical elements are there? Ask teens to invent a fantasy world of their own. They can work together to build a model or draw a mural of this new world.

9. **Fantastic Careers.** Discuss some jobs that would be of interest to fantasy-lovers. These can include writers of fantasy novels, short stories and magazines, and the publishers that produce them. Also include writers of fantasy TV shows and movies, plus numerous film production jobs including special effects technicians, set designers, costume designers, actors, directors and others. In addition to fields in literature and film, other creative people who work in a fantasy world are artists, cartoonists, puppeteers, doll manufacturers, performing magicians and people who explore unexplained phenomena. You can also provide information on fantasy fan clubs for teens to join.

10. **Magicians' Convention.** Fantasy novels are often populated by magical folk such as wizards, sorcerers and witches. Invite teens to come to a dance party dressed in the garb of a magic person of their choice from a specific novel they have read. Teens should try to act and speak in character. Later during the party, patrons can try to guess each other's identities.

Curriculum Tie-Ins

1. **English Literature/Composition.** Ask students to name some elements of fantasy novels, such as dragons, wizards, quests, magic, etc. List all on the board and compare these elements in various short stories. Then tell students to select any ten elements and use them in a story. Or, have students write a sequel to a fantasy novel or movie.

2. **Science.** Witches and sorcerers in fantasy novels often whip up some interesting potions and concoctions. In real life, there are many plants, roots, and herbs that have medicinal or healing powers. Explore some of these plants with the class. What medicinal properties do they have and why? Go to a health food store and look up books on herbs to find out more about some natural remedies.

3. **History/Geography.** List some popular creatures in fantasy stories, such as dragons, unicorns, and witches. Students can choose one of these and research how it is treated in the customs, folklore, and history of a particular nation. For example, dragons are celebrated in Chinese culture, unicorns are legendary in Ireland, and witches have been historically condemned in many countries. Students can relate some historical events, beliefs, and traditional activities associated with their fantasy characters and creatures.

4. Math. Time travel is an element in some fantasy novels, such as in Madeleine L'Engle's *A Wrinkle in Time*. Prepare some math exercises involving time for students to solve. Questions can be based on Earth's time zones (If it is 6:00 A.M. in New York City, what time is it in Hong Kong?) or involve crossing time zones (If it takes X number of hours to fly from London to San Francisco and you leave on Monday at 11:00 P.M., what day and time will it be when you reach San Francisco?) You can also have students read a fantasy novel that deals with time travel and have them answer time questions that are specific to the book.

Activity Sheet Ideas

1. Word search or crossword puzzles of: a) fantasy character types, b) plot elements, or c) genre terms.

2. Word scrambles or cryptograms of: a) titles of popular fantasy books or movies, b) verses or spells spoken by magical folk in fantasy novels, or c) names of fantasy series or trilogies.

3. Matching activities: match a) characters to the book, movie or TV show in which they appear, b) authors to their books, c) movie and TV characters to the actors who portrayed them.

Suggested Resources

Reference and Nonfiction

Card, Orson Scott. *How to Write Science Fiction and Fantasy*. Writer's Digest, 1990.

Cawthorn, James, and Moorcock, Michael. *Fantasy: The 100 Best Books*. Carroll & Graf, 1989.

Datlow, Ellen, and Windling, Terri, eds. *The Year's Best Fantasy and Horror: Eighth Annual Collection*. St. Martin's, 1995.

Egoff, Sheila A. *Worlds Within: Children's Fantasy from the Middle Ages to Today*. ALA, 1988.

Foster, Robert. *The Complete Guide to Middle-Earth: From the Hobbit to the Silmarillion*. Ballantine, 1985.

Fricke, John, et al. *The Wizard of Oz: The Official 50th Anniversary Pictorial History*. Warner, 1989.

Galloway, Bruce, ed. *Fantasy Wargaming*. Stein and Day, 1982.

Goldberg, Lee, et al. *The Dreamweavers: Interviews with Fantasy Filmmakers of the 1980s*. McFarland, 1995.

Hammacher, Abraham Marie. *Phantoms of the Imagination: Fantasy in Art and Literature from Blake to Dali*. Abrams, 1981.

Kies, Cosette. *Supernatual Fiction for Teens: More Than 1300 Good Paperbacks to Read for Wonderment, Fear, and Fun*. Libraries Unlimited, 1993.

Le Guin, Ursula K. *The Language of the Night: Essays on Fantasy and Science Fiction*. Berkley, 1979.

Lynn, Ruth Nadelman. *Fantasy Literature for Children and Young Adults: An Annotated Bibliography*. Bowker, 1995.

Maitre, Doreen. *Literature and Possible Worlds*. Pembridge, 1983.

Nigg, Joe. *Wonder Beasts: Tales and Lore of the Phoenix, the Griffin, the Unicorn, and the Dragon*. Libraries Unlimited, 1995.

Nye, Jody Lynn, and McCaffrey, Anne. *The Dragonlover's Guide to Pern.* Ballantine, 1989.

Ouellette, William, compiler. *Fantasy Postcards.* Doubleday, 1975.

Page, Michael F., and Ingpen, Robert R. *Encyclopedia of Things That Never Were: Creatures, Places, and People.* Viking, 1987.

Platt, Charles. *Dream Makers: Science Fiction and Fantasy Writers at Work.* Ungar, 1987.

Robertson, Bruce. *Fantasy Art.* North Light, 1988.

Schiff, Gert. *Images in Horror and Fantasy.* Abrams, 1978.

Searles, Baird, et al. *A Reader's Guide to Fantasy.* Avon, 1982.

The Tourist's Guide to Transylvania. Octopus, 1981.

Vallejo, Boris. *Fantasy Art Techniques.* Arco, 1985.

Wullschlager, Jackie. *Inventing Wonderland: The Lives and Fantasies of Lewis Carroll, Edward Lear, J.M. Barrie, Kenneth Grahame, and A.A. Milne.* Free Press, 1995.

Zelazny, Roger, and Randall, Neil. *Roger Zelazny's Visual Guide to Castle Amber.* Avon, 1988.

Fiction

Alexander, Lloyd. *The Remarkable Journey of Prince Jen.* Dutton, 1991.

Ball, Margaret. *The Shadow Gate.* Baen, 1991.

Bradshaw, Gillian. *The Dragon and the Thief.* Greenwillow, 1991.

Brooks, Terry. *The Scions of Shannara.* Ballantine, 1990.

Cooper, Susan. *Over Sea, Under Stone.* Harcourt, 1966.

Downer, Ann. *The Glass Salamander.* Atheneum, 1989.

Fletcher, Susan. *Dragon's Milk.* Atheneum, 1989.

Garden, Nancy. *The Door Between.* Farrar, 1987.

Hilgartner, Beth. *Colors in the Dreamweaver's Loom.* Houghton, 1989.

Hill, Douglas. *Master of Fiends.* Macmillan, 1988.

Hughes, Monica. *The Promise.* Simon & Schuster, 1992.

Jacques, Brian. *Mariel of Redwall.* Putnam, 1992.

Jones, David Lee. *Unicorn Highway.* Avon, 1992.

Jones, Diana Wynne. *Castle in the Air.* Greenwillow, 1991.

Jordan, Robert. *Eye of the World.* Tor, 1990.

Kerr, Katharine. *The Bristling Wood.* Doubleday, 1989.

Kisling, Lee. *The Fool's War.* HarperCollins, 1992.

Kurtz, Katherine. *The Harrowing of Gwynedd.* Ballantine, 1989.

Lee, Tanith. *The Black Unicorn.* Atheneum, 1991.

Le Guin, Ursula K. *A Wizard of Earthsea.* Parnassus, 1968.

L'Engle, Madeleine. *A Wrinkle in Time.* Farrar, 1962.

Lillington, Kenneth. *Jonah's Mirror.* Faber and Faber, 1988.

Lucas, George, and Claremont, Chris. *Shadow Moon.* Bantam, 1995.

McCaffrey, Anne. *Dragonflight.* Ballantine, 1981.

McGowen, Tom. *The Magical Fellowship.* Lodestar, 1991.

Mayne, William. *Antar and the Eagles.* Delacorte, 1990.

Morpurgo, Michael. *King of the Cloud Forests.* Viking, 1988.

Pattou, Edith. *Hero's Song.* Harcourt, 1991.

Pfeffer, Susan Beth. *Rewind to Yesterday.* Delacorte, 1988.

Rawn, Melanie. *Stronghold.* DAW, 1990.

Smith, Sherwood. *Wren to the Rescue*. Harcourt, 1990.
Strickland, Brad. *Dragon's Plunder*. Atheneum, 1992.
Tolkien, J.R.R. *The Hobbit; or, There and Back Again*. Ballantine, 1982.
Williams, Tad. *The Dragonbone Chair*. New American Library, 1988.
Wilson, David Henry. *The Coachman Rat*. Carroll & Graf, 1989.
Wrede, Patricia C. *Dealing with Dragons*. Harcourt, 1990.
Yep, Laurence. *Dragon of the Lost Sea*. HarperCollins, 1982.
Yolen, Jane. *Dragon's Blood*. Delacorte, 1982.
Zelazny, Roger. *Nine Princes in Amber*. Avon, 1972.

(Also other fantasy books by these authors.)

Periodicals

Amazing Stories. TSR, Inc.
Magazine of Fantasy and Science Fiction. Mercury Press.
Marion Zimmer Bradley's Fantasy Magazine. Marion Zimmer Bradley.
Oracle Science Fiction and Fantasy Magazine. Science Fiction and Fantasy Productions.
Weird Tales. Terminus Publishing Co.

Feature-Length Films

Dragonslayer. Paramount, 1981. (G)
Journey to the Center of the Earth. Cannon, 1988. (PG)
Labyrinth. Sultan Entertainment, 1986. (PG)
Legend. MCA/Universal, 1986. (PG)
The Princess Bride. Columbia Tristar, 1987. (PG)
Time Bandits. Paramount, 1988. (PG)

Computer Software

Companions of Xanth. Legend Entertainment, 1994.
Dragon Lore—The Legend Begins. Mindscape, 1994.
Fables & Fiends: The Legend of Kyrandia. Virgin Interactive Entertainment, 1992.
Fantasy Fest. Mindscape, 1994.
The Lord of the Rings CD-ROM. Interplay Productions, 1993.
Myst. Broderbund, 1994.

17

Go in Style

If you want to keep up with the latest fashions, come into the library. We have books and magazines for gals interested in exciting make-up, fantastic hairstyles, kicky fashion accessories and clothes ranging from sporty to glamorous. Guys can look up grooming tips and outfits that suit their lifestyles. You can also read about modeling and fashion fads from the past. Whether you're looking to follow a fashion trend or set one of your own, you should always Go in Style.

Display Idea

Set aside nonfiction books on beauty, grooming, fashion and modeling, along with related magazines and fiction. Props such as a vanity mirror, hairstyling equipment, and magazine photos of fashions and hairstyles for young men and women should attract attention to the display.

Sponsorship for Prizes

1. Ask a local hairstylist or salon to donate certificates for free or reduced-price services.
2. Ask a natural cosmetics boutique to donate soaps, skin lotion and other merchandise.
3. Ask a bookstore to donate paperback books or magazines about beauty, grooming, fashion, modeling or other related topics.
4. Ask a clothing store to donate discount merchandise certificates.

Program Game

Give each patron a sheet of paper, folded in half. Head one side "Best Dressed List" and the other side "Worst Dressed List." For each point earned, patrons can add the name of a celebrity to either list. Points can be earned for completing the activities mentioned in the General Guidelines, and for:
1. Reading a novel and completing a Fiction Book Review Form.
2. Reading a nonfiction book about some aspect of fashion, beauty, or grooming and completing a Fashion Nonfiction Book Review Form.
3. Reading a nonfiction book and completing a Nonfiction Book Review Form.
4. Reading two men's or women's fashion magazines and comparing them in a Fashion Magazine Comparison Form.

Program Forms

1. Fiction Book Review Form
Title:
Author:
Publisher and date:
Brief summary of plot:
I would rate this book: "The personification of beauty," "Has exquisite features," "Looks good," "In need of a makeover," "Ugly."

2. Fashion Nonfiction Book Review Form
Title:
Author:
Publisher and date:
Brief description of information:
What was the most interesting part of the book?
Did this book contain information that you found useful? Why or why not?

3. Nonfiction Book Review Form
Title:
Author:
Publisher and date:
Brief description of information:
I would rate this book: "The ultimate in fine fashion," "Bold and trend-setting," "Stylish," "Mismatched and irregular," "Bargain basement reject."

4. Fashion Magazine Comparison Form
Name and date of magazine #1:
To whom would this magazine appeal?
Name and date of magazine #2:
To whom would this magazine appeal?
What are some similarities between these magazines?
What are some differences?
Which one do you prefer and why?

Program Activities

1. Fashion on Film. Show a movie about the fashion industry, beauty pageants, modeling, or a related topic.

2. Attractive Opposites. Have girls complete a survey of the styles they like for boys. For example, do they prefer boys with moustaches or clean-shaven faces, with or without earrings, using or not using cologne, with long or short hair? Meanwhile, boys can complete a similar survey about styles they like for girls. Tabulate the results, and let teens discuss their responses.

3. Makeover Magic. Ask a beautician to demonstrate make-up and hairstyling techniques on one or more female volunteers. (Make sure the volunteers have parental permission first!) The beautician can discuss proper skin and hair care for girls, and advise them on which colors suit them best. Patrons can sample various cosmetics to enhance their appearance.

4. Good Grooming for Guys. Invite an expert in male grooming to talk to boys about looking good. He can give guys tips on how to have healthy skin, hair, and bodies. Perhaps the guest can bring in product samples for patrons to try.

5. Take a Whiff of This. There are many perfumes and colognes on the market for men and women. Give teens a chance to smell several of these and pick their favorite. Ahead of time, saturate squares of porous paper with different fragrances of perfume. Make sure each sample is labeled on the back so you can identify the brand. During the library program, patrons can sniff these cards to decide which scent they prefer. Take a poll to determine the most popular brands for girls and boys.

6. Trés Chic Trivia. Use pictures and photos from magazines and books as visual questions in a game show for teens. Contestants must identify who or what the pictures show, in categories such as Famous Models (from magazine covers and layouts), Fashions from the Past (such as hoop skirts and Nehru jackets), Designer Labels (such as Guess?), What's That Hairstyle? (beehives and bobs), Footwear Fads (clogs, Earth Shoes), and Men's Facial Hair (sideburns, goatees).

7. Teens à la Mode. Teen volunteers can model the latest in youth fashions at a Teen Scene Fashion Show in the library. Ask a popular youth clothing store to lend dressy and sporty outfits and accessories, and a local hairdresser to style models' hair for the show. Play upbeat music to set the pace. You can also have members of the audience act as fashion critics, and write their opinions of the clothes that are modeled.

8. Accessorize! Ask a boutique to lend an assortment of vests, hats, scarves, ties, headbands and other fashion accessories for teens to try on. A representative from the shop can give pointers on compatible color schemes and offer other advice on how to get the most out of fashion accessories.

9. Beautiful People. Showcase occupations in fashion and grooming at a career day program. Set up tables with information on becoming a hairstylist, theater make-up artist, cosmetician, fashion designer, fashion critic, model, fashion photographer, manicurist, plastic surgeon and other related fields. Also include jobs of people who develop, manufacture, and sell health and beauty aids. Supply a list of model agencies, cosmetology programs, and schools of fashion design. Have books on these subjects available for patrons to borrow.

10. For the Fashion-Impaired Only. Sponsor a Nerd Dance Party at the library. Teens must come dressed in the most unstylish, mismatched, or outdated outfits they can assemble. Play novelty songs and encourage patrons to talk in character. Award prizes for Worst Dressed Male and Female.

Curriculum Tie-Ins

1. English Literature/Composition. Select several passages in novels in which a character's physical appearance is described. Can readers get a clear mental picture of what these characters look like from the authors' descriptions? Give each student a different picture or photograph of a person. Have them write physical descriptions of these people. Display the pictures as students read their passages aloud, and see if students can guess each picture that was described.

2. Science. In modern American culture, thin is considered beautiful. In reality, what is the perfect weight of males and females of various heights? Students can study some weight-related health problems, such as anorexia, bulimia, obesity, and fad dieting. What kinds of foods should people eat to nurture healthy skin, hair and teeth?

3. History/Geography. The concept of beauty has changed over the years. Compare what was considered beautiful at various times in the past, to what modern Americans think of as the perfect figure, weight, facial features, hairstyles, etc. Students can also trace the history of the fashion industry. What styles did American teens wear in the past?

4. Math. Health and beauty products come in packages of various sizes. Base a math lesson on finding the best consumer value of several brands of items. Each student should choose a different product, such as shampoo, and pick four brands to compare. They should list the number of ounces in every size package available for these brands, along with their prices. Students can determine the price per ounce of these items, and graph the results.

Activity Sheet Ideas

1. Word search or crossword puzzles of: a) fashion terms, b) types of make-up, or c) types of fabric.

2. Word scrambles or cryptograms of: a) names of fashion and grooming magazines, b) advertising jingles or slogans for health and beauty products, or c) names of famous fashion designers.

3. Matching activities: match a) brand names of health and beauty products to their manufacturers, b) American fashions to the decade in which they were popular, or c) foreign language fashion terms to their literal meanings.

Suggested Resources

Reference and Nonfiction

Anderson, Marie Philomene. *Model: The Complete Guide to Becoming a Professional Model.* Doubleday, 1989.

Beckelman, Laurie. *Body Blues.* Crestwood, 1994.

The Body Shop International. *The Body Shop Book: Skin, Hair, and Body Care.* Dutton, 1994.

Bolognese, Don, and Raphael, Elaine. *Drawing Fashions: Figures, Faces, and Techniques.* Watts, 1985.

Bowen-Woodward, Kathy. *Coping with a Negative Body Image.* Rosen, 1989.

Brumberg, Elaine. *Save Your Money, Save Your Face: What Every Cosmetics Buyer Needs to Know.* Facts on File, 1986.

Cantwell, Mary. *Manhattan, When I Was Young.* Houghton, 1995.

Feldman, Elaine. **Fashions of a Decade** series. Facts on File, 1992.

Feldon, Leah. *Dress Like a Million—on Considerably Less: A Trend-Proof Guide to Real Fashion.* Villard, 1993.

Gearhart, Susan Wood. *Opportunities in Beauty Culture.* VGM, 1996.

_____. *Opportunities in Modeling.* VGM, 1991.

Grimble, Frances. *After a Fashion: How to Reproduce, Restore, and Wear Vintage Styles.* Lavolta, 1993.

Jackson, Victoria, and Calistro, Paddy. *Redefining Beauty: Discovering Your Individual Beauty, Enhancing Your Self-Esteem.* Warner, 1993.

Landau, Elaine. *The Beauty Trap.* Macmillan, 1994.

Lasch, Judith. *The Teen Model Book.* Messner, 1985.

McCoy, Kathy, and Wibbelsman, Charles. *The New Teenage Body Book.* Perigee, 1992.

Marano, Hara Estroff. *Style Is Not a Size: Looking and Feeling Great in the Body You Have.* Bantam, 1991.

Martin, Nancie S. *Miss America Through the Looking Glass.* Messner, 1985.

Martin, Richard, ed. *Contemporary Fashion.* St. James, 1995.

Mathis, Darlene. *Women of Color: The Multicultural Guide to Fashion and Beauty*. Ballantine, 1994.

Mauro, Lucia. *Careers for Fashion Plates and Other Trendsetters*. VGM, 1996.

Newman, Leslea. *Fat Chance*. Putnam's, 1994.

Peacock, John. *20th Century Fashion: The Complete Sourcebook*. Thames & Hudson, 1993.

Reybold, Laura. *Everything You Need to Know About the Dangers of Tattooing and Body Piercing*. Rosen, 1996.

Scheman, Andrew J., and Severson, David L. *Cosmetics Buying Guide*. Consumer Reports, 1993.

Schnurnberger, Lynne Edelman. *Let There Be Clothes: 40,000 Years of Fashion*. Workman, 1991.

Schorr, Lia, and Sims, Shari Miller. *Lia Schorr's Skin Care Guide for Men*. Prentice, 1985.

Shaw, Diana. *Make the Most of a Good Thing, You!* Atlantic Monthly, 1985.

Wadeson, Jacki. *Hairstyles: Braiding and Haircare*. Crescent, 1994.

Wilson, William. *Man at His Best: The Esquire Guide to Style*. Addison-Wesley, 1985.

Zamkoff, Bernard, and Price, Jeanne. *Basic Pattern Skills for Fashion Design*. Fairchild, 1987.

Zeldis, Yona. *Coping with Beauty, Fitness, and Fashion: A Girl's Guide*. Rosen, 1987.

Fiction

Anderson, Mary. *Who Says Nobody's Perfect?* Delacorte, 1987.

Blume, Judy. *Deenie*. Bradbury, 1973.

Busselle, Rebecca. *Bathing Ugly*. Orchard, 1989.

Callan, Jamie. *Over the Hill at Fourteen*. NAL, 1982.

Clark, Mary Higgins. *While My Pretty One Sleeps*. Simon & Schuster, 1989.

Conford, Ellen. *The Things I Did for Love*. Bantam, 1987.

Cooney, Caroline B. *Twenty Pageants Later*. Bantam, 1991.

Dygard, Thomas J. *Game Plan*. Morrow, 1993.

Ford Supermodels of the World series. Random.

Greene, Constance. *Monday I Love You*. Harper, 1988.

Joose, Barbara A. *The Pitiful Life of Simon Schultz*. HarperCollins, 1991.

Katz, William. *Facemaker*. McGraw, 1988.

Kerr, M. E. *Dinky Hocker Shoots Smack!* Harper, 1989.

Klass, Sheila Soloman. *Rhino*. Scholastic, 1993.

Klein, Daniel. *Beauty Sleep*. St. Martin's, 1990.

Koertge, Ronald. *The Boy in the Moon*. Little, 1990.

Levenkron, Steven. *The Best Little Girl in the World*. Warner, 1989. (Also *Kessa*.)

Littke, Lael. *Prom Dress*. Scholastic, 1989.

McNamara, John. *Model Behavior*. Dell, 1987.

Michaels, Barbara. *Shattered Silk*. Berkley, 1988.

Myers, Walter Dean. *Crystal*. Viking, 1987.

Park, Barbara. *Beanpole*. Knopf, 1983.

Peck, Richard. *Representing Super Doll*. Dell, 1982.

Perl, Lila. *Fat Glenda Turns Fourteen*. Clarion, 1991.

Rabinowich, Ellen. *Underneath I'm Different*. Delacorte, 1983.

Tamar, Erika. *High Cheekbones*. Viking, 1990.

Taylor, Theodore. *The Weirdo*. Harcourt, 1991.

Woodson, Jacqueline. *Between Madison and Palmetto*. Delacorte, 1993.

Young, Alida E. *The Klutz Is Back*. Willowisp, 1990.

Periodicals

Elle. Murdoch Magazines.
Essence: The Magazine for Today's Black Woman. Essence Communications, Inc.
GQ (Gentlemen's Quarterly). Esquire Publications.
Mademoiselle. Conde Naste Publications, Inc.
Radiance: The Magazine for Large Women. Radiance.
Seventeen. Triangle Publications.
Teen. Petersen Publications Co.

Feature-Length Films

Designing Woman. MGM/UA, 1957.
Funny Face. Paramount, 1957.
Hairspray. Columbia Tristar, 1988. (PG)
It Should Happen to You. Good Times/Kids Klassics, 1954.
Lovely to Look At. MGM/UA, 1952.
Smile. MGM/UA, 1975.

Computer Software

Cameron's Fashion and Glamour. Cameron, 1994.
The Face. Brigalow Digital Publishing, 1993.
Poser. Fractal Design, 1995.

18
Get in Shape

Are you physically fit? A balanced diet and regular exercise are necessary for your body's health. The library has lots of books, magazines and videos on nutrition and fitness, and some great music for you to work out to. And if you're starving for a good story, you can supplement your diet with a satisfying variety of fiction and nonfiction. So treat yourself right. Let the library help you to Get in Shape!

Display Idea

Nonfiction books on health, diet, nutrition, physical fitness and exercise can be displayed with fiction, magazines and videos on these topics. Post weight and nutrition charts and posters of people exercising. Include small props, such as a calorie counter or wrist weights.

Sponsorship for Prizes

1. Ask a bookstore to donate paperbacks on health, diet, nutrition, physical fitness, and exercise.
2. Ask a local health club to donate free passes.
3. Ask a health food store to donate merchandise coupons.
4. Ask a sporting goods or sportswear store to donate coupons for exercise equipment or clothing.

Program Game

The game board is in the shape of the food pyramid, with the number of suggested servings for dairy, meat, vegetables, fruit, and grains listed. Patrons will add a picture representing one serving for each point earned. Points can be earned for completing the activities mentioned in the General Guidelines, and for:

1. Reading a novel and completing a Fiction Book Review Form.
2. Reading a nonfiction book related to physical fitness or nutrition and completing a Fitness Nonfiction Book Review Form.
3. Reading a nonfiction book not related to the fitness theme and completing a Nonfiction Book Review Form.
4. Exercising to a workout video or book and completing an Exercise Program Review Form.

Program Forms

1. Fiction Book Review Form
Title:
Author:
Publisher and date:
Brief summary of plot:
I would rate this book: "A stimulating workout," "Good exercise," "Not too much of a strain," "Physically exhausting," "Painful."

2. Fitness Nonfiction Book Review Form
Title:
Author:
Publisher and date:
Brief description of information:
What was the most interesting or useful part of this book, and why?
To whom would this book appeal and why?

3. Nonfiction Book Review Form
Title:
Author:
Publisher and date:
Brief description of information:
I would rate this book: "Meets 100% RDA," "Has many important nutrients," "Contains some vitamins but no protein," "High in artificial sweeteners, fat and cholesterol," "Junk food."

4. Exercise Program Review Form
Title:
Exercise Instructor:
Publisher and date:
Who is the target audience of this video or book?
Is this a good workout for you? Why or why not?

Program Activities

1. Diet-Rate. There are many prepared diet foods on the market. Have teens conduct a consumer poll to decide which foods are the best choices. Participants can compare the tastes of various diet "meal-in-a-drink" products, frozen dinners, diet cookies and snack bars. Rank foods on a scale of 1 (tastes awful) to 5 (tastes great) and post all scores on a wall chart. Then compare these foods for nutritional value, taking into consideration all items listed on the package labels, and again rank them from 1 (low in nutrients) to 5 (very nutritious). Add these figures to determine which foods score the highest in each category.

2. Healthy Image. Provide old magazines, newspapers and pamphlets that can be cut up. Give each patron a sheet of construction paper, scissors and glue. Tell teens to look through the reading materials and cut out any pictures, recipes, exercise tips, healthful hints or other information that they think will motivate them to take care of their bodies and watch their diet. Teens can use these materials to create a collage which reflects a healthy image of themselves.

3. Workout. Invite a physical fitness expert to conduct a low-impact aerobics session with teens. Print instructions for the exercises used for patrons to take with them.

4. **Sporty Duds.** Ask a sportswear store to provide leotards, sneakers, and other exercise clothing for teens to model. Play upbeat music for models to strut to during the fashion show.

5. **Nutri-Snacks.** Plan a cooking and tasting party to introduce teens to healthy snacks. Let them experiment with yogurt, lowfat milk, and assorted fresh fruits to whip up a frothy drink. Combine dried fruits, nuts and seeds to make a trail mix. Blend yogurt-based dips for vegetables and unsalted chips. Encourage teens to create their own recipes for nutritious treats.

6. **Which is Better for You?** Teens can compete in a game show that reinforces making healthy food choices. Ask multiple choice questions that challenge patrons to pick from a list of four foods the one that has the least number of calories, cholesterol, fat, or sodium; the highest amount of iron, protein, calcium, or a particular vitamin; or the highest overall nutritional value.

7. **Equipment Demo.** Ask a sporting goods store to set up several different exercise machines, mats and other items. A store representative can supervise teens who want to try working out with the equipment.

8. **Physical Fitness Council.** Make lists of the members and recommendations of the President's Council on Physical Fitness. If your state has a similar association, gather information on that as well. Discuss these recommendations with teens. Are they realistic? Does the Council provide a worthwhile service? Ask teens to make their own physical fitness guidelines and recommendations for teenagers.

9. **Healthy Jobs.** Present a program of career opportunities in the fields of health and fitness, such as professional athlete, sports trainer, aerobics or physical education instructor, nutritionist, weight loss counselor, dietician, nurse, doctor or other medical professional. Provide books about related occupations and a list of schools that offer majors in these fields.

10. **Exercise Video Previews.** Run five-minute clips from several exercise videos, and have teens work out (as much as possible) to them. Pause after each video and ask patrons for their comments. Were the exercises too easy, too hard, or about right for them? Was the instructor a fitness pro or not? After all videos have been previewed, let teens vote on which one(s) they would most likely want to use themselves.

Curriculum Tie-Ins

1. **English Literature/Composition.** Ask students to help you list some unhealthy habits and conditions that can harm their bodies, such as doing drugs, smoking, taking steroids and anorexia. Have them choose one of these topics and read a nonfiction article and a fiction story or book about it. Then have them write a short story or article about a teen dealing with this problem.

2. **Science.** Discuss how various vitamins and minerals are important to the human body, and some sources of these nutrients. Define other nutritional terms, such as fiber, fat, cholesterol, sodium, calorie and RDA. Talk about how problems caused by dietary deficiencies, such as scurvy, can be avoided by maintaining a healthy diet. Have students look at a chart of muscles in the human body, and note some exercises to tone up selected muscles.

3. **History/Geography.** Malnutrition is a serious problem in many parts of the world. Have students locate on a map areas where large segments of the population are starving. Have students choose one of these places and research the cause(s) of this problem.

4. Math. Show students a chart of recommended calorie intakes and let them note how many calories they should be consuming per day. Then pass out a list of foods and their calorie counts. Tell students to plan five days worth of nutritious meals, keeping within their recommended calorie limits.

Activity Sheet Ideas

1. Word search or crossword puzzles of: a) dietary terms, b) physical fitness terms, or c) related occupations.

2. Word scrambles or cryptograms of: a) types of exercise equipment, b) famous diet or fitness personalities, or c) titles of books and videos produced by these people.

3. Matching activities: match a) vitamins and minerals to foods that are good sources of them, b) high-fat or cholesterol foods to nutritious alternatives, or c) muscles and ligaments to the parts of the body in which they are located.

Suggested Resources

Reference and Nonfiction

Arnold, Caroline. *Too Fat? Too Thin? Do You Have a Choice?* Morrow, 1984.

Brems, Marianne. *The Fit Swimmer: 120 Workouts and Training Tips.* Contemporary, 1984.

Caldwell, Carol Coles. *Opportunities in Nutrition Careers.* VGM, 1992.

Camenson, Blythe. *Careers for Health Nuts and Others Who Like to Stay Fit.* VGM, 1996.

Carroll, Stephen, and Smith, Tony. *Complete Family Guide to Healthy Living.* Dorling Kindersley, 1995.

Eagles, Douglas. *Nutritional Diseases.* Watts, 1987.

Gans, Janet. *America's Adolescents, How Healthy Are They?* American Medical Association, 1990.

Human Fuel Handbook: Nutrition for Peak Athletic Performance. Health for Life, 1988.

Iknonian, Therese. *Fitness Walking.* Human Kinetics, 1995.

Jackowski, Edward. *Hold It! You're Exercising Wrong.* Simon & Schuster, 1995.

Kane, June Kozak. *Coping with Diet Fads.* Rosen, 1990.

Kolodny, Nancy J. *When Food's a Foe: How to Confront and Conquer Eating Disorders.* Little, 1992.

Lee, Sally. *New Theories on Diet and Nutrition.* Watts, 1990.

Lyons, Pat, and Burgard, Debby. *Great Shape: The First Exercise Guide for Large Women.* Arbor, 1988.

The Marshall Cavendish Encyclopedia of Health. 14 vols. Marshall Cavendish, 1995.

McCoy, Kathy. *The New Teenage Body Book.* Body Press, 1992.

Mercer, Nelda, and Orringer, Carl. *Grocery Shopping Guide: A Consumer's Manual for Selecting Foods Lower in Dietary Saturated Fat and Cholesterol.* University of Michigan Medical Center, 1989.

Newman, Leslea. *Fat Chance.* Putnam, 1994.

Ojeda, Linda. *Safe Dieting for Teens.* Hunter, 1993.

Peterson, Jane A., et al. *Strength Training for Women.* Human Kinetics, 1995.

Rosas, Debbie, and Rosas, Carlos. *Non-Impact Aerobics: Introducing the NIA Technique.* Avon, 1988.

Rosenberg, Ellen. *Growing Up Feeling Good: A Growing Up Handbook Especially for Kids.* Puffin, 1996.

_____. *Opportunities in Fitness Careers*. VGM, 1991.

Salter, Charles. *Looking Good, Eating Right*. Millbrook, 1991.

_____. *The Nutrition-Fitness Link*. Millbrook, 1993.

Schwarzenegger, Arnold, and Dobbins, Bill. *Encyclopedia of Modern Bodybuilding*. Simon & Schuster, 1985.

The Shopper's Guide to Natural Foods. Avery, 1987.

Silverstein, Alvin, et al. *So You Think You're Fat?* HarperCollins, 1991.

Simon, Nissa. *Good Sports: Plain Talk About Health and Fitness for Teens*. Harper, 1990.

Slap, Gail B., and Jablow, Martha M. *Teenage Health Care*. Pocket, 1994.

Thompson, Trisha. *Maintaining Good Health*. Facts on File, 1989.

Yacenda, John. *Fitness Cross-Training*. Human Kinetics, 1994.

Fiction

Boyle, T. Coraghessan. *The Road to Wellville*. Signet, 1993.

Busselle, Rebecca. *Bathing Ugly*. Orchard, 1989.

Cavallaro, Ann. *Blimp*. Dutton, 1983.

Cooper, Ilene. *Stupid Cupid*. Viking, 1995.

Crutcher, Chris. *Staying Fat for Sarah Byrnes*. Greenwillow, 1993.

_____. *Stotan!* Greenwillow, 1986.

Greenberg, Jan. *The Pig-Out Blues*. Farrar, 1982.

Greene, Constance C. *Monday I Love You*. Harper, 1988.

Hautzig, Deborah. *Second Star to the Right*. Greenwillow, 1981.

Holland, Isabelle. *Dinah and the Green Fat Kingdom*. Lippincott, 1978.

Hopper, Nancy J. *Wake Me Up When the Band Starts Playing*. Lodestar, 1988.

Kassem, Lou. *Secret Wishes*. Avon, 1989.

Kerr, M.E. *Dinky Hocker Shoots Smack!* HarperCollins, 1972.

Kirshenbaum, Binnie. *Short Subject*. Watts, 1989.

Knudson, R.R. *Fox Running*. Avon, 1977.

_____. *Just Another Love Story*. Farrar, 1983.

Levy, Marilyn. *The Girl in the Plastic Cage*. Ballantine, 1982.

Lipsyte, Robert. *One Fat Summer*. HarperCollins, 1977.

McDaniel, Lurlene. *A Season for Goodbye*. Bantam, 1995.

Miklowitz, Gloria D. *Anything to Win*. Delacorte, 1989.

Nixon, Joan Lowery. *The Dark and Deadly Pool*. Delacorte, 1987.

Perl, Lila. *Fat Glenda Turns Fourteen*. Clarion, 1991. (Also *Hey, Remember Fat Glenda?*)

Pinsker, Judith. *A Lot Like You*. Bantam, 1988.

Saul, John. *Creature*. Bantam, 1989.

Strasser, Todd. *How I Changed My Life*. Simon & Schuster, 1995.

Stren, Patti. *I Was a Fifteen-Year-Old Blimp*. NAL, 1986.

Taha, Karen T. *Marshmallow Muscles, Banana Brainstorms*. Harcourt, 1988.

Periodicals

American Fitness. Aerobics and Fitness Association of America.

Current Health 2: The Continuing Guide to Health Education. Weekly Reader Corp.

FDA Consumer. Food and Drug Administration.
Hippocrates: The Magazine of Health and Medicine. Hippocrates, Inc.
Prevention. Rodale Press, Inc.
Shape Magazine. Joe Weider Publications.

Feature-Length Films

American Flyers. Warner, 1985. (PG-13)
Pumping Iron. Columbia Tristar, 1976. (PG)
Rocky. MGM/UA, 1976. (PG)
See How She Runs. 1978.
Vision Quest. Warner, 1985. (R)

Computer Software

Better Homes and Gardens Healthy Cooking CD Cookbook. Multicom Publishing, 1993.
Fitness Partner. Computer Directions, 1993.
Mayo Clinic Sports Health and Fitness. IVI Publishing, 1994.
Multimedia Express: Health. Minisoft, 1990.
SimHealth: The National Health Care System. Maxis, 1994.
Total Health—Body and Mind. Softkey International, 1994.

19

A Feast of Fun

Come see what's on the menu in the library! For an appetizer, nibble on a selection of gourmet magazines. Fill your plate with a smorgasbord of international and domestic cookbooks. Indulge in a satisfying novel for dessert, and wash it down with a thirst-quenching video. There's even some ear-candy for you music-lovers to snack on. If you're looking for a tasty yet nourishing treat, the library is the place for A Feast of Fun.

Display Idea

Display a selection of fiction and nonfiction books about food and cooking, plus related magazines, pamphlets, and videos. Cooking utensils, posters picturing foods, and various food charts can decorate the display.

Sponsorship for Prizes

1. Ask local restaurants to donate gift certificates.

2. Ask a housewares store to donate items such as refrigerator magnets, potholders, and small utensils.

3. Ask a bookstore to donate paperback cookbooks.

4. Ask a health food store or specialty food store to donate merchandise coupons.

Program Game

Give each participant a game board that resembles a round pizza with outlines drawn on it to show where the pizza toppings should go. Patrons will add one topping to their pizzas for each point earned. Points can be earned for completing the activities mentioned in the General Guidelines, and for:

1. Reading a fiction book and completing a Fiction Book Review Form.

2. Reading a nonfiction book about food or cooking and completing a Food Nonfiction Book Review Form.

3. Reading a nonfiction book not related to the food theme and completing a Nonfiction Book Review Form.

4. Reading two feature food or cooking articles from two different magazines and completing a Food Articles Review Form.

Program Forms

1. Fiction Book Review Form
Title:
Author:
Publisher and date:
Brief summary of plot:
I would rate this book: "A glorious banquet," "Delicious," "Sustaining," "Half-baked," "Tasteless."

2. Food Nonfiction Book Review Form
Title:
Author:
Publisher and date:
Brief description of information:
Why did you choose to read this book?
What was the most interesting or useful part of the book?

3. Nonfiction Book Review Form
Title:
Author:
Publisher and date:
Brief description of information:
I would rate this book: "A 5-layer, beautifully decorated wedding cake," "A selection of freshly-baked pies, served à la mode," "A plate of brownies," "A half-eaten box of store-bought cookies," "A stale jelly donut with all the jelly sucked out."

4. Food Articles Review Form
Article #1:
Source and date:
Summary of Article #1:
Article #2:
Source and date:
Summary of Article #2:
Which article is easier to read? Which has more information?
Would you want to try the food mentioned in either article? Why or why not?

Program Activities

1. Food TV. Some of television's most hilarious comic moments involve food. For example, *I Love Lucy* had several, and *Saturday Night Live* often satirizes food commercials. Present a program of funny food shows and skits.

2. Playing With Your Food. Plan an indoor or outdoor food fun day. Teens can participate in races carrying an egg on a spoon, passing an orange from under one person's chin to another, or balancing donuts on their heads. Have contests such as bobbing for apples, pie-eating, or spitting watermelon seeds. For really messy fun, create food games or an obstacle course like those shown on the television show *Double Dare*.

3. Chef Toujours. Invite a cook or baker to present a cooking demonstration. Perhaps teens can help in the preparation of some foods. Leave time for a question and answer period, and to sample the results.

4. Food for the Hungry. Get your patrons involved in helping to feed people who are in need. Sponsor a canned and packaged food drive—teens can collect food and deliver it to a food distribution agency. As a speaker, invite someone who works to feed the poor. Plan a cooking party and have teens bake biscuits or cupcakes that will be donated to a soup kitchen.

5. Super Sub. Organize teens to bring in rolls, cold cuts, sliced cheese, lettuce and other sandwich fillings, and have them build a giant submarine sandwich. Measure it, photograph it, and let everyone eat it! For dessert, they can make ice cream sundaes.

6. What Food is This? Teens can participate in a food-themed game show with categories such as Edible Song Titles (such as "American Pie"), Food Commercials (match the food to its advertisement), What's It Mean? (define foreign cooking terms such as "al dente"), Name the Condiment (identify it after hearing a list of the ingredients), Weird Foods (such as, What is calamari?), and Origins (name country where food originated).

7. Spice Up Your Life. Conduct a food fair to demonstrate how to use various herbs and spices. Let teens experiment with sprinkling different seasonings on simple foods such as sliced tomatoes. Start with a plain tomato sauce and allow patrons to sample some as each new ingredient is added on the way to making spaghetti sauce. Have teens mix their own curry, Italian seasoning, flavored bread crumbs, or tea leaves. Give each participant a spice chart to take home.

8. Taste-O-Meter. Teens can form consumer panels to rate various taste and texture factors of different foods. They can sample five brands of chocolate chip cookies and rate them on how sweet, chewy, salty, crisp, or soggy they are, and the quality and quantity of their chocolate chips. How crunchy, spicy, salty, sweet and full of vegetables are different brands of salsa? How sour, sweet, watery, bitter, pulpy and artificial-tasting are some types of fresh, frozen, and powdered lemonades? Have teens record their preferences and compare them to similar polls done in consumer magazines.

9. Careers in the Kitchen. Inform teens of some jobs that involve food preparation, such as baker, chef, short order cook, and butcher, as well as jobs in fast food places, restaurant management, deli counters, and companies that process and package foods. Additional careers include cookbook author, restaurant critic, food buyer, nutritionist, dietician and food inspector. Have books on these topics available, and provide a list of schools that offer majors in culinary arts, restaurant management, and nutrition.

10. Family Recipes. Many families have special recipes that have been handed down from one generation to the next. Each culture also has its own traditional dishes. Ask patrons to obtain one recipe that is a favorite in their families. Combine these in a cookbook to distribute to the contributors. Then ask everyone to bring in a sample of their recipes and have a tasting party at the library.

Curriculum Tie-Ins

1. English Literature/Composition. Have students read passages of food descriptions from several novels. Then read magazine or newspaper articles written by food or restaurant critics. Discuss the phrases and descriptions that are used. Then ask students to write an article critiquing or describing a meal served in the school cafeteria, a restaurant, or at home.

2. Science. Students can research a cooking-related science topic: For example: What is the difference between baking soda and baking powder? How do microwave ovens work? What chemical reactions cause bread and cakes to rise when they bake? How are condensed, freeze-dried, or dehydrated foods made? How are foods canned or vacuum-packed, and why do they stay fresh?

   3. History/Geography. List some traditional foods served in other nations and cultures. Tell students to choose one food and find out what it is, what nationality/culture originated it, the occasion for which it is served, and any other information they can find. On a world map, locate the lands from which these foods came.

   4. Math. Discuss cooking measurements with the class and let them experiment with measuring liquids and dry foods. Have them calculate how to double a recipe, cook for a crowd, determine how much dry rice and water will yield a certain amount of cooked rice, convert quarts to liters, and do other cooking-related math problems.

Activity Sheet Ideas

   1. Word search and crossword puzzles of: a) cooking utensils, b) foods, or c) spices and herbs.

   2. Word scrambles or cryptograms of: a) famous chefs, b) popular local restaurants, or c) TV cooking shows.

   3. Matching activities: match a) popular cookbook titles to their authors, b) cooking measurements to their equivalents, and c) cooking terms to their meanings.

Suggested Resources

Reference and Nonfiction

Albyn, Carole Lisa, and Webb, Lois Sinaiko. *The Multicultural Cookbook for Students.* Oryx, 1993.

Baggett, Nancy. *The International Cookie Cookbook.* Stewart, 1988.

Benarde, Melvin A. *The Food Additives Dictionary.* Pocket, 1987.

Betty Crocker's Step-by-Step Cookbook. Prentice, 1988.

Bissell, Frances. *The Book of Food.* Holt, 1994.

Chmelynski, Carol Caprine. *Opportunities in Food Service Careers.* VGM, 1992.

Claiborne, Craig. *Craig Claiborne's The New York Times Food Encyclopedia.* Random, 1985.

Clark, Ann. *Quick Cuisine: Easy and Elegant Recipes for Every Occasion.* Penguin, 1995.

Clifton, Claire. *Edible Gifts.* McGraw, 1983.

Cobb, Vicki. *Science Experiments You Can Eat.* Harper, 1972.

Donovan, Mary. *Careers for Gourmets and Others Who Relish Food.* VGM, 1993.

Ehberts, Marjorie, and Gisler, Margaret. *Fast Food Careers.* VGM, 1989.

Ettlinger, Steve. *The Kitchenware Book.* Macmillan, 1992.

Franck, Irene M., and Brownstone, David M. *Restaurateurs and Innkeepers.* Facts on File, 1989.

Hill, Barbara. *The Cook's Book of Indispensable Ideas: A Kitchen Sourcebook.* Summer, 1988.

Igoe, Robert S. *Dictionary of Food Ingredients.* Van Nostrand, 1989.

Jacobson, Michael F., and Fritschner, Sarah. *The Fast-Food Guide: What's Good, What's Bad, and How to Tell the Difference.* Workman, 1986.

Kowalchik, Claire, and Hylton, William H. *Rodale's Illustrated Encyclopedia of Herbs.* Rodale, 1987.

Krescholleck, Margie. *The Guaranteed Goof-Proof Microwave Cookbook.* Bantam, 1988.

Mindell, Earl. *Unsafe at Any Meal.* Warner, 1987.

Murdich, Jack. *Buying Produce: A Greengrocer's Guide to Selecting and Storing Vegetables.* Hearst, 1986.

Nidetch, Jean. *Weight Watchers Quick Success Program Cookbook*. NAL, 1989.

Patrick, William. *The Food and Drug Administration*. Chelsea, 1988.

Perl, Lila. *Junk Food, Fast Food, Health Food: What America Eats and Why*. Clarion, 1980.

Schneider, Carol E., and Schneider, Andrew. *Midnight Snacks: The Cookbook That Glows in the Dark*. Clarkson Potter, 1994.

The Shopper's Guide to Natural Foods. Avery, 1987.

Tchudi, Stephen. *Soda Poppery: The History of Soft Drinks in America*. Macmillan, 1986.

Trager, James. *The Food Chronology: A Food Lover's Compendium of Events and Anecdotes, from Prehistory to the Present*. Holt, 1995.

Visser, Margaret. *Much Depends on Dinner: The Extraordinary History and Mythology, Allure and Obsessions, Perils and Taboos of an Ordinary Meal*. Grove, 1988.

Webb, Lois Sinaiko. *Holidays of the World Cookbook for Students*. Oryx, 1995.

Wood, Jacqueline, and Gilchrist, Joclyn Scott. *The Campus Survival Cookbook #2*. Morrow, 1981.

Zisman, Honey, and Zisman, Larry. *The Burger Book*. St. Martin's, 1987.

Fiction

Angell, Judie. *Leave the Cooking to Me*. Bantam, 1990.

Blair, Cynthia. *The Hot Fudge Sunday Affair*. Ballantine, 1985.

Collier, James Lincoln, and Collier, Christopher. *With Every Drop of Blood*. Delacorte, 1994.

Danziger, Paula. *The Pistachio Prescription*. Delacorte, 1978.

Davidson, Diane Mott. *The Last Suppers*. Bantam, 1994. (Also others in series.)

Davis, Jenny. *Checking on the Moon*. Orchard, 1991.

Dubosarsky, Ursula. *High Hopes*. Viking, 1990.

Duffy, James. *Cleaver and Company*. Scribner, 1991.

Flagg, Fannie. *Fried Green Tomatoes at the Whistle Stop Cafe*. Random, 1987.

Gilson, Jamie. *Can't Catch Me, I'm the Gingerbread Man*. Lothrop, 1981.

Greenberg, Jan. *Just the Two of Us*. Farrar, 1988.

Ho, Minfong. *Rice Without Rain*. Lothrop, 1990.

Keller, Beverley. *Fowl Play, Desdemona*. Lothrop, 1989.

Korman, Gordon. *The Zucchini Warriors*. Scholastic, 1988.

Laurence, Janet. *Recipe for Death*. Doubleday, 1993. (Also others in series.)

Lutzeier, Elizabeth. *The Coldest Winter*. Holiday, 1991.

Pascal, Francine. *Love and Betrayal and Hold the Mayo!* Viking, 1985.

Paulsen, Gary. *The Cookcamp*. Orchard, 1991.

Roberts, Gillian. *Philly Stakes*. Scribner, 1989.

Ruby, Lois. *Pig-Out Inn*. Houghton, 1987.

Springstubb, Tricia. *Eunice Gottlieb and the Unwhitewashed Truth About Life*. Delacorte, 1987.

Stout, Rex. *The Doorbell Rang*. Bantam, 1992.

Stren, Patti. *I Was a Fifteen-Year-Old Blimp*. Harper, 1985.

Sweeney, Joyce. *Piano Man*. Dell, 1994.

Taha, Karen T. *Marshmallow Muscles, Banana Brainstorms*. Harcourt, 1988.

Tamar, Erika. *It Happened at Cecilia's*. Atheneum, 1989.

Tchudi, Stephen. *The Burg-O-Rama Man*. Delacorte, 1983.

Wojciechowski, Susan. *Patty Dillman of Hot Dog Fame*. Orchard, 1989.

Yep, Laurence. *The Star Fisher*. Morrow, 1991.

Periodicals

Bon Appetit. American Colortype Co.
Creative Ideas for Living. Southern Living.
Food News for Consumers. U.S. Department of Agriculture, Food Safety and Quality Service.
Gourmet. Conde Nast Publications.
The Herb Quarterly. Uphill Press.

Feature-Length Films

Eat a Bowl of Tea. Columbia Tristar, 1989. (PG-13)
Fried Green Tomatoes. MCA/Universal, 1991. (PG-13)
The Grapes of Wrath. CBS/Fox, 1940.
Killer Tomatoes Strike Back. Fox/Lorber, 1990.
Untamed Heart. MGM/UA, 1993. (PG-13)
Who Is Killing the Great Chefs of Europe? Warner, 1988. (PG)

Computer Software

Better Homes and Gardens Healthy Cooking CD Cookbook. Multicom Publishing, 1993.
Cookbook USA. J&D Publishing, 1994.
Food and Human Nutrtion. Silver Platter Information, semiannual.
Great Restaurants, Wineries and Breweries. Deep River Publishing, 1994.
Key Home Gourmet. Softkey International, 1994.
Natural Foods Cookbook. Rodale Press, 1992.

20
Cultivate an Interest in Gardening

"Mary, Mary, quite contrary, how does your garden grow?" At the library, it grows in rows of books about gardening, agriculture, landscaping and other nonfiction topics. It blooms in stacks of fiction and racks of magazines. And it blossoms when you find just the book you're looking for. So plant yourself in a cozy chair and nurture your mind with a good book. You don't need a green thumb to Cultivate an Interest in Gardening.

Display Idea

Small gardening tools, seed packets and potted plants can be placed near a display of nonfiction books and magazines about indoor and outdoor gardening. Novels that mention flower or vegetable gardens and related themes can be included, along with gardening and landscaping videos.

Sponsorship for Prizes

1. Ask a local gardening store to donate seed packets, plants, or small gardening tools.
2. Ask a bookstore to donate gardening books.
3. Ask a magazine stand to donate gardening and landscaping magazines.
4. Ask a kitchenware store to donate potholders, aprons and other items that have a gardening motif.

Program Game

A landscaped terrace, without plants, serves as the game board. For each point earned, add a sticker or stamp of a plant, flower, or tree to the scene. Points can be earned for completing the activities mentioned in the General Guidelines, and for:
1. Reading a novel and completing a Fiction Book Review Form.
2. Reading a nonfiction book related to the gardening theme and completing a Gardening Nonfiction Book Review Form.
3. Reading a nonfiction book not related to the gardening theme and completing a Nonfiction Book Review Form.
4. Reading two gardening magazines and completing a Gardening Magazine Comparison Form.

Program Forms

1. Fiction Book Review Form
Title:
Author:
Publisher and date:
Brief summary of plot:
I would rate this book: "A large, thriving garden," "A healthy, good-sized garden," "A small but well-cared for plot," "A couple of neglected plants," "Weeds and bugs."
2. Gardening Nonfiction Book Review Form
Title:
Author:
Publisher and date:
Brief description of information:
Why did you choose to read this book?
What section interested you the most and why?
3. Nonfiction Book Review Form
Title:
Author:
Publisher and date:
Brief description of information:
I would rate this book: "Fully blossomed and beautiful," "A thriving plant," "Lots of leaves but no fruit," "Barely sprouted," "A rotten seed."
4. Gardening Magazine Comparison Form
Magazine #1:
Publisher and date:
Magazine #2:
Publisher and date:
What are some similarities between these two magazines?
What are some differences?
Which one do you consider to be more useful and why?

Program Activities

1. Green Screen. Show a movie which takes place in a garden or flower shop, such as *Little Shop of Horrors*, or which contains gardening scenes, such as *Edward Scissorhands*.

2. Terrariums. Provide gardening tools, large jars or bottles, gravel, soils and small plants for teens to use in making terrariums. Or, if you prefer, use bowls to make dish gardens. Instruct patrons on how to care for their indoor gardens.

3. Patch Work. If possible, arrange for teens to adopt a small patch of earth near the library to raise a garden. Participants can plan ahead of time which flowers, shrubs, or vegetables they want to plant and take turns caring for the garden. If they plant vegetables, teens can split the harvest or eat the food at another library-sponsored event.

4. Harvest Fair. If this program is held in the fall, you can encourage patrons to bring in samples of any flowers, vegetables or other plants they have grown during the summer. Display these in a public area, as well as any flower arrangements, homemade preserves, or other garden product made by teens. You may want to award prizes for the best item in each category.

5. **Can Do.** Do a program on how to preserve home-grown fruits and vegetables. Show teens how to blanch, freeze and can foods. You can also demonstrate how to make preserves and ices with fresh fruits and berries. Allow teens to participate in these activities and to take samples home with them.

6. **How Does Your Garden Grow?** Sponsor a game show that features questions involving gardening, agriculture and various plants. Sample categories: Plant Relatives (artichokes are members of the *thistle* family), Seasons (crocuses bloom in the *spring*), Picker Beware! (which plants are safe or poisonous), Medicinal Plants (which plants have what type of healing power), Bulbs, Seeds, or Tubers? (plant reproduction), Plant Physiology (identify plant parts).

7. **Flower Power.** Ask a local horticulturist to conduct a workshop on making floral arrangements. Provide either fresh or artificial flowers and various bowls, baskets, and vases so that teens can have hands-on experience designing attractive floral displays.

8. **Garden Party.** Arrange to have an outdoor program of lawn games. Teens can play croquet, boccie, or horseshoes, run races, go on a scavenger hunt and participate in other outdoor games. They can make floral wreaths to wear and enjoy a picnic lunch on the lawn.

9. **Earthy Careers.** Plan a job fair which specializes in occupations that relate to plants, such as gardening, landscaping, horticulture, agriculture, botany, forestry, herbology. Provide information about job requirements and where teens can go to learn more about these fields.

10. **Rock Garden.** Invite teens to come to a dance where all the music played is by acts with names that match the cultivation theme, such as Soundgarden. You can also play music with related titles, such as "The Rose." Decorate the room with artificial flowers and serve veggie snacks and fruit.

Curriculum Tie-Ins

1. **English Composition/Literature.** Have students look up the meanings of several idioms and metaphors that use gardening or plant terms, such as "garden variety," "green thumb," "rosy cheeks," etc. Read passages of prose or poetry that use these phrases and have students comment on the effectiveness of the image the author was trying to convey. Then tell students to create their own descriptive garden phrases and use them in a story or poem.

2. **Science.** Students can conduct a variety of experiments using plants for a school science fair. Some project suggestions: experiment with hydroponics, compare plants grown under various lighting conditions, study the effects of acid rain on plants, test various types of fertilizers, or graft two plants together.

3. **History/Geography.** Give students a list of unusual plants and have them look up where in the world they grow. Make another list of extinct plants and have students research where they grew and why they became extinct. Compile another list of plants that had special uses in the past (such as papyrus). Where did they grow and how were they used?

4. **Math.** Planning a garden requires some calculations. Pass out various vegetable seed packets that tell the amount of space they need in order to grow. Have students open the packages and count their seeds. How big a plot will they need in order to plant all their seeds? Students should plan how many rows they would plant, estimate how many seeds would germinate, and how much produce they could expect to harvest.

Activity Sheet Ideas

1. Word search or crossword puzzles of: a) garden vegetables, b) flowers, or c) trees and shrubs.

2. Word scrambles or cryptograms of: a) famous botanical gardens and where they are located, b) gardening or agricultural organizations, or c) local orchards and nurseries.

3. Matching activities: match a) endangered plants to the part of the world they came from, b) common plant names to their scientific (genus and species) names, or c) gardening tools to their uses.

Suggested Resources

Reference and Nonfiction

Adams, Abby. *The Gardener's Gripe Book: Amusing Advice and Comfort for Anyone Who Has Ever Suffered the Loss of a Tulip or Petunia.* Workman, 1995.

Asimov, Isaac. *How Did We Find Out About Photosynthesis?* Walker, 1989.

Better Homes and Gardens New Garden Book. Meredith, 1990.

Bonnet, Robert L., and Keen, G. Daniel. *Botany: 49 Science Fair Projects.* TAB, 1989.

Burpee Complete Gardener. Macmillan, 1995.

Camenson, Blythe. *Careers for Plant Lovers and Other Green Thumb Types.* VGM, 1995.

Cook, Hal. *Arranging: The Basics of Contemporary Floral Design.* Morrow, 1985.

Cox, Jeff, et al. *How to Grow Vegetables Organically.* Rodale, 1988.

Creasy, Rosalind. *The Gardener's Handbook of Edible Plants.* Sierra, 1986.

Dowden, Anne Ophelia. *The Clover and the Bee: A Book of Pollination.* Harper, 1990.

_____. *From Flower to Fruit.* Harper, 1984.

Ehberts, Marjorie. *Nature.* VGM, 1996.

Eck, Joe. *Elements of Garden Design.* Holt, 1996.

Ettlinger, Steve. *The Complete Illustrated Guide to Everything Sold in Garden Centers (Except the Plants).* Macmillan, 1990.

Garden Lovers Quotations. Exley, 1992.

Garner, Jerry. *Careers in Horticulture and Botany.* VGM, 1996.

Hemphill, John, and Hemphill, Rosemary. *Herbs: Their Cultivation and Usage.* Borgo, 1987.

Hessayon, D.G. *The House Plant Expert.* Sterling, 1990.

Lerner, Carol. *Dumb Cane and Daffodils: Poisonous Plants in the House and Garden.* Morrow, 1990.

McClure, Susan. *The Herb Gardener.* Prentice, 1996.

Martin, Alexander C. *Weeds.* Wester, 1973.

Newcomb, Duane, and Newcomb, Karen. *The Complete Vegetable Gardener's Sourcebook.* Prentice, 1989.

Paterson, John, and Paterson, Katherine. *Consider the Lilies: Plants of the Bible.* Harper, 1986.

Rahn, Joan Elma. *More Plants That Changed History.* Macmillan, 1985.

Reader's Digest editors. *Magic and Medicine of Plants.* Random, 1986.

Southern Living Garden Guide series. Oxmoor.

Step-by-Step Gardening Techniques Illustrated. Storey, 1996.

Taylor's Guide to Ground Covers, Vines and Grasses. Houghton, 1987.

Woods, Sylvia. *Plant Facts and Fancies.* Faber, 1985.

Fiction

Alcock, Vivien. *The Stonewalkers*. Delacorte, 1983.
Beaton, M.C. *Agatha Raisin and the Potted Gardener*. St. Martin's, 1994.
Bosse, Malcolm J. *The 79 Squares*. Crowell, 1979.
Burnett, Frances Hodgson. *The Secret Garden*. Dell, 1962.
Carlson, Dale. *Plant People*. Dell, 1983.
Christopher, John. *The Lotus Caves*. Macmillan, 1969.
Collette, Paul, and Wright, Robert. *Huddles*. Players, 1985.
Craig, Alisa. *The Grub-and-Stakers House a Haunt*. Morrow, 1993.
Dunlop, Eileen. *Green Willow*. Holiday, 1993.
Garden Tales: Classic Stories from Favorite Writers. Viking, 1990.
Godden, Rumer. *An Episode of Sparrows*. Puffin, 1989.
Hayes, Sheila. *Speaking of Snapdragons*. Lodestar, 1982.
Ho, Minfong. *Rice Without Rain*. Lothrop, 1990.
Horning, Doug. *The Dark Side*. Mysterious, 1986.
Josipovici, Gabriel. *In a Hotel Garden*. New Directions, 1995.
Kosinski, Jerzy. *Being There*. Bantam, 1985.
L'Engle, Madeleine. *A Wind in the Door*. Farrar, 1973.
Phipson, Joan. *The Watcher in the Garden*. Macmillan, 1982.
Quattlebaum, Mary. *Jackson Jones and the Puddle of Thorns*. Delacorte, 1994.
Roosevelt, Elliott. *Murder in the Rose Garden*. St. Martin's, 1990.
Rowlands, Avril. *Milk and Honey*. Oxford University, 1989.
Sherwood, John. *Bones Gather No Moss*. Scribner, 1994.
Smith, Alison. *Reserved for Mark Anthony Crowder*. Dutton, 1978.
Thesman, Jean. *Nothing Grows Here*. HarperCollins, 1994.
Tsukiyama, Gail. *The Samurai's Garden*. St. Martin's, 1995.
Wyndham, John. *The Day of the Triffids*. Ballantine, 1985.

Periodicals

Better Homes and Gardens. Meredith.
Fine Gardening. Taunton Press.
Flower and Garden: The Home Gardening Magazine. Modern Handcraft, Inc.
House and Garden. Conde Nast Publications.
National Gardening: The Gardener's Newsmagazine. National Gardening Association.
Organic Gardening. Rodale Press.

Feature-Length Films

Bed of Roses. New Line, 1996. (PG)
Little Shop of Horrors. Warner, 1986. (PG-13)
Edward Scissorhands. Fox, 1990. (PG-13)
Invasion of the Body Snatchers. MGM/UA, 1978. (PG)
The Secret Garden. Republic Pictures, 1987. (PG)
The Spanish Gardener. Nostalgia, 1957.

Computer Software

Better Homes and Gardens Complete Guide to Gardening. Multicom Publishing, 1994.
Gardenfax—Fruit, Vegetables and Herbs. Commadore Business Machines, 1991. (Also others in series.)
Gardening Encyclopedia. Books-on-Disk, 1994.
Key Home Gardener. Soft Key, 1994.
The Urban Gardener (Growing Pains and How to Avoid Them). PMEP.
Western Garden. Sunset New Media, 1995.

21
Discover Your Heritage

If you've ever wanted to dig up information about your roots, the library is a good place to start. Along with materials about how to research your family tree, you can find sources such as city directories and census records, and learn about other people and places to contact. We even have some ideas for making family keepsakes that you can pass on to your future generations. Our librarians are ready to help you Discover Your Heritage.

Display Idea

Display nonfiction books and magazines that give sources and instructions for researching a family's ancestry, plus books on heraldry, origins of names, and biographies of people who have researched their own roots. Add fiction that includes the history of a family in the plot, and appropriate videos. A sample family tree and pictures of coats of arms can be posted by the books.

Sponsorship for Prizes

1. Ask a bookstore to donate books about genealogy.
2. Ask a department store to donate blank video cassettes for patrons with camcorders.
3. Ask a camera store to donate film, photo developing, photo albums, or frames.
4. Ask a photographer to donate a free family photo session and discount photographs.

Program Game

Make up a chart that resembles a pedigree ancestor index or a family tree chart with room for several entries. Patrons can write in the titles of each book they read and each activity in which they participate on the chart. Points can be gained for these entries, including the activities mentioned in the General Guidelines, and for:

1. Reading a novel and completing a Fiction Book Review Form.
2. Reading a nonfiction book related to the genealogy theme and completing a Genealogy Nonfiction Book Review Form.
3. Reading a nonfiction book not related to the genealogy theme and completing a Nonfiction Book Review Form.
4. Reading a genealogy magazine and completing a Genealogy Magazine Report Form.

Program Forms

1. Fiction Book Review Form
Title:
Author:
Publisher and date:
Brief summary of plot:
I would rate this book: "A timeless story for all generations," "Holds appeal for people of all ages," "People from certain generations may be able to identify with the story," "Out of touch with my generation," "A crummy story, no matter when you were born."

2. Genealogy Nonfiction Book Review Form
Title:
Author:
Publisher and date:
Brief description of information:
How can this book be of use to a genealogist?
What was the most interesting information you found and why?

3. Nonfiction Book Review Form.
Title:
Author:
Publisher and date:
Brief description of information:
I would rate this book: "A prized family heirloom," "A valuable keepsake," "A useful hand-me-down," "An odd trinket from the past," "A worthless piece of old junk."

4. Genealogy Magazine Report Form
Magazine name and date:
Brief description of information:
What is the focus of this magazine?
Was the information of interest to you? Why or why not?

Program Activities

1. Family Film. Show a film about a person's or family's ancestry. A marathon screening of the episodes of *Roots* may be of interest to teens.

2. History Book. Ask teens to bring in interesting photos, newspaper articles, and other memorabilia of their family members to share with the group. Then have patrons make scrap books in which they can save mementos from their own lives: Punch two holes along one side of several large sheets of construction paper. Cover two pieces of cardboard with wallpaper samples to serve as front and back covers. Tie these together with strong lacing. Teens may want to glue a photograph or letters spelling out the family name on the cover of their albums.

3. How to Get Started. Invite a genealogist to talk to teens about how to research their family trees. The speaker can hand out reference family data sheets, pedigree ancestor index sheets and other forms to aid in recording a family's lineage. The genealogist can explain various record-keeping details in addition to suggesting methods of gathering information.

4. What's in a Name. Tell teens to find out, before they come to the program, how their parents determined what to name them. Then provide an assortment of books on the origins of surnames and meanings of given names (baby-naming books are good for this). Make sure you have sources that represent the ethnic, national, and cultural backgrounds of your patrons. Teens can look through these books and find out the meanings of their names. If you include books on heraldry and art materials, you can have teens create a coat of arms for their family or their individual names.

5. Family Buffet. Sponsor a luncheon buffet at the library. Each young adult must bring along an older family member (parent, grandparent, aunt or uncle), a favorite family recipe (preferably one that was passed down through the generations), and a sample of that recipe for everyone to taste. Play music that was popular during different years and ask people to say what memories they associate with the songs.

6. Generations. Select teens who have a good knowledge of history to participate in this game show program. The categories can be: Your Generation (1980s-1990s), Your Parents' Generation (1950s–1970s), Your Grandparents' Generation (1920s–1940s), Your Great-Grandparents' Generation (1890s–1910s), etc. Questions can focus on some of the defining events that helped to shape the world during each generation's youth.

7. Programmed Genealogy. Several software programs are available for genealogists who want to keep track of their relatives on computer. Ask a computer software sales representative or a genealogist who is familiar with one such program to demonstrate its features to young adult patrons.

8. The Record Business. Some good sources for genealogists include census records, federal records such as military papers, city directories, church records, and vital records (birth, marriage, death), among others. Provide samples of several types of records and show patrons how they can be used to trace a family's history. If possible, invite clerks or archivists from associated agencies to discuss how these records are kept.

9. Jobs in the Genes. Genealogist is the most obvious career, but there are other genealogy-related jobs. These include historian, archivist, biographer, census-taker, town clerk, librarian, state or federal records-keeper, immigration or naturalization officer, cataloger, recorder of court or military documents, etc. Since many records are kept on microfilm and computer disks, there are jobs available in these areas, too. There are many sources for researching genealogy—and each one must be recorded by somebody!

10. Keepsake Quilt. Young adults who like to sew can start a keepsake quilt to commemorate the lives of families. Tell teens to bring in scraps of material from used clothing and other fabrics that have special meaning for themselves and family members (such as a baby blanket, favorite shirt, dress worn in a family photo, etc.). Display some simple quilt patterns and have patrons choose one to follow. Help them cut out and arrange their patches, which can be sewn by hand or on a sewing machine. Teens can make their quilts an ongoing project, adding patches for years to come; eventually they will become family heirooms.

Curriculum Tie-Ins

1. English Literature/Composition. Read a historical novel that encompasses several generations of a family's history. Then have students create a family tree that includes all related characters in the book. On a separate page, students can write brief biographies of each character. You can also have students write a story based on a true event that happened to someone in their family.

2. Science. Most people have collections of family photographs. One way to preserve these pictures is to transfer them to videotape. Show students how to film some photos, edit them on tape, and add a soundtrack.

3. History/Geography. Ask students to interview an older family member or acquaintance to gather information about that person's family history. Compile a list of suggested interview questions, such as dates of birth, marriage and death, maiden name, birthplace, etc. Give them forms on which to record the responses. Students should draw up a family tree from the information they gather.

4. Math. When recording information about one's family, it is very important to assign each person an ID number in order to file and retrieve the information accurately and easily. Review how to use *ahnentafel* (or ancestor) numbering in recording family data. You can also show students how to use descendancy numbering, which is another system used by genealogists.

Activity Sheet Ideas

1. Word search or crossword puzzles of: a) types of genealogy sources, b) genealogy-related terms, or c) historically prominent family surnames where you live.

2. Word scrambles or cryptograms of: a) genealogy or historical societies, b) titles of genealogy books or magazines, or c) names of local genealogy sources.

3. Matching activities: match a) names to their meanings, b) surnames to their cultural or national origins, or c) surnames to their coats-of-arms.

Suggested Resources

Reference and Nonfiction

Baselt, Fonda, compiler. *The Sunny Side of Genealogy: A Humorous Collection of Anecdotes, Poems, Wills, Epitaphs, and Other Miscellany from Genealogy.* Genealogical Publishing Co., 1986.

Beller, Susan. *Roots for Kids: A Genealogy Guide for Young People.* Betterway, 1989.

Crandall, Ralph J. *Shaking Your Family Tree: A Basic Guide to Tracing Your Family's Genealogy.* Yankee, 1986.

Croom, Emily. *The Genealogist's Companion and Sourcebook.* Betterway, 1994.

_____. *Unpuzzling Your Past: A Basic Guide to Genealogy.* Betterway, 1989.

Doane, Gilbert H. *Searching for Your Ancestors.* University of Minnesota, 1980.

Dollarhide, William. *Managing a Genealogical Project.* Genealogical Publishing Co., 1989.

Fletcher, William. *Recording Your Family History: A Guide to Preserving Oral History.* Ten Speed, 1989.

Frazier, Ian. *Family.* HarperPerennial, 1994.

Galeener-Moore, Laverne. *Collecting Dead Relatives: An Irreverent Romp Through the Field of Genealogy.* Genealogical Publishing Co., 1987.

Genealogical and Local History Books in Print. Genealogical Books in Print.

Gutnik, Martin J. *Genetics.* Watts, 1985.

Haley, Alex. *Roots.* Doubleday, 1976.

Hoobler, Dorothy, and Hoobler, Thomas. **American Family Albums** series. Oxford University Press.

Hook, J.N. *Family Names.* Macmillan, 1982.

Krause, Carol. *How Healthy Is Your Family Tree? A Complete Guide to Tracing Your Family's Medical and Behavioral Tree.* Simon & Schuster, 1995.

Kurzweil, Arthur. *From Generation to Generation: How to Trace Your Jewish Genealogy and Personal History*. Schocken, 1982.

Lainhart, Anne S. *State Census Records*. Genealogical Publishing Co., 1992.

Meltzer, Milton. *A Book About Names*. Harper, 1984.

Olesky, Walter. *Miracles of Genetics*. Childrens, 1986.

Oryx American Family Tree series. Oryx.

Perl, Linda. *The Great Ancestor Hunt: The Fun of Finding Out Who You Are*. Clarion, 1989.

Polking, Kirk. *Writing Family Histories and Memoirs*. Writer's Digest, 1995.

Silverstein, Alvin, and Silverstein, Virginia. *Genes, Medicine, and You*. Enslow, 1989.

Stryker-Rodda, Harriet. *How to Climb Your Family Tree: Genealogy for Beginners*. G.K. Hall, 1990.

Thomas, Frank P. *How to Write the Story of Your Life*. Betterway, 1989.

U.S. Vital Records Catalog: An Invaluable Aid to Genealogical Research. Ancestry, 1985.

Westin, Jeane Eddy. *Finding Your Roots: How Every American Can Trace His Ancestors At Home and Abroad*. St. Martin's, 1988.

Westridge Young Writers Workshop. *Kids Explore the Heritage of Western Native Americans*. John Muir, 1995.

Wolfman, Ira. *Do People Grow on Family Trees? Genealogy for Kids and Other Beginners*. Workman, 1991.

Worth, Richard. *The American Family*. Watts, 1984.

Fiction

Brown, Irene Bennett. *Answer Me, Answer Me*. Macmillan, 1985.

Burchard, Peter. *Sea Change*. Farrar, 1984.

Clark, Ann Nolan. *Secret of the Andes*. Viking, 1970.

Cookson, Catherine. *The Black Candle*. Summit, 1990.

Cooney, Caroline B. *Family Reunion*. Bantam, 1989.

Coper, J. California. *Family*. Doubleday, 1991.

Cormier, Robert. *Fade*. Delacorte, 1988.

Doherty, Berlie. *Granny Was a Buffer Girl*. Orchard, 1988.

_____. *The Snake-Stone*. Orchard, 1996.

Dorris, Michael. *A Yellow Raft in Blue Water*. Warner, 1988.

Dunlop, Eileen. *The Valley of Deer*. Holiday, 1989.

Evernden, Margery. *The Dream Keeper*. Lothrop, 1985.

Fleischman, Paul. *The Borning Room*. HarperCollins, 1991.

Gleeson, Libby. *Eleanor, Elizabeth*. Holiday, 1990.

Halter, Marek. *The Book of Abraham*. Dell, 1987.

Houston, James. *Drifting Snow: An Arctic Search*. McElderry, 1992.

Johnston, Norma. *Carlisle's Hope*. Bantam, 1986.

Leonard, Alison. *Tina's Chance*. Viking, 1988.

Macdonald, Caroline. *Speaking to Miranda*. HarperCollins, 1992.

Meyer, Carolyn. *Denny's Tapes*. Macmillan, 1987.

Miller, Alex. *The Ancestor Game*. Graywolf, 1994.

Miller, Jim Wayne. *Newfound*. Orchard, 1989.

Paulsen, Gary. *The Winter Room*. Watts, 1989.

Pilcher, Rosamunde. *September*. St. Martin's, 1990.

Reiss, Kathryn. *The Glass House People*. Harcourt, 1992.
Rowntree, Kathleen. *The Haunting of Willow Dasset*. Little, 1989.
Voigt, Cynthia. *Sons from Afar*. Macmillan, 1987.
Wallin, Luke. *Ceremony of the Panther*. Macmillan, 1987.
West, Michael Lee. *Crazy Ladies*. Longstreet, 1990.
Yolen, Jane. *Briar Rose*. Tor, 1992.

Periodicals

The American Genealogist. American Genealogist.
The Genealogical Helper. Everton Publishers.
Genealogist. William Pollard and Co.
Genealogy Digest. Genealogical Club of America.

Feature-Length Films

The Addams Family. Paramount, 1991. (PG-13)
Big Business. Touchstone, 1988. (PG)
Roots (6 tapes). Warner, 1977.
Table Setting. RKP Pictures, 1984.
Twins. MCA/UA, 1988. (PG)

Computer Programs

Census '90. Slater Hall Information Products, 1993.
Family History Collection series. Banner Blue Software.
Family History Collections series. Automated Archives.
Marriage Records series. Automated Archives.
Family Tree Maker Deluxe CD-ROM Edition. Banner Blue Software, 1994.
Your Mythic Journey. JourneyWare Media, 1995.

22

Relive the Past

If you have ever wanted to experience life in a bygone time, then you will enjoy reading historical fiction. The library has many novels set in the past, as well as plays and videos. You can march with Joan of Arc in *Dove and Sword*, witness the burning of Atlanta with Scarlett O'Hara in *Gone with the Wind*, and encounter other historical adventures. So come into the library, where you can Relive the Past.

Display Idea

Set up a selection of historical fiction, arranged by periods in history. By each section, place some nonfiction titles and videos that correspond to that time frame. Add related posters and magazines, plus articles about local history and historical figures to the display.

Sponsorship for Prizes

1. Ask a bookstore to donate paperback historical fiction.
2. Ask a video rental store to donate free rental certificates for historical movies.
3. Ask a costume rental shop to donate certificates for free rentals of historical outfits.
4. Ask a stationery store to donate blank books or diaries for patrons to record their own histories.

Program Game

Draw a game board that involves pictures representing various historical novels, such as a gabled house for *The House of Seven Gables*. Make a trail of spaces that travels through these areas and identifies each book that is represented. Patrons will move one space along the board for each point earned. Points can be earned for completing the activities mentioned in the General Guidelines, and for:

1. Reading a historical novel or play and completing an Historical Fiction Book Review Form.
2. Reading a novel that is not historical fiction and completing a Fiction Book Review Form.
3. Reading a nonfiction book and completing a Nonfiction Book Review Form.
4. Watching a historical film or play and completing an Historical Fiction Performance Review Form.

Program Forms

1. Historical Fiction Book Review Form
Title:
Author:
Publisher and date:
Brief summary of plot:
Where and when did this book take place?
Would you read this type of book again? Why or why not?
2. Fiction Book Review Form
Title:
Author:
Publisher and date:
Brief summary of plot:
This book will go down in history as: "A great work of literature," "A good book," "An OK book," "Not very memorable," "It will die quietly and be forgotten."
3. Nonfiction Book Review Form
Title:
Author:
Publisher and date:
Brief description of information:
I would rate this book: "An important historical document," "A work of some historical significance," "Noteworthy to local historians only," "Of very little historical interest," "Historically inaccurate and insignificant."
4. Historical Fiction Performance Form
Name of film or play:
Was this a film or a play? (circle one)
Brief summary of plot:
Where and when did the story take place?
Would you want to see this type of film or play again? Why or why not?

Program Activities

1. Historical Flick. Show a historical movie that would appeal to teens, such as *Glory*.

2. Historical Drama. If a local theater is performing a play that takes place in the past, arrange to take teens to a performance. Or, ask teens to read scenes from historical plays for the group.

3. Local History. Make a list of historical novels that are set in your town or state and encourage teens to read them. If possible, invite the author of one of these books to speak at the library. Discuss how your area was portrayed in the books, and compare this to newspaper articles, photographs, postcards and other memorabilia from those times in history.

4. Visiting the Past. If you live near a historical museum, take a group of teens there for a visit. As you tour rooms that hold objects from different periods in history, booktalk some novels that are set in those times. Or, invite a representative from the museum to talk to teens about exhibits that relate to popular historical novels.

5. Old Food. Many types of food that were consumed by people in the past are rarely seen in twentieth-century America. Make a list of foods from medieval times, America's pioneer days, etc., and provide some books in which they are mentioned. If possible, prepare some of these dishes for patrons to sample.

6. Time Trivia. In this trivia game show, teens who are historical fiction buffs can answer questions about novels set in various time periods, such as the Depression, the Civil War, and World War II. For each time period, devise questions for categories such as Heroes and Heroines, Climactic Scenes, Plays, Newbery Winners, Books Made into Movies, or Where It All Happened.

7. Future History. Ask young adults to suggest contemporary books that they would include in a time capsule for people to discover 50 or 100 years from now. What books do they think accurately portray life for today's teens?

8. Great Books. Invite teens to bring in their favorite works of historical fiction. Participants can discuss their books and annotate them. Publish a list of recommended reading and distribute it to patrons.

9. Past Lives. Present a job fair of careers in history-related fields such as archeology, historical research, teaching history, paleontology, genealogy, writing historical novels, dramaturgy, biography and various jobs in museums. Provide information on these careers and on colleges that offer related majors.

10. Dance Into History. Teens can come to a dance party dressed as famous historical figures or characters from historical fiction. Teach them how to dance to music that was popular in the past, such as the minuet or the Charleston. Teens can try to guess the identities of the people portrayed at the party.

Curriculum Tie-Ins

1. English Literature/Composition. Provide students with a list of recommended historical novels representing a variety of time periods. Or choose one period in history, such as colonial America or World War II, and have students read books set in that time. Students can write a paper on how the author uses historical details to portray the world as it was during the time of the novel.

2. Science. Many historical novels include scenes in which people suffer illnesses, such as plague, tuberculosis, polio and nutrition-related diseases. Have students compare how these health problems were treated in the past to modern medical cures. What significant scientific breakthroughs enable today's doctors to successfully combat diseases that were fatal in the past?

3. History/Geography. Have the class create a timeline of great literature throughout history. Include such classics as *Don Quixote*, *War and Peace* and *A Tale of Two Cities*.

4. Math. Have students take an inventory of historical novels owned by the library. They can record the number of books on various time periods or historical events. Then have them make a chart or graph to compare these figures. How does this compare to what is being taught in the history classes?

Activity Sheet Ideas

1. Word search or crossword puzzles of: a) names given to periods in history, b) famous figures from history, or c) great civilizations from the past.

2. Word scrambles or cryptograms of: a) notable historical events, b) titles of historical novels, or c) plays that take place in a bygone era.

3. Matching activities: match a) fictional characters to the historical novels in which they appear, b) historical fiction to the time period in which it takes place, or c) actors to the roles they played in movies based on historical fiction.

Suggested Resources

Reference and Nonfiction

Arnold-Foster, Mark. *The World at War*. Scarborough, 1986.

Asimov, Isaac, and White, Frank. *The March of the Millennia: A Key to Looking at History*. Walker, 1990.

Axelrod, Alan, and Phillips, Charles. *What Every American Should Know About American History: 200 Events That Shaped the Nation*. Adams, 1992.

Camenson, Blythe. *Careers for History Buffs and Others Who Learn from the Past*. VGM, 1994.

Carey, John, ed. *Eyewitness to History*. Harvard University Press, 1988.

Clinton, Catherine. *Tara Revisited*. Abbeville, 1995.

Edelman, Bernard, ed. *Dear America: Letters Home from Vietnam*. Norton, 1985.

Eggenberger, David. *An Encyclopedia of Battles*. Dover, 1985.

Faber, Doris, and Faber, Harold. *The Birth of a Nation: The Early Years of the United States*. Macmillan, 1989.

Greenberg, Judith E., and McKeaver, Helen Cary. *A Pioneer Women's Memoir*. Watts, 1995.

Heide, Robert, and Gilman, John. *Home Front America: Popular Culture of the World War II Era*. Chronicle, 1995.

Hobhouse, Henry. *Forces of Change: An Unorthodox History*. Arcade, 1990.

Howard, Elizabeth F. *America as Story: Historical Fiction for Secondary Schools*. ALA, 1988.

Karl, Jean. *America Alive: A History*. Philomel, 1994.

Killingray, David. *The Transatlantic Slave Trade*. Batsford, 1987.

Levine, Ellen. *A Fence Away from Freedom: Japanese Americans and World War II*. Putnam, 1995.

Levinson, Nancy Smiler. *Turn of the Century: Our Nation One Hundred Years Ago*. Lodestar, 1995.

Lewin, Rhoda G., ed. *Witness to the Holocaust: An Oral History*. Twayne, 1990.

Lord, Walter. *Day of Infamy*. Bantam, 1987.

McEvedy, Colin. *The World History Factfinder*. Smith, 1989.

Marrin, Albert. *The War for Independence: The Story of the American Revolution*. Macmillan, 1988.

Meltzer, Milton, ed. *Voices from the Civil War: A Documentary History of the Great American Conflict*. Harper, 1989.

Parker, Thomas. *Day-by-Day: The Sixties*. Facts on File, 1983. (Also other books in series.)

Rogasky, Barbara. *Smoke and Ashes: The Story of the Holocaust*. Holiday, 1988.

Singleman, Jeffrey L. *Daily Life in Elizabethan England*. Greenwood, 1995.

Smith, Ronald D. *Fascinating People and Astounding Events from the History of the Western World*. ABC-CLIO, 1990.

Vadney, T.E. *The World Since 1945: A Complete History of Global Change from 1945 to the Present*. Facts on File, 1987.

Wetterau, Bruce. *The New York Public Library Book of Chronologies*. Prentice, 1990.

Winter, J.M. *The Experience of World War I*. Oxford University Press, 1989.

Wright, David. *War in Vietnam*. 4 vols. Childrens, 1989.

Fiction

Alexander, Lloyd. *The Philadelphia Adventure*. Dutton, 1990.

Banks, Lynne Reid. *One More River*. Morrow, 1992.

Beatty, Patricia. *Be Ever Hopeful, Hannalee*. Morrow, 1988. (Also *Turn Homeward, Hannalee*.)

Bell, William. *Forbidden City: A Novel of Modern China*. Bantam, 1990.

Broner, Peter. *Night of the Broken Glass*. Station Hill, 1991.

Carter, Peter. *Borderlands*. Farrar, 1990.

Choi, Sook Nyul. *Year of Impossible Goodbyes*. Houghton, 1991.

Conlon-McKenna, Marita. *Wildflower Girl*. Holiday, 1992.

Conrad, Pam. *Prairie Songs*. HarperCollins, 1985.

Cooney, Caroline B. *Operation: Homefront*. Bantam, 1992.

Corbin, William. *Me and the End of the World*. Simon & Schuster, 1991.

Forman, James D. *Becca's Story*. Scribner, 1992.

Garden, Nancy. *Dove and Sword*. Farrar, 1995.

Hansen, Joyce. *Out from This Place*. Walker, 1988.

Hawthore, Nathaniel. *The House of the Seven Gables*. Houghton, 1966.

Holland, Cecelia. *The Bear Flag*. Houghton, 1990.

Hudson, Jan. *Dawn Rider*. Philomel, 1990.

Jones, Douglas C. *Remember Santiago*. Holt, 1988.

Keehn, Sally. *I Am Regina*. Philomel, 1991.

Kendall, Jane. *Miranda and the Movies*. Crown, 1989.

Kincaid, Nanci. *Crossing Blood*. Putnam, 1992.

Koller, Jackie French. *Nothing to Fear*. Harcourt, 1991.

Leonard, Hugh. *Parnell and the Englishwoman*. Atheneum, 1991.

Luhrmann, Winifred Bruse. *Only Brave Tomorrows*. Houghton, 1989.

Lutzeier, Elizabeth. *The Coldest Winter*. Holiday, 1991.

Lyons, Mary E. *Letters from a Slave Girl: The Story of Harriet Jacobs*. Scribner, 1992.

McGraw, Eloise. *The Striped Ships*. Macmillan, 1991.

Matas, Carol. *Lisa's War*. Scribner, 1989.

Mitchell, Margaret. *Gone with the Wind*. Warner, 1993.

Nelson, Theresa. *And One for All*. Orchard, 1989.

O'Brien, Tim. *The Things They Carried*. Houghton, 1990.

Orlev, Uri. *The Man from the Other Side*. Houghton, 1991.

Paterson, Katherine. *Lyddie*. Lodestar, 1991.

Penman, Sharon Kay. *Falls the Shadow*. Holt, 1988.

Rinaldi, Ann. *The Secret of Sarah Revere*. Gulliver, 1995.

Ruemmler, John. *Smoke on the Water*. Shoe Tree, 1992.

Salisbury, Graham. *Under the Blood-Red Sun*. Delacorte, 1994.

Smith, Claude Clayton. *The Stratford Devil*. Walker, 1985.

Stolz, Mary. *Bartholomew Fair*. Greenwillow, 1990.

Whelan, Gloria. *Once on This Island*. HarperCollins, 1995.

Wisler, G. Clifton. *Piper's Ferry*. Lodestar, 1990.

Periodicals

American Heritage. Heritage, Inc.

American History Illustrated. National Historical Society.

Calliope. Cobblestone Publishing Co.
Early American Life. Early American Society.
History Today. History Today.
The Smithsonian. Smithsonian Associates.

Feature-Length Films

Bill and Ted's Excellent Adventure. Columbia Tristar, 1989. (PG)
Far and Away. MCA/Universal, 1992. (PG-13)
Forrest Gump. Paramount, 1994. (PG-13)
Glory. Columbia Tristar, 1989. (R)
Little Big Man. Fox, 1970. (PG)
The Longest Day. Fox, 1962.
Malcolm X. Warner, 1992. (PG-13)

Computer Software

Eyewitness History of the World. Dorling Kindersley Multimedia, 1995.
The Grolier Multimedia Encyclopedia of American History. Grolier Electronic Publishing, 1995.
Lessons from History. Quanta Press, 1993.
Time Almanac of the 20th Century. Compact Publishing, 1994.
Time Traveler CD. Orange Cherry New Media, 1992.
Who Built America. Voyager Company, 1993.

23
Find Your Hobby at the Library

If you're looking for something interesting to do, then go to the library. You will find lots of great books on hobbies of all sorts. How about starting a special collection? Perhaps you would like a hobby that will take you outdoors. Maybe a creative endeavor, such as a handicraft, would be more to your liking. Our shelves are brimming with terrific ideas. Take a look and Find Your Hobby at the Library.

Display Idea

Display samples of hobbies next to nonfiction materials on that subject, such as a framed stamp collection along with books about philately and brochures from the post office with ideas for collectors. Include books on all types of collectibles, information on how to start a collection, and price guides. Additional hobbies, such as bird-watching and other outdoor activities, building models, cooking, photography, handicrafts and other artistic endeavors should be represented. Include magazines and fiction that have hobby themes.

Sponsorship for Prizes

1. Ask a craft or hobby store to donate coupons for materials.
2. Ask a bookstore to donate books on hobbies or collections.
3. Ask a museum to donate free passes to special exhibits.
4. Ask a sports memorabilia store to donate merchandise.

Program Game

The game board should resemble a page in a stamp collector's album, with several stamp outlines drawn. For every point earned, patrons can paste a stamp (sticker) onto the page, until the page is filled. Points can be earned for completing the activities mentioned in the General Guidelines, and for:

1. Reading a novel and completing a Fiction Book Review Form.
2. Reading a nonfiction book related to the hobby theme and completing a Hobby Nonfiction Book Review Form.
3. Reading a nonfiction book not related to the hobby theme and completing a Nonfiction Book Review Form.
4. Watching a hobby or "how to" video and completing a Hobby Video Review Form.

Program Forms

1. Fiction Book Review Form
Title:
Author:
Publisher and date:
Brief summary of plot:
I would rate this book: "A valuable addition to the collection," "In good condition," "Of some interest," "For fanatical collectors only," "Worthless."

2. Hobby Nonfiction Book Review Form
Title:
Author:
Publisher and date:
Brief description of information:
After reading this book, are you interested in learning more about this hobby? Why or why not?
Would you want to try this hobby or make something shown in this book? Why or why not?

3. Nonfiction Book Review Form:
Title:
Author:
Publisher and date:
Brief description of information:
I would rate this book: "Superb craftsmanship," "Good quality," "Nice construction," "Not a good sample," "Fell apart."

4. Hobby Video Review Form
Type of hobby:
Name of video:
Producer and date:
Brief summary of video:
Did you find this video information useful? Why or why not?
Would you like to try this hobby? Why or why not?

Program Activities

1. Hobby Film. Show a feature film or documentary that involves some type of hobby, such as *A River Runs Through It*.

2. Crafty Kids. Some of your young adult patrons may have a talent for a particular craft. Ask for volunteers to run workshops on activities such as embroidery, origami, stenciling, flower arranging, stringing beads or other simple handicrafts. If there is enough interest, you may want to sponsor a craft show so that teens can sell their handmade goods.

3. Hobby Fair. Set up tables for people in the community to display their collectibles, samples of their crafts, photographs of outdoor activities, or other examples of their hobbies. Teens can visit these to learn how to take up hobbies of their own.

4. Museum Trip. Museums house many types of collections. Arrange to take teens on a field trip to a museum that offers exhibits of interest.

5. Getting Back to Nature. Hobbies such as camping or bird-watching stress an appreciation of nature. Present a talk or film of some nature hobbies. Afterwards, you can have hobbyists demonstrate any equipment they might use. Teens can also make a nature craft, such as a floral wreath.

6. What's My Hobby? Some people have very unusual hobbies. Invite local hobbyists to be guests in a game show based on the TV game show *What's My Line?* Teens can ask questions that require "yes" or "no" answers in an attempt to guess the person's hobby. Or, you can have young adults pretend to be experts on certain hobbies, and have them play the game with their peers.

7. Puzzle Party. Making jigsaw puzzles is a popular pastime. Host an all-day or all-night puzzle marathon. Teens can bring in their own jigsaw and 3D puzzles and work in groups to complete them. You can also post a wall-size crossword puzzle and pass out sheets of mazes to challenge kids. Let participants change activities as needed so they don't get bored or dizzy.

8. Sports Card Convention. A common hobby among sports fans is collecting trading cards. Reserve a day for teens to bring in their collections of cards to show and trade. Set up a display of books on collecting trading cards and sports memorabilia. If possible, invite a local athlete to speak and sign autographs.

9. Collectors' Gallery. Ask patrons if they have any collections they would like to put on display in the library. Take care to protect any loaned items and label the display(s) to acknowledge the donor(s). Perhaps you can have the donor(s) speak to teens about the collection(s).

10. Talented Teens. Invite teens whose hobbies include singing, dancing, playing a musical instrument, performing magic, juggling, acting, gymnastics and other performance activities to participate in a talent show at the library. Have available books on related topics for patrons to check out.

Curriculum Tie-Ins

1. English Literature/Composition. Have students read "how-to" articles about starting a hobby/collection, or instructions for a particular craft. Then let them choose a hobby, collection, or craft that interests them, and write their own "how-to" article about it.

2. Science. Some hobbies are related to a science, such as rock collecting and geology. Ask students to name other hobby-science connections. Then have a class discussion on how studying a particular science can make a hobby even more fascinating.

3. History/Geography. Have students choose a popular hobby, such as collecting baseball cards, and explore its history. Questions to consider: How did the hobby start? When did it become popular? What items are considered valuable and why? Where is this hobby popular? If there are any conventions or shows associated with this hobby, tell where and when they occur.

4. Math. Collectibles can be worth a lot of money. List the value of several items when they are in perfect, good, and fair condition. Have students draw graphs to show how the monetary value of these items changes according to their condition.

Activity Sheet Ideas

1. Word search or crossword puzzles of: a) crafts, b) types of collectibles, or c) hobby activities.

2. Word scrambles or cryptograms of: a) special collections or exhibits, b) names of hobby or collectors' magazines, and c) museums which feature special exhibits.

3. Matching activities: match a) hobby magazines to their hobby, b) specialized terms to their hobby, c) hobby equipment to its hobby.

Suggested Resources

Reference and Nonfiction

Allmen, Diane. *The Official Identification and Price Guide to Postcards.* Ballantine, 1991.

Armke, Ken. *Hummel: An Illustrated Handbook and Price Guide.* Wallace-Homestead, 1995.

Bawden, Juliet. *Jewelry and Accessories: Beautiful Designs to Make and Wear.* North Light, 1995.

Bial, Raymond. *With Needle and Thread: A Book About Quilts.* Houghton, 1996.

Boyd, Margaret, ed. *The Crafts Supply Sourcebook: A Comprehensive Shop-By-Mail Guide.* North Light, 1994.

Camenson, Blythe. *Opportunities in Museum Careers.* VGM, 1996.

Cockrill, Pauline. *The Teddy Bear Encyclopedia.* Dorling Kindersley, 1993.

Fink, Nancy, and Ditzler, Maryalice. *Buttons: The Collector's Guide to Selecting, Restoring and Enjoying New and Vintage Buttons.* Courage Books, 1993.

Finnigan, Dave. *The Complete Juggler.* Random, 1987.

Gunnell, John. *A Collector's Guide to Automobiles.* Krause, 1994.

Hobson, Burton, and Obojski, Robert. *Stamp Collecting as a Hobby.* Sterling, 1986.

Horovitz, Marc, and Larson, Ross. *Beginner's Guide to Large Scale Model Railroading.* Greenburg, 1994.

Krause, Barry. *Collecting Coins for Pleasure and Profit: A Comprehensive Guide and Handbook for Collectors and Investors.* Betterway, 1991.

_____. *Collecting Stamps for Pleasure and Profit.* Betterway, 1988.

Larson, Mark K. *101 Sports Card Investments: Best Buys From $5 to $500.* Krause, 1993.

O'Brien, Richard. *Collecting Toy Soldiers No. 2: An Identification and Value Guide.* Books Americana, 1992.

Paint Craft. North Light, 1995.

Paper Craft. North Light, 1995.

Rees-Mogg, William. *How to Buy Rare Books: A Practical Guide to the Antiquarian Book Market.* Christie's, 1985.

Retskin, Bill, and Williams, John. *The Matchcover Collectors Price Guide.* WorldComm, 1993.

Richter, Lydia, and Richter, Joachim Franz. *Collecting Antique Dolls: Fashion Dolls, Doll Curiosities, Exclusive Dolls.* Hobby House, 1991.

Rinker, Harry L. *Collector's Guide to Toys, Games, and Puzzles.* Wallace-Homestead, 1991.

Rowh, Mark. *Careers for Crafty People and Other Dexterous Types.* VGM, 1993.

Sanders, George R., et al. *Collector's Guide to Autographs.* Wallace-Homestead, 1990.

Schleicher, Robert. *Building and Flying Model Aircraft.* Dover, 1988.

Stewart, Mark. *House of Cards: The Insider's Guide to Baseball Cards.* Crown, 1993.

Stine, G. Harry. *Handbook of Model Rocketry.* Prentice, 1983.

Swartz, Jon David, and Reinehr, Robert C. *Handbook of Old-Time Radio: A Comprehensive Guide to Golden Age Radio Listening and Collecting.* Scarecrow, 1993.

Ward, K. Anthony. *First Editions: A Field Guide for Collectors of English and American Literature.* Scolar, 1994.

Zalkin, Estelle. *Zalkin's Handbook of Thimbles and Sewing Implements: A Complete Collector's Guide with Current Prices.* Warman, 1988.

Fiction

Anderson, Mary. *You Can't Get There from Here*. Ace, 1983.
Baehr, Patricia. *Falling Scales*. Morrow, 1987.
Baird, Thomas. *Walk Out a Brother*. Harper, 1983.
Banks, Ian M. *The Player of Games*. St. Martin's, 1989.
Brenner, Barbara. *A Killing Season*. Macmillan, 1981.
Budbill, David. *Snowshoe Trek to Otter River*. Bantam, 1979.
Callan, Jamie. *Just Too Cool*. NAL, 1987.
Carey, M.V. *The Mystery of the Cranky Collector*. 1987.
Curry, Jane Louise. *The Lotus Cup*. Macmillan, 1986.
Duncan, David James. *The River Why*. Sierra, 1983.
Haynes, Mary. *Catch the Sea*. Bradbury, 1989.
Hemingway, Ernest. *The Old Man and the Sea*. Macmillan, 1977.
Hermann, Spring. *Flip City*. Watts, 1988.
Howe, Fanny. *Race of the Radical*. Viking, 1985.
Klein, Norma. *Snapshots*. Dial, 1984.
Knudson, R.R. *Just Another Love Story*. Farrar, 1983.
Lee, Mildred. *The Skating Rink*. Houghton, 1969.
LeMieux, A.C. *T-H-E TV Guidance Counselor*. Tambourine, 1993.
Livingston, Alan W. *Ronnie Finkelhof, Superstar*. Fawcett, 1988.
MacLachlan, Patricia. *Journey*. Delacorte, 1991.
Mark, Jan. *Thunder and Lightenings*. Harper, 1976.
Mazer, Harry. *The Girl of His Dreams*. Harper, 1987.
Moynes, Patricia. *A Six-Letter Word for Death*. Holt, 1983.
Paulsen, Gary. *The Island*. Orchard, 1988.
Ramus, David. *Thief of Light*. HarperCollins, 1995.
Smith, Doris Buchanan. *Karate Dancer*. Putnam, 1987.
Smith, Kay. *Skeeter*. Houghton, 1989.
Tevis, Walter. *The Queen's Gambit*. Dell, 1983.
Ure, Jean. *What If They Saw Me Now?* Delacorte, 1984.
Werbsa, Barbara. *Crazy Vanilla*. Harper, 1986.

Periodicals

American Craft. AmericanCraft Council.
Antiques and Collecting Magazine. Lightner Publishing Group.
Coins: The Complete Magazine for Coin Collectors. Krause Publications, Inc.
Fine Gardening. Taunton Press.
Games. B & P Publishing, Inc.
Linn's Stamp News. Amos Press.
Model Railroader. A.C. Kalmbach and Co.
Workbench. Modern Handcraft.

Feature-Length Films

Breaking Away. CBS/Fox, 1979. (PG)
The Dollmaker. Fox, 1984.

A River Runs Through It. Columbia Tristar, 1992. (PG)
Searching for Bobby Fischer. Paramount, 1993. (PG)
The Secret Garden. Republic Pictures, 1987.

Computer Software

Antique Toys. Gazelle Technologies, 1992.
Bicycle: the CD-ROM Collection. Swifte International, 1994.
Bobby Fischer Teaches Chess. Mission Studios, 1995.
Hobby Corner. Save-on Software, 1993.
Millennium Auction. Eidolon, 1994.
Stamps—Windows on the World. PMEP.

24

Have a Horrorble Time

Beware: Vampires, evil spirits, homicidal maniacs, spooks, mad scientists, zombies and other ghoulish creatures are lurking in the library. They have been buried in books, vanquished to videos, and imprisoned in magazines and music. You can let loose these tales of horror and the supernatural with your own library card. So if you're not afraid of gore, psychos, or curses, come to the library and Have a Horrorble Time.

Display Idea

Display several horror and supernatural novels and short story collections for young adults. Include nonfiction titles, magazines, eerie sound-effects recordings and videos of this genre. Spooky-looking posters, horror masks and props will draw teens to this display.

Sponsorship for Prizes

1. Ask a local video rental store to donate free rental certificates for horror and supernatural movies.

2. Ask a bookstore to donate paperback copies of horror and supernatural novels.

3. Ask a magazine stand to donate issues of horror fanzines or comic books.

4. Ask a novelty store to donate horror masks and accessories.

Program Game

Design a picture of the interior of a haunted house. Draw a four-story staircase leading from the front door steps to the attic door, which is closed. Blood is seeping out from underneath the attic door and dripping down the staircase. Starting from the front door steps, patrons will advance one drop of blood for every point they earn, until they reach the attic door. Points can be earned for completing the activities mentioned in the General Guidelines, and for:

1. Reading a horror or supernatural novel or short story collection and completing a Horror Fiction Book Review Form.

2. Reading a novel not related to the horror theme and completing a Fiction Book Review Form.

3. Reading a nonfiction book and completing a Nonfiction Book Review Form.

4. Watching a horror or supernatural feature-length movie, reading a critic's review of the film, and completing a Horror Film Review Form.

Program Forms

1. Horror Fiction Book Review Form
Title:
Author:
Publisher and date:
Brief summary of plot:
How does this book compare to other horror or supernatural books you have read?
Would you read other books by this author? Why or why not?

2. Fiction Book Review Form
Title:
Author:
Publisher and date:
Brief summary of plot:
I would rate this book: "Exciting enough to raise the dead," "A spine-tingling page turner," "Shows some spirit," "Frightfully bad," "The author should take a stab at another career."

3. Nonfiction Book Review Form
Title:
Author:
Publisher and date:
Brief description of information:
I would rate this book: "A perfect specimen," "It shows signs of intelligence," "A moderately successful experiment," "The author has created a monster," "Kill it before it multiplies."

4. Horror Film Review Form
Name of film:
Date released:
Director:
Brief summary of plot:
Name of critic:
Source and date:
Brief summary of critic's opinion:
Did you agree with the critic? Why or why not?

Program Activities

1. Horror Flicks. Horror films are especially popular with teens. Welcome them to a showing of one movie from this genre or a compilation of horror film excerpts. Or, you can plan an all-day or all-night marathon of scary movies.

2. Masks of Terror. Provide teens with materials to create their own spooky or gory masks. Start with plain paper, clay, or rubber masks. Supply paints and brushes, wig materials, rubber cement, clay, Styrofoam and an assortment of theater make-up for patrons to use. If possible, invite a person who is skilled in designing horror make-up or masks to demonstrate how to make realistic-looking scars and other gruesome features.

3. Master of Doom. Invite an author of horror/supernatural stories to speak to teens about writing for this genre. Or, ask a storyteller to present a program of spooky stories and legends.

4. **Classic Horror Shows.** Ask for volunteers to take parts in a readers' theater program. Choose scenes from classic horror movies, plays, and radio shows for teens to read. Set up props for making sound effects. Dim the lights and have participants read their lines by flashlight.

5. **Fright Night.** Sponsor a spooky sleepover at the library. Play haunting soundtrack music from films and plays such as *Phantom*. Dim the lights and tell ghost stories. Lead partygoers through a haunted house tour. Watch videos of spooky TV shows, such as *The Twilight Zone* or *Dark Shadows*. Serve "Witches' Brew Punch" (chilled with dry ice), gummy worms and other ghoulish treats.

6. **Wheel of Misfortune.** Teens can participate in a trivia game show where the category is chosen by spinning a wheel. Categories of questions can include Classic Horror Novels (Who wrote *Frankenstein?*), Horror Film Actors (Who played Jason in the *Halloween* movies?), Causes of Death (spell words such as 'asphyxiation' or 'bludgeon'), Fill-in-the-Blank Horror Cliches (I vant to bite your——-), Masters of the Genre (Who wrote *Chain Letter?*), and Creature Features (match supernatural characters to their descriptions).

7. **Phenomenal Ingredients.** Many horror and supernatural stories contain elements of parapsychology or paranormal phenomena. Set up several tables, each with information on a different topic, such as telekenetics, reincarnation, Ouija boards, ESP, channeling, poltergeists, the tarot, etc. Have available videos, fiction and nonfiction books on each topic at the tables for patrons to check out. If possible, include some interactive materials, such as a deck of tarot cards, for patrons to use.

8. **Evil Books?** Some people object to books with occult or supernatural themes because they believe these materials are evil and promote Satanism. Prepare a list of supernatural books that have been banned or challenged, along with the charges that have been brought against them. Invite teens to discuss specific book challenges, as well as the general issue of censoring books of this genre. Is there such a thing as "Satanism," and do supernatural books subject teenagers to bad influences?

9. **Favorite Haunts.** Teens can discuss the plots of several horror novels and films they have read and seen. Then they can vote for their favorites in categories such as Best Horror Film, Scariest Story, Most Diabolical Author, Most Twisted Plot, Goriest Movie Makeup, Most Evil Series Character, Spookiest Special Effects, Eeriest Actor.

10. **Monster Mash.** Host a costume party and dance. Tell patrons to dress as monsters, vampires and other creepy creatures. Play haunted house sounds and let them dance to spook-themed music, such as "Thriller." For more fun, have groups of teens act out short skits, playing roles based on their costumes.

Curriculum Tie-Ins

1. **English Literature/Composition.** Read a classic horror novel, such as *Frankenstein*, with the class. Discuss some common plot elements of supernatural stories, such as blood, haunted houses, vampires, etc. Have students write stories using several of these plot devices.

2. **Science.** Base a chemistry lesson on the theme of "Dr. Jekyll's Laboratory." Demonstrate how to mix fake blood, use dry ice, distill various liquids, create "green slime," or perform other mad scientist–type experiments.

3. **History/Geography.** Is there any truth to stories of vampires and werewolves? Have students research the historical backgrounds of these legends. Where is Transylvania and what is its history? Locate places around the world where there have been rumored sightings of supernatural creatures.

4. Math. Certain numbers, such as 13 and 666, have supernatural connotations. Discuss some of these with the class. Then demonstrate some math tricks or assign math problems involving these numbers.

Activity Sheet Ideas

1. Word search or crossword puzzles of: a) genre creatures and characters, b) plot elements, or c) supernatural phenomena.

2. Word scrambles or cryptograms of: a) genre novels, b) authors, or c) films.

3. Matching activities: match a) fiction titles to their authors or series, b) horror film actors to their most famous roles, or c) classic horror quotes to the characters who said him.

Suggested Resources

Reference and Nonfiction

Beahm, George, ed. *The Stephen King Companion.* Andrews & McMeel, 1989.
Carceau, Jenn-Luc, and Donner, Cecile. *The Dictionary of Superstitions.* Granada, 1987.
Cohen, Daniel. *The Encyclopedia of the Strange.* Dodd, 1985.
_____. *Master of Horror.* Clarion, 1984.
Fairley, John, and Welfare, Simon. *Arthur C. Clarke's World of Strange Powers.* Putnam, 1984.
Fischer, Dennis. *Horror Film Directors, 1931-1990.* McFarland, 1991.
Garden, Nancy. *Devils and Demons.* Harper, 1976.
Go Fango: How to Be a Vampire. Western, 1993.
Guiley, Rosemary Ellen. *The Encyclopedia of Ghosts and Spirits.* Facts on File, 1993.
Jarvis, Sharon, ed. *The Uninvited: True Tales of the Unknown, Vol II.* Bantam, 1989.
Jones, Stephen, and Newman, Kim, eds. *Horror: 100 Best Books.* Carroll & Graf, 1989.
Knight, David C. *The Moving Coffins: Ghosts and Hauntings Around the World.* Prentice, 1987.
McHargue, Georgess. *Meet the Werewolf.* Harper, 1976.
Marsden, Simon. *The Haunted Realm: Ghosts, Spirits and Their Uncanny Abodes.* Dutton, 1987.
Monroe, Lucy. *Creepy Cuisine: Revolting Recipes That Look Disgusting but Taste Divine.* Random, 1993.
Myers, Arthur. *The Ghostly Register.* Contemporary, 1986.
Mysteries of the Unexplained. Reader's Digest, 1983.
Nickell, Joe, and Fischer, John F. *Secrets of the Supernatural: Investigating the World's Occult Mysteries.* Prometheus, 1988.
Pitts, Michael R. *Horror Film Stars.* 2nd ed. McFarland, 1991.
Powers, Tom. *Horror Movies.* Lerner, 1989.
_____. *Movie Monsters.* Lerner, 1989.
Riccio, Dolores, and Bingham, Joan. *Haunted Houses.* Pocket, 1989.
Rovin, Jeff. *The Encyclopedia of Monsters.* Facts on File, 1989.
Skal, David J. *Hollywood Gothic: The Tangled Web of Dracula from Novel to Stage to Screen.* Norton, 1990.
Sullivan, Jack, ed. *The Penguin Encyclopedia of Horror and the Supernatural.* Viking, 1986.
Warren, William E. *The Screaming Skull.* Prentice, 1987.
Weaver, Tom. *They Fought in the Creature Features: Interviews with 23 Classic Horror, Science Fiction and Serial Stars.* McFarland, 1995.

Williamson, J.N., ed. *How to Write Tales of Horror, Fantasy & Science Fiction.* Writer's Digest, 1991.
Wilson, Colin. *Poltergeist: A Study in Destructive Haunting.* Putnam, 1983.
Winter, Douglas R. *Faces of Fear: Encounters with the Creators of Modern Horror.* Berkley, 1985.

Fiction

Aiken, Joan. *A Fit of Shivers: Tales for Late at Night.* Delacorte, 1992.
Barker, Clive. *The Thief of Always.* HarperCollins, 1992.
Bloch, Robert. *Lori.* Tor, 1989.
Brodien-Jones, Chris. *The Dreamkeepers.* Bradbury, 1992.
Campbell, Ramsey. *Midnight Sun.* Tor, 1991.
Clarke, J. *The Torment of Mr. Gully: Stories of the Supernatural.* Holt, 1990.
Cooney, Caroline B. *The Fog.* Scholastic, 1989.
Cusick, Richie Tankersley. *Vampire.* Archway, 1991.
Farris, John. *Fiends.* Tor, 1990.
Gallo, Donald R., ed. *Short Circuits: Thirteen Shocking Stories by Outstanding Writers for Young Adults.* Delacorte, 1992.
Garden, Nancy. *Mystery of the Night Menace.* Farrar, 1988.
Haaf, Beverly T. *The Chanting.* Popular Library, 1991.
Hambly, Barbara. *Those Who Hunt the Night.* Ballantine, 1988.
Huff, Tanya. *Blood Price.* DAW, 1991.
James, Peter. *Possession.* Doubleday, 1988.
King, Stephen. *Nightmares and Dreamscapes.* Signet, 1993.
Lake, Simon. *Daughter of Darkness.* Bantam, 1992.
Littke, Lael. *Prom Dress.* Scholastic, 1989.
Lovecraft, H.P. *At the Mountains of Madness and Other Novels.* Arkham, 1985.
McDonald, Collin. *The Chilling Hour: Tales of the Real and Unreal.* Dutton, 1992.
McKissack, Patricia. *The Dark Thirty: Southern Tales of the Supernatural.* Knopf, 1992.
Mahy, Margaret. *The Changeover.* Atheneum, 1984.
Masterton, Graham. *The Burning.* Tor, 1991.
Morgan, Helen. *The Witch Doll.* Viking, 1992.
Nixon, Joan Lowery. *Whispers From the Dead.* Delacorte, 1989.
Pike, Christopher. *Die Softly.* Pocket, 1991.
Rice, Anne. *The Mummy; or, Ramses the Damned.* Ballantine, 1989.
Saul, John. *Sleepwalk.* Bantam, 1990.
Shelley, Mary Wollstonecraft. *Frankenstein.* Dell, 1964.
Sleator, William. *The Duplicate.* Dutton, 1988.
Stevenson, Robert Louis. *The Strange Case of Dr. Jekyll and Mr. Hyde.* University of Nebraska Press, 1990.
Stine, R.L. **Fear Street** series. Archway, 1991.
Vance, Steve. *Spook.* Soho, 1990.

(Also other horror titles by these authors.)

Periodicals

Amazing Stories. TSR, Inc.
Bizarre Bazaar. TAL Publications.

Haunts. Nightshade Publications.
Horror. Wildside Press.
Midnight Zoo. Experiences Unlimited.

Feature-Length Films and Series

The Birds. MCA/Universal, 1963.
Gremlins. Warner, 1984. (PG)
Halloween. Media Home Entertainment, 1978. (R)
Night of the Living Dead. Columbia Tristar, 1968.
Poltergeist. MGM/UA, 1982. (PG)
Psycho. MCA/Universal, 1960.
Twilight Zone: The Movie. Warner, 1983. (PG)

Computer Software

Alone in the Dark 3. I-MOTION, 1995.
Bureau 13. Take 2 Interactive Software, 1994.
Classic Clips: Horrors. Starlite Productions, 1995.
Ghosts. Media Design Interactive, 1995.
Poe's Tales of Terror. Queue, 1992.
Terror T.R.A.X. Track of the Vampire. 3 Prong Plug, 1995.

25

Do It Yourself

Some day in the not-too-distant future, you will move out of your parents' house and be on your own. When that time comes, will you be able to set up an apartment, make simple household repairs, manage your personal finances, cook, clean your clothes and accomplish other basic chores? You will find out what you need to know in the library. We have books, magazines and videos with instructions on how to do just about anything. So roll up your sleeves and learn a new skill. With a little practice, you will be able to Do it Yourself.

Display Idea

Gather several nonfiction "handyman" and "how-to" books, cookbooks and collections of helpful hints, as well as related magazines. Display these with "do-it-yourself" videos and novels about people who are learning to manage on their own, or who have taken on a construction or repair project. Add some workman's tools, such as a tire jack or paintbrush, to draw attention to the display.

Sponsorship for Prizes

1. Ask a bookstore to donate how-to books and magazines with do-it-yourself projects.
2. Ask a hardware store to donate merchandise certificates.
3. Ask a video rental store to donate certificates for free rentals of do-it-yourself videos.
4. Ask a craft store to donate craft supplies and instructions.

Program Game

Make a blueprint of a house to use as the game board. Throughout the house, there will be various do-it-yourself projects to accomplish, such as painting the ceiling, replacing a fuse, sewing on a button, etc. Draw a path from one end of the house to the other, passing through each room and project. Patrons will advance one space along the path for each point earned. Points can be earned for completing the activities mentioned in the General Guidelines, and for:

1. Reading a novel and completing a Fiction Book Review Form.
2. Reading a nonfiction book related to the do-it-yourself theme and completing a Do It Yourself Nonfiction Book Review Form.
3. Reading a nonfiction book not related to the theme and completing a Nonfiction Book Review Form.

4. Reading a "how-to" magazine article and watching a video about a similar project, and comparing them on a Do It Yourself Project Comparison Form.

Program Forms

1. Fiction Book Review Form
Title:
Author:
Publisher and date:
Brief summary of plot:
I would rate this book: "A superbly-crafted work of art," "A job well done," "Looks good," "Held together with duct tape," "It fell apart."

2. Do It Yourself Nonfiction Book Review Form
Title:
Author:
Publisher and date:
Brief description of information:
Are the instructions in this book easy or difficult to follow?
Why do you think so?
Do you think you will attempt to do any of the projects in this book? If so, which one?

3. Nonfiction Book Review Form
Title:
Author:
Publisher and date:
Brief description of information:
I would rate this book: "A skilled craftsman," "Very handy," "Can complete a project with help," "Has trouble following directions," "Is all thumbs."

4. Do It Yourself Project Comparison Form
Name of article:
Magazine and date:
Name of video:
What type of project was described?
Which set of instructions do you think would be easier to follow and why?

Program Activities

1. Cars. Ask an auto mechanic to demonstrate how to change a flat tire, replace the windshield wipers, change the oil, and perform other routine auto maintenance chores.

2. Fun Stuff. You can run how-to workshops on one or more craft activities. Some ideas are stenciling, carving pumpkins, decoupage, basket weaving, calligraphy, building model cars, tie-dyeing T-shirts, ceramics, knitting and other needlecrafts.

3. Furniture. Hold a workshop on how to refinish furniture. A woodworker can show teens how to safely remove old paint or varnish from a table, sand it down, and apply a fresh coat of paint, stain, or varnish. An upholsterer can demonstrate how to cover chair cushions with new fabric.

4. Electrical. Invite an electrician to review safety tips with young adults and teach them some basic maintenance tasks. For example, teens can learn how to change a fuse, fix a frayed lamp cord, replace a wall outlet and remove a stuck light bulb.

5. Kid Care. Sponsor a babysitting class for teens. Contact the Red Cross to have a qualified person lead one or more sessions in child care, safety, and first aid or CPR.

6. Task Masters. Teens can participate in a game show program to determine how good they are at accomplishing manual and household tasks. Rather than simply telling the answers, contestants will have to actually show how to do each task. Each of the following categories includes a sample task: Call a Plumber (the player must demonstrate how to replace a washer in a faucet), Kitchen Chores (separate an egg), Home Decorating (put curtains on a curtain rod), Electronics Wiz (program a VCR), Handicrafts (thread a needle), or Sports Stuff (get a bicycle chain back on track). Provide all the materials needed to complete the chores, and set a time limit for each one.

7. Clothes. Teens who want to look their best should learn how to take care of their clothes. Young women and men can be shown how to properly sort and wash their laundry, sew on buttons and make hems, iron, and hang freshly cleaned and pressed clothes so that they will stay neat.

8. Gardening. This activity can be adapted to an indoor or outdoor program. Teens can get hands-on gardening experience by making compost, preparing the soil, measuring areas to be planted, and planting seeds, bulbs or larger plants.

9. Handy Work. Discuss several jobs for people who like to build or fix things themselves, such as carpenter, upholsterer, plumber, electrician, tailor, auto mechanic, mason, wallpaper hanger or house painter. Other jobs for people who like to create things can include engineer, architect, fashion designer, photographer, chef, gardener, jeweler or craftsperson. Provide information on schools that offer training in these areas, as well as short-term courses for teens interested in pursuing some of these endeavors as hobbies.

10. Library Skills. Use this opportunity to instruct teens in the use of any computer programs, research tools, or electronic equipment on which they have not yet been trained. You can also show them how to use certain reference sources, follow the Dewey decimal system, or accomplish other library skills.

Curriculum Tie-Ins

1. English Literature/Composition. Provide several how-to articles for students to read. Discuss the basic format of these articles with the class. Then let teens choose a manual task or craft that they know something about, and have them write their own how-to articles.

2. Science. Choose a how-to project that involves some scientific knowledge to accomplish. For example, you can teach students how to develop black and white film as part of a chemistry unit.

3. History/Geography. Students can make a chart of tools used by several cultures throughout history, such as Neanderthals, Philistines, Eskimos and Ancient Egyptians. Teens can note the materials from which the tools were fashioned, how the tools were made, and how they were used. How did geography help to determine the type of tools made by each culture or civilization?

4. Math. People living on their own must know how to accomplish some basic financial chores. Prepare students for this by showing them how to budget their money, write a check and balance a monthly statement, invest in a savings bond, etc. Or, you can teach measuring skills in conjunction with an activity such as carpentry or gardening.

Activity Sheet Ideas

1. Word search or crossword puzzles of: a) handyman skills, b) carpentry (or plumbing, electrical, etc.) terms, or c) tools.
2. Word scrambles or cryptograms of: a) how-to projects, b) helpful hints, or c) magazines that publish do-it-yourself projects.
3. Matching activities: match a) the fix-it chore to its solution, b) craft, construction, or repair projects to the tools needed to complete them, or c) do-it-yourself celebrities to the types of projects they do.

Suggested Resources

Reference and Nonfiction

Armstrong, Dorinne, and Armstrong, Richard. *Leaving the Nest: Mom's Guide to Living on Your Own*. Morrow, 1986.
Ashton, Betsy. *Betsy Ashton's Guide to Living on Your Own*. Little, 1988.
Bial, Raymond. *With Needle and Thread: A Book About Quilts*. Houghton, 1996.
Branson, Gary D. *The Complete Guide to Lumber Yards and Home Centers: A Consumer Guide to Choosing and Using Building Materials and Tools*. Betterway, 1991.
Brown, Rachel. *The Weaving, Spinning, and Dyeing Book*. Knopf, 1983.
Burpee Complete Gardener. Macmillan, 1995.
Chaback, Elaine, and Fortunato, Pat. *The Official Kids' Survival Kit: How to Do Things on Your Own*. Little, 1981.
The Complete Book of Needlecrafts. Chilton, 1990.
Cosentino, Peter. *The Encyclopedia of Pottery Techniques*. Running Press, 1990.
Creating Your Home series. Betterway.
Erickson, Mary Anne, and Cohen, Eve. *Knitting by Design: A Step-by-Step Guide to Designing and Knitting Your Own Clothes*. Bantam, 1986.
Finney, Mark. *The Stanley Book of Woodworking Tools, Techniques and Projects*. Betterway, 1995.
Ford, Marianne. *Copycats and Artifacts: 42 Creative Artisan Projects to Make*. Godine, 1986.
Heloise. *Heloise from A to Z*. Perigee, 1992.
James, Elizabeth, and Barkin, Carol. *A Place of Your Own*. Dutton, 1981.
Johnson, Kay. *Canework*. Dyrad, 1987.
Kitagawa, Yoshiko. *Creative Cards: Wrap a Message with a Personal Touch*. Kodansha, 1987.
Marlow, A.W. *Fine Furniture for the Amateur Cabinetmaker*. Scarborough, 1990.
Musheno, Elizabeth J. *Fast and Easy Home Decorating*. St. Martin's, 1986.
Paradis, Adrian A. *Opportunities in Vocational and Technical Careers*. VGM, 1992.
Philbin, Tom. *The Complete Illustrated Guide to Everything Sold in Hardware Stores*. Macmillan, 1993.
Reid, John. *From One Sheet of Plywood*. Sterling, 1987.
Rheingold, Howard, ed. *The Millennium Whole Earth Catalog: Access to Tools and Ideas*. HarperSanFrancisco, 1994.

Rombauer, Irma S., and Becker, Marion Rombauer. *The Joy of Cooking*. Macmillan, 1986.
Sew It Yourself Home Decorating: Creative Ideas for Beautiful Interiors. Prentice, 1986.
Sheldon, Roger. *Opportunities in Carpentry Careers*. VGM, 1993.
Time-Life Books editors. *Working with Metal*. Silver Burdett, 1990.
Time-Life Complete Fix-It-Yourself Manual. Prentice, 1989.
Wood, Robert. *Opportunities in Electrical Trades Careers*. VGM, 1996.
Zamkoff, Bernard, and Price, Jeanne. *Basic Pattern Skills for Fashion Design*. Fairchild, 1987.

Fiction

Berry, Liz. *Mel*. Puffin, 1991.
Cole, Brock. *Celine*. Farrar, 1989.
Cooney, Caroline B. *The Party's Over*. Scholastic, 1991.
Corcoran, Barbara. *Family Secrets*. Atheneum, 1992.
Grant, Cynthia D. *Kumquat May, I'll Always Love You*. Macmillan, 1986.
Hall, Lynn. *The Leaving*. Macmillan, 1980.
_____. *The Solitary*. Macmillan, 1986.
Korman, Gordon. *Losing Joe's Place*. Scholastic, 1990.
Lo, Steven C. *The Incorporation of Eric Chung*. Algonquin, 1989.
Lowry, Lois. *Anastasia on Her Own*. Houghton, 1985.
Murray, Marguerite. *Like Seabirds Flying Home*. Atheneum, 1988.
Myers, Walter Dean. *The Young Landlords*. Viking, 1979.
Naylor, Phyllis Reynolds. *Alice in Lace*. Atheneum, 1996.
Oldham, June. *Moving In*. Delacorte, 1987.
Pfeffer, Susan Beth. *Kid Power*. Watts, 1977.
Ross, Rhea Beth. *The Bet's On, Lizzie Bingman!* Houghton, 1988.
Shura, Mary Francis. *The Sunday Doll*. Dodd, 1988.
Voight, Cynthia. *Seventeen Against the Dealer*. Atheneum, 1989.
Williams, Jeanne. *Lady of No Man's Land*. St. Martin's, 1988.
Wood, Marcia. *The Search for Jim McGwynn*. Atheneum, 1989.
Zeier, Joan T. *The Elderberry Thicket*. Atheneum, 1990.

Periodicals

Better Homes and Gardens. Meredith.
Choices: The Magazine for Personal Development and Practical Living Skills. Scholastic, Inc.
The Family Handyman: The Do-It-Yourself Home Improvement Magazine. Home Service Publications.
Good Housekeeping. International Magazine Co.
House Beautiful. Hearst Corp.
Teen Times. Future Homemakers of America.

Feature-Length Films

George Washington Slept Here. MGM/UA, 1942.
How to Make a Monster. Columbia Tristar, 1958.

The Karate Kid. Columbia Tristar, 1984. (PG)
The Money Pit. MCA/Universal, 1986. (PG)
Mr. Blandings Builds His Dream House. Turner Home Entertainment, 1948.

Computer Software

The Complete Home Suite. Alpha Software.
The Home Repair Encyclopedia. Books That Work, 1994.
Hometime Weekend Home Projects. IVI Publishing, 1994.
Key Home Gardener. Softkey, 1994.
The Life Skills CD. Queue, 1992.
Physics Explorer: AC/DC Circuits. Logical Software, 1992.

26
A Lot of Laughs

What's so funny? Come to the library and find out! There are humorous novels, farcical plays, riotous comedy albums, satirical magazines and hilarious videos. You can check out nonfiction books on comedy classics, humor collections and biographies of merry men and women. You can even pick up some "punderful" joke books that could help you be the life of the party. If you're looking for something to tickle your funnybone, you'll find A Lot of Laughs at the library.

Display Idea

Set up a display of humorous fiction, short stories, plays, poetry and satire. Add nonfiction books about comedy, books of humorous observations, joke and riddle books, and biographies of comedians. Include humor magazines, funny videos, recordings by comedians and tapes of comedy shows. Post pictures of famous comedians and gag props such as a rubber chicken to enliven the display.

Sponsorship for Prizes

1. Ask a joke shop to donate gag items and novelties.
2. Ask a bookstore to donate humorous fiction and nonfiction.
3. Ask a local theater or cinema to donate tickets to a humorous play or movie.
4. Ask a video rental store to donate free rental certificates for humorous films.

Program Game

Design a board game to look like the inside of a funhouse. Draw a trail past distorted mirrors, laughing figures, crazy walk-ways, tilted rooms, etc. Along the way, mark spaces with jokes, tricks and famous punch lines. The trail can end with a slide into a vat of gelatin or some other goopy stuff. Patrons can advance one space along the trail for each point. Points can be earned by completing the activities mentioned in the General Guidelines, and for:

1. Reading a humorous novel and completing a Humor Fiction Book Review Form.
2. Reading a novel that is not humorous and completing a Fiction Book Review Form.
3. Reading a nonfiction book related to the humor theme and completing a Humor Nonfiction Book Review Form.
4. Completing a nonfiction book not related to the theme and completing a Nonfiction Book Review Form.

Program Forms

1. Humor Fiction Book Review Form
Title:
Author:
Publisher and date:
Brief summary of plot:
I would rate this book: "I laughed my head off," "It cracked me up," "It brought a smile to my lips," "So funny I forgot to laugh," "Yawn."
2. Fiction Book Review Form
Title:
Author:
Publisher and date:
Brief summary of plot:
Did you like this book? Why or why not?
What was your favorite scene in the book and why?
3. Humor Nonfiction Book Review Form
Title:
Author:
Publisher and date:
Brief description of information:
I would rate this book: "The king of comedy," "Headlines at comedy clubs," "Makes people laugh at parties," "Can never remember the punchline," "Has no sense of humor whatsoever."
4. Nonfiction Book Review Form
Title:
Author:
Publisher and date:
Brief description of information:
Why did you choose this book?
What was the most interesting part of the book and why?

Program Activities

1. Comedy Classics. Play clips of classic comedy routines, such as Abbott and Costello's "Who's on First?" Or you may want to have a movie marathon showing several generations of comedy films, such as a Marx Brothers movie, *The Pink Panther*, and *Buffy the Vampire Slayer*.

2. The Funnies. Let teens discuss and take a poll of their favorite comic strips. What makes them so popular? Provide books of comic strip collections as well as the Sunday funnies from several weeks' worth of various newspapers so teens can read ones they've missed. Show some comics that were popular in the past and ask teens for their reactions.

3. Editorials. Political cartoons are humorous, but they often have a serious message. Invite a political cartoonist from a local newspaper or magazine to speak to teens about his work. If that isn't possible, show several political cartoons using an overhead projector. Teens can discuss how the cartoons make fun of serious issues. Is humor an effective way to relay an important message?

4. Play Time. Treat students to a program of comedy theater at the library or at a local playhouse. The play can be a musical comedy, farce, comic revue or another type of theater comedy.

5. Musical Comedy. Some songwriters specialize in composing humorous songs and parodies. Play tunes from past funnymen such as Alan Sherman and Ray Stevens, and contemporary lampooners such as "Weird" Al Yankovic. For songs that are parodies, play the original song along with the spoof so teens can compare the two versions. You can also play comical songs from musical plays or films, such as "Make'em Laugh" from the film *Singin' in the Rain.*

6. The Joke's on You. Everyone should have a fun time with this hilarious and messy game show. Teen contestants can demonstrate their sense of humor by supplying the punch-lines to jokes, creating captions to one-frame cartoons, improvising with funny props, coming up with puns, etc. The game show host will present a comic situation. Each contestant will have a chance to come up with a humorous retort or routine. The audience will clap and cheer for their favorite response to each situation. The winner will receive points, while the losers receive a pie in the face, a squirt of seltzer, a handshake with a joy buzzer, and other gag punishments as the audience shouts, "The joke's on you!" You can add funny sound effects and other slapstick jokes to add humor to the game.

7. Clown School. Some hospitals and service groups encourage clown volunteers to cheer up their clients. Ask a volunteer to hold a clown workshop. Patrons can learn how to apply make-up and other basics of clowning. Supply gaudy, oversized clothes and accessories or let teens bring in their own clown costumes. With additional training, teens may be able to perform skits for various public service organizations.

8. Jokers and Riddlers. It takes skill to tell a joke well. Invite someone who has mastered this art to give pointers to a teen audience. Provide several joke and riddle books for patrons to use at the program and to check out afterward.

9. Funny Business. Introduce patrons to careers in comedy at a job fair program. Career opportunities can include stand-up comedian, comic actor, gag writer, political satirist, author of humorous fiction or nonfiction, cartoonist, playwright, circus clown, etc. Include a list of local comedy clubs and books on writing, drawing and performing humor.

10. Comedy Tonight. Allow teens to put on a comedy variety show for their peers. Young adults can perform comic skits, funny songs, stand-up comedy routines, impersonations, etc. (Audition participants ahead of time to screen out any inappropriate acts.)

Curriculum Tie-Ins

1. English Literature/Composition. Satire is a special form of comedy. Discuss elements of satire with the class. Have students read a satirical novel and talk about the author's intentions. Students can then write a satirical short story about a contemporary issue. You may also want to discuss other forms of humor (irony, farce, parody, sarcasm, etc.)

2. Science. Have students poll their family and friends to answer the question: "Is laughter the best medicine?" Students can ask people to rate how often they laugh, on a scale of 1 (very little) to 5 (a lot). Then ask them to rate how often they get sick, and chart the results. The class can look in medical books and journals to see if there is any scientific documentation to prove that laughter is healthy.

3. History/Geography. Each student can choose a different comedian or comic actor to study, then write a biography of that person, including landmarks in the comic's career and relating the person's comedy to what was happening in the world at the time. (Example: In *The Great Dictator*, Charlie Chaplin satirized Hitler's ambition to take over the world.) Students should also note important places in the person's life (place of birth and death, where he or she performed, etc.)

4. Math. Show an episode of two comparable TV sitcoms, such as *I Love Lucy* and *Roseanne* or *The Mary Tyler Moore Show* and *Murphy Brown*. Have each student keep a record of how many times he or she laughed during each show. The class can plot these numbers on a graph to compare which show was funnier. You can also use this method to compare stand-up comic routines, comic recordings or movies.

Activity Sheet Ideas

1. Word search or crossword puzzles of: a) types of humor and comedy, b) humorous props, or c) comic characters.

2. Word scramble or cryptograms of: a) jokes and puns, b) names of comedy clubs, or c) names of comedians.

3. Matching activities: match a) humorous films to their comic actors, b) famous comic routines to the people who originated them, or c) riddles to their answers.

Suggested Resources

Reference and Nonfiction

Allen, Woody. *Without Feathers*. Ballantine, 1987.

Bombeck, Erma. *The Grass Is Always Greener Over the Septic Tank*. Fawcett, 1986.

Borns, Betsy. *Comic Lives: Inside the World of Stand-Up Comedy*. Simon & Schuster, 1987.

Buchwald, Art. *Whose Rose Garden Is It Anyway?* Putnam, 1989.

Burnett, Carol. *One More Time*. Avon, 1987.

Eisner, Joel, and Krinsky, David. *Television Comedy Series: An Episode Guide to 153 TV Sitcoms in Syndication*. McFarland, 1984.

Finnigan, Dave. *The Complete Juggler*. Random, 1987.

Helitzer, Melvin. *Comedy Writing Secrets*. Writer's Digest, 1987.

Keillor, Garrison. *Leaving Home: A Collection of Lake Woebegon Stories*. Penguin, 1990.

Keller, Charles, ed. *Growing Up Laughing: Humorists Look at American Youth*. Prentice, 1981.

Kerr, Walter. *The Silent Clowns*. Da Capo, 1975.

Langman, Larry, and Gold, Paul. *Comedy Quotes from the Movies: Over 4,000 Bits of Humorous Dialogue from All Film Genres, Topically Arranged and Indexed*. McFarland, 1994.

McManus, Patrick F. *The Night the Bear Ate Goombaw*. Holt, 1989.

Martin, Linda, and Segrave, Kerry. *Women in Comedy*. Citadel, 1986.

Muir, Frank, ed. *The Oxford Book of Humorous Prose: William Caxton to P.G. Wodehouse—A Conducted Tour*. Oxford University Press, 1990.

Novak, William, et al., eds. *The Big Book of New American Humor: The Best of the Past 25 Years*. Harper, 1990.

Palin, Michael. *Around the World in 80 Days with Michael Palin*. Parkwest, 1990.

Pinkwater, Daniel. *Fish Whistle: Commentaries, Uncommentaries, and Vulgar Excesses*. Addison-Wesley, 1989.

Radner, Gilda. *It's Always Something*. Simon & Schuster, 1989.

Ritchard, Dan, and Moloney, Kathleen. *Ventriloquism for the Total Dummy*. Random, 1987.

Sarrantonio, Al, ed. *Fireside Treasury of Great Humor*. Simon & Schuster, 1987.

_____. *The National Lampoon Treasury of Humor*. Simon & Schuster, 1991.

Schwartz, Alvin, compiler. *Flapdoodle: Pure Nonsense from American Folklore*. Harper, 1980.

Shalit, Gene, ed. *Laughing Matters: A Celebration of American Humor*. Doubleday, 1987.

Seinfeld, Jerry. *SeinLanguage*. Bantam, 1993.

Smirnoff, Yakov. *America on Six Rubles a Day: Or, How to Become a Capitalist Pig*. Random, 1987.

Vorhaus, John. *The Comic Toolbox: How to Be Funny Even When You're Not*. Silman-James, 1994.

Winokur, Jon, ed. *The Portable Curmudgeon*. NAL, 1987.

Fiction

Bauer, Joan. *Squashed*. Delacorte, 1992.

Byers, Betsy. *Bingo Brown and the Language of Love*. Viking, 1989.

Clarke, Judith. *The Heroic Life of Al Capsella*. Holt, 1990.

Conford, Ellen. *Lenny Kandell, Smart Aleck*. Pocket, 1983.

Cresswell, Helen. **The Bagthorpe Saga** series. Macmillan.

Fine, Anne. *My War with Goggle-Eyes*. Little, 1989.

Fleischman, Paul. *A Fate Totally Worse Than Death*. Candlewick, 1995.

Gaiman, Neil, and Pratchett, Terry. *Good Omens: The Nice and Accurate Prophecies of Agnes Nutter, Witch*. Workman, 1990.

Gale, David, ed. *Funny You Should Ask*. Delacorte, 1992.

Gilden, Mel. *Outer Space and All That Junk*. Lippincott, 1989.

Grant, Cynthia D. *Keep Laughing*. Atheneum, 1991.

Hall, Lynn. *Murder in a Pig's Eye*. Harcourt, 1990.

Haseley, Dennis. *Dr. Gravity*. Farrar, 1992.

Hurwitz, Johanna. *Class Clown*. Morrow, 1987.

Korman, Gordon. *A Semester in the Life of a Garbage Bag*. Scholastic, 1987.

Lantz, Francess. *Dear Celeste, My Life Is a Mess*. Bantam, 1992.

McFann, Jane. *No Time for Rabbits*. Avon, 1991.

Manes, Stephen. *Comedy High*. Scholastic, 1992.

Naylor, Phyllis Reynolds. *The Agony of Alice*. Atheneum, 1985.

Nixon, Joan Lowery. *Star Baby*. Bantam, 1989.

Oldham, June. *Moving In*. Delacorte, 1990.

Paulsen, Gary. *The Boy Who Owned the School*. Orchard, 1990.

Pinkwater, Daniel. *Borgel*. Macmillan, 1990.

Sachar, Louis. *Dogs Don't Tell Jokes*. Knopf, 1991.

Salzman, Mark. *The Laughing Sutra*. Random, 1991.

Schwartz, Joel L. *Upchuck Summer*. Delacorte, 1982.

Sutton, Jane. *Definitely Not Sexy*. Little, 1988.

Taylor, William. *Agnes the Sheep*. Scholastic, 1991.

Ustinov, Peter. *The Old Man and Mr. Smith*. Arcade, 1991.

Wolitzer, Meg. *This Is Your Life*. Crown, 1988.

Periodicals

Mad Magazine. E. C. Publications, Inc.
National Lampoon. NL Communications, Inc.

Feature-Length Films

Airplane! Paramount, 1980. (PG)
And Now for Something Completely Different. Columbia Tristar, 1972. (PG)
Buffy the Vampire Slayer. Fox/Lorber, 1992. (PG-13)
Golden Age of Comedy. VidAmerica, 1958.
Horsefeathers. MCA/Universal, 1932.
The Pink Panther. MGM/UA, 1964.
This Is My Life. Fox/Lorber, 1992. (PG-13)

Computer Software

Dating and Mating. Time-Warner Interactive, 1994.
Funny: The Movie in QuickTime. Time Warner Interactive, 1993.
Hilarious Sports Bloopers. Chestnut, 1994.
A Million Laughs. Future Visions Multimedia, 1993.
Monty Python's Complete Waste of Time. 7th Level, 1994.
QuickLaffs Volume 1. Gazelle Technologies, 1993. (Also Vol. 2.)

27

Invention Adventures

If you've ever had the urge to create, tinker, experiment, build or design something, then you could be a budding scientist or inventor. You'll find plenty of nonfiction books in the library to inspire you, plus novels, magazines and videos about great and not-so-great inventions and experiments. And if you're looking for an idea for an interesting science project, you've come to the right place. The library has just what you need to help you embark on your own Invention Adventures.

Display Idea

Find nonfiction books about inventors and inventions, scientists and their experiments to display along with magazines devoted to these subjects. Several novels and videos—both fiction and documentary—related to the theme should be available for patrons to check out.

Sponsorship for Prizes

1. Ask a local bookstore to donate fiction and nonfiction books about inventions, experiments, and the people who worked on them.

2. Ask a video rental store to donate free rental certificates for videos about science experiments and inventions.

3. Ask a hobby store to donate chemistry sets, electronics kits, and other items for teens who like to create things.

4. Ask a science or technology museum to donate free passes.

Program Game

Draw a diagram of the inner workings of a complex machine, such as the automatic transmission of a car (see *The Way Things Work* for ideas). Use arrows to indicate direction and lines to section off spaces. Patrons can advance one space for each point earned. Points can be earned for completing the activities mentioned in the General Guidelines, and for:

1. Reading a novel about inventors, inventions, scientist, or experiments and completing Inventions Fiction Book Review Form.

2. Reading a novel not related to the inventions theme and completing a Fiction Book Review Form.

3. Reading a nonfiction book related to the inventions theme and completing an Inventions Nonfiction Book Review Form.

4. Reading a nonfiction book not related to the theme and completing a Nonfiction Book Review Form.

Program Forms

1. Inventions Fiction Book Review Form
Title:
Author:
Publisher and date:
Brief summary of plot:
How did the invention or experiment affect the main character?
Did you enjoy reading this book? Why or why not?
2. Fiction Book Review Form
Title:
Author:
Publisher and date:
Brief summary of plot:
I would rate this book: "Performs beyond all expectations," "Works well," "Does an adequate job," "Breaks down occasionally," "Won't work at all."
3. Inventions Nonfiction Book Review Form
Title:
Author:
Publisher and date:
Brief description of information:
What was the most interesting part of the book?
Would you like to read more about this subject? Why or why not?
4. Nonfiction Book Review Form
Title:
Author:
Publisher and date:
Brief description of information:
I would rate this book: "An incredible discovery," "An important find," "An interesting development," "A questionable proposition," "A complete failure."

Program Activities

1. Creative Film. Teens can watch a movie about a scientist or inventor, such as *Tucker: The Man and His Dream*.

2. Thingamajig. As a group project, have teens create a complicated machine that goes to great lengths to perform a minor task, such as those designed by Rube Goldberg. Teens can use marbles, dominoes, ramps, pulleys, toy cars and a variety of other items to make their invention.

3. Auto-Mation. Ask teens to consider: if they could design a car (or other transportation vehicle), what would it look like? Place patrons with similar ideas in groups and let them draw up plans for their inventions. They can incorporate features that are currently available, as well as creating new ones. Encourage teens to use their imaginations; they can invent anything they want, even if the technology for it does not yet exist. When the designs are completed, each group can explain its concept.

4. Exhibits. If there is a science or technology museum in your area, arrange to take a group of teens there to view exhibits on great inventions.

5. Creative Cooking. Give patrons an opportunity to invent a great new dessert. Provide recipes for a basic cookie dough, brownie mix, pie filling or other dessert, along with measuring tools, baking pans and ingredients. Also supply a variety of extra mix-ins, such as crushed candy bars, canned fruit, shredded coconut, nuts, etc. Let teens add 1 to 3 ingredients to the basic recipe to create something new. Make sure they write down the exact measurements and items they used, so they can repeat their recipes at home. Teens can taste-test each other's new desserts, and compile the best recipes into a cookbook.

6. What's the Question? Young adults can participate in a *Jeopary*-style game show in which they must invent the question to fit the answer in categories such as American Inventors, Adventures in Technology and Communications, Scientists and Their Experiments, The Industrial Revolution, Household Wonders, or Inventions That Changed the World.

7. Working Inventions. Base a program on David Macaulay's book *The Way Things Work*. Set up exhibits of some of the "things" illustrated in the book for teens to work, or provide materials for some of the machines and let teens build them.

8. Fasten-Ating Inventions. We take simple-looking fasteners for granted, but many were revolutionary inventions. Provide books and articles about everyday inventions and assign each teen one item to look up. Subjects can include zipper, Velcro, screw-top jar lid, button, safety pin, vacuum-pack can, hook and eye, nut and bolt, lock and key, etc. Give patrons a few minutes to find the information they need. Then they can share what they discovered about their inventions with the group.

9. Inventive Minds. Sponsor a job fair program featuring careers involving scientific experimentation or invention. Suggested areas include chemistry, physics, engineering, medical research, food science, biology, agriculture, computer programming and software design, electronics, space technology, mechanics, communications, and many more. Make a list of creative careers and provide books on these subjects for patrons to check out.

10. Game Plans. Place teens in groups and allow them to brainstorm ideas for inventing their own board, video, or computer games. Provide paper and drawing materials so they can draw game boards or video screens, accompanying instructions, and playing materials. Each team can pitch their ideas to the rest of the group.

Curriculum Tie-Ins

1. English Literature/Composition. Occasionally, science experiments go wrong and have disastrous results. This is a popular theme in stories such as *Frankenstein* and *The Strange Case of Dr. Jekyll and Mr. Hyde*. Read one of these novels or another book on this theme with the class. Discuss the consequences of experiments that backfired. How did the scientist in the novel deal with the problem? Then have students write their own endings to the story, in which the scientist tries another approach to solving the problem.

2. Science. Assign students the project of creating their own great inventions. Students must identify a need for a product and invent a device to fill that need. Require each student to draw a blueprint or diagram of the invention, build a working model, have several people test the invention, and evaluate how well it works. The class can present their inventions to the school at a project fair. You may want to award prizes for the best inventions.

3. History/Geography. Make a list of notable inventions. Have each student choose a different one to research and write a paper about. Or, choose a period in history, such as the Industrial Revolution, and ask students to draw a timeline of important inventions that were patented during this time. In each case, students can note where the inventors worked.

4. Math. Teach a unit of math formulas an inventor may use, such as problems involving watts, voltage, and other electrical units; problems involving weights and measurements; etc.

Activity Sheet Ideas

1. Word search or crossword puzzles of: a) inventions that use electricity, b) inventions powered by fossil fuels, or c) inventions used for recreation.

2. Word scrambles of cryptograms of: a) documentary films about inventions or inventors, b) types of inventions that failed, c) or quotes about invention, discovery or experimentation.

3. Matching activities: match a) famous inventions to their inventors, b) important scientific experiments to their scientists, or c) inventions to the years they were patented.

Suggested Resources

Reference and Nonfiction

Aaseng, Nathan. *Better Mousetraps: Product Improvements That Led to Success.* Lerner, 1990.

Bolick, Nancy O'Keefe, and Randolph, Sallie G. *Shaker Inventions.* Walker, 1990.

Brown, Kenneth A. *Inventors at Work: Interviews with 16 Notable American Inventors.* Tempus, 1988.

Brown, Travis. *Historical First Patents: The First United States Patent for Many Everyday Things.* Scarecrow, 1994.

Caney, Steven. *Steven Caney's Invention Book.* Workman, 1985.

Coe, Lewis. *The Telephone and Its Several Inventors.* McFarland, 1995.

Crump, Donald J., ed. *Small Inventions That Make a Big Difference.* **Books for World Explorers** series. National Geographic, 1984. (Also others in series.)

Flatow, Ira. *They All Laughed.* HarperCollins, 1992.

Freedman, Russell. *The Wright Brothers: How They Invented the Airplane.* Holiday, 1991.

Gardner, Robert. *Experimenting with Inventions.* Watts, 1990.

Goldberg, Rube. *The Best of Rube Goldberg.* Prentice, 1979.

Great Modern Inventions. Larousse Kingfisher Chambers, 1992.

Griffen, Gordon D. *How to Be a Successful Inventor: Turn Your Ideas Into Profit.* Wiley, 1991.

Growing Up with Science: The Illustrated Encyclopedia of Invention. 28 vols. Marshall Cavendish, 1985.

Haskins, James. *Outward Dreams: Black Inventors and Their Inventions.* Walker, 1991.

Johnson, Steven M. *Public Therapy Buses, Information Specialty Bums, Solar Cook-a-Mats and Other Visions of the 21st Century.* St. Martin's, 1991.

_____. *What the World Needs Now.* Ten Speed, 1984.

Karnes, Frances A., and Bean, Suzanne M. *Girls and Young Women Inventing.* Free Spirit, 1995.

Macaulay, David. *The Way Things Work.* Houghton, 1988.

Murphy, Jim. *Guess Again: More Weird and Wacky Inventions.* Bradbury, 1986.

Newhouse, Elizabeth, ed. *Inventors and Discoverers: Changing Our World.* National Geographic, 1988.

Noonan, Jon. *Nineteenth-Century Inventors.* Facts on File, 1992.

Olsen, Frank H. *Inventors Who Left Their Brands on America.* Bantam, 1991.

Oxford Illustrated Encyclopedia, Vol 6: Invention and Technology. Oxford University Press, 1992.

Park, Robert. *The Inventor's Handbook*. Betterway, 1990.

Peek, Stephen. *The Game Inventor's Handbook*. Betterway, 1993.

Platt, Richard. *The Smithsonian Visual Timeline of Inventions*. Dorling Kindersley, 1994.

Rose, Sharon, and Schlager, Neil. *CD's, Super Glue and Salsa: How Everyday Products Are Made*. UXL, 1995.

Schlager, Neil. *How Products Are Made: An Illustrated Guide to Product Manufacturing*. Gale, 1994.

Showell, Ellen, and Amram, Fred M.B. *Women Invent in America: From Indian Corn to Outer Space*. Cobblestone, 1995.

Travers, Bridget, ed. *World of Invention*. Gale, 1994.

Tucker, Tom. *Brainstorm! The Stories of Twenty American Kid Inventors*. Farrar, 1995.

Wilkinson, Philip, and Dineen, Jacqueline. *The Early Inventions*. **Ideas That Changed the World** series. Chelsea, 1995. (Also others in series.)

Williams, Trevor Illtyd. *The History of Invention*. Facts on File, 1987.

Yankee Magazine editors. *The Inventive Yankee: From Rockets to Roller Skates, 200 Years of Yankee Inventors and Inventions*. Yankee, 1989.

Fiction

Asimov, Isaac, ed. *Wild Inventions*. Raintree, 1981.

Bechko, P.A. *Blown to Hell*. Curley, 1994.

Bethancourt, T. Ernesto. *The Great Computer Dating Caper*. Crown, 1984.

Bunn, T. Davis. *Dangerous Devices*. Chariot, 1994.

Cramer, John. *Twistor*. Morrow, 1989.

Dennard, Deborah. *Travis and the Better Mousetrap*. Dutton, 1996.

Haas, Dorothy. *Burton's Zoom Zoom Va-Room Machine*. Simon & Schuster, 1990.

Heinlein, Robert A. *The Door Into Summer*. Ballantine, 1986.

Lillington, Kenneth. *Jonah's Mirror*. Faber and Faber, 1988.

Martin, Valerie. *Mary Reilly*. Doubleday, 1990.

Melendez, Francisco. *The Mermaid and the Major: Or, The True Story of the Invention of the Submarine*. Abrams, 1991.

Neville, Susan. *The Invention of Flight*. University of Georgia Press, 1984.

Peck, Richard. *Lost in Cyberspace*. Dial, 1995.

Percy, Walker. *Love in the Ruins*. Farrar, 1971.

Shelley, Mary Wollstonecraft. *Frankenstein*. Dell, 1964.

Skinner, David. *The Wrecker*. Simon & Schuster, 1995.

_____. *You Must Kiss a Whale*. Simon & Schuster, 1992.

Stevenson, Robert Louis. *The Strange Case of Dr. Jekyll and Mr. Hyde*. University of Nebraska Press, 1990.

Thomas, Donald. *Jekyll, Alias Hyde: A Variation*. St. Martin's, 1988.

Willard, Mildred Wilds. *The Man Who Had to Invent a Flying Bicycle*. Stackpole, 1967.

Wise, Ted. *Tesla: A Novel*. Turner, 1994.

Yep, Laurence. *Dragonwings*. Harper, 1975.

Periodicals

Inventors' Digest. Affiliated Inventors Foundation.

Inventor's Gazette. Inventors Association of America.

Popular Mechanics. Hearst Magazines.
Popular Science. Times Mirror Magazines, Inc.

Feature-Length Films

Honey, I Shrunk the Kids. Walt Disney, 1989. (G)
Man in the White Suit. HBO, 1951.
The Manhattan Project. HBO, 1986 (PG-13)
Race the Sun. Columbia Tristar, 1996. (PG)
Remote. Paramount, 1993. (PG)
The Time Machine. MGM/UA, 1960.
Tucker: The Man and His Dream. Paramount, 1988. (PG)

Computer Software

How Things Work. Aimtech Corp., 1991.
Ideas That Changed the World. Integrated Communications Entertainment, 1994.
The Incredible Machine. Dynamix, 1993.
Leonardo, The Inventor. Interactive Electronic Publishing, 1994.
Simple Machines. Science for Kids, 1994.
The Time Table History: Science and Innovation. Xiphias, 1992.
The Way Things Work. Dorling Kindersley Multimedia, 1994.

28
Magical Mysteries

You're in for a magical, mystical time at the library. Books, magazines, music and videos of all types appear on our shelves. You can spirit away stories of sorcerers, wizards, witches and other magical characters, and books on a variety of mystic arts. Check out a book on magic and learn some tricks that will amaze your friends. So come to the library and conjure up some Magical Mysteries.

Display Idea

Feature novels that have a magic theme or magical characters such as genies, wizards, and witches. Add nonfiction books on magic and card tricks, hypnotism, mysticism, illusion, and other magical arts, as well as related videos and music. Include some magic props, such as a deck of cards, a wand, and a top hat, to make the display more intriguing.

Sponsorship Ideas

1. Ask a local magic store to donate simple trick items.
2. Ask a bookstore to donate books of magic and card tricks, or other related fiction and nonfiction.
3. Ask a video rental store to donate free rental certificates for magic-themed movies.
4. Ask a costume store or rental shop to donate certificates for magic-related costumes and props.

Program Game

Use a floor plan of a mansion for the game board. Draw a trail through the house that passes several rooms that hold magical surprises, such as a piano that plays by itself, a trick mirror, talking framed pictures of magicians, etc. The trail can lead from the outside steps, through the house, and end at the theater where a magic show is being performed. Patrons can advance a space along the trail for each point earned. Points can be earned for completing the activities mentioned in the General Guidelines, and for:

1. Reading a novel with a magic theme or magical characters and completing a Magic Fiction Book Review Form.
2. Reading a novel not related to the magic theme and completing a Fiction Book Review Form.
3. Reading a nonfiction book related to the magic theme and completing a Magic Nonfiction Book Review Form.

4. Reading a nonfiction book not related to the magic theme and completing a Nonfiction Book Review Form.

Program Forms

1. Magic Fiction Book Review Form
Title:
Author:
Publisher and date:
Brief summary of plot:
What reference(s) to magic was (were) in the book?
How did magic advance the plot?
2. Fiction Book Review Form
Title:
Author:
Publisher and date:
I would rate this book: "A master of mysticism," "A sorcerer's apprentice," "A talented amateur," "A sidewalk con artist," "A no-talent fake."
3. Magic Nonfiction Book Review Form
Title:
Author:
Publisher and date:
Brief description of information:
What interested you most about this book?
Would you recommend it to a friend? Why or why not?
4. Nonfiction Book Review Form
Title:
Author:
Publisher and date:
Brief description of information:
I would rate this book: "An astounding illusion," "A marvelous bit of conjuring," "An interesting sleight-of-hand trick," "A bungled attempt at a dime-store diversion," "Should have been a disappearing act."

Program Activities

1. **Mystic Flick.** Show teens a movie with a magical theme, such as *Houdini.*
2. **Good Luck Signs.** Magic and superstition are closely related. Some people believe that magical objects, such as talismans and hex signs, can bring them good luck. Supply sheets of colored paper, stencils, scissors, and glue so teens can makes their own good luck talismans or hex signs. (Symbols and explanations for these can be found in *Magical Arts*.) Patrons can use traditional symbols or make up their own lucky charms.
3. **Card Sharks.** Invite a master of card tricks to put on a show and teach teens some simple tricks.
4. **Elusive Illusions.** Some magicians' tricks are really optical illusions. Teens can have fun with some visual deceptions at this library program. Use an overhead projector to enlarge pictures that create optical illusions and ask teens to tell you what they see. Look in books

to find illusions to project on a screen or to demonstrate to a group. You can also have available some of the *Magic Eye* books for patrons to check out.

5. Magic Potions. Teens can help conjure an assortment of treats and drinks that supposedly have magical powers. Find simple recipes for love potions, health remedies, foods to bring you good luck or strength, or brews to ward off evil. Make a list of herbs and other foods which are said to have a magical effect which patrons can take home.

6. Mystic Revelations. A simple magic trick can be used to conjure up the answers in this magical game show. Use a black marker to write each question on an individual sheet of white paper. Use lemon juice to write the answer beneath the question. When the juice dries, it will be invisible. During the game, post the current question so everyone can see it. Read it aloud as usual to the person whose turn it is. After the contestant has replied, pass a hot light bulb or iron in front of the invisible answer. The heat will cause the lemon juice to burn, and the answer will magically appear. Categories of questions can include Magical Characters in Literature (literary figures such as Merlin), Magic Terminology (terms used by magicians), Magical Sitcoms (TV shows that have featured magic), Superstitions (the reasons behind popular ones), The Mystic Arts (such as palm reading and astrology), Famous Magicians (and the tricks that made them famous).

7. Magic Class. Ask a magician to perform a show of sleight-of-hand tricks, illusions, and manipulations. Afterward, the guest can show teens how a few of these were accomplished and conduct a workshop on basic magic.

8. Magical Arts Fair. Ask volunteers to set up several booths or tables, each of which has an activity or information on a different magic-related subject. Possible ideas: a Ouija board, tarot card reading, palm reading, ventriloquism, hypnotism, mind-reading, superstitions, astrology, etc. Teens can visit the booths to participate in the activities, observe a demonstration, or take part in a discussion. Have books on related subjects available for patrons to borrow.

9. Magic in Your Life. Inform patrons of some occupations associated with magic during a special program. Performers may earn money as professional or amateur magicians, but there are also people who make their living writing about magic, building props and stage apparatus for magicians, selling magic items, designing and producing special effects, filming magic acts for the media, publicizing and staging magic shows, etc. Supply a list of magic societies and magazines available to serious magic enthusiasts.

10. Magic's in the Music. Sponsor a dance party during which all the music played has a mystical or magic theme. Play oldies such as "Do You Believe in Magic?" by the Lovin' Spoonful as well as newer tunes like "Mrs. Rita" by the Gin Blossoms. Teens can come costumed as magicians, sorcerers, gypsies or other magical folk.

Curriculum Tie-Ins

1. English Literature/Composition. Magic is a theme in many classic novels and plays. Read one of these with the class, and discuss the importance of magic to the plot. Note some magical creatures and spirits that appear in literature, such as fairies, leprechauns, witches, etc. Have students write short stories using one or more of these characters.

2. Science. Many magic tricks rely on simple scientific principles of chemistry, magnetism, physics and optical illusion. Consult a number of magic books to find several science-based magic tricks for students to do.

3. History/Geography. The class can learn about soothsayers, conjurers, gypsy fortune tellers, shamans, mystics, escape artists and other magic practitioners from various times in history and throughout the world. Assign each student a different country. Does its folklore include tales of magic (such as Arabian genies or Irish leprechauns)? What are or were some popular feats of magic? Students should include an explanation of a typical magic stunt that is or was popular in their country.

4. Math. A favorite trick of magicians who claim to be mind-readers is to guess the number that a person is thinking of. The magician is not actually reading the volunteer's mind at all, but performing a simple mathematical trick. Show the class several math tricks in which a person is manipulated into coming up with a specific number, which a magician can pretend to guess.

Activity Sheet Ideas

1. Word search or crossword puzzles of: a) types of magicians, b) magicians' terminology, or c) types of magic.

2. Word scrambles and cryptograms of: a) magic societies, b) magic words and chants, or c) names of famous magic tricks.

3. Matching activities: match a) magicians from the past or present to their stage names, b) magicians to their most famous act, or c) actors to the magical characters they played on TV or film.

Suggested Resources

Reference and Nonfiction

Ashley, Leonard R.N. *The Wonderful World of Magic and Witchcraft*. Dembner, 1986.

Baker, James W. *Illusions Illustrated: A Professional Magic Show for Young Performers*. Lerner, 1984.

Blackstone, Harry, Jr. *The Blackstone Book of Magic and Illusion*. Newmarket, 1985.

Cavendish, Richard. *Man, Myth, and Magic: The Illustrated Encyclopedia of Mythology, Religion, and the Unknown*. 21 vols. Marshall Cavendish, 1994.

Cobb, Vicki. *Magic ... Naturally! Science Entertainments and Amusements*. Harper, 1976.

Cunningham, Scott. *The Magic of Food: Legends, Lore and Spellwork*. Llewellyn, 1996.

Dolnick, Barrie. *Simple Spells for Love: Ancient Practices for Emotional Fulfillment*. Harmony, 1995.

Dunninger, Joseph. *Dunninger's Complete Encyclopedia of Magic*. Gramercy, 1987.

Frederick, Guy. *One Hundred One Best Magic tricks*. NAL, 1985.

Friedhoffer, Bob. *More Magic Tricks, Science Facts*. Watts, 1990.

Gibson, Walter Brown. *Mastering Magic: One Hundred Secrets of the Great Magicians*. Lifetime, 1995.

Hay, Henry. *The Amateur Magician's Handbook*. NAL, 1982.

Knoles, David. *Spooky Magic Tricks*. Sterling, 1994.

Lamb, Geoffrey. *Illustrated Magic Dictionary*. Elsevier/Nelson, 1979.

McGill, Ormond. *Balancing Magic and Other Tricks*. Watts, 1986.

Magical Arts. Time-Life, 1990.

N.E. Thing Enterprises and King Features Syndicate. *Best of the Sunday Comics Magic Eye*. Morrow, 1995. (Also other *Magic Eye* books.)

Niehaus, Joseph, and Sakora, Mary. *Hypnosis Unveiled*. PPI, 1994.

Nimier, Marie. *Hypnotism Made Easy*. Four Walls Eight Windows, 1996.

Ramsland, Katherine M., and Rice, Anne. *The Witches Companion: The Official Guide to Anne Rice's Lives of the Mayfair Witches*. Ballantine, 1994.

Ritchard, Dan, and Moloney, Kathleen. *Ventriloquism for the Total Dummy*. Random, 1987.

Russell, Jeffrey B. *A History of Witchcraft: Sorcerers, Heretics and Pagans*. Peter Smith, 1983.

Scarne, John. *Scarne on Card Tricks*. NAL, 1986.

Schindler, George. *Magic with Everyday Objects*. Scarborough, 1980.

Severn, Bill. *Bill Severn's Best Magic: 50 Top Tricks to Entertain and Amaze Your Friends on All Occasions*. Stackpole, 1990.

Time-Life Book editors. *Spells and Bindings*. Silver Burdett, 1985. (Also books in **Enchanted World** series.)

Townsend, Charles B. *World's Best Magic Tricks*. Sterling, 1992.

Van Rensselaer, Alexander. *Your Book of Magic*. Transatlantic, 1968.

Waters, T.A. *The Encyclopedia of Magic and Magicians*. Facts on File, 1988.

Williams, Randall. *The Rosen Photo Guide to a Career in Magic*. Rosen, 1988.

Wilson, Mark, and Gibson, Walter Brown. *Mark Wilson's Complete Course in Magic*. Courage, 1988.

Fiction

Aamodt, Donald. *Name to Conjure With*. Avon, 1989.

Avi. *Bright Shadow*. Bradbury, 1985.

Babbitt, Lucy Cullyford. *The Oval Amulet*. Farrar, 1985.

Brittain, Bill. *The Fantastic Freshman*. Harper, 1988.

Brooks, Terry. *The Elf Queen of Shannara*. Del Rey, 1992.

Charnas, Suzy McKee. *The Golden Thread*. Bantam, 1989.

Chetwin, Grace. *The Crystal Stair*. Bradbury, 1988.

Dickenson, Peter. *The Devil's Children*. Dell, 1988.

Duane, Diane. *So You Want to Be a Wizard?* Delacorte, 1983.

Furlong, Monica. *Juniper*. Knopf, 1991.

Goldstein, Lisa. *Travellers in Magic*. Tor, 1994.

Jones, Diana Wynne. *A Sudden Wild Magic*. Greenwillow, 1992.

Jordan, Robert. *Eye of the World*. Tor, 1990.

Kerr, M.E. *Fell Down*. HarperCollins, 1991.

Lackey, Mercedes. *Winds of Fate*. DAW, 1991.

Lee, Tanith. *The Black Unicorn*. Atheneum, 1991.

Le Guin, Ursula. *A Wizard of Earthsea*. Parnassus, 1968.

McGowen, Tom. *A Trial of Magic*. Lodestar, 1992.

McKinley, Robin. *The Blue Sword*. Greenwillow, 1982.

Mahy, Margaret. *The Changeover*. Macmillan, 1987.

Norton, Andre, and Lackey, Mercedes. *Elvenblood*. Tor, 1995.

Pierce, Tamora. *Wild Magic*. Atheneum, 1992.

Rice, Anne. *Taltos: Tales of the Mayfair Witches*. Knopf, 1994.

Sherman, Josepha. *Child of Faerie, Child of Earth*. Walker, 1992.

Shinn, Sharon. *The Shape-Changer's Wife*. Ace, 1995.

Tarr, Judith. *Ars Magica*. Bantam, 1989.

Watt-Evans, Lawrence. *With a Single Spell*. Ballantine, 1987.

Wolf, Joyce. *Between the Cracks*. Dial, 1992.
Wrede, Patricia C. *Searching for Dragons*. Harcourt, 1991.
Yolen, Jane. *Here There Be Witches*. Harcourt, 1995.
Zambreno, Mary Frances. *A Plague of Sorcerers*. Harcourt, 1991.
(Also other series books by these authors.)

Periodicals

The Linking Ring. International Brotherhood of Magicians.
Magic. Stan Allen and Associates.
The Magic Circular. The Magic Circle, London, England.

Feature-Length Films

Black Magic. MCA/Universal, 1992. (PG-13)
Eternally Yours. Nostalgia, 1939.
Houdini. Paramount, 1953.
Magic. Sultan Entertainment, 1978. (R)
Max Maven's Mindgames. MCA/Universal, 1984.
Wizards. CBS/Fox, 1977. (PG)

Computer Software

The Alchemist. Enteractive, 1995.
The Amazing Zoltan. PMEP.
King's Quest VII: The Princess Bride. Sierra On-Line, 1995. (Also others in series.)
Magic Carpet. Electronic Arts, 1995.
The Magic Death. Creative Multimedia Corp., 1993.
Max Magic. PMEP, 1994.
Pandemonium. Crystal Dynamics, 1996.

29

Cruising the Mall

If you like to hang out at the local mall, you're going to love what we have in store for you at the library! We've got books and activities to show you how to shop smart and get the best stuff for the best price. You can even find out how to get a job at the mall. So come into the library and stroll the aisles of books, magazines, music and videos. Our great selection and friendly service will make you feel like you're Cruising the Mall.

Display Idea

Books dealing with shopping, advice to consumers, outlet guides, and related career books can be displayed next to some flashy advertisements from stores that are located in nearby malls and plazas. Add any novels and videos that have scenes that take place in a shopping area, as well as consumer magazines.

Sponsorship for Prizes

1. Ask several shops and restaurants in a local mall or plaza to donate gift certificates and discount coupons.

2. Ask a bookstore to donate books and magazines that offer advice to consumers.

3. Ask a movie theater in a local mall to donate free passes.

4. If there is a members-only shopping warehouse in your area, ask them to donate membership passes.

Program Game

Use the floor plan of a local mall for the game board. For each point earned, the patron can fill in the name of one of the businesses and color in the space. Points can be earned for completing the activities mentioned in the General Guidelines, and for:

1. Reading a novel and completing a Fiction Book Review Report.

2. Reading a nonfiction book and completing a Nonfiction Book Review Report.

3. Reading a sales circular from a store located in a mall, comparing one item listed in it to its write-up in a consumer magazine or book, and completing a Wise Consumer Report.

4. Reading a feature article about a store, restaurant, or shopping area in a newspaper or magazine and completing a Site Report.

Program Forms

1. Fiction Book Review Report
Title:
Author:
Publisher and date:
Brief summary of plot:
I would rate this book: "A shopper's paradise," "A classy department store," "A trendy boutique," "A bargain basement," "Out of business."

2. Nonfiction Book Review Report
Title:
Author:
Publisher and date:
Brief description of information:
I would rate this book: "Great selection and excellent service," "Good assortment and friendly staff," "Doesn't carry everything, but prices are reasonable," "You really have to look, but you may find something worthwhile," "Thrift store rejects."

3. Wise Consumer Report
Store that circular is from:
Item reviewed and price advertised:
Consumer source (title and date):
How did this item rate in the consumer source?
How did its price in the circular compare to the price quoted in the consumer source?
Would you purchase this item, based on this evaluation? Why or why not?

4. Site Report
Name of store, restaurant, or shopping area:
Where it is located:
Source and date of article:
Brief summary of article:
Was the article favorable or not, and why?
Based on this article, would you do business at this place? Why or why not?

Program Activities

1. The Cinema. Show a movie that includes some scenes that were filmed in a mall, such as *The Blues Brothers.*

2. Shop Till You Drop. Collect sales circulars from several stores in local malls and plazas. Divide teens into small groups and give each group the same list of ten or more specific brand-name items to buy. Tell the groups to look through the store ads for these items. When they find an item on the list, they should write down the store that is selling it, the price, and the date of the ad. Give participants a certain amount of time to complete this scavenger hunt. When the time is up, have the teams compare answers. The winning group is the one that found the most items at the best prices.

3. Prize Drawings. Occasionally, malls have special contests and giveaways. Conduct a similar contest with young adult program participants. Collect patrons' book review forms in a large container. Each week of the program, draw out a winning slip and award the person a gift item or certificate from a local mall.

4. Smart Shoppers. Provide a stack of consumer magazines and books for this activity. Ask teens to name some items that can be bought at the local mall, such as washing machines, basketball sneakers and sunglasses. Ask them to write down which brands of these items they would most likely want to buy. Then have patrons look through the consumer information to see which brands received the best ratings. Would they change their minds about what to buy based on what they read?

5. Food Court. Malls often have several fast food restaurants and sometimes fancy eateries. Imitate a mall food court in the library. Ask teens to bring in a variety of food dishes to share. Set them up in individual booths to represent different restaurants, such as you might find at a mall.

6. Mall IQ. Find out how well teens know the local mall in this fun game show. Ask players questions that only a serious mall cruiser would know, such as "Name three shoe stores at the mall," "What are the two anchor stores?" "What is the nearest restaurant to the public rest rooms?" "Which store is running a special on in-line skates this week?" "How much does it cost to get a wash, cut, and blow dry at the mall hair salon?" etc. Start off with easy questions, and advance to the more obscure ones. Make sure to cruise the mall yourself the day before the game to be sure your answers are correct!

7. Clothing Boutiques. Arrange for one or more clothing stores from a local mall or plaza to sponsor a fashion show at the library. Teen models can show off new seasonal styles of clothing and accessories. Ask store personnel to provide descriptions of the modeled outfits.

8. The Malling of America. Some people argue that there are too many malls and it isn't necessary to build any more. Others say that mall development should be encouraged. In some municipalities, this is a very hot topic. Provide some written pro and con arguments, or ask local citizens representing both sides of the issue to come to the library for a discussion. Allow teens to offer their opinions and reasoning.

9. A Nice Place to Work. There are many employment opportunities at the mall. Teens can find jobs in restaurants, stores, cinemas, arcades and parking garages. Additional jobs include custodial services and groundskeeping. Ask businesses that hire teens to provide job descriptions and applications. High school or college graduates can find mall-related employment in retail or restaurant management, sales, security, maintenance, architecture, construction, landscaping, advertising, window-dressing, banking, publicity, and more. Have information available for patrons on various professional and non-professional mall jobs.

10. Design-a-Mall. All malls have a variety of large and small stores and restaurants. Some also have cinemas, arcades, and special events and attractions. The Clackamas Town Centre mall in Clackamas, Oregon, even has an Olympic-size skating rink and the town library! Ask teens what they would include if they could design the perfect mall. Have them name specific businesses, services and features they would like to see there. Encourage them to think creatively, making up new technology and adding whatever they like (moving sidewalks, virtual reality shopping, etc.). If possible, have teens draw a blueprint or construct a model of their ideal mall.

Curriculum Tie-Ins

1. English Literature/Composition. Have students read some restaurant reviews written by food critics. If possible, have them also read critical articles about stores. Then tell students to visit a store, restaurant, or other business in a local mall and write an article about it. Writers should describe, as specifically as possible, the decor of the business and give their opinions about the quality of the products and service. They should rate the business on a scale of * to **** and tell whether they would recommend doing business there.

2. Science. Most stores ring up sales on computerized cash registers. Study how these machines work. How can scanners pick up the price of an item from its barcode? Compare today's sophisticated technology to older cash registers. Many stores also have security alarms that will go off if an item is stolen. Discuss how these systems work.

3. History/Geography. Malls didn't always exist in America. Many countries don't have any malls. Have students research how people shop in other countries, and how early Americans acquired the items they needed. Some things to discuss: peddlers, market places, bartering. You can also compare prices of items today to how much similar items cost in the past.

4. Math. Create various math problems about shopping for items at the mall. Sample questions: a) Calculate the amount of money you would pay in credit card interest when buying an expensive item, b) Figure out if buying three regular-size packages versus one giant-size is more economical (before and after using double coupons), c) Determine the prices of clothing on sale at 20 percent, 30 percent, and 40 percent off, d) How long will it take to pay off an item that was put on layaway at various payment plans?

Activity Sheet Ideas

1. Word search or crossword puzzles of: a) things that can be bought at a mall, b) jobs people can find there, or c) design features of a mall.

2. Word scrambles and cryptograms of: a) chain stores often found in malls, b) things to do at a mall, or c) current sales promotions running at mall businesses.

3. Matching activities: match a) names of malls to the city or town and state in which they are located, b) store names to the type of merchandise they sell, or c) (if there is more than one mall nearby) stores to the mall in which they are located.

Suggested Resources

Reference and Nonfiction

Boundy, Donna. *When Money Is the Drug: The Compulsion for Credit, Cash, and Chronic Debt.* HarperSanFrancisco, 1993.

Brox, Andrea. *Brox's Ultimate Outlet Guide to New England.* Pleasant Street, 1994.

Bruner, Pat A. *How to Own and Operate a Retail Cart in a Shopping Mall.* Trump, 1995.

Burnstiner, Irving. *Run Your Own Store: From Raising the Money to Counting the Profits.* Prentice, 1989.

Buy Me, Buy Me. Pantheon, 1987.

Campbell, Sally R. *The Confident Consumer.* Goodheart-Willcox, 1988.

Chaiet, Donna. *Staying Safe While Shopping.* Rosen, 1995.

Consumer Reports editors. *Consumer Reports Buying Guide Issue.* Consumers Union, annual.

_____. *I'll Buy That!* Consumers Union, 1986.

Council on Economic Priorities. *Shopping for a Better World: A Quick and Easy Guide to Socially Responsible Supermarket Shopping.* Ballantine, 1990.

Dolber, Roslyn. *Opportunities in Retailing Careers.* VGM, 1996.

Ellis, Iris. *Fabulous Finds: The Sophisticated Shopper's Guide to Factory Outlet Centers.* Writer's Digest, 1991.

Francis, Dorothy B. *Shoplifting: The Crime Everybody Pays For*. Lodestar, 1980.

Garbarino, James. *The Future as If It Really Mattered*. Bookmakers, 1988.

Goldstein, Sue. *Secrets from the Underground Shopper: The Only Book to Tell You What Retailers Won't*. Taylor, 1986.

Green, Mark J. *The Consumer Bible: 1001 Ways to Shop Smart*. Workman, 1994.

Hamburg, Joan, et al. *Our Little Black Book of Shopping Secrets*. Joan and Gerry, 1993.

Kidd, W.A. *Cash from Coupons: Plan, Organize, and Save with Manufacturer's Coupons and Store Specials*. Practical Information Distributing, 1992.

King, Judith. *The Greatest Gift Guide Ever*. Betterway, 1993.

Kowinski, William Severini. *The Malling of America: An Inside Look at the Great Consumer Paradise*. Morrow, 1985.

Joyce, Marion. *The Frugal Shopper: Save Money on Everything with Coupons, Refunds, Rebates and Free Offers*. Putnam, 1986.

Luxenberg, Stan. *Roadside Empires: How the Chains Franchised America*. Viking, 1985.

Mandell, Lewis. *The Credit Card Industry: A History*. Twayne, 1990.

Marketing and Sales Career Directory. Career Press, 1987.

Milios, Rita. *Shopping Savvy*. Rosen, 1992.

1,001 Helpful Tips, Facts and Hints from Consumer Reports. Consumers Union, 1989.

Rathbun, Robert Davis. *Shopping Centers and Malls*. Retail Reporting Corp., 1990.

Roberts, William. *How to Save Money on Just About Anything*. Strebor, 1991.

Schmitt, Lois. *Smart Spending: A Young Consumer's Guide*. Scribner, 1989.

Singer, Arlene. *Take It Back: The Art of Returning Almost Anything*. National, 1990.

Steinberg, Margery. *Opportunities in Marketing Careers*. VGM, 1994.

Tasaday, Laurence. *Shopping for a Better Environment: A Brand Name Guide to Environmentally Responsible Shopping*. Simon & Schuster, 1991.

Walz, Michael K. *The Law and Economics: Your Rights as a Consumer*. Lerner, 1990.

Wesson, Carolyn. *Women Who Shop Too Much: Overcoming the Urge to Splurge*. St. Martin's, 1990.

Fiction

Brodmann, Aliana. *Gifts*. Simon & Schuster, 1993.

Colman, Hila. *Forgotten Girl*. Crown, 1990.

Cusick, Richie Tankersley. *The Mall*. Pocket, 1992.

Hamilton, Dorothy. *Amanda Fair*. Herald, 1981.

Haynes, Betsy. *Mall Mania*. Bantam, 1991.

Kaye, Marilyn. *Cassie*. Harcourt, 1987.

Kehret, Peg. *Cages*. Dutton, 1991.

Kenyon, Kate. *The Night the Eighth Grade Ran the Mall*. Scholastic, 1989.

Landis, J.D. *Looks Aren't Everything*. Bantam, 1990.

Lasky, Kathryn. *Prank*. Macmillan, 1984.

Mauser, Pat Rhodes. *Rip-Off*. Macmillan, 1985.

Peck, Richard. *Bel-Air Bambi and the Mall Rats*. Delacorte, 1993.

_____. *Secrets of the Shopping Mall*. Delacorte, 1979.

Pratchett, Terry. *Truckers*. Delacorte, 1990.

Robinson, Kevin. *Mall Rats*. Walker, 1992.

Tchudi, Stephen. *The Green Machine and the Frog Crusade*. Delacorte, 1987.

Periodicals

CD-ROM Shopper's Guide. DDRI, Inc.
Cheapskate Monthly. Cheapskate Monthly.
Consumer Reports. Consumers Union of the United States, Inc.
Consumers Digest. Consumers Digest, Inc.
Consumers' Research Magazine. Consumers' Research, Inc.

Feature-Length Films

Big Store. MGM, 1941.
The Blues Brothers. MCA/Universal. 1980. (R)
How to Beat the High Cost of Living. Live Home Video, 1980. (PG)
Mannequin. Critic's Choice, 1987. (PG)
Rosalie Goes Shopping. Ingram International, 1989. (PG-13)

Computer Software

Consumer Information. Quanta Press, annual.
Consumers Reference Disc. NISC, semi-annual.
Focus on the Customer. CD-I Training, 1993.
The Kids Study. Simmons Market Research.
Selling in the 90's and Changing the Game: The New Way to Sell. Compton's NewMedia.

30
Journey to the Middle Ages

Chivalry is not dead—it's waiting for you at the library, along with books about kings, empires, knights, the crusades and other stories from medieval history. Our kingdom holds a treasury of historical fiction, classical literature, nonfiction, videos and music, and our staff and pages are eager to serve. You'll find epic tales of romance and adventure, plus much more, when you Journey to the Middle Ages.

Display Idea

Set up a display of historical fiction and classical literature pertaining to the Middle Ages. Include nonfiction, such as books of medieval architecture and costumes, as well as videos set in medieval times and CDs of music from that era. Posters of artwork from the Middle Ages can adorn the display.

Sponsorship for Prizes

1. Ask a bookstore to donate historical fiction and classical literature from the Middle Ages.
2. Ask a costume rental shop to lend medieval costumes.
3. Ask a music store to donate tapes and CDs of period music.
4. Ask a video rental store to donate free rental certificates for films or video games with medieval themes.

Program Game

Copy a map of medieval Europe to use as the game board. Starting from a castle somewhere in England, draw a route through France, the Holy Roman Empire, the Byzantine Empire, and finally to Jerusalem to represent the First Crusade. Players can advance one space along the route for each point earned. Points can be earned for completing the activities mentioned in the General Guidelines, and for:
1. Reading a historical novel set in the Middle Ages and completing a Medieval Fiction Book Review Form.
2. Reading a novel not set in the Middle Ages and completing a Fiction Book Review Form.
3. Reading a nonfiction book related to some aspect of medieval history, and completing a Medieval Nonfiction Book Review Form.
4. Reading a nonfiction book and completing a Nonfiction Book Review Form.

Program Forms

1. Medieval Fiction Book Review Form
Title:
Author:
Publisher and date:
Brief summary of plot:
What was your favorite scene in the book?
Would you recommend this book to a friend? Why or why not?
2. Fiction Book Review Form
Title:
Author:
Publisher and date:
Brief summary of plot:
I would rate this book: "King," "Lord," "Squire," "Servant," "Peasant."
3. Medieval Nonfiction Book Review Form
Title:
Author:
Publisher and date:
Brief description of information:
What was the most interesting fact in the book?
Would you want to learn more about this period in history? Why or why not?
4. Nonfiction Book Review Form
Title:
Author:
Publisher and date:
Brief description of information:
I would rate this book: "An illuminated manuscript," "A scroll of some importance," "A sealed missive," "Barely legible and lacking in grace," "The scribbling of an illiterate boor."

Program Activities

1. Cinema. Screen a movie that takes place during the Middle Ages, such as *First Knight*.

2. Hark the Herald. Provide color construction paper, glue and markers for teens to use in creating a coat-of-arms banner for themselves. Have available several books on heraldry for teens to look through when planning their designs.

3. Classical Art. Use slides and art reproductions to illustrate a program on artwork from the Middle Ages. Include samples of painting, Romanesque and Gothic architecture, stained glass, sculpture, manuscript illustration, castles and cathedrals. Play Gregorian chants as background music. Photocopy pages from a medieval art coloring book for teens to color, and display completed pictures.

4. Journey. Arrange to visit a historical museum with a group of young adults to view exhibits dealing with the Middle Ages. Have a museum guide discuss subjects such as medieval clothing and armor, weaponry, art, religious articles and other topics related to what you observe.

5. Drama. Some popular plays are set in Medieval Europe. Play songs from musicals such as *Camelot*, *Man of La Mancha*, and *Pippin*. Provide scripts of historical dramas such as

The Lark or Shakespeare's *Richard II*. Teens can volunteer to read scenes from these and other period plays.

6. Medieval Quest. Host a game show in which players must answer questions about the Middle Ages. Categories can include Arthurian Legend (sample: Who was Arthur's father?), Kings and Their Kingdoms (What area did Charlemagne rule?), the Feudal System (What did a squire do?), Good Knights (Was Sir Gawain a member of Arthur's Round Table?), Robin Hood Lore (Where did Robin Hood and his men live?), and Dragon Tales (In Chinese lore, are dragons good or evil?).

7. Tournament. Chess was a popular game of strategy during the Middle Ages, as it is now. In fact, the chess pieces are named for medieval positions. Sponsor a chess tournament for teens at the library. You can invite a chess expert to explain the medieval background of the game and offer some tips on strategy.

8. Mind Your Manors. Set aside an area in which participants can build a replica of a medieval estate. Teens can work on building a castle, the surrounding town and the countryside as an ongoing craft project, using recycled items such as Styrofoam blocks, wood scraps, cardboard tubes, and other materials. Provide glue, tape, paint and brushes.

9. Middle-Aged Work. Inform teens of some careers of people who study the Middle Ages, such as artist, historian, musician and composer, writer, architect, actor, clergyman, clothes designer, museum curator, interior decorator, antiques collector, as well as political and military strategists. Provide books on these subjects for patrons to check out.

10. Medieval Feast. Assign teens various roles, such as lord or lady, squire, knight, cobbler, serf, peasant, scullery maid, princess, etc. Each person must come to the feast in costume (these can be homemade or borrowed) and act out his or her role. Minstrels, troubadours and jesters can entertain guests, and peasants can beg for food. Ask partygoers to provide food for the banquet.

Curriculum Ideas

1. English Literature/Composition. Select an epic poem, play or novel written during or about the Middle Ages. As you read it with the class, relate the events in the story to what was happening during that period in history. Then have students choose a character from the story and write a scene from the book from that person's perspective.

2. Science. The Middle Ages were marred by terrible diseases and plagues, often due to poor sanitary conditions. Discuss the causes of some of these sicknesses and the treatments used at the time. Have students compare these to today's knowledge of disease prevention and treatment.

3. History/Geography. The Middle Ages stretched over a period of time from approximately 400 A.D. through the 1500s. During this time, the geography of western Europe changed several times. Have students create a series of historical maps that reflect the various empires, kingdoms, invasions, and wars of the Middle Ages. Note which lands were claimed by which civilizations on each of the maps.

4. Math. Devise math problems for students to solve using medieval settings. For example, if a king has X much land, which he divides among his sons, which is divided among their lords and then among the lord's knights—how much land does each person own? Other problems can involve figuring out how much tax money would be owed to the king by his subjects, the number of miles traveled during a crusade, etc.

Activity Sheet Ideas

    1. Word search or crossword puzzles of: a) feudal terms, b) names of medieval kings, or c) important people who lived during the Middle Ages.

    2. Word scrambles or cryptograms of: a) lines from medieval poetry, b) wars and other events, or c) famous castles and cathedrals.

    3. Matching activities: match a) works of medieval literature to their authors, b) works of art to their artists, or c) kings to the years during which they reigned.

Suggested Resources

Reference and Nonfiction

Andronik, Catherine M. *Quest for a King: Searching for the Real King Arthur*. Macmillan, 1989.

Barron, W.R., ed. *Sir Gawain and the Green Knight*. Barnes & Noble, 1976.

Billings, Malcolm. *The Cross and the Crescent: A History of the Crusades*. Sterling, 1988.

Brooks, Polly Scholyer. *Beyond the Myth: The Story of Joan of Arc*. Harper, 1990.

Brown, R. Allen. *The Architecture of Castles: A Visual Guide*. Facts on File, 1985.

Bunson, Matthew. *The Encyclopedia of the Middle Ages*. Facts on File, 1995.

Burrow, J.A. *Medieval Writers and Their Work: Middle English Literature and Its Background*. Oxford University Press, 1982.

Caselli, Giovanni. *The Roman Empire and the Dark Ages*. Bedrick, 1985.

Corbishley, Mike. *The Middle Ages*. Facts on File, 1990.

Day, David. *The Search for King Arthur*. Facts on File, 1995.

Gies, Joseph. *The Knight in History*. Harper, 1984.

Gies, Joseph, and Gies, Frances. *Life in a Medieval Village*. Harper, 1990.

Gottfried, Robert S. *The Black Death: Natural and Human Disaster in Medieval Europe*. Free Press, 1983.

Harpur, James. *Revelations: The Medieval World*. Holt, 1995.

History of the Ancient and Medieval World. 12 vols. Marshall Cavendish, 1996.

Kaplan, Zoe Coralnik. *Eleanor of Aquitaine*. Chelsea, 1986.

Kenyon, Sherrilyn. *The Writer's Guide to Everyday Life in the Middle Ages*. Writer's Digest, 1995.

Labarge, Margaret Wade. *A Small Sound of the Trumpet: Women in the Medieval Life*. Beacon, 1988.

Macaulay, David. *Castle*. Houghton, 1977.

Malory, Thomas. *Le Morte d'Arthur*. Macmillan, 1975.

Matthew, Donald. *Atlas of Medieval Europe*. Facts on File, 1983.

Miles, Bernard. *Robin Hood: His Life and Legend*. Macmillan, 1979.

Pyle, Howard. *Merry Adventures of Robin Hood*. NAL, 1986.

Sancha, Sheila. *The Luttrell Village: Country Life in the Middle Ages*. Harper, 1983.

_____. *Walter Dragun's Town: Crafts and Trade in the Middle Ages*. Harper, 1989.

Singleman, Jeffrey L., and McLean, Will. *Daily Life in Chaucer's England*. Greenwood, 1995.

Snyder, James. *Medieval Art: Painting, Sculpture, Architecture—4th-14th Century*. Abrams, 1989.

Steinbeck, John. *The Acts of King Arthur and His Noble Knights*. Ballantine, 1986.

Time-Life Books editors. *Dragons*. Silver Burdett, 1984.

Westwood, Jennifer. *Stories of Charlemagne*. Phillips, 1976.

Yue, Charlotte, and Yue, David. *Armour*. Houghton, 1994.

Fiction

Ashley, Mike, ed. *The Pendragon Chronicles*. Bedrick, 1990.
Attanasio, A.A. *Kingdom of the Grail*. HarperCollins, 1992.
Berry, James. *Magicians of Erianne*. Harper, 1988.
Bradley, Marion Zimmer. *The Mists of Avalon*. Ballantine, 1985.
Cochran, Molly, and Murphy, Warren. *The Forever King*. Tor, 1992.
Curry, Ann. *The Book of Brendan*. Holiday, 1990.
Cushman, Karen. *Catherine, Called Birdie*. Clarion, 1994.
_____. *The Midwife's Apprentice*. Clarion, 1995.
Fleischman, Sid. *The Whipping Boy*. Greenwillow, 1986.
Follett, Ken. *Pillars of the Earth*. Morrow, 1989.
Garden, Nancy. *Dove and Sword*. Farrar, 1995.
Gray, Elizabeth Janet. *Adam of the Road*. Viking, 1942.
Holland, Cecelia. *The Lord of Vaumartin*. Houghton, 1988.
Kaufman, Pamela. *Banners of Gold*. Crown, 1986.
Konigsburg, E.L. *A Proud Taste for Scarlet and Miniver*. Atheneum, 1973.
Lawhead, Stephen R. *Arthur*. Crossway, 1989.
McKinley, Robin. *The Outlaws of Sherwood*. Greenwillow, 1988.
Peters, Ellis. *A Morbid Taste for Bones*. Fawcett, 1985.
Quick, Amanda. *Mystique*. Bantam, 1995.
Rice, Robert. *The Last Pendragon*. Walker, 1991.
Riley, Judith Merkle. *A Vision of Light*. Delacorte, 1989.
Stewart, Mary. *The Crystal Cave*. Fawcett, 1970.
Strauss, Victoria. *The Lady of Rhoddesmere*. Warne, 1982.
Sutcliffe, Rosemary. *The Road to Camlann*. Dutton, 1982.
Temple, Frances. *The Ramsay Scallop*. Orchard, 1994.
Tomlinson, Theresa. *The Forest Wife*. Orchard, 1995.
Twain, Mark. *A Connecticut Yankee in King Arthur's Court*. Bantam, 1977.
White, Steve. *Debt of Ages*. Baen, 1995.
White, T.H. *The Once and Future King*. Berkley, 1968.
Woolley, Persia. *Queen of the Summer Stars*. Simon & Schuster, 1990.

(Also sequels to these novels.)

Periodicals

Journal of Medieval History. Elsevier Science.
Medieval Folklore. Edwin Mellen Press.
Parabola. Society for the Study of Myth and Tradition.
Studies in Medieval Culture. Medieval Institute Publications.

Feature-Length Films

Camelot. Warner, 1967.
Excalibur. Warner, 1981. (R)
First Knight. Columbia Tristar, 1995. (PG-13)
Ivanhoe. MGM/UA, 1952.

The Lion in Winter. Columbia Tristar, 1968. (PG)
Robin Hood: Prince of Thieves. Warner, 1991. (PG-13)

Computer Programs

Art and Music: The Medieval Era. Zane, 1994.
Castles II: Siege and Conquest. Interplay, 1994.
Fantasy Fiefdom: Medieval England. Software Sorcery, 1993.
King Arthur's Magic Castle. Orange Cherry New Media, 1993.
Lords of the Realm. Impressions Software, 1994.
Middle Ages. Queue, 1992.

31

You Get Your Money's Worth at the Library

Everyone is interested in money, but do you have much dollar sense? Do you know the history of money, how it is made, or what types of currency are used in different countries? You can find out in the library. You can also look up job information to help you earn money, financial advice to help you invest it, and consumer news to help you spend it wisely. So hit the books for big bucks. To coin a phrase: You Get Your Money's Worth at the Library.

Display Idea

Replicas of United States dollars and currency from around the world can adorn a display of nonfiction books on the history of money, how it is made, consumer information, coin collecting, job ideas for young adults, money management, finance. Biographies of successful business people may be included. Add some videos and fiction titles with money themes, and related periodicals.

Sponsorship for Prizes

1. Ask a local bank to donate calendars or coin banks.
2. Ask a store to donate Velcro wallets or fanny packs.
3. Ask various businesses to donate "Buy 1, get 1 free" coupons.
4. Ask a magazine store to donate copies of magazines with money themes.

Program Game

Give each patron a "savings certificate." Each point earned is another deposit into the account, and extra "interest points" can be awarded if deposits are made on a regular basis. Set a goal of points needed to win the game. Points can be earned for completing the activities mentioned in the General Guidelines, and for:

1. Reading a novel and completing a Fiction Book Review Form.
2. Reading a nonfiction book on a money-related theme and completing a Money Nonfiction Book Review Form.
3. Reading a nonfiction book not related to the money theme and completing a Nonfiction Book Review Form.
4. Reading an article from a consumer magazine or financial periodical and completing a Money Article Report Form.

Program Forms

1. Fiction Book Review Form
Title:
Author:
Publisher and date:
Brief summary of plot:
I would rate this book: "Worth its weight in gold," "Meets high standards," "A good value," "No great bargain," "Not worth the paper its printed on."
2. Money Nonfiction Book Review Form
Title:
Author:
Publisher and date:
Brief description of information:
Why did you choose to read this book?
What was the most interesting or helpful part of the book and why?
3. Nonfiction Book Review Form
Title:
Author:
Publisher and date:
Brief description of information:
I would rate this book: "Blue chip stock," "In the Fortune 500," "A wise investment," "Declining interest rates," "Stock market crash."
4. Money Article Report Form
Name of article:
Source and date:
Brief summary of article:
Do you think this article offers good financial advice? Why or why not?
Who do you think would benefit most from this information, and why?

Program Activities

1. Pay Per View. Show a movie with a plot that revolves around money, such as *It Could Happen to You.*

2. Play Dough. Prepare cookie dough and chill it inside frozen juice cans so that it can easily be cut into circles. Each teen can be given a roll of dough or several pre-sliced pieces. They can decorate or imprint their cookies to represent coins of their own design. Bake the cookies and let patrons trade cookie coins with each other. Pack the coins carefully in wax paper and give to patrons to take home.

3. Take a Collection. Invite a coin collector to speak about the hobby of numismatics, including what makes a coin valuable and what some rare coins are worth. The talk may also include collecting paper money or money from other countries. Have available nonfiction books on these topics for patrons to borrow.

4. Play Money. Set up several tables in a room. On each one, place a different money game, such as "Monopoly," for teens to play. If your town allows it, you may let teens try their luck at a roulette game or a penny pitch. You can award prizes to winners, and any profits realized can be donated to the Young Adult Department.

5. **Bucks for Books.** Let teens participate in a fund-raising activity for the library, such as a car wash, book sale or bake sale. Encourage each volunteer to set a personal monetary goal (such as the price of a specific book). Or you could set a group goal and allow teens to have a say in what the money would purchase.

6. **The Price Is Better.** Teach teens some consumer smarts by conducting a game show that demonstrates the value of shopping for sales. Divide the group into teams and give them actual sales ads for local stores or mail-order catalogs. Each group should choose a different store or catalog, and ads need not be from the same week. Call out some specific brands of merchandise kids would consider buying (Sony Walkman, a particular video game, etc.). All items you ask for should appear in every team's ads. Each team will tell the group the price they found for these items, and a scorekeeper will list all prices so that patrons can make comparisons. Afterwards, let teens discuss which stores offer the best values for certain types of merchandise.

7. **Money Management Seminar.** Offer young adults some financial advice by arranging for accountants and other professionals to conduct a workshop in money management. Set up several booths for teens to learn how to balance a checkbook, fill out a financial aid application, apply for a credit card, buy and cash in a savings bond, understand the legalities of a sales agreement, complete a standard tax return, etc.

8. **Gambling Debate.** Until recently, most forms of gambling were illegal in many states. Now, several states have loosened their restrictions on gambling and gaming laws. Invite some pro- and anti-gambling advocates to argue both sides of this issue. Then allow teens to offer their views.

9. **High Finance Jobs.** Ask a banker, stockbroker, insurance agent, accountant, finance manager, investor, and other professional money managers to speak at a career day program. Have available books on the banking industry, investments, government finance jobs, real estate, wholesale and retail management, accounting and other money management occupations. Make a list of colleges that offer degrees in these areas. Also supply information on jobs for teens, how to find a job, and the job outlook for various careers.

10. **Money Music.** Many songs have been written about money throughout the years, such as "Brother Can You a Spare a Dime?," and "Tax Man." Invite teens to a dance party where these and other money-related songs are played. You can also let teens participate in a lip synch or kareoke contest.

Curriculum Tie-Ins

1. **English Literature/Composition.** There are many popular quotes about money, such as "The love of money is the root of all evil." Have students write a story or essay on a theme related to money or wealth. If the class is studying Shakespeare, read *The Merchant of Venice* and discuss the character Shylock and his role in the play.

2. **Science.** Talk about the various metals used around the world to make coins. How has the metal composition of United States coins changed over the years? How do coin-operated vending machines work, and why can't Canadian coins be used in machines in America?

3. **History/Geography.** Trace the history of money, including what people did before money was used, how and why it came into use, early forms of money, and how it has since developed. Discuss what can make the value of money rise and fall, and compare the worth of monetary units in other countries to the United States dollar. How did the Stock Market crash of 1929 affect the American and world economy?

4. Math. Teach the class how to read the stock market report from the *Wall Street Journal* or the *New York Times*. Let each student choose three companies among which they can (on paper) invest a total of $1,000. Have students follow their financial investments by keeping a daily graph for each stock they own, and calculating how much money they have gained or lost. At the end of the unit, students should determine the cash-in value of their stocks, and report on their experiences.

Activity Sheet Ideas

1. Word search or crossword puzzles of: a) terms relating to finance and investments, b) careers in those fields, or c) how money is used.
2. Word scrambles or cryptograms of: a) quotes about money, b) movies with money-related plots, or c)names of Fortune 500 companies.
3. Matching activities: match a) monetary units to the countries in which they are used, b) United States presidents to the coins or bills on which they appear, or c) currency from other countries to their worth in United States dollars.

Suggested Resources

Reference and Nonfiction

Bruce, Colin R. *Collecting World Coins: A Century of Monetary Issues*. Krause, 1994.
Cribb, Joe, et al. *The Coin Atlas*. Facts on File, 1990.
Estess, Patricia Schiff, and Barocas, Irving. *Kids, Money, and Values*. Betterway, 1994.
Folbre, Nancy. *A Field Guide to the U.S. Economy*. Pantheon, 1988.
Friedberg, Robert. *Paper Money of the United States: A Complete Illustrated Guide with Valuations*. Coin & Currency, 1989.
Getting a Raise Made Easy. VGM, 1996.
Godfrey, Joline. *No More Frogs to Kiss: 99 Ways to Give Economic Power to Girls*. Harper-Business, 1995.
Kingstone, Brett. *The Student Entrepreneur's Guide: How to Start and Run Your Own Business*. McGraw, 1989.
Krause, Barry. *Collecting Coins for Pleasure and Profit: A Comprehensive Guide and Handbook for Collectors and Investors*. Betterway, 1991.
Kyte, Kathy S. *The Kids' Complete Guide to Money*. Knopf, 1984.
Lee, Richard S., and Lee, Mary Price. *Coping with Money*. Rosen, 1988.
Lee, Susan. *Susan Lee's ABZs of Money and Finance*. Watts, 1986.
Little, Jeffrey B. *Reading the Financial Pages*. Chelsea, 1988.
Maybury, Richard J. *Whatever Happened to Penny Candy? For Students, Business People and Investors*. Bluestocking, 1989.
Moore, Carl H., and Russell, Alvin E. *Money: Its Origin, Development and Modern Use*. McFarland, 1987.
O'Neill, Terry, ed. *Opposing Viewpoints: Economics in America*. Greenhaven, 1986.
Paradis, Adrian A. *Opportunities in Banking Careers*. VGM, 1993.
_____. *Opportunities in Part-Time and Summer Jobs*. VGM, 1987.
Ring, Trudy. *Careers in Finance*. VGM, 1993.
Roberts, William. *How to Save Money on Just About Everything*. Strebor, 1991.

Schmitt, Lois. *Smart Spending: A Young Consumer's Guide*. Scribner, 1989.

Skousen, Mark. *Scrooge Investing: The Bargain Hunter's Guide to Discounts, Free Services, Special Privileges, and 99 Other Money-Saving Tips*. Dearborn Financial, 1992.

Smith, Allan. *Teenage Moneymaking Guide*. Success, 1984.

Sobel, Robert, and Sicilia, David B. *The Entrepreneurs: An American Adventure*. Houghton, 1986.

Stine, Jane, and Stine, Bob. *Everything You Need to Survive: Money Problems*. Random, 1983.

Sumichrast, Michael. *Opportunities in Financial Careers*. VGM, 1991.

Taylor, Gary. *The Federal Reserve System*. Chelsea, 1989.

Wallace, G. David. *Money Basics*. Prentice, 1984.

Wesson, Carolyn. *Women Who Shop Too Much: Overcoming the Urge to Splurge*. St. Martin's, 1990.

Wood, Heather. *101 Marvelous Money-Making Ideas for Kids*. Tor, 1995.

Fiction

Bennett, Jay. *The Skeleton Man*. Watts, 1986.

Brancato, Robin F. *Uneasy Money*. Knopf, 1986.

Brooks, Terry. *Magic Kingdom for Sale—Sold!* Ballantine, 1986.

Dygard, Thomas. *Wilderness Peril*. Morrow, 1985.

Forbes, Kathryn. *Mama's Bank Account*. Harcourt, 1968.

Hailey, Arthur. *The Moneychangers*. Dell, 1986.

Haseley, Dennis. *The Counterfeiter*. Macmillan, 1987.

Hawks, Robert. *The Richest Kid in the World*. Avon, 1992.

Karr, Kathleen. *Oh Those Harper Girls! Or Young and Dangerous*. Farrar, 1992.

Klass, Sheila Solomon. *Credit-Card Carole*. Macmillan, 1983.

Korman, Gordon. *No Coins, Please*. Scholastic, 1989.

Levoy, Myron. *Kelly 'n' Me*. HarperCollins, 1992.

McCrumb, Sharyn. *Missing Susan*. Ballantine, 1991.

Mazer, Harry, and Mazer, Norma Fox. *The Solid Gold Kid*. Dell, 1978.

Miklowitz, Gloria D. *Suddenly Super Rich*. Bantam, 1989.

Moore, Yvette. *Freedom Songs*. Orchard, 1991.

Mooser, Stephen. *The Hitchhiking Vampire*. Delacorte, 1989.

Muller, Marcia. *Trophies and Dead Things*. Mysterious, 1990.

Myers, Walter Dean. *The Mouse Rap*. Harper, 1990.

Pease, William D. *Playing the Dozens*. NAL, 1990.

Pfeffer, Susan Beth. *Claire at Sixteen*. Bantam, 1989.

Pullman, Philip. *The Shadow in the North*. Knopf, 1988.

Raskin, Ellen. *The Westing Game*. Avon, 1984.

Roos, Stephen. *My Favorite Ghost*. Macmillan, 1988.

Snyder, Anne, and Pelletier, Louis. *The Best That Money Can Buy*. Signet, 1983.

Taylor, Theodore. *The Hostage*. Delacorte, 1988.

Tilly, Nancy. *Golden Girl*. Farrar, 1985.

Watson, Harvey. *Bob War and Poke*. Houghton, 1991.

Wersba, Barbara. *The Farewell Kid*. Harper, 1990.

Westlake, Donald E. *Drowned Hopes*. Mysterious, 1990.

Periodicals

Cheapskate Monthly. Cheapskate Monthly.
Coins: The Complete Magazine for Coin Collectors. Krause Publications, Inc.
Dollars and Sense. Economic Affairs Bureau.
The Economist. Economist Newspaper, Ltd.
Money. Time, Inc.

Feature-Length Films

The Freshman. Columbia Tristar, 1990. (PG)
How to Marry a Millionaire. CBS/Fox, 1953.
It Could Happen to You. Columbia Tristar, 1994. (PG)
Mr. Deeds Goes to Town. Columbia Tristar, 1936.
Slither. MGM/UA, 1973. (PG)
Who's Minding the Mint? Goodtimes/Kids Klassics, 1967.

Computer Software

Consumer Information. Quanta Press, annual.
Corporate Affiliations Plus. Reed Reference Publishing, quarterly.
Gazillionaire. Spectrum Holobyte, 1995.
Government Giveaways for Entrepreneurs. InfoBusiness, 1993.
Money, Money, Money! Aris Entertainment, 1992.
Quicken Financial Suite. Intuit, 1996.

32
Read a Good Movie Today

Have you read a good movie lately? Lots of great movies started out as books: *Jaws*, *Gone with the Wind*, *Forrest Gump*, *Jurassic Park* and many, many more. Sometimes, novelizations are written after the movie is made, such as *Love Story* and the *Star Wars* books. Have you ever seen a movie that you liked a lot but wanted to know more about the characters or sub-plots? Read the book that it's based on to catch up on those extra details. You'll discover that it's fun to Read a Good Movie Today.

Display Idea

Set up a display of books that have been made into movies. Be sure to include books on which current box office hits were based. The display can also include nonfiction titles about the film industry, Hollywood, famous screen actors and directors, movie-making equipment, as well as related periodicals, and novels with film plots. Ask a local movie theater or video rental store to donate movie posters or other publicity materials to add to the display.

Sponsorship for Prizes

1. Ask a local movie theater to donate free movie passes or posters.
2. Ask a video rental store to donate free movie rental certificates or posters.
3. Ask a bookstore to donate paperback copies of books that were made into movies.
4. Ask a record or music store to donate merchandise certificates for CDs or cassettes of movie soundtracks.

Program Game

Make a game board that resembles a winding loop of film footage. Patrons can advance one frame for each point they earn until the entire loop has been completed. Points can be earned for completing the activities mentioned in the General Guidelines, and for:
1. Reading a novel and completing a Fiction Book Review Form.
2. Reading a nonfiction book and completing a Nonfiction Book Review Form.
3. Watching a movie and completing a Movie Review Form.
4. Watching a movie, reading the book on which it is based, and completing a Book vs. Movie Comparison Form.

Opinion Forms

1. Fiction Book Review Form
Title:
Author:
Publisher and Date:
Brief summary of plot:
What is your opinion of this book?
Would you recommend this book to a friend? Why or why not?

2. Nonfiction Book Review Form
Title:
Author:
Publisher and date:
Brief description of information:
I would rate this book: "Two thumbs up—a blockbuster book!," "A surprise hit!," "Rated PG for Pretty Good," "For selected audiences only," or "A bomb."

3. Movie Review Form
Name of movie or feature-length video:
Year it was released:
Director:
Brief description of plot:
I would rate this movie: "Super—I'd see it again," "A great date movie," "Good, but not an Oscar contender," "The previews were better than the film," or "Stinks—I left when I ran out of popcorn."

4. Book vs. Movie Comparison Form
Title of Book:
Author:
Publisher and date:
Name of movie:
Year it was released:
Director:
Does the movie version differ from the book? If so, how?
Which version do you prefer, and why?

Program Activities

1. Behind-the-Scenes. Show some videos of how popular movies, such as *Raiders of the Lost Ark*, were made. Tell teens to look for special effects, make-up application, stunts, addition of soundtrack, and other elements of the filmmaking process. Or show a movie about making a movie, such as *Singin' in the Rain*.

2. And the Winners Are... Make a list of movies that have been released in the past year. Have teens come up with categories, such as Best Action Movie, Best Comedy or Musical, Best Date Movie, Most Intense Drama, Most Gorgeous Actor/Actress, Best Hairstyles, Most Danceable Movie Soundtrack, Best Song, Best Special Effects, Wildest Costumes, Most Unusual Make-up, etc. Then let them vote for their favorites. Tabulate the results and post them in the library.

3. Movie Pro. If possible, invite a local resident who has worked in the film industry to talk to teens. Even if you can't catch a famous Hollywood star, you may be able to find someone who has worked behind the scenes of a movie or is knowledgeable about some aspect of film production.

4. Documentary Workshop. Show some short or full-length documentaries. Discuss how a documentary differs from a movie with a fictitious plot. If video equipment is available, have participants film their own simple documentary. For example, select one person to be the interviewer, and have him or her ask the other teens for their opinions on an issue that concerns them. Teens can also assume various production tasks, such as operating the video camera, setting up props, adjusting lighting and assisting in editing. The documentary can be presented at a film showing held later on.

5. Make-Up Call. Invite a beautician or make-up artist to do a program on movie make-up. Teens can have hands-on practice applying special-effects make-up, or volunteer to be made up as a movie monster, an elderly person, etc.

6. Film Buffs Trivia. Invite teens to participate in a game show program about movies. Suggested categories: Name That Film Tune, Oscar Winners, Great Directors, Classic Lines, Movie Sequels, Box Office Bombs.

7. The Reel Things. Ask a film expert to bring in a 35mm camera, a reel-to-reel movie projector, editing and splicing machines, and other movie-making equipment, and to demonstrate how they are used.

8. Film Festival. Many young adults have access to video equipment. Invite teens to make their own movies and present them at a film festival held in the library. Viewers can vote for best comedy, documentary, drama, direction, special effects, etc. (Note: It may be wise to have participants submit their films in advance for the library staff to preview.)

9. Reel Life. Hold a career day that highlights occupations associated with the film industry. Patrons can find out what it takes to become a director, actor, sound or lighting technician, costume designer, camera operator, film editor, stunt person, special effects coordinator, screenwriter, etc. Invite people who are knowledgeable about these occupations to speak. Have available several nonfiction books about these careers for patrons to borrow. Make a list of colleges that offer related majors.

10. Cinematic Dance. Encourage teens to come to a party dressed as popular movie characters. They can dance to music from movie soundtracks and try to guess each other's identities. Decorate the room with movie posters that can be given away as door prizes.

Curriculum Tie-Ins

1. English Literature/Composition. Many movies were made from classical literature. Read one or more of these books or plays. Ask students to compare the literature to the movie version. What was added, changed, or deleted? Or, show a movie to the class that they are not likely to have seen, but do not show the ending. Let students write their own endings. How do these compare with the film's conclusion?

2. Science. Study the technology of the motion picture process. How is film made? How is sound added? What are some types of special effects and how are they achieved? What are some technological possibilities for the future of filmmaking?

3. History/Geography. Have students trace the history of the motion picture industry. Questions to consider: Who invented the first projectors and how did they work? How were movies presented in the theaters? When were "talkies" and other new cinematic techniques introduced? List some famous directors and and classic foreign films, and locate their countries of origin on a map of the world.

4. Math. Motion picture film comes in different sizes (8mm, etc.) Have students look up how many frames flash by per minute for each type of film, and how much film is contained on an average reel. Then have them work out problems of how many frames and reels would be needed for films of specific lengths of time, and for different sizes of film.

Activity Sheet Ideas

1. Word search or crossword puzzles of: a) terms relating to the film industry, b) moviemaking equipment, or c) related occupations.

2. Word scrambles or cryptograms of: a) titles of books that have been made into movies, b) names of movie actors or directors, or c) famous quotes from movies.

3. Matching Activities: match a) actors to the movie roles they played, b) foreign films to their American versions, or c) remakes to their original films.

Suggested Resources

Reference and Nonfiction

Armstrong, Richard B., and Armstrong, Mary Willems. *The Movie List Book*. Betterway, 1994.

Betrock, Alan. *The I Was a Teenage Juvenile Delinquent Rock 'n' Roll Horror Beach Party Movie Book*. St. Martin's, 1986.

Bloom, Ken. *Hollywood Song: The Complete Film Musical Companion*. 3 vols. Facts on File, 1995.

Bohn, Thomas W., and Stromgren, Richard L. *Light and Shadows: A History of Motion Pictures*. Mayfield, 1987.

Bone, Jan. *Opportunities in Film Careers*. VGM, 1990.

Brestoff, Richard. *The Camera Smart Actor*. Smith and Kraus, 1994.

Brouwer, Alexandra, and Wright, Thomas Lee. *Working in Hollywood*. Crown, 1990.

Bushnell, Brooks. *Directors and Their Films: A Comprehensive Reference, 1895–1990*. McFarland, 1993.

Chell, David. *Moviemakers at Work: Interviews*. Microsoft, 1987.

Cohen, Daniel. *Masters of Horror*. Houghton, 1984.

Eastman, John. *Retakes: Behind the Scenes of 500 Classic Movies*. Ballantine, 1989.

Everson, William K. *American Silent Film*. Oxford University Press, 1978.

Finler, Joel W. *The Hollywood Story*. Crown, 1988.

Fraser, George MacDonald. *The Hollywood History of the World*. Morrow, 1988.

Greenspon, Jaq. *Careers for Film Buffs and Other Hollywood Types*. VGM, 1993.

Helfer, Ralph. *The Beauty of the Beasts: Tales of Hollywood's Wild Animal Stars*. Tarcher, 1990.

Herbert, Katherine Atwell. *Writing Scripts Hollywood Will Love: An Insider's Guide to Film and Television Scripts That Sell*. Allworth, 1994.

Hunter, Nigel. *The Movies*. Raintree, 1990.

Maltin, Leonard. *Leonard Maltin's Movie and Video Guide*. Signet, annual.

Medved, Harry, and Medved, Michael. *The Golden Turkey Awards*. Putnam, 1980. (Also *Son of the Golden Turkey Awards: More of Hollywood's Worst Achievements*.)

Moss, Joyce, and Wilson, George, eds. *From Page to Screen: Children's and Young Adult Books on Film and Video*. Gale, 1992.

Osborne, Robert. *60 Years of the Oscar: The Official History of the Academy Awards.* Abbeville, 1989.

Peary, Danny. *Cult Movies 3: 50 More of the Classics, the Sleepers, the Weird, and the Wonderful.* Simon & Schuster, 1988. (Also earlier editions.)

Quinlan, David. *Wicked Women of the Screen.* St. Martin's, 1988.

Rimmer, Ian. *Movies F/X.* Rourke, 1988.

Rosenblum, Joseph, and Karen, Robert. *When the Shooting Stops ... the Cutting Begins: A Film Editor's Story.* DaCapo, 1986.

Searles, Baird. *Films of Science Fiction and Fantasy.* Abrams, 1988.

Staskowski, Andrea. *Movie Musicals.* Lerner, 1992.

Taub, Eric. *Gaffers, Grips and Best Boys: An Inside Look at Who Does What in the Making of a Motion Picture.* St. Martin's, 1987.

Time-Life Books editors. *Life Goes to the Movies.* Crown, 1987.

VideoHound's Golden Movie Retriever. Visible Ink, annual.

Fiction About Movies

Daniel, Kate. *Teen Idol.* HarperPaperbacks, 1992.

Green, Constance C. *Star Shine.* Viking, 1985.

Greene, Yvonne. *Headliners.* Bantam, 1986.

Kendall, Jane. *Miranda and the Movies.* Crown, 1989.

Kirshenbaum, Binnie. *Short Subject.* Watts, 1989.

Korman, Gordon. *Macdonald Hall Goes to Hollywood.* Scholastic, 1991.

Murphy, Barbara Beasley, and Wolkoff, Judie. *Ace Hits the Big Time.* Dell, 1982.

Robinson, Nancy K. *The Phantom Film Crew.* Scholastic, 1986.

Shaw, Diana. *Gone Hollywood: A Carter Colborn Mystery.* Little, 1988.

Books That Were Made Into Movies

Alcott, Louisa May. *Little Women.* Putnam, 1947.

Armstrong, William H. *Sounder.* Harper, 1969.

Austen, Jane. *Emma.* Bantam, 1984.

Benchley, Peter. *Jaws.* Bantam, 1991.

Blake, Michael. *Dances with Wolves.* Fawcett, 1988.

Boulle, Pierre. *Planet of the Apes.* Vanguard, 1963.

Chiel, Debora. *A Walk in the Clouds.* NAL, 1995.

Christie, Agatha. *Murder on the Orient Express.* Putnam, 1985.

Clancy, Tom. *Patriot Games.* Putnam, 1987.

Crichton, Michael. *Jurassic Park.* Knopf, 1990.

Clarke, Arthur C. *2001: A Space Odyssey.* NAL, 1968.

Cook, Robin. *Outbreak.* Berkley, 1988.

Fine, Anne. *Alias Madame Doubtfire.* Little, 1988.

Fisher, Carrie. *Postcards from the Edge.* Pocket, 1990.

Fleischer, Leonore. *Rain Man.* NAL, 1989.

Fossey, Dian. *Gorillas in the Mist.* Houghton, 1983.

Goldman, William, reteller. *The Princess Bride: S. Morgenstern's Classic Tale of True Love and High Adventure.* Ballantine, 1982.

Groom, Winston. *Forrest Gump*. Pocket, 1994.
Heller, Joseph. *Catch-22*. Dell, 1961.
Herbert, Frank. *Dune*. Putnam, 1984.
Hinton, S.E. *Tex*. Delacorte, 1979.
King, Stephen. *The Shining*. Doubleday, 1977.
Kinsella, W.P. *Shoeless Joe*. Ballantine, 1995.
Lucas, George. *Star Wars: From the Adventures of Luke Skywalker*. Ballantine, 1977.
Maclean, Norman. *A River Runs Through It and Other Stories*. University of Chicago Press, 1979.
Martin, Valerie. *Mary Reilly*. Doubleday, 1990.
Mitchell, Margaret. *Gone with the Wind*. Macmillan, 1936.
Rice, Anne. *Interview with a Vampire*. Ballantine, 1986.
Segal, Erich. *Love Story*. Bantam, 1988.
Tyler, Anne. *The Accidental Tourist*. Random, 1986.
Waller, Robert J. *The Bridges of Madison County*. Warner, 1992.
Wharton, Edith. *The Age of Innocence*. Macmillan, 1920.

Periodicals

American Film. American Film Institute.
Entertainment Weekly. Entertainment Weekly, Inc.
Films in Review. National Board of Review of Motion Pictures, Inc.
Movie Club Magazine. Gateway Entertainment, Inc.
Movie Weekly. EWA Publications.
Premiere. K-III Magazines.

Feature-Length Films

From "Star Wars" to "Jedi": The Making of a Saga. CBS/Fox, 1983.
Great Movie Stunts and the Making of Raiders of the Lost Ark. Paramount, 1981.
Hollywood Outtakes and Rare Footage. Columbia Tristar, 1983.
The Purple Rose of Cairo. Live Home Video, 1985. (PG)
Silent Movie. CBS/Fox, 1976. (PG)
Singin' in the Rain. MGM/UA, 1952.
The Stunt Man. CBS/Fox, 1980. (R)

Computer Software

Gametek Cinema: "Metropolis." Gametek, 1994.
Hollywood. Theatrix, 1995.
Hollywood Encyclopedia Volume 2. ScanRom Publications, 1994. (Also Volume 1.)
Microsoft Cinema. Microsoft, annual.
MovieSelect. Paramount Digital Entertainment, 1993.
Oscar Story CD-ROM. MGE Communications, 1994.

33

Multicultural America

The United States of America is a land of many peoples. Our residents include representatives of a wide variety of nationalities, races, religions and ethnic groups. In the library, you can find novels and nonfiction books that reflect our country's rich diversity, as well as the traditional music of many lands. Learn more about our varied heritage as you celebrate Multicultural America.

Display Idea

Young adult novels, short story collections, and videos with multicultural themes should be featured. Add nonfiction books on traditional music, art, dance, foods, holidays, festivals and clothing, as well as issues of concern, such as immigration and the problems of assimilating into America's society. Props such as traditional holiday decorations can be added to the display.

Sponsorship for Prizes

1. Ask a bookstore to donate young adult novels with multicultural themes.

2. Ask a video rental store to donate free rental certificates for videos with multicultural themes.

3. Ask restaurants that specialize in ethnic foods to donate certificates for free meals.

4. If there is a local museum, exhibit, dance or theater troupe that represents an ethnic or cultural group, ask them to donate free passes.

Program Game

Many people from different nationalities arrived in the United States as immigrants through Ellis Island. Draw a map of the east coast of North America, the Atlantic Ocean, and the west coasts of Europe and Africa to serve as the game board. Measure off spaces for one or more routes from European and African cities to Ellis Island. Patrons can begin at the foreign point of their choice and advance one space toward the United States for each point earned. Points can be earned for completing the activities mentioned in the General Guidelines, and for:

1. Reading a multicultural novel and completing a Multicultural Fiction Book Review Form.

2. Reading a novel not related to the multicultural theme and completing a Fiction Book Review Form.

3. Reading a nonfiction book related to the theme and completing a Multicultural Nonfiction Book Review Form.

4. Reading a nonfiction book not related to the theme and completing a Nonfiction Book Review Form.

Program Forms

1. Multicultural Fiction Book Review Form
Title:
Author:
Publisher and date:
Brief summary of plot:
What was the cultural background of the main character(s)?
Was the character's culture an issue in the plot? If so, how?
2. Fiction Book Review Form
Title:
Author:
Publisher and date:
Brief summary of plot:
I would rate this book: "A wonderful tradition," "A meaningful ritual," "A nice custom," "A nearly-forgotten practice," "A cultural loss."
3. Multicultural Nonfiction Book Review Form
Title:
Author:
Publisher and date:
Brief description of information:
Tell one interesting fact from the book:
Why did this interest you?
4. Nonfiction Book Review Form
Title:
Author:
Publisher and date:
Brief description of information:
I would rate this book: "Working together in peace and harmony," "Accepting of cultural differences," "Peaceful coexistence," "Culture clash," "Riots."

Program Activities

1. Cultured Film. Teens can view a film about one or more ethnic groups in the United States, such as *The Joy Luck Club.*

2. What's in a Name. Provide books on heraldry and the meanings of first and last names for teens to consult, as well as construction paper, glue, scissors and markers. Teens can use these materials to create a banner or coat-of-arms that they feel represents their cultural heritage or their image of themselves.

3. Story Time. Invite a storyteller to relate folktales from many cultures to a group of teens. Provide several collections of multicultural folklore and supernatural tales for patrons to check out after the program.

4. **Holidays.** Take a look at how holidays are celebrated by different cultures. Provide books and articles on holidays that are specific to a particular culture, ethnic group, or religion, such as the Day of the Dead or Purim. Also have information available on how various cultures celebrate common holidays, such as Christmas or the New Year. Teens can choose a holiday tradition that interests them to tell the group about. You can also present a film or slide show of celebrations and festivals of various cultures.

5. **Foods.** Ask teens to contribute traditional foods that represent their own cultural heritage to a multicultural buffet. They can also bring in the recipes for these dishes. Recipes can be compiled into a cookbook to give to patrons.

6. **Culture Clues.** Teams of young adults can compete in a game show program that focuses on the traditions of various cultural groups. Categories may include Traditional Clothing (identify which cultures wear certain clothing items), Symbolic Objects (what is this item and who uses it), Famous Americans (their cultural backgrounds), Folk Songs and Traditional Music (sound clues), Language Enhancements (words from other countries that have become part of our language), or Works of Art (art object is representative of which culture).

7. **Exhibit.** Ask teens to bring in items from home that symbolize their cultural heritage to be exhibited in a library display representing multicultural America. Supplement these items with pictures from library resource materials and captions written by teen contributors.

8. **Culture Clash.** Although most Americans believe that diversity is good, it is still a challenge for people of different nationalities, religions, and ethnic groups to live together peacefully. This culture clash has spawned many debates. Choose one issue, such as "Should English be made the official language of the Unites States?" or "Should states refuse health care and schooling to illegal aliens?" Teens can read arguments for both sides of the issue, and then join in a discussion or debate on the topic.

9. **Such Talent!** Many immigrants brought a knowledge about their trades to the United States. Present a program about people who moved to this country and the talents they brought with them. For example, you could mention German scientist Werner Von Braun or Ukrainian ice skater Oksana Baiul. Provide biographies of famous immigrants for patrons to read.

10. **Let's Dance.** Host a multicultural dance party at the library. Invite guests who can teach teens traditional dances from different cultures. Guests should provide recordings of the music they need for their dances.

Curriculum Tie-Ins

1. **English Literature/Composition.** Provide a list of multicultural novels and let each student choose a different one to read. Have students note information about the main character's cultural heritage, family, customs and traditions, problems assimilating into American society and what the character does to solve these problems, etc. Then ask students to choose a secondary character and write that character's opinion of the main character.

2. **Science.** Use this opportunity to acknowledge the accomplishments of scientists and inventors who either immigrated to the United States, or were born in the United States but are strongly identified with a certain cultural group. Students can research information on one of these people to present in a written or oral report.

3. **History/Geography.** Choose several cultural, ethnic, or racial groups that have large populations living in the United States. Have students find out where large concentrations

of these groups live, and draw areas on a map of the United States to reflect these patterns. When did large numbers of people from these nations immigrate to the U.S. and why?

4. Math. Look up population statistics to find out the percentages of various ethnic groups and nationalities in your town or city, county and state. Students can draw up charts or graphs to compare these numbers to each other and to the cultural breakdown of the entire United States population.

Activity Sheet Ideas

1. Word search and crossword puzzles of: a) traditional foods, b) holidays, celebrations and festivals, or c) American words derived from the languages of other nations.

2. Word scrambles or cryptograms of: a) traditional sayings, toasts or curses, b) translations of verses from multicultural songs, or c) historical events that resulted in a great influx of immigrants to the United States.

3. Matching activities: match a) multicultural young adult novels to their authors, b) traditional celebrations to their calendar dates, or c) traditional holiday foods to their holidays.

Suggested Resources

Reference and Nonfiction

Albyn, Carole Lisa, and Webb, Lois Sinaiko. *The Multicultural Cookbook for Students.* Oryx, 1993.
Alicea, Gil C., and DeSena, Carmine. *The Air Down Here: True Tales from a South Bronx Boyhood.* Chronicle, 1995.
Brownstone, David M. *The Irish-American Heritage.* Facts on File, 1989. (Also others in series.)
Chan, Sucheng. *Asian Americans: An Interpretive History.* Twayne, 1990.
Costabel, James M. *The Pennsylvania Dutch: Craftsmen and Farmers.* Macmillan, 1986.
Daniels, Roger. *Coming to America: A History of Immigration and Ethnicity in American Life.* Harper, 1990.
Day, Frances Ann. *Multicultural Voices in Contemporary Literature.* Heineman, 1994.
di Franco, J. Philip. *The Italian Americans.* Chelsea, 1987. (Also others in series.)
Dolan, Edward F., Jr. *Anti-Semitism.* Watts, 1985.
Encyclopedia of Multiculturalism. 6 vols. Marshall Cavendish, 1994.
Footsteps to America series. New Discovery.
Galens, Judy, et al., eds. *Gale Encyclopedia of Multicultural America.* 2 vols. Gale, 1995.
Gay, Kathlyn. *Bigotry.* Enslow, 1989.
Helbig, Elizabeth, and Perkins, Agnes Regan. *This Land Is Our Land: A Guide to Multicultural Literature for Children and Young Adults.* Greenwood, 1994.
Hoobler, Dorothy, and Hoobler, Thomas. *The Jewish American Family Album.* Oxford University Press, 1995. (Also others in series.)
Krull, Kathleen. *City Within a City: How Kids Live in New York's China Town.* Lodestar, 1994. (Also *The Other Side: How Kids Live in a California Latino Neighborhood.*)
Langley, Lester D. *MexAmerica: Two Countries, One Future.* Crown, 1988.
Larsen, Ronald J. *The Puerto Rican Americans.* Lerner, 1989.
Leone, Bruno, ed. *Opposing Viewpoints: Racism.* Greenhaven, 1986.
McKissack, Patricia, and McKissack, Fredrick. *Taking a Stand Against Racism and Racial Discrimination.* Watts, 1990.

Mazer, Anne. *Going Where I'm Coming from: Memoirs of American Youth*. Persea, 1995.

Meltzer, Milton, ed. *The Black Americans: A History in Their Own Words*. Harper, 1984. (Also other books by this author.)

Miller-Lachmann, Lyn. *Our Family, Our Friends, Our World: An Annotated Guide to Significant Multicultural Books for Children and Teenagers*. Bowker, 1992.

Morrison, Joan, and Zabusky, Charlotte. *American Mosaic: The Immigrant Experience in the Words of Those Who Lived It*. Dutton, 1985.

Multicultural Biography series. Mitchell Lane.

Nash, Renea D. *Everything You Need to Know About Being a Biracial/Biethnic Teen*. Rosen, 1995.

Reimers, David M. *The Immigrant Experience*. Chelsea, 1989.

Rochman, Hazel. *Against Borders: Promoting Books for a Multicultural World*. ALA, 1993.

Slaight, Craig, and Sharrar, Jack, eds. *Multicultural Scenes for Young Actors*. Smith and Kraus, 1995.

Stedman, Raymond William. *Shadows of the Indian: Stereotypes in American Culture*. University of Oklahoma Press, 1982.

White, Robert H. *Tribal Assets: The Rebirth of Native America*. Holt, 1990.

Winters, Paul, ed. *Opposing Viewpoints: Race Relations*. Greenhaven, 1996.

Wright, David. *A Multicultural Portrait of Life in the Cities*. Marshall Cavendish, 1993.

Fiction

Bethancourt, T. Ernesto. *The Me Inside of Me*. Lerner, 1985.

Blair, Cynthia. *Crazy in Love*. Ballantine, 1988.

Bosse, Malcolm J. *Ganesh*. Harper, 1981.

Bryson, Jamie S. *The War Canoe*. Alaska Northwest, 1990.

Cannon, A.E. *The Shadow Brothers*. Delacorte, 1990.

Chin, Frank. *Donald Duk*. Coffee House, 1991.

Cisneros, Sandra. *Woman Hollering Creek and Other Stories*. Random, 1991.

Crew, Linda. *Children of the River*. Delacorte, 1989.

Dubosarsky, Ursula. *High Hopes*. Viking, 1990.

Hamilton, Virginia. *The People Could Fly: American Black Folk Tales*. Knopf, 1985.

Houston, James. *Drifting Snow: An Arctic Search*. McElderry, 1992.

Irwin, Hadley. *Kim/Kimi*. Macmillan, 1987.

Jordan, Mildred. *Proud to Be Amish*. Crown, 1968.

Lee, Gus. *China Boy*. Dutton, 1991.

Lee, Marie G. *Finding My Voice*. Houghton, 1992.

Lo, Steven C. *The Incorporation of Eric Chung*. Algonquin, 1989.

Meyer, Carolyn. *Denny's Tapes*. Macmillan, 1987.

Mohr, Nicholasa. *Felita*. Dial, 1979.

Nixon, Joan Lowery. *Land of Hope*. Bantam, 1992.

Pitts, Paul. *Racing the Sun*. Avon, 1988.

Sebestyen, Ouida. *Words by Heart*. Little, 1979.

Singer, Marilyn. *Several Kinds of Silence*. Harper, 1988.

Soto, Gary. *Baseball in April: And Other Stories*. Harcourt, 1990.

_____. *Taking Sides*. Harcourt, 1991.

Thomas, Joyce Carol. *A Gathering of Flowers: Stories About Being Young in America*. Harper, 1990.

Uchida, Yoshiko. *The Happiest Ending*. Macmillan, 1985.

Weissenberg, Fran. *The Streets Are Paved with Gold*. Harbinger, 1990.

Woodson, Jacqueline. *Maizon at Blue Hill*. Delacorte, 1992.

Yee, Paul. *Tales from the Gold Mountain: Stories of the Chinese in the New World*. Macmillan, 1990.

Yep, Laurence. *Thief of Hearts*. HarperCollins, 1995.

Periodicals

Asian Week: An English Language Journal for the Asian American Community. Pan Asian Venture Capital Corp.

Daybreak. Oren Lyons.

Ebony. Johnson Publishing Co.

Faces: The Magazine About People. Cobblestone Publishing.

Heritage. Heritage News Service.

Hispanic. Hispanic Publishing Corp.

Interrace: The Source for Interracial Living. Interrace Magazine.

Feature-Length Films

Dances with Wolves. Orion, 1990. (PG-13)

The Joy Luck Club. Hollywood Pictures, 1994. (R)

Popi. Wood Knapp, 1969 (PG)

A Raisin in the Sun. Columbia Tristar, 1961. (PG-13)

School Ties. Paramount, 1992. (PG-13)

Witness. Paramount, 1985. (R)

Computer Software

The African American Experience. Quanta, 1992.

The American Indian: A Multimedia Encyclopedia. Facts on File, 1993.

Discovering Multicultural America. Gale Research, annual.

The History of Music: Music and Culture. Zane, 1994.

One Tribe. Virgin Sound and Vision, 1994.

Smithsonian's America. Creative Multimedia Corp., 1994.

34

Whole Lotta Music Goin' On!

What kind of music do you like—rap, rock, jazz, classical, country, R&B or something else? Whatever your interest, you can find out more about it at the library. From music history to how instruments are made to lyrics of Broadway tunes to your favorite rock 'n' roll magazines, it's all here. Why not check out a biography of your favorite musician to read when you listen to a cassette or CD by that artist? Listen up—there's a Whole Lotta Music Goin' On at the library!

Display Idea

Set up a display of books about the music industry, musical instruments, types of music, musical plays and films, musicians, composing and songwriting, music videos and other related subjects. Add popular music magazines, posters of rock stars, replicas of musical instruments, and a selection of CDs and music videos. A list of the current "Top 10" albums and singles, updated weekly, will keep young adults interested in the program.

Sponsorship for Prizes

1. Ask a record or music store to donate coupons for free merchandise.
2. Ask a video rental store to donate certificates for free music video rentals.
3. Ask a local cinema or theater to donate free passes to a musical film or play.
4. Ask a concert hall or other music venue to donate tickets to an upcoming performance.

Program Game

Make a game board in the shape of a large CD or long-playing record. Starting at the outside edge of the disc, measure out spaces along a spiral pattern until they reach the center. Players can advance one space for each point earned. Points can be earned for completing the activities mentioned in the General Guidelines, and for:

1. Reading a novel that involves music in the plot and completing a Music Fiction Book Review Form.
2. Reading a novel not related to the music theme and completing a Fiction Book Review Form.
3. Reading a nonfiction book and completing a Nonfiction Book Review Form.
4. Listening to an album-length tape or CD, reading a review of that recording, and completing a Music Critique Form.

Program Forms

1. Music Fiction Book Review Form
Title:
Author:
Publisher and date:
Brief summary of plot:
How is music important to the story?
Would you recommend this book to a friend? Why or why not?

2. Fiction Book Review Form
Title:
Author:
Publisher and date:
Brief summary of plot:
I would rate this book: "A number one hit!" "On the Top Ten List," "Barely broke into the Top 40," "Off the charts," "Should have scrapped the demo."

3. Nonfiction Book Review Form
Title:
Author:
Publisher and date:
Brief summary of information:
I would rate this book: "Worthy of playing at Carnegie Hall," "Well-orchestrated," "Has a good rhythm," "Out of tune," "You call that music?"

4. Music Critique Form
Name of recording:
Artist:
Brief summary of critic's review:
Do you agree with this review or not, and why?
What is your own opinion of this recording?

Program Activities

1. In Concert. Ask a local band, choral group or orchestra to perform at the library. Or, invite local teens who belong to rock groups to compete in a Battle of the Bands, to be judged by the audience.

2. The Top Twenty. Ask teens to list some of their favorite songs of all time. For each song, they should list the artist who performed it and the year it was a hit. Then have them vote for twenty songs. Compile all votes to come up with a master list of twenty favorite songs.

3. DJ for a Day. Invite a local disc jockey to bring in some radio equipment, demonstrate its use and answer questions about broadcasting. Perhaps teens can be allowed to select music and introduce songs on the radio. If possible, have the radio station broadcast live from the library.

4. Lip Synch or Kareoke Contest. Contestants must provide their own music cassettes and may compete as single performers or in a group. Hold auditions beforehand, and print up a program listing the performer(s), the song, and the original artist. Allow the audience to vote for their favorite acts.

5. **Smells Like "Weird Al."** "Weird" Al Yankovich has made a career out of writing parodies of popular songs. Play some of his tunes, such as "Smells Like Nirvana," along with the songs they spoof. Discuss what makes a good parody. Then encourage teens to write and sing their own parodies of popular songs.

6. **So You Think You Know Music?** Invite teens to compete in a game show in which all questions deal with some aspect of music. Sample categories may be the Sixties, Country Songs, Female Singers, Piano Men, Complete the Lyric, British Bands, Number One Singles, One-Hit Wonders. You can play music clips for categories such as Name That Instrument, Show Tunes, or Famous Guitar Riffs.

7. **Music Video.** Encourage teens with access to video equipment to shoot their own music videos. Present them at a live MTV-type show at the library, with other young adults acting as VJs. Viewers can vote for their favorites. (Library staff and VJs should preview the videos for appropriate content, to decide on the order in which to show them, and to write the introductions.)

8. **Banned in the USA.** Censorship of music lyrics and videos is a major concern for many people. Hold a discussion or debate on this topic. Young adults can look up information about people and organizations who want to ban or place restrictions on controversial music, and why. What types of music are most frequently challenged? Encourage teens to consider both sides of the question before they formulate their opinions.

9. **Music in Your Life.** Hold a career day of music-related occupations such as songwriter, orchestra conductor, concert musician, singer, concert promoter, "roadie," record industry executive, music store owner, DJ or VJ, music video director, sound technician, etc. Set out nonfiction books about music careers for patrons to borrow. Provide a list of addresses where people can write for more information.

10. **Dance Craze.** Sponsor a youth dance at the library. Choose a theme, such as "Disco Fever" or "At the Sock Hop," and play appropriate records. Encourage teens to dress to match the theme, and teach them some of the dances that were the rage of whatever era you have chosen.

Curriculum Tie-Ins

1. **English Literature/Composition.** Many popular songs are quite poetic. Read the lyrics of "Dangling Conversation" by Paul Simon, "All I Wanna Do" by Sheryl Crow, and songs by other artists. Analyze them for meter, rhythm and other poetic elements. Have students write poetry to go along with music you play in class.

2. **Science.** Study how strings, woodwinds, percussion and other types of instruments make music. How do electric instruments, such as guitars or synthesizers, work? How do amplifiers, speakers, microphones, earphones, CDs, cassettes, and other forms of music technology work?

3. **History/Geography.** Have students research different types of music, such as jazz, baroque, chamber music, etc. Where and when was each musical form created? Name some musical instruments that are typical of certain kinds of music, past and present, around the world.

4. **Math.** Musical notes can be used to review a unit on fractions. Have students "translate" whole, half, quarter notes, etc., into numbers, then "add" verses of sheet music together.

Activity Sheet Ideas

1. Word search or crossword puzzles of: a) names of rock groups, b) musical instruments, or c) music terms.

2. World scrambles or cryptograms of: a) song titles, b) album names, or c) classical music compositions or operas.

3. Matching activities: match a) songs to the artists who originally recorded them, b) show tunes to the play or movie they came from, or c) songs to the composers who wrote them.

Suggested Resources

Reference and Nonfiction

Berger, Melvin. *The Science of Music*. HarperCollins, 1989.

Bradley, Jack. *How to Read, Write, and Understand Music: A Practical Guide*. Hill Springs, 1986.

Collier, James Lincoln. *Jazz: The American Theme Song*. Oxford University Press, 1993.

Copland, Aaron. *What to Listen for in Music*. Dutton, 1989.

Erlewine, Michael, and Bultman, Scott. *All Music Guide: The Best CD's, Albums and Tapes*. Miller Freeman, 1992.

Escott, Colin, and Hawkins, Martin. *Good Rockin' Tonight: Sun Records and the Birth of Rock 'n' Roll*. St Martin's, 1991.

Gerardi, Robert. *Opportunities in Music Careers*. VGM, 1991.

Goulding, Phil G. *Classical Music: The 50 Greatest Composers and Their 1,000 Greatest Works*. Fawcett, 1992.

Johnson, Jeff. *Careers for Music Lovers and Other Tuneful Types*. VGM, 1996.

Jones, K. Maurice. *Say It Loud! The Story of Rap Music*. Millbrook, 1994.

Kay, Ernest. *International Who's Who in Music and Musicians' Directory*. Melrose, annual.

Karlin, Fred. *Listening to Movies: The Film Lover's Guide to Film Music*. Macmillan, 1994.

Kennedy, Rosemary G. *Bach to Rock: An Introduction to Famous Composers and Their Music*. Rosemary, 1989.

Kettlekamp, Larry. *Electronic Musical Instruments: What They Do, How They Work*. Morrow, 1984.

Kimpel, Dan. *Networking in the Music Business*. Writer's Digest, 1993.

Kogan, Judith. *Nothing but the Best: The Struggle for Perfection at the Julliard School*. Random, 1987.

Leikin, Molly-Ann. *How to Write a Hit Song*. Hal Leonard, 1995.

Levine, Michael. *The Music Address Book: How to Reach Anyone Who's Anyone in Music*. Harper-Perennial, 1994.

Livingston, Myra Cohn. *Call Down the Moon: Poems of Music*. Simon & Schuster, 1995.

Luck, Oliver W. *Music Is Math*. Owl, 1987.

McLaughlin, Patrick F. **The Practical Musical Instrument Owner's Guide** series. Instrument Press.

Meigs, James B., and Stern, Jennifer A. *Make Your Own Music Video*. Watts, 1986.

Nite, Norm N. *Rock on Almanac: The First Four Decades of Rock 'n' Roll: A Chronology*. Harper, 1989.

Powell, Stephanie. *Hit Me with Music: How to Start, Manage, Record, and Perform with Your Own Rock Band*. Millbrook, 1995.

Rabin, Carol Price. *Music Festivals in America*. Berkshire Traveller, 1990.

Santoro, Gene. *Dancing in Your Head: Jazz, Blues, Rock and Beyond*. Oxford University Press, 1994.

The Songwriter's Market Guide to Song and Demo Submission Formats. Writer's Digest, 1994.

Stone, Cliffie, and Stone, Joan Carol. *Everything You Always Wanted to Know About Songwriting but Didn't Know Who to Ask*. Showdown, 1991.

Umphred, Meal. *Goldmine's Price Guide to Collectible Record Albums, 1950-1979*. Krause, 1991.

Wacholtz, Larry E. *Inside Country Music*. Billboard, 1986.

Fiction

Barnes, Linda. *Steel Guitar*. Delacorte, 1991.

Bell, Mary S. *Sonata for Mind and Heart*. Macmillan, 1992.

Brooks, Bruce. *Midnight Hour Encores*. Harper, 1986.

Casely, Judith. *Kisses*. Knopf, 1990.

Childress, Mark. *Tender*. Crown, 1990.

Christian, Mary Blount. *Singin' Somebody Else's Song*. Macmillan, 1988.

Cooney, Caroline B. *Don't Blame the Music!* Putnam, 1986.

Ferry, Charles. *One More Time!* Houghton, 1985.

Frank, Elizabeth B. *Couder Cutlas*. HarperCollins, 1987.

Hart, Bruce, and Hart, Carole. *Strut*. Avon, 1992.

Higginsen, Vy, and Bolden, Tonya. *Mama, I Want to Sing*. Scholastic, 1992.

Kidd, Ronald. *Second Fiddle: A Sizzle and Splat Mystery*. Lodestar, 1988.

Lackey, Mercedes. *The Lark and the Wren*. Baen, 1992.

Landis, J.D. *The Band Never Dances*. HarperCollins, 1989.

Levoy, Myron. *Kelly 'n' Me*. HarperCollins, 1992.

Livingston, Alan W. *Ronnie Finkelhof, Superstar*. Fawcett, 1988.

Major, Kevin. *Dear Bruce Springsteen*. Delacorte, 1988.

Paterson, Katherine. *Come Sing, Jimmy Jo*. Dutton, 1985.

Paulsen, Gary. *Woodsong*. Puffin, 1991.

Ritz, David. *Family Blood*. Donald I. Fine, 1991.

Scarbourough, Elizabeth Ann. *Phantom Banjo*. Bantam, 1991.

Smith, Alison. *Billy Boone*. Scribner, 1989.

Strasser, Todd. *Rock 'n Roll Nights*. Dell, 1983.

Sweeney, Joyce. *Piano Man*. Delacorte, 1992.

Tamar, Erika. *Out of Control*. Atheneum, 1991.

Thesman, Jean. *Cattail Moon*. Houghton, 1994.

Thomas, Joyce Carol. *When the Nightingale Sings*. HarperCollins, 1992.

Voight, Cynthia. *Orfe*. Scholastic, 1992.

Vos, Ida. *Dancing on the Bridge at Avignon*. Houghton, 1995.

Wolff, Virginia Euwer. *The Mozart Season*. Scholastic, 1993.

Periodicals

Billboard. BPI Communications, Inc.

CD Review Digest. Connell Communications.

Circus. Circus Enterprises.

Computer Music Journal. The MIT Press.
Down Beat. Maher Publications.
Rolling Stone. Straight Arrow Publishers Co.

Feature-Length Films

Amadeus. HBO, 1984. (PG)
Mr. Holland's Opus. Hollywood Pictures, 1995. (PG)
Rolling Stone Presents Twenty Years of Rock and Roll. MGM/UA Home Video.
Some Like It Hot. MGM/UA, 1959.
Tender Mercies. HBO, 1983. (PG)
This Is Spinal Tap. Music Video, 1984. (R)

(Also various films of Broadway and classic MGM musicals.)

Computer Software

Apple Pie: Music of American History/History of American Music. Linotronics, 1994.
The Grammys. Mindscape, 1995.
History of Music: The Art of Listening. Zane, 1994. (Also others in series.)
Melody Maestro. Blue Ribbon Soundworks, 1994.
Microsoft Musical Instruments. Microsoft, 1993.
Microsoft Multimedia Stravinsky: The Rite of Spring. Microsoft, 1993. (Also others in series.)
Noteplay for Windows. IBIS Software, 1992.

35

Uncover a Mystery

Murderers, kidnappers, pick-pockets and other criminals are lurking in the library. But don't worry—the world's most famous detectives, secret agents, and law enforcement officers are hot on their trails. Check out a mystery novel or true crime story and gather clues, trail suspects, engage in international espionage, and face danger as your sleuth toils to solve the case. Whodunit? Find out when you Uncover a Mystery.

Display Idea

Display mystery, suspense and detective novels by popular genre authors, as well as other "whodunits." Nonfiction books of true crime and unsolved mysteries, biographies of genre writers, as well as related short story collections, magazines and videos should be included. Props such as a magnifying glass, a Sherlock Holmes hat, and pictures of murder weapons will draw patrons' attention.

Sponsorship for Prizes

1. Ask a video rental store to donate certificates for free mystery, suspense and detective movies.

2. Ask a bookstore to donate paperback novels of mystery, suspense, detective and true crime stories.

3. Ask department stores to donate mystery and detective board games, such as "Clue."

4. Ask a movie theater to donate free passes for current mystery, suspense, or detective films.

Program Game

The game board should look like a house plan, similar to the "Clue" game, with a dead body lying in one room. Footprints make a path from the corpse through all the rooms, picking up clues along the way, such as the murder weapon and notes hinting at the motive. The footprints finally lead to the murderer. Patrons will move one footprint for each point earned. Points can be earned for completing the activities mentioned in the General Guidelines, and for:

1. Reading a mystery, suspense, detective or crime novel and completing a Mystery Fiction Book Review Form.

2. Reading any non-genre novel and completing a Fiction Book Review Form.

3. Reading a nonfiction book and completing a Nonfiction Book Review Form.

4. Reading a collection of mystery, suspense, detective or crime short stories or a magazine of this genre and completing a Mystery Stories Review Form.

Program Forms

1. Mystery Fiction Book Review Form
Title:
Author:
Publisher and date:
Brief summary of plot:
I would rate this book: "The perfect crime!" "Super sleuthing," "A typical whodunit," "Reading this book was murder," "The author doesn't have a clue."

2. Fiction Book Review Form
Title:
Author:
Publisher and date:
Brief summary of plot:
I would rate this book: "I detect a winner," "Evidently well-written," "There's a good motive to read this book," "The plot was elementary," "It's a mystery how this book ever got published."

3. Nonfiction Book Review Form
Title:
Author:
Publisher and date:
Brief description of information:
Why did you chose to read this book?
What was your opinion of it?

4. Mystery Stories Review Form
Title of book or magazine:
Publisher and date:
Title and author of your favorite story:
Brief summary of plot:
Why did you like this story?
Was this story typical of the other stories in this collection? How or how not?

Program Activities

1. Mystery Movie. Show a mystery, suspense, spy or crime movie, or a film adaptation of a genre novel or play. You may want to show a series of films, or even have an all-night mystery movie marathon.

2. Cracking Codes. Deciphering codes and cryptic messages is a main element of spy and crime stories. Teens can hone their decoding skills during a special program in the library. Look through nonfiction books to devise ciphers for your patrons to crack. Graeme Base's *The Eleventh Hour: A Curious Mystery* also includes a variety of imaginative codes. Young adults can create their own cryptic messages for their peers to decipher.

3. Crime Lab. Invite a detective or other crime expert to conduct a crime lab workshop. Start with a fictitious crime. Teens can analyze hair samples and cloth fibers under a microscope, dust a surface for fingerprints and match them to the criminal's records, etc. The guest can talk about crime-solving methods used by real detectives, and answer questions from patrons.

4. Brilliant Deductions. Challenge teens to use visual and listening skills in solving mysteries. Allow patrons one minute to study a picture, then quiz them to see how many details they remembered and what conclusions they can draw from the visual clues that were given. Read a short mystery story and ask teens to solve it. Ask a group of teens to act out a mystery scene for other patrons to solve.

5. Library Search. Young adults will reinforce their reference skills as they gather clues to solve this mystery. First, pose a question, such as "What movie was Mr. Deadman watching when he was murdered?" Then place teens in teams of two to four people. Give each one a scavenger hunt list of reference questions and an answer sheet on which to record their findings. When the list is completed, the first letter of each answer should spell out the solution to the mystery.

6. Mystery Trivia. Set up a game board game similar to "Concentration," with a layer of cards covering a rebus or other puzzle to be solved. The outside surface of each card on the board is numbered, with no hint of the type of question it contains. (Since this is a mystery game, players will not know what category they have selected until the card is read.) Players or teams will earn a point for each correct answer. Categories can include Who Wrote Whom? (match author to his famous detective), True Crime (match details of an infamous true crime case to the name given to it by the press), Spy TV (match TV secret agent to the name of the show or the person who played that role), and Cop TV (same, but with TV police shows). At any time during the game, players or teams can try to guess the rebus as it is revealed. An incorrect answer means a loss of 5 points; a correct answer means a gain of 10 points. The player or team with the most points after the puzzle has been solved is the winner.

7. Mystery Theater. Agatha Christie's *Mousetrap* is England's longest-running play. Ask for teen volunteers to perform scenes from this or another mystery play.

8. Murder in the Library. Involve the library staff in a murder in the library scenario. Teens must interview various staff members and get their testimonies in order to piece together clues and solve the mystery. Some clues can require young adults to look up information in reference books that have been put aside for this game. Offer a reward to the sleuth who solves the crime.

9. A Life of Crime. Provide information on careers in criminology, police and detective work, criminal law, and other occupations related to preventing or solving crimes. Also include careers of people who write about crime, such as newspaper reporters, suspense novelists, and authors of true crime books. Provide a list of schools that offer related majors. Have books on these topics available for patrons to borrow.

10. Mystery Ball. Young adults can come to a costume party dressed as a famous detective, suspect or other character from a novel, movie or play. Have them role-play mystery skits, acting in character according to their outfits.

Curriculum Tie-Ins

1. English Literature/Composition. Let each student choose a classic detective novel author to study. Review the typical patterns of a detective story and an inverted detective story. Have students list the defining characters of a popular detective their author wrote about, and chart how one novel followed one of the story patterns. Then have students write a scene in the style of their chosen author.

2. Science. Fictional secret agents have many special gizmos to help them track suspects and solve crimes. Discuss some equipment used by James Bond and other characters. How, in theory, do they work? Then have students design their own spy equipment, explaining its use and how, in theory, it would work.

3. History/Geography. Have students trace globe-trotting routes taken by various fictional detectives and spies in some of their novels. If the book is set in the past, how would the locations have appeared at the time? What are some historical events that were relevant to the plots of these novels?

4. Math. Students can decipher secret codes based on mathematical progressions, formulas, or measurements.

Activity Sheet Ideas

1. Word search or crossword puzzles of: a) weapons and tools used by criminals, b) equipment used by detectives, police, or spies, or c) general terms used by writers of the genre.

2. Word scrambles or cryptograms of: a) popular genre writers, b) phrases uttered by famous fictional detectives or spies, or c) TV police, spy, or detective stories.

3. Matching activities: match a) movie detectives or spies to the actor(s) who portrayed them, b) popular genre fiction characters to the books in which they appear, and c) true crime cases to the year(s) in which they occurred.

Suggested Resources

Reference and Nonfiction

Ashton, Christina. *Codes and Ciphers: Hundreds of Unusual and Secret Ways to Send Messages.* Betterway, 1993.

Berger, Gilda. *Violence and Drugs.* Watts, 1989.

Binyon, T.J. *Murder Will Out.* Oxford University Press, 1989.

Camenson, Blythe. *Careers for Mystery Buffs and Other Snoops and Sleuths.* VGM, 1996.

Collingwood, Donna, ed. *Mystery Writer's Marketplace and Sourcebook.* Writer's Digest, annual.

Colman, Penny. *Spies! Women in the Civil War.* Shoe Tree, 1992.

Crimes and Punishment: The Illustrated Crime Encyclopedia. 28 vols. Marshall Cavendish, 1994.

Deacon, Richard. *Spyclodepedia: The Comprehensive Handbook of Espionage.* Morrow, 1989.

De Sola, Ralph. *Crime Dictionary.* Facts on File, 1982.

Dulles, Allen. *Great True Spy Stories.* Ballantine, 1989.

Flowers, R. Barri. *The Adolescent Criminal: An Examination of Today's Juvenile Offender.* McFarland, 1990.

Grafton, Sue, ed. *Writing Mysteries: A Handbook by the Mystery Writers of America.* Writer's Digest, 1992.

Gustafson, Anita. *Guilty or Innocent?* Holt, 1985.

Hardwick, Michael. *The Complete Guide to Sherlock Holmes.* St. Martin's, 1987.

Hart, Anne. *The Life and Times of Hercule Poirot.* Putnam, 1990.

Howdunit series. Writer's Digest.

Jones, Richard Glyn, ed. *Unsolved! Classic True Murder Cases.* Bedrick, 1987.

Kurland, Michael. *The Spy Master's Handbook*. Facts on File, 1988.

Marrin, Albert. *The Secret Armies: Spies, Counterspies, and Saboteurs in World War II*. Macmillan, 1985.

Murder a la Carte: Host Your Own Mystery Party. Lombarde Marketing.

Riley, Dick, and McAllister, Pam, eds. *The New Bedside, Bathtub and Armchair Companion to Agatha Christie*. Ungar, 1986.

Silverstein, Herma. *Spies Among Us: The Truth About Modern Espionage*. Watts, 1988.

Stinchcomb, James. *Opportunities in Law Enforcement and Criminal Justice Carers*. VGM, 1990.

Symons, Julian. *Bloody Murder: From the Detective Story to the Crime Novel*. Viking, 1985.

Warner, Penny, and Warner, Tom. *A Deadly Game of Klew*. St. Martin's, 1986.

_____. *Greetings from the Grave*. St, Martin's, 1986.

Wilson, Kirk. *Unsolved: Great Mysteries of the 20th Century*. Carroll & Graf, 1990.

Woeller, Waltrand, and Cassidy, Bruce. *The Literature of Crime and Detection: An Illustrated History from Antiquity to the Present*. Ungar, 1988.

Yost, Graham. *The CIA*. Facts on File, 1989. (Also *The KGB*.)

_____. *Spies in the Sky*. Facts on File, 1989.

Fiction

Avi. *The Man Who Was Poe*. Orchard, 1989.

Barnes, Linda. *Coyote*. Delacorte, 1990.

Base, Graeme. *The Eleventh Hour: A Curious Mystery*. Abrams, 1988.

Beck, K.K. *Peril Under the Palms*. Walker, 1989.

Bloch, Robert. *Psycho House*. St. Martin's, 1990.

Childress, Mark. *V Is for Victor*. Knopf, 1989.

Christie, Agatha. **Hercule Poirot** and **Miss Marple** mysteries.

Clancy, Tom. *The Cardinal of the Kremlin*. Putnam, 1988.

Clark, Mary Higgins. *All Around the Town*. Simon & Schuster, 1992.

Conan Doyle, Sir Arthur. *The Adventures of Sherlock Holmes*. Bantam, 1985.

Cork, Barry. *Laid Dead*. Scribner, 1991.

Douglas, Carole Nelson. *Good Night, Mr. Holmes*. Tor, 1990.

Duncan, Lois. *Don't Look Behind You*. Delacorte, 1989.

Ebisch, Glen. *Lou Dunlop: Private Eye*. Crosswinds, 1988.

Francis, Dick. *The Edge*. Putnam, 1989.

Grafton, Sue. *I Is for Innocent*. Holt, 1992.

Grisham, John. *The Pelican Brief*. Doubleday, 1992.

Hillerman, Tony. *A Thief of Time*. Harper, 1988.

Inglehart, Donna Walsh. *Breaking the Ring*. Little, 1991.

Kerr, M.E. *Fell Down*. HarperCollins, 1991.

Lasky, Kathryn. *Double Trouble Squared*. Harcourt, 1991.

Le Carre, John. *Our Game*. Knopf, 1995.

Levitt, J.R. *Ten of Swords*. St. Martin's, 1991.

Locke, Joseph. *Kill the Teacher's Pet*. Bantam, 1991.

Michaels, Barbara. *Smoke and Mirrors*. Simon & Schuster, 1989.

Muller, Marcia. *Trophies and Dead Things*. Mysterious, 1990.

Nixon, Joan Lowery. *Secret, Silent Screams*. Delacorte, 1988.

Paretsky, Sara. *Burn Marks*. Delacorte, 1990.
Pease, William D. *Playing the Dozens*. Viking, 1990.
Wilson, F. Paul. *Dydeetown World*. Baen, 1989.

(Also other mystery, suspense, detective and crime titles from these authors.)

Periodicals

Alfred Hitchcock's Mystery Magazine. Davis Publications.
Ellery Queen's Mystery Magazine. Davis Publications.
Enigma. National Puzzlers' League.

Feature-Length Films

Clear and Present Danger. Paramount, 1994. (PG)
Goldeneye. MCA/Universal, 1995. (PG-13)
The Maltese Falcon. MGM/UA, 1941.
Murder by Death. Columbia Tristar, 1976. (PG)
The Seven Percent Solution. MCA/Universal, 1976. (PG)
Sleuth. Home Vision Cinema, 1972. (PG)
Strangers on a Train. Warner, 1951.

Computer Software

Conspiracy. Virgin Interactive Entertainment, 1993.
Crime Patrol. American Laser Games, 1994.
Great Mystery Classics. World Library, 1993.
The Lost Files of Sherlock Holmes. Electronic Arts.
Where in the World Is Carmen Sandiego? Junior Detective Edition. Broderbund, 1995.
Who Killed Sam Rupert? Creative Multimedia Corp., 1993. (Also others in series.)

36

Focus on Photography

Picture this: The library has loads of books to help you get a sure shot every time you use a camera. In addition to books on all facets of photography, the library has lots of flashy fiction, expertly developed nonfiction, perfectly processed magazines and other print materials. You can zoom in on some great music and videos, too. Now is the time to expose yourself to all the library has to offer, as we Focus on Photography.

Display Idea

Include novels with photography themes in a display of nonfiction about various aspects of photography and photographers. Add photography magazines and related videos. You can place various pieces of camera equipment in a showcase alongside the books and feature some interesting black and white and color photographs.

Sponsorship for Prizes

1. Ask a portrait studio to donate certificates for free photo sessions.
2. Ask a bookstore to donate photography books.
3. Ask a camera shop to donate film and discounts for camera supplies.
4. Ask a photo developer to offer free or discount services.

Program Game

Start with a black and white photograph of a large group of people, such as a sports team or a class picture. Make a duplicate of this photo, but with the faces blanked out. Patrons can glue on one face for every point earned. Points can be earned for completing the activities mentioned in the General Guidelines, and for:

1. Reading a novel and completing a Fiction Book Review Form.
2. Reading a nonfiction book about photography and completing a Photography Nonfiction Book Review Form.
3. Reading a nonfiction book not related to the photography theme and completing a Nonfiction Book Review Form.
4. Reading a photography magazine and completing a Photography Magazine Information Form.

Program Forms

1. Fiction Book Review Form
Title:
Author:
Publisher and date:
Brief summary of plot:
I would rate this book: "Picture perfect," "Good composition and depth," "Interesting, but not the artist's best work," "Lacks focus," "Overexposed and underdeveloped."
2. Photography Nonfiction Book Review Form
Title:
Author:
Publisher and date:
Brief description of information:
What did you like most about this book and why?
What did you learn from reading it?
3. Nonfiction Book Review Form
Title:
Author:
Publisher and date:
Brief description of information:
I would rate this book: "A nationally syndicated Pulitzer-Prize winning photo," "A magazine cover shot," "Good enough to publish in the local newspaper," "Bury the photo in a drawer," "Destroy the negatives."
4. Photography Magazine Information Form
Title:
Author:
Publisher and date:
Brief summary on one feature article:
What was the most interesting thing in this magazine and why?
How could you use the information contained in this magazine?

Program Activities

1. Picture Show. Play a feature film with a photography theme, such as *The Year of Living Dangerously*, for teens to enjoy.

2. Cover Shots. Teens can make customized photograph albums during a special craft workshop. Provide materials and patterns for a variety of album cover designs, including embroidery and needlepoint patterns, decoupage materials, paints, fabric scraps, wallpaper samples, etc. Help teens to decorate the album covers and allow them to bring home materials if they do not finish their projects during the workshop.

3. Photo Talk. Invite a photographer to talk to teens about various aspects of the craft, such as how to set up shots, when to use a zoom lens, etc. The guest can show slides of photos of his or her work and answer questions from the audience.

4. Gallery. Some of your patrons may have a talent for photography. In a designated area in the library, allow teens to display photos they have taken. Label each entry with the photographer's name, school and grade, and a title or brief description of the subject.

5. I've Been Framed. A good frame can add to the beauty and value of a picture. Ask teens to bring in some 8 × 10 photographs. Provide a variety of mats and frames, and let teens experiment with placing photos in the different frames, with or without mats, to see which combinations they like the best. Discuss the various types of frames and suggest creative things kids can do to design their own frames.

6. Camera Quiz. Sponsor a game show during which teens must answer multiple-choice questions on an assortment of photography-related topics. Categories can include Cover Girls (identify the pictured model), What's Wrong with This Picture? (tell why the photo came out badly), Photo Finishes (guess which horse or person won a close race—the answer is in a photo taken at the finish line), Famous Photographers (tell who took the picture shown), What Does It Do? (give the purpose of the named camera part), and Photo Lingo (define photography terms).

7. Shutter Bugs. Ask a camera shop representative to bring several demonstration models for teens to try out. The guest can explain the various features available on different cameras, optional equipment, and how to buy a camera. Provide consumer information so patrons can compare the cost and value of the sample photography equipment.

8. Big Shots. Discuss the works of several renowned photographers during a slide show or video about photographers. Ask teens to identify themes or styles that are characteristic of each person's work. Have available several books of photograph collections for patrons to look through and check out. You can also show samples of award-winning photos and let teens offer their opinions on what made these shots special.

9. Photo Opportunities. Arrange a career day program that focuses on jobs in photography. There are opportunities for photographers in the fields of journalism, police work, entertainment, nature, fashion, advertising and publishing. Photographers can also work in photography studios or film special events such as weddings. Related jobs include creating and manufacturing photography equipment, developing film, framing and exhibiting photographs. Provide books on these subjects and a list of schools where patrons can go to study photography.

10. Period Portraits. Many fairs have a photography booth where customers can dress up in old-fashioned outfits and have their pictures taken. Provide a variety of costumes and props, and ask a photographer to take portraits of costumed teens. The photographer will most likely want to be paid for his work, so advise patrons ahead of time about the cost of the photo sessions.

Curriculum Tie-Ins

1. English Literature/Composition. It is said that "one picture is worth a thousand words." Show students some Pulitzer Prize–winning photos, photos taken by renowned photographers, and photos that depict aspects of everyday life in the past and present. Have students write a short story or essay based on one or more of these photos.

2. Science. Study how a camera works. Discuss what each part does and how variations in factors such as light or distance can affect the outcome of the photograph. Compare the capabilities and limitations of different types of cameras and film. If possible, set up a darkroom and demonstrate how photos are developed.

3. History/Geography. Trace the history of photography from the *camera obscura* and early inventions to modern and future technology. Have students look up information about notable photographers and inventors around the world, and explain their contributions to the art of photography.

4. Math. Math is involved in photography in several ways, such as figuring out the proper speed film to use under certain lighting conditions, the distance that a flash will be effective, the capabilities of various sizes of lens, depth of focus, etc. Create several math problems based on these aspects of photography.

Activity Sheet Ideas

1. Word search or crossword puzzles of: a) photography terms, b) photo equipment, or c) photography styles and techniques.

2. Word scrambles or cryptograms of: a) photography magazines, b) manufacturers of film and photography equipment, or c) advertising slogans for camera and film companies.

3. Matching activities: match a) photographers to their famous works, b) inventors to their inventions, or c) camera parts to their usage.

Suggested Resources

Reference and Nonfiction

The Art of Photography. Yale University Press, 1989.
Bennett, Stuart. *How to Buy Photographs*. Christie's, 1987.
Busselle, Michael. *The Complete 35mm Sourcebook*. Amphoto, 1988.
Conrad, Pam. *Prairie Visions: The Life and Times of Solomon Butcher*. HarperCollins, 1991.
Cumming, David. *Photography*. Steck-Vaughn, 1989.
Gernsheim, Helmut. *A Concise History of Photography*. Dover, 1986.
Gleason, Roger. *Seeing for Yourself: Techniques and Projects for Beginning Photographers*. Chicago Review, 1992.
Grimm, Tom, et al. *The Basic Darkroom Book*. NAL, 1986.
Henderson, Kathy. *Market Guide for Young Artists and Photographers*. F & W Publishing, 1995.
Hoy, Frank P. *Photojournalism: The Visual Approach*. Prentice, 1986.
Hughes, Jerry. *The World's Simplest Photography Book*. Philips Lane, 1993.
Johnson, Bervin. *Opportunities in Photography Careers*. VGM, 1991.
Kodak Library of Creative Photography series. Silver Burdett, 1984.
Leekley, Sheryle, and Leekley, John. *Moments: The Pulitzer Prize Photographs*. Crown, 1978.
McLean, Cheryl. *Careers for Shutterbugs and Other Candid Types*. VGM, 1994.
Make Color Work for You. Silver Burdett, 1983.
Mark, Mary Ellen. *The Photo Essay: Photographs*. Smithsonian Institution, 1990.
Pinkard, Bruce. *The Photographer's Bible: An Encyclopedic Reference Manual*. Arco, 1983.
Platt, Richard. *The Photographer's Idea Book: How to See and Take Better Pictures*. Amphoto, 1985.
Rowell, Galen. *Galen Rowell's Vision: The Art of Adventure Photography*. Sierra Club, 1993.
Schaub, George. *Using Your Camera: A Basic Guide to 35mm Photography*. Amphoto, 1989.
Silverman, Ruth, ed. *Athletes: Photographs*. Knopf, 1987.
Simon, Seymour. *Hidden Worlds: Pictures of the Invisible*. Morrow, 1983.
Smith, Peter. *The First Photography Book*. Sterling, 1988.
Suess, Bernhard J. *Mastering Black-and-White Photography: From Camera to Darkroom*. Allworth, 1995.
Suffrin, Mark. *Focus on America: Profiles of Nine Photographers*. Macmillan, 1987.

Van Wormer, Joe. *How to Be a Wildlife Photographer*. Lodestar, 1982.
Wignall, Jeff. *Landscape Photography*. McGraw, 1988.
Willins, Michael, ed. *Photographer's Market*. Writer's Digest, annual.
Wolf, Sylvia. *Focus: Five Women Photographers*. Whitman, 1994.

Fiction

Bauer, Joan. *Thwonk*. Delacorte, 1995.
Buselle, Rebecca. *A Frog's-Eye View*. Orchard, 1990.
Calhoun, B.B. *The New Me*. Random, 1994.
Fergus, Charles. *Shadow Catcher*. Soho, 1991.
Gilman, Dorothy. *Mrs. Pollifax on Safari*. Fawcett, 1988.
Girion, Barbara. *Portfolio to Fame: Cameron's Story*. Dell, 1987.
Gregory, Kristiana. *Earthquake at Dawn*. Harcourt, 1992.
Kavanaugh, Michelle. *Emerald Explosion*. Pineapple, 1988.
Kelly, Mary Anne. *Park Lane South, Queens*. St. Martin's, 1990.
King, Thomas. *Medicine River*. Viking, 1990.
Klein, Norma. *Snapshots*. Dial, 1984.
Krishner, Trudy. *Spite Fences*. Delacorte, 1994.
LeMieux, A.C. *T-H-E TV Guidance Counselor*. Tambourine, 1993.
Levoy, Myron. *Pictures of Adam*. Harper, 1986.
MacLachlan, Patricia. *Journey*. Delacorte, 1991.
Nixon, Joan Lowery. *Overnight Sensation*. Bantam, 1990.
Robertson, Keith, and Cuffari, Richard. *In Search of a Sandhill Crane*. Viking, 1973.
Rose, Malcolm. *The Highest Form of Killing*. Harcourt, 1992.
Sachs, Marilyn. *Class Pictures*. Dutton, 1980.
Schulman, Audrey. *The Cage*. Algonquin, 1994.
Sonnenmark, Laura A. *The Lie*. Scholastic, 1992.
Soto, Gary. *Crazy Weekend*. Scholastic, 1994.
Tamar, Erika. *High Cheekbones*. Viking, 1990.
Townsend, John Rowe. *Cloudy-Bright: A Novel*. Lippincott, 1984.
Wersba, Barbara. *Crazy Vanilla*. Harper, 1986.
_____. *The Farewell Kid*. Harper, 1990.
Westcott, Earle. *Winter Wolves*. Yankee, 1988.

Periodicals

American Photo. Diamandis Communications, Inc.
Aperture. Aperture Foundation, Inc.
Darkroom Photography. Melrose Publications.
Exposure. Society for Photographic Education.
Petersen's Photographic Magazine. Petersen Publishing Co.
Popular Photography. Diamandis Communications, Inc.

Feature-Length Films

The Cameraman. MGM/UA, 1928.
Double Exposure: The Story of Margaret Bourke-White. Turner Home Entertainment, 1989.

The Eyes of Laura Mars. Goodtimes/Kids Klassics, 1978. (R)
Love That Bob. Movies Unlimited, 1955.
Running Wild. Media Home Entertainment, 1973. (G)
The Year of Living Dangerously. MGM/UA, 1982. (PG)

Computer Software

The Blue Ribbon Photography Series, Volume 1. Pacific Publishing Group, 1994. (Also Volume 2.)
I Photograph to Remember. Voyager Company.
Material World: A Global Family. Star Press Multimedia, 1995.
Photo Factory for Windows. Multimedia Store, 1994.
Time-Life Photography. Time, Inc.
Understanding Exposure: How to Shoot Great Photographs. DiAMar Interactive Corp.

37
Raves for Radio Waves

What do cellular phones, remote control devices, broadcast radio, CBs and microwave ovens have in common? They all work with radio waves! The library has books and magazines on all these topics, plus information ranging from Marconi to the Golden Age of Radio to modern and future radio technology. Whether you're more interested in listening to the top forty on FM radio, or searching for new stars using radio astronomy, you'll have Raves for Radio Waves.

Display Idea

Nonfiction books on the history of radio and how radios work, as well as magazines and related fiction, can be set up with a display of sound recordings of old radio shows. Fill a showcase with some old-fashioned radios and modern ones. Also include materials about other forms of radio technology, such as radar, microwaves, radio astronomy, remote control devices, etc.

Sponsorship for Prizes

1. Ask a bookstore to donate books on the history of radio or other related topics.

2. Ask an electronics store to donate portable radios, headsets, or discount certificates for audio merchandise.

3. Ask a music store to donate sound recordings of old radio shows.

4. Ask a local radio station to donate free passes to movie openings and other events they sponsor.

Program Game

The game should resemble an old-fashioned FM radio dial, showing broadcast bands ranging from 88 megahertz to 108 megahertz, in a horizontal line. The vertical line indicating the station to which the radio is tuned should be set at 88. For each point earned, the vertical line will be drawn one increment to the right along the dial. Points can be earned for completing the activities mentioned in the General Guidelines, and for:

1. Reading a novel and completing a Fiction Book Review Form.

2. Reading a nonfiction book about the history of broadcast radio, radio technology, or another related area and completing a Radio Nonfiction Book Review Form.

3. Reading a nonfiction book not related to the radio theme and completing a Nonfiction Book Review Form.

4. Listening to a sound recording of an old radio show and completing a Radio Show Review Form.

Program Forms

1. Fiction Book Review Form
Title:
Author:
Publisher and date:
Brief summary of plot:
I would rate this book: "A strong FM signal with excellent sound quality," "A good AM transmission that can be heard far away," "A small broadcast station heard locally," "Poor transmitter—lots of static," "The FCC revoked the license."

2. Radio Nonfiction Book Review Form
Title:
Author:
Publisher and date:
Brief description of information:
Why did you choose to read this book?
What did you like best about this book?

3. Nonfiction Book Review Form
Title:
Author:
Publisher and date:
Brief description of information:
I would rate this book: "The #1 station in the nation," "Has many devoted fans," "Pulls in a decent market share," "Boring format," "Take it off the air."

4. Radio Show Review Form
Name of series and episode title:
Producer and date:
Brief description of plot:
What is your opinion of this recording?
Would you like to listen to more old radio shows? Why or why not?

Program Activities

1. Visual Radio. Show a movie with a radio plot, such as *Radio Days*.

2. Easy Listening. Treat young adults to an evening of old radio programs. Play recordings of classic shows such as *The Shadow* or *Fibber McGee and Molly*. You may want to present *War of the Worlds* by Orson Welles and discuss all the fuss it caused when it originally aired.

3. On the Air. Invite a local radio station to broadcast live from the library for a day. DJs can talk to teens and show them how radio equipment works. Perhaps teens can have an opportunity to introduce a record or read a news report.

4. Radio Poll. Teens can complete a survey in which they vote for their favorite radio personality (DJ), local radio station, and preferred radio format (top 40, alternative, oldies, country, etc.). You can ask additional questions, such as where and when they like to listen to the radio, and compare the number of hours they listen to radio to the number of hours they watch television or listen to tapes and CDs. Tabulate the results of this poll and discuss it with the group.

5. Hams. There may be a ham radio club in your area. Invite people with short band radios and CBs to demonstrate their use. What distant radio broadcasts can they pick up? How can people communicate with each other using a CB radio? Hobbyists can discuss how to get an amateur radio license, demonstrate the Morse Code, and discuss examples of CB language.

6. Caller Number One. Many radio stations have call-in quizzes. Often, a DJ will play a few seconds from a record and ask listeners to call in to identify the song and performer. Base a library game show on this concept. The first contestant to dial in on a toy phone (the kind that jingles) will have the first chance to offer an answer. Play music in categories such as Songs About Radio, Number One Hits from the Eighties, Country Classics, Instrumentals, One-Hit Wonders, and Movie Soundtrack Songs.

7. Shop Talk. Invite an electronics store to bring in demonstration models of various radio devices. A store representative can answer questions about portable headset radios, boom boxes, remote control devices, cellular phones, beepers, etc. Teens can try these out to compare sound quality and other features. Have consumer reports of these items available for patrons to browse.

8. Broadcast News. Radio stations receive news copy from the various wire services. Ask a local radio station to save several days' worth of news copy to give to you. There should be many long sheets of paper, with local and world news, weather and sports. Show teens this "raw" news and let them decide how they would edit this information down to present a five-minute news report for each day.

9. Radio Personalities. Careers in broadcast radio and other fields of radio technology can be featured in a Radio Job Fair. Broadcasting opportunities can include on-air jobs such as disc jockey and sports reporter, as well as behind-the-scenes jobs in sales and marketing, engineering and station management. Also provide information on careers in radio technology as it relates to fields such as navigation, astronomy, product development, medical science and communications. Supply a list of broadcasting schools and colleges that offer these majors. Books on these subjects should be available for patrons to check out.

10. Remote Control. Radio waves are used to power remote-controlled devices. Ask a hobby shop to provide remote control cars and trains for an indoor program, or airplanes for an outdoor show. Invite patrons who own remote-controlled toys to bring their items in for others to see. Teens can learn how these devices work, and have a chance to try them out.

Curriculum Tie-Ins

1. English Literature/Composition. Read some scripts of old radio programs in class. Students can read the various roles and create sound effects. Discuss the format of these scripts and how a radio play differs from a play that is watched. Then have students adapt a short story or chapter from a book to a radio script format. These can also be read aloud in class.

2. Science. Have the class study how radios work. Take apart old radios and compare their inner workings to modern ones. How are sound waves transmitted and received? In addition to communications, study some other ways that radio waves are used, such as radiology and radar. What differences do changes in frequency and wavelength make in the applications of radio waves?

3. History/Geography. Have students draw a timeline of radio technology. Note some scientific pioneers in the field, technological advances, and some important events in the history of radio communications. Locate on a map where these highlights occurred.

4. Math. Have students draw up charts or graphs identifying the range of frequencies and wavelengths of various radio waves. For example, where on the chart would AM and FM waves be? Measure these waves in megahertz or kilohertz, as applicable.

Activity Sheet Ideas

1. Word search or crossword puzzles of: a) broadcast radio terms, b) terms relating to how radio waves work, or c) radio equipment.

2. Word scrambles or cryptograms of: a) radio shows from the 1950s, b) names of radio broadcasting networks, or c) radio celebrities from the past and present.

3. Matching activities: match a) radio parts to their functions, b) various radio devices (such as walkie talkies) to their uses, or c) names of scientists and inventors to their contributions to radio technology.

Suggested Resources

Reference and Nonfiction

The ARRL Handbook, 1990. American Radio Relay League, 1989.

Barker, Larry M. *Scanner Radio Guide.* HighText, 1993.

Broadcasting and Cable Yearbook. R.R. Bowker, annual.

Crisfield, Deborah. *Radio.* Silver Burdett, 1995.

Dearborn, Laura. *Good Sound: An Uncomplicated Guide to Choosing and Using Audio Equipment.* Morrow, 1987.

Douglas, George H. *The Early Days of Radio Broadcasting.* McFarland, 1987.

Edmonds, I.G., and Gebhardt, William H. *Broadcasting for Beginners.* Holt, 1980.

Eisenson, Henry L. *Scanners and Secret Frequencies.* Index, 1993.

Ellis, Elmo I. *Opportunities in Broadcasting Careers.* VGM, 1992.

Erbe, Maureen. *Made in Japan: Transistor Radios of the 50s and 60s.* Chronicle, 1993.

Finkelstein, Norman H. *Sounds in the Air: The Golden Age of Radio.* Macmillan, 1993.

Fitzgerald, Merni Ingrassia. *The Voice of America.* Putnam, 1987.

Harmon, Jim. *The Great Radio Comedians.* Doubleday, 1970.

_____. *Radio Mystery and Adventure and Its Appearances in Film, Television and Other Media.* McFarland, 1992.

Helms, Harry L. *All About Ham Radio.* High Text, 1992.

Johnson, David, and Johnson, Betty. *Guide to Old Radios: Pointers, Pictures, and Prices.* Wallace-Homestead, 1995.

Kaufman, Milton. *Radio Operator's License Q & A Manual.* Hayden, 1989.

Kearman, Jim, et al., eds. *Now You're Talking! Discover the World of Ham Radio.* American Radio Relay League, 1991.

Lackman, Ron. *Same Time ... Same Station: An A to Z Guide to Radio from Jack Benny to Howard Stern.* Facts on File, 1996.

Mayo, Jonathan L. *The Radio Amateur's Digital Communications Handbook.* TAB, 1992.

Mott, Robert L. *Radio Sound Effects: Who Did It, and How, in the Era of Live Broadcasting.* McFarland, 1993.

Nourse, Alan E. *Radio Astronomy*. Watts, 1989.

Passport to World Band Radio. International Broadcasting Services, 1987.

Pratt, Douglas R. *The Beginner's Guide to Radio Control Sport Flying*. TAB, 1988.

Siposs, George G. *Building and Racing Radio Control Cars and Motorcycles*. Kalmbach, 1981.

Sklar, Rick. *Rocking America: An Insider's Story: How the All-Hit Radio Stations Took Over*. St. Martins, 1984.

Swartz, Jon David, and Reinehr, Robert C. *Handbook of Old-Time Radio: A Comprehensive Guide to Golden Age Radio Listening and Collecting*. Scarecrow, 1993.

Terrace, Vincent. *Radio's Golden Years: The Encyclopedia of Radio Programs, 1930-1960*. A.S. Barnes, 1981.

Wertheimer, Linda, ed. *Listening to America: Twenty-Five Years in the Life of a Nation, as Heard on National Public Radio*. Houghton, 1995.

Wong, Michael A. *A Day in the Life of a Disc Jockey*. Troll, 1988.

Fiction

Avi. *Who Was That Masked Man, Anyway?* Orchard, 1992.

Brancato, Robin F. *Come Alive at 505*. Knopf, 1980.

Carter, Alden R. *Up Country*. Putnam, 1989.

Conford, Ellen. *Strictly for Laughs*. Berkley, 1986.

Cooney, Caroline B. *The Voice on the Radio*. Delacorte, 1996.

Gilson, Jamie. *Dial Leroi Rupert*. Lothrop, 1979.

Hall, Lynn. *Dagmar Schultz and the Angel Edna*. Scribner, 1989.

Hamilton, Virginia. *Willie Bea and the Time the Martians Landed*. Macmillan, 1983.

Jordan, Mildred. *Proud to Be Amish*. Crown, 1968.

Keillor, Garrison. *WLT: A Radio Romance*. Viking, 1991.

Qualey, Marsha. *Everybody's Daughter*. Houghton, 1991.

Periodicals

Amateur Radio. WGE Publishing Co.

CQ: The Radio Amateurs' Journal. CQ Publishing, Inc.

Radio Control Car Action. Air Age, Inc.

Radio-Electronics. Gernsback Publications.

Radio Ink. Streamline Publishing, Inc.

Worldradio. Martin Publications, Inc.

Sound Recordings of Radio Programs

Abbott and Costello. Abbott & Costello Enterprises, 1987.

Agnes Moorehead in "Sorry, Wrong Number"; Orson Welles in "The Hitchhiker." Great American Audio Corp.

Amos 'n' Andy. Camco Enterprises, 1989.

Baby Snooks Show. Jabberwocky, 1983.

Buck Rogers in the 25th Century: The Origin of Buck Rogers. Golden Age, 1979.

Dragnet, Starring Jack Webb. Mind's Eye, 1983.

Elliot, Bob, and Goulding, Ray. *The Best of Bob and Ray*. Radioart, 1986.

Fields, W.C. *In Some of His Greatest Routines*. Mind's Eye, 1985.

Golden Age Radio Blockbusters series. Metacom.
The Haunting Hour. Metacom, 1977.
Keillor, Garrison. *Prairie Home Companion Tourists.* Minnesota Public Radio, 1983. (Also other titles by Keillor.)
Koch, Howard. *The War of the Worlds: The Complete, Unedited, Original Radio Broadcast Exactly as Heard on CBS Radio, October 30, 1938.* Nostalgia Lane, 1982.
The Lone Ranger. Mind's Eye, 1983.
Ma Perkins. Radio Reruns, 1978.
Marx, Groucho. *You Bet Your Life.* Mind's Eye, 1983.
Mercury Theater. Metacom, 1990.
Oboler, Arch. *Arch Oboler's Lights Out Everybody.* Metacom, 1986.
Old-Time Radio Comedy Favorites. Radio Spirits, 1994.
Radio's Greatest Detectives. Great American Audio Corp., 1987.
Radio's Greatest Sitcoms series. MMP International, 1992. Includes titles such as *The Best of Edgar Bergen and Charlie McCarthy, The Best of Fibber McGee and Molly, The Best of George Burns and Gracie Allen, The Best of Jack Benny, The Best of Our Miss Brooks, Sherlock Holmes, The Adventures of Ozzie and Harriet, The Bickersons.*
Rogers, Will. *"All I Know Is Just What I Read in the Papers": Comments from His Radio Show of the Thirties.* Golden Age, 1979.
Suspense. Metacom, 1980.

Feature-Length Films

Good Morning, Vietnam. Touchstone Pictures, 1987. (R)
Radio Days. HBO, 1987. (PG)
Radioland Murders. MCA/Universal, 1994. (PG)
The Shadow. MCA/Universal, 1994. (PG-13)
Sleepless in Seattle. Columbia Tristar, 1993. (PG)
Straight Talk. Hollywood Pictures, 1992. (PG)

Computer Software

Ham Radio. American Software and Hardware Distributors, 1993.
The Ham Radio and Scanner Companion. John O'Connor Publishing, 1994.
Hamcall. Buckmaster Publishing, 1989.
Physics Explorer: Waves. Logical Software, 1992.
Radio Active: The Music Trivia Game Show. Sanctuary Woods, Multimedia Corp., 1994.

38
Romance Is in the Air

If you want to add some romance to your life, then come into the library. You'll find romance novels, love poems, romantic comedies, plus movies and music to set the mood. And if you like nonfiction, magazines, stories of adventure and other types of fiction, there's a lot more to love in the library. Wherever you look, you'll find that Romance Is in the Air.

Display Idea

Place teen romance novels and other YA fiction with romantic themes at the center of this display. Add books of love poems and romantic plays. Post valentine decorations, clippings from romance advice columns, and lovey-dovey greeting cards around the books. Include romantic videos and music CDs, as well as related nonfiction and magazines.

Sponsorship for Prizes

1. Ask a bookstore to donate paperback romance novels.
2. Ask a card store to donate romantic or friendship greeting cards.
3. Ask a florist to donate flowers or discount certificates.
4. Ask a local restaurant to donate two free dinners, and a theater or cinema to donate two tickets for Dating Game prizes.

Program Game

The reading game will be represented by a valentine with an arrow going through it. The valentine is a maze, with the arrow as the start and end points. Patrons can advance through the maze with points earned. Points can be earned by completing the activities mentioned in the General Guidelines, and for:

1. Reading a romance novel or love story and completing a Romance Fiction Book Review Form.
2. Reading a novel not related to the romance theme and completing a Fiction Book Review Form.
3. Reading a nonfiction book and completing a Nonfiction Book Review Form.
4. Reading a book of love poems or a romantic play (happy or sad) and completing a Romance Literature Form.

Program Forms

1. Romance Fiction Book Review Form
Title:
Author:
Publisher and date:
Brief summary of plot:
Was the story really romantic? Why or why not?
Do you think the story was a satisfying romance? Why or why not?
2. Fiction Book Review Form
Title:
Author:
Publisher and date:
Brief summary of plot:
I would rate this book: "A candlelight dinner for two and an evening of dancing," "Reservations at a nice restaurant and tickets to the theater," "Dinner at a fast food place and going to the movies," "Popcorn and pretzels while watching a video on TV," "Splitting a candy bar in the school cafeteria."
3. Nonfiction Book Review Form
Title:
Author:
Publisher and date:
Brief description of information:
I would rate this book: "I loved it!," "I liked it," "I thought it was OK," "I disliked it," "I hated it."
4. Romance Literature Form
Title:
Author:
Publisher and date:
Brief description of literature:
What is your favorite scene or poem and why?
Would you want to read more of this type of literature? Why or why not?

Program Activities

1. Love on the Big Screen. *Romancing the Stone* is a romantic action movie about a novelist who writes romances. Show this film, or another romantic movie that would appeal to teens.

2. Wear Your Heart. Young adult patrons can bring in their own T-shirts and announce their romances to the world with this craft program. Provide transfers of hearts and other appropriate pictures, an assortment of letters, and an iron or pressing machine. Teens can write messages such as "Bobby's girl," "Tom and Lisa forever," etc. For safety reasons, an adult should operate the iron.

3. How Do I Love Thee? Poetry is often considered to be very romantic. Invite teens to write original love poems (happy and sad). Collect and print the best ones to distribute to patrons.

4. **Love on Stage.** Many plays are romantic comedies. If a local theater company is performing one of these, sponsor a trip to see the play. Or, select scenes from various romantic comedies, such as *The Importance of Being Earnest*, and ask teen volunteers to read the parts.

5. **A Table for Two.** Certain foods are considered romantic. Conduct a cooking program to show teens how to make some of these dishes. What other elements, such as dining by candlelight, can help to make eating a romantic experience?

6. **The Dating Game.** Ahead of time, ask teens to submit their names (boys and girls in separate boxes) to be contestants on a *Dating Game*–type show. Randomly select enough names for two games—one in which a girl will ask questions of three unseen boys, and another in which a boy will ask questions of three unseen girls. The questioner can ask ten queries and hear answers from each of the three competitors before deciding on whom to pick. You can award each of the two couples a package "date" that was donated by program sponsors. The competitors can disguise their voices so the questioners won't guess their identities ahead of time. You may want to screen the questions before the show for appropriate content.

7. **Drawn-Out Romances.** A popular syndicated cartoon is the "Love Is..." drawings. Encourage young adult artists to draw their own "Love Is..." cartoons, or create their own romantic comic strips. Display these in the library for all to enjoy.

8. **What They Really Think.** Let teens take a survey about relationships that is similar to ones found in women's magazines. Statements can be open-ended, such as "The thing that really turns me off about a guy is...," or multiple choice, such as "The first thing I notice about a girl's face is her: eyes, smile, hair, complexion." Teens can make up the questions, tabulate the answers, and publish a list of the top responses. You may want to have a follow-up program in which teens can discuss the survey results.

9. **Love Life.** Teens can learn about the occupations of people who are involved in planning weddings at a mock bridal fair. Showcase jobs in photography, bridal magazine publishing, catering, music, fashion design (for gowns and tuxedos), hall rental, and cake decorating. There are also jobs selling wedding gowns, jewelry, china, furniture, flowers, honeymoon travel plans and wedding invitations. Provide information on these and other romance-related jobs.

10. **Valentines Dance.** Even if it isn't February, you can still hold a Valentines Dance at the library. Decorate the room with hearts and flowers, and play only love songs (romantic or silly).

Curriculum Tie-Ins

1. **English Literature/Composition.** Have the class think of some possible romance novel scenarios, such as "Boy meets girl, boy loses girl, boy gets girl." Then have each student read a different romantic story and tell which category the book falls into. Discuss what makes a satisfying love story, and let students write short romance stories of their own.

2. **Science.** Since teens (and often, adults) confuse love with sex, this may be a good time to teach a unit on sex education. Discuss what happens to boys' and girls' bodies when they are attracted to someone. Also talk about safe and responsible behavior.

3. **History/Geography.** Study mating customs in other countries. What are some traditional marriage customs and ceremonies practiced today around the world? Also have students research mating rituals from the past, and among different religions.

4. Math. Ask students to graph statistics on the number of marriages for various years, states and counties. You might also have them graph statistics on birth and divorce rates. What conclusions can be drawn from these numbers?

Activity Sheet Ideas

1. Word search and crossword puzzles of: a) synonyms for "love," b) authors of romance novels, or c) romantic items one lover might send to another.

2. Word scrambles or cryptograms of: a) TV shows with "Love" in the title, b) titles of romance novels, and c) romantic advertising slogans.

3. Matching activities: match a) song lyrics to the titles of the love songs from which they came, b) actors and actresses who play opposite each other in romantic movies, or c) romantic couples in fiction.

Suggested Resources

Reference and Nonfiction

Beyer, Kay. *Coping with Teen Parenting*. Rosen, 1990.

Bode, Janet. *Kids Having Kids: The Unwed Teenage Parent*. Watts, 1980.

Booher, Dianna Daniels. *Love: First Aid for the Young*. Messner, 1985.

Bradshaw, John. *Creating Love: The Next Great Stage of Growth*. Bantam, 1994.

Browning, Elizabeth Barrett. *Sonnets from the Portuguese, and Other Love Poems*. Hanover, 1954.

Buscaglia, Leo. *Love*. Fawcett, 1985. (Also *Personhood*.)

Cahn, Julie. *The Dating Book: A Guide to the Social Scene*. Simon & Schuster, 1983.

Curtis, Robert H. *Mind and Mood: Understanding and Controlling Your Emotions*. Macmillan, 1986.

Ephron, Delia. *Teenage Romance: Or, How to Die of Embarrassment*. Ballantine, 1982.

Filichia, Peter. *A Boy's-Eye-View of Girls*. Scholastic, 1983.

Fromm, Erich. *The Art of Loving*. Harper, 1956.

Goodman, Linda. *Linda Goodman's Love Signs: A New Approach to the Human Heart*. Harper-Perennial, 1992.

Keene, Irene Krause. *Love and Dishes: Scene Stealing Recipes from Your Favorite Soap Stars*. Hearst, 1996.

Kingma, Daphne Rose. *Coming Apart: Why Relationships End and How to Live Through the Ending of Yours*. Conari, 1987.

Janeczko, Paul B., ed. *Going Over to Your Place: Poems for Each Other*. Macmillan, 1987.

Laner, Mary Riege. *Dating: Delights, and Dilemmas*. Sheffield, 1995.

McCullough, Frances, ed. *Love Is Like a Lion's Tooth: An Anthology of Love Poems*. Harper, 1984.

McShane, Claudette. *Warning! Dating May Be Hazardous to Your Health*. Mother Courage, 1988.

Paludan, Eve. *Romance Writer's Pink Pages: The Insider's Guide to Getting Your Romance Novel Published*. Prima, annual.

Pianka, Phyllis Taylor. *How to Write Romances*. Writer's Digest, 1988.

Quiri, Patricia Ryon. *Dating*. Watts, 1989.

Ramsdall, Kristin. *Happily Ever After: A Guide to Reading Interests in Romance Fiction.* Libraries Unlimited, 1987.

Rue, Nancy. *Coping with Dating Violence.* Rosen, 1989.

Scheider, Meg F. *Romance! Can You Survive It? A Guide to Sticky Dating Situations.* Dell, 1984.

_____. *Two in a Crowd: How to Find Romance Without Losing Your Friends.* Putnam, 1985.

Stallworthy, Jon, ed. *A Book of Love Poems.* Oxford University Press, 1974.

Stefoff, Rebecca. *Friendship and Love.* Chelsea, 1989.

Vedral, Joyce L. *Boyfriends: Getting Them, Keeping Them, Living Without Them.* Ballantine, 1990.

Wallace, Carol M. *Should You Shut Your Eyes When You Kiss?* Little, 1983.

Weston, Carol. *Girltalk About Guys.* Harper, 1988.

Fiction

Anthony, Evelyn. *The Scarlet Thread.* Harper, 1990.

Applegate, Katherine. *June Dreams.* Archway, 1995. (Also *July's Promise* and *August Magic.*)

Avi. *Romeo and Juliet Together Again (and Alive!) At Last.* Orchard, 1987.

Bauer, Joan. *Squashed.* Delacorte, 1992.

Beckman, Delores. *Who Loves Sam Grant?* Dutton, 1983.

Bunting, Eve. *Janet Hamm Needs a Date for the Dance.* Bantam, 1987.

Caseley, Judith. *Kisses.* Knopf, 1990.

Clements, Bruce. *Tom Loves Anna Loves Tom.* Farrar, 1990.

Cohen, Barbara. *Lovers' Games.* Atheneum, 1983.

Conford, Ellen. *Loving Someone Else.* Bantam, 1991.

Cooney, Caroline B. *The Girl Who Invented Romance.* Bantam, 1988.

Fields, Terri. *Recipe for Romance.* Scholastic, 1986.

Foley, June. *Susanna Siegelbaum Gives Up Guys.* Scholastic, 1991.

Gerber, Merrill Joan. *Handsome as Anything.* Scholastic, 1990.

Gingher, Marianne. *Teen Angel: And Other Stories of Young Love.* Atheneum, 1988.

Goudge, Eileen. *Don't Say Good-Bye.* Dell, 1985.

Kaplow, Robert. *Alessandra in Love.* Lippincott, 1989.

Kerr, M.E. *Him She Loves?* Harper, 1984.

Killien, Christi. *Fickle Fever.* Houghton, 1988.

Leroe, Ellen. *Meet Your Match, Cupid Delaney.* Lodestar, 1990.

Lewis, Linda. *My Heart Belongs to That Boy.* Archway, 1989.

Lowry, Lois. *Your Move, J.P.!* Houghton, 1990.

Mazer, Harry. *The Girl of His Dreams.* Crowell, 1987.

Marlin, J. *Appeal to the Heart.* Berkley, 1986.

Neenan, Colin. *In Your Dreams.* Harcourt, 1995.

Plummer, Louise. *The Unlikely Romance of Kate Bjorkman.* Delacorte, 1995.

Rylant, Cynthia. *A Couple of Kooks and Other Stories About Love.* Orchard, 1990.

Sharmat, Marjorie. *He Noticed I'm Alive...And Other Hopeful Signs.* Delacorte, 1984.

Singer, Marilyn. *The Course of True Love Never Did Run Smooth.* Harper, 1983.

West, Beverly, and Peske, Nancy. *Frankly Scarlett, I Do Give a Damn! A Parody: Classic Romances Retold.* HarperCollins, 1995.

Zable, Rona S. *Love at the Laundromat.* Bantam, 1988.

Periodicals

Bride's. Conde Nast Publications.
Modern Bride. Cahner's Publishing Co.
Modern Romance. Sterling-Macfadden Partnership.
Romantic Times. Romantic Times Publishing Group.
True Romance. Sterling-Macfadden Partnership.

Feature-Length Films

Ghost. Paramount, 1990. (PG-13)
I.Q. Paramount, 1994. (PG)
Love Affair. Warner, 1994. (PG-13)
Love Story. Paramount, 1970. (PG)
Romancing the Stone. CBS/Fox, 1984. (PG)
Say Anything. CBS/Fox, 1989. (PG13)
Sleepless in Seatle. Columbia Tristar, 1993. (PG)

Computer Software

Blind Date. Trimark Interactive, 1994.
Cooking to Seduce. Procomad.
Dating and Mating. Time Warner Interactive, 1994.

39

The Science Fiction Frontier

Attention Trekkies, Jedis, and other science fiction aficionados! The library is the place to check out the best sci fi novels, videos and soundtracks. And for these of you who like the "science" part as much as the "fiction," there are books on astronomy, computers, robotics, rocketry, technology and other fascinating subjects. There are new worlds to explore, aliens to greet, time zones to travel, and dimensions to cross in The Science Fiction Frontier.

Display Idea

Set up a display of science fiction novels, short story collections and magazines. Include a variety of nonfiction science books in subject areas such as aeronautics, computers, robotics, communications technology, space exploration, and other science concepts used in science fiction. Add videos of sci fi TV shows and movies, plus recordings of sci fi soundtracks. Use posters and novelty items of sci fi entertainments to add interest to the display.

Sponsorship for Prizes

1. Ask video rental stores to donate free movie rental certificates for science fiction movies, TV shows and video games.
2. Ask bookstores to donate paperback copies of science fiction titles.
3. Ask a local movie theater to donate movie posters or passes to science fiction movies.
4. Ask a department store or novelty store to donate trademark merchandise (T-shirts, cups, etc.) for sci fi movies and TV shows.

Program Game

The game board can depict a track through an amusement park ride. Along the sidelines, draw pictures of science fiction story elements such as aliens, cyborgs, portals into other dimensions, computers, space ships, planets, etc. Patrons can advance one space along the track for each point earned. Points can be earned for completing the activities mentioned in the General Guidelines, and for:
1. Reading a science fiction novel and completing a Science Fiction Book Review Form.
2. Reading a novel not related to the science fiction theme, and completing a Fiction Book Review Form.
3. Reading a nonfiction book and completing a Nonfiction Book Review Form.

4. Reading a science fiction magazine or short story collection and completing a Science Fiction Stories Review Form.

Program Forms

1. Science Fiction Book Review Form
Title:
Author:
Publisher and date:
Brief summary of plot:
What was your favorite part of the book and why?
Would you like to read more sci fi books by this author? Why or why not?

2. Fiction Book Review Form
Title:
Author:
Publisher and Date:
Brief summary of plot:
I would rate this book: "Moves at warp speed," "May it live long and prosper," "Meets Starfleet regulations," "Highly illogical," "Transport me to another book."

3. Nonfiction Book Review Form
Title:
Author:
Publisher and date:
Brief description of information:
I would rate this book: "Out of this world!," "Technologically advanced," "OK special effects," "Strictly for aliens," "Place it in suspended animation and don't revive it."

4. Science Fiction Stories Review Form
Title:
Author or editor:
Publisher and date:
Name and author of your favorite story:
Brief description of plot:
Why is it your favorite?
Do you enjoy reading this type of literature? Why or why not?

Program Activities

1. Sci Fi Flick. Treat teens to a showing of one or more science fiction movies, such as the *Star Trek* films.

2. Space Crafts. Many science fiction stories involve space ships, space exploration, and colonization of other planets. Reserve an area where teens can set up a model space station or settlement of their own design. Provide various scrap materials to use in constructing space ships and a futuristic city. Builders should consider energy sources, the atmosphere, and other factors that could influence the design of their settlement. Patrons can work on this project throughout the duration of the science fiction program.

3. Robot Shop. Robots are featured in many science fiction stories. Show slides or film clips of famous movie robots and actual working robots. Ask teens what type of robot they would like to see invented. Invite an electronics expert to talk about how robots are made. Perhaps the guest can guide teens in constructing a simple remote-controlled machine.

4. Look to the Stars. Ask members of a local astronomy club to invite teens along for an evening of star-gazing. Teens can have a chance to look through a telescope, and astronomers can point out various constellations, stars and planets.

5. Aliens. Provide theater costume materials, such as make-up, rubber masks, wigs, and an assortment of odd-looking accessories, for teens to use as they transform themselves into space aliens or monsters. Photograph these alien invaders and display the pictures in the library.

6. Sci Fi Smarts. In this game show, science fiction buffs can answer questions about sci fi elements in past and present forms of entertainment and literature. Categories can include Sci Fi Novels, Movies, TV Shows, Pop and Soundtrack Music, Video and Computer Games or Comic Books.

7. Cyberspace. Advanced computer technology is a standard element in science fiction novels. Invite a local computer store to sponsor a technology fair and demonstrate the capabilities of some state-of-the-art computers. Allow teens to sample several types of software. Have a computer expert speak about future technology and career opportunities in this growing field. Create a bibliography of related books to hand out.

8. Virtual Experience. Some science fiction stories, such as the movie *Total Recall*, feature the concept of virtual reality. Discuss virtual reality with group participants. What is it? How can it be used? Have them tell you what ideas they would incorporate if they were to create a virtual reality arcade game.

9. Spaced-Out Jobs. Present a program of career opportunities that have come about due to the exploration of outer space, such as jobs in space technology, communications, computers and several areas of science. Also provide information for jobs related to the genre of science fiction, such as writing stories and scripts; designing special effects, costumes and make-up for movies and television shows; and marketing conventions and various goods based on popular characters, books and media.

10. Sci Fi Convention. Invite teens to come to a science fiction convention dressed as characters from books, movies and TV shows. Show episodes of sci fi television shows. Play music from genre movies and have patrons invent dances to them. Let a devoted Trekkie give a lesson on how to speak Klingon. Teens can display and trade memorabilia.

Curriculum Tie-Ins

1. English Literature/Composition. Read several science fiction stories or novels with the class to get them familiar with the genre. Then read one more novel or story, but do not let students read the ending. Have students write their own endings, in the style of the story. Students can compare their conclusions with the author's. Which ending is their favorite and why?

2. Science. Many inventions first written about in science fiction stories are actually in use today. Explore some of these, such as robots, computer technology and lasers. How are they made and how do they work? List some other inventions and science fiction concepts, such as time travel, that are still only fiction. Let students discuss the possibility of these and other ideas becoming reality in the near future.

3. History/Geography. Have students make a list of classic or ground-breaking science fiction. Include movies, important works by Jules Verne and other authors, and sci fi "laws" such as Isaac Asimov's Rules for Robots. Be sure to include authors and films from other countries as well as the United States. Students can also note sci fi works that predicted scientific discoveries and inventions, and the time and place in which these predictions were realized.

    4. Math. In *Star Trek*, the space crafts fly at various levels of warp speed. Look up how fast these speeds supposedly are. Also list the locations of several star systems and planets. Have students determine the distances between the various locations. Then ask students to solve math problems of how long it would take a space ship to fly from Planet X to Planet Y at warp Z.

Activity Sheet Ideas

    1. Word search or crossword puzzles of: a) typical genre terms, b) plot elements, or c) terms used in the *Star Trek* shows.

    2. Word scrambles or cryptograms of: a) titles of popular phrases from sci fi TV shows and movies, b) titles of sci fi movies, or c) titles or series of sci fi novels.

    3. Matching activities: match a) movie and TV sci fi characters to the movies and TV shows they are from, b) actors to the sci fi characters they have portrayed, or c) sci fi authors to their novels.

Suggested Resources

Reference and Nonfiction

Asimov, Isaac, and White, Frank. *Think About Space: Where Have We Been and Where Are We Going?* Walker, 1989.

Barlowe, Wayne Douglas. *Barlowe's Guide to Extraterrestrials.* Workman, 1987.

Berger, Melvin. *UFOs, ETs and Visitors from Space.* Putnam, 1988.

Blumberg, Rhoda. *The First Travel Guide to the Moon: What to Pack, How to Go, and What to See When You Get There.* Macmillan, 1980.

Bone, Jan. *Opportunities in Laser Technology Careers.* VGM, 1989.

_____. *Opportunities in Robotics Careers.* VGM, 1993.

Clareson, Thomas D. *Understanding Contemporary American Science Fiction: The Formative Period, 1926-1970.* University of South Carolina, 1990.

Clute, John. *Science Fiction: The Illustrated Encyclopedia.* DK, 1995.

Gibberman, Susan R. *Star Trek: An Annotated Guide to Resources on the Development, the Phenomenon, the People, the Television Series, the Films, the Novels and the Recordings.* McFarland, 1991.

Goldberg, Lee, et al. *Science Fiction Filmmaking in the 1980s: Interviews with Actors, Directors, Producers and Writers.* McFarland, 1995.

Gutman, John W. *Robot Hobby: The Complete Manual for Individuals and Clubs.* Machine Press, 1992.

Heckman, Philip. *The Magic of Holography.* Macmillan, 1986.

Jackson, Francis, and Moore, Patrick. *Life in the Universe.* Norton, 1989.

Kennedy, DayAnn M., et al. *Science and Technology in Fact and Fiction: A Guide to Young Adult Books.* Bowker, 1990.

Lambert, Mark. *Living in the Future.* Bookwright, 1986.

Lampton, Christopher. *New Theories on the Birth of the Universe.* Watts, 1990.

MacNee, Marie J., ed. *Science Fiction, Fantasy, and Horror Writers*. Gale, 1995.

Moravec, Hans. *Mind Children: The Future of Robot and Human Intelligence*. Harvard University Press, 1988.

Ochoa, George, and Osier, Jeff. *The Writer's Guide to Creating a Science Fiction Universe*. Writer's Digest, 1993.

Phillips, Mark, and Garcia, Frank. *Science Fiction Television Series: Episode Guides, Histories, and Casts and Credits for 62 Prime Time Shows, 1959 Through 1989*. McFarland, 1995.

Platt, Charles. *Dream Makers: Science Fiction and Fantasy Writers at Work*. Ungar, 1987.

Sargent, Pamela, ed. *Nebula Awards 29*. Harcourt, 1995.

Spangenburg, Ray, and Moser, Diane. *Exploring the Reaches of the Solar System*. Facts on File, 1990.

_____. *Opening the Space Frontier*. Facts on File, 1989.

Spielberg, Nathan, and Anderson, Bryon D. *Seven Ideas That Shook the Universe*. Wiley, 1987.

Swift, David W. *SETI Pioneers: Scientists Talk About Their Search for Extraterrestrial Intelligence*. University of Arizona Press, 1990.

Taylor, L.B., Jr. *Space: Battleground of the Future?* Watts, 1988.

Tompkins, David, ed. *Science Fiction Writer's Marketplace and Sourcebook*. Writer's Digest, 1994.

Vallee, Jacques. *Confrontations: A Scientist's Search for Alien Contact*. Ballantine, 1990.

Walters, Ed, and Walters, Frances. *The Gulf Breeze Sightings: The Most Astounding Multiple Sightings of UFOs in U.S. History*. Morrow, 1990.

Wickelgren, Ingrid. *Ramblin' Robots: Building a Breed of Mechanical Beasts*. Watts, 1996.

Fiction

Arnason, Eleanor. *A Woman of the Iron People*. Morrow, 1991.

Asimov, Isaac. *Foundation Trilogy*. Doubleday, 1982.

Baird, Thomas. *Smart Rats*. Harper, 1990.

Barron, Thomas A. *Heartlight*. Philomel, 1990.

Bear, Greg. *Queen of Angels*. Warner, 1990.

Blackwood, Gary L. *Beyond the Door*. Atheneum, 1991.

Bradbury, Ray. *Fahrenheit 451*. Ballantine, 1953.

Brin, David. *Earth*. Bantam, 1990.

Caraker, Mary. *The Faces of Ceti*. Houghton, 1991.

Card, Orson Scott. *Ender's Game*. Tor, 1985.

Clarke, Arthur C. *Imperial Earth*. Ballantine, 1976.

Farmer, Nancy. *The Ear, the Eye, and the Arm*. Orchard, 1994.

Foster, Alan Dean. *To the Vanishing Point*. Warner, 1988.

Heinlein, Robert A. *Stranger in a Strange Land*. Putnam, 1961.

Herbert, Frank. *Dune*. Putnam, 1984.

Hughes, Monica. *Invitation to the Game*. Simon & Schuster, 1991.

Le Guin, Ursula K. *The Left Hand of Darkness*. Ace, 1969.

Lowry, Lois. *The Giver*. Houghton, 1993.

McCaffrey, Anne. *Crystal Line*. Ballantine, 1992.

Macdonald, Caroline. *The Lake at the End of the World*. Dial, 1989.

Maguire, Gregory. *I Feel Like the Morning Star*. Harper, 1989.

Mayhar, Ardath. *A Place of Silver Silence*. Walker, 1988.

Moulton, Deborah. *Children of Time*. Dial, 1989.
Ryan, Mary C. *Me Too*. Little, 1991.
Sanders, Scott Russell. *The Engineer of Beasts*. Orchard, 1988.
Sargent, Pamela. *Alien Child*. Harper, 1988.
Service, Pamela F. *Under Alien Stars*. Atheneum, 1990.
Shatner, William. *TekWar*. Putnam, 1989.
Silverberg, Robert. *Letters from Atlantis*. Atheneum, 1990.
Wells, H.G. *War of the Worlds*. Heinemann, 1984.

(Also sequels and other science fiction works by these authors.)

Periodicals

Analog Science Fiction and Fact. Dell Magazines.
Asimov's Science Fiction. Dell Magazines.
Magazine of Fantasy and Science Fiction. Mercury Press.
Robotics World. Communications Chanels, Inc.
Science Fiction Age. Sovereign Media.
Starlog. Starlog Group, Inc.

Feature-Length Films

Blade Runner. Warner, 1982. (R)
Close Encounters of the Third Kind. Columbia Tristar, 1977. (PG)
Independence Day. CBS/Fox, 1996. (PG-13)
Star Trek: The Motion Picture. Paramount, 1980. (G)
Stargate. MGM/UA, 1994. (PG-13)
THX 1138. Warner, 1971. (PG)
Total Recall. Live Home Video, 1990. (R)

Computer Software

Alien Legacy. Sierra On-Line, 1995.
Classic Clips: Science Fiction. Starlite Productions, 1995.
The Hugo and Nebula Anthology 1993. ClariNet Communications, 1994.
Klingon Immersion Studies. Simon & Schuster/Prentice-Hall, 1995.
The Journeyman Project II. Sanctuary Woods Multimedia, 1994.
The Multimedia Encyclopedia of Science Fiction. Grolier Electronic Publishing, 1995.
Outpost. Sierra On-Line, 1994.
Star Trek Omnipedia. Simon & Schuster Interactive, 1995.

40

High Seas Adventures

Now is the time to chart a course for the library, where an ocean of books is waiting for you. Read true and fictitious stories about the sea, ships, pirates, marine life, shipwrecks, sailing, sea lore and other seafaring subjects. Ride a tide of seaworthy videos and enjoy smooth sailing by listening to songs of the seas. So drop anchor at the library and experience some High Seas Adventures.

Display Idea

Provide a selection of fiction and nonfiction books about ships, seas and oceans, sailing, submarines, sunken treasure, pirates, marine life and other related topics. Include videos in which the action takes place on or by the sea. Display posters and props such as model ships and ocean scenes, as well as CDs of songs about the seafaring life.

Sponsorship for Prizes

1. Ask a bookstore to donate novels about ships, the sea, or another related topic.
2. Ask a hobby store to donate model ships.
3. Ask a video rental store to donate free rental certificates for videos set on the high seas.
4. Ask a seafood restaurant to donate coupons for free or discount meals.

Program Game

Use a map of the world as the game board. Draw lines to represent the route of a clipper ship, sea explorer, pirate ship or submarine. Place the appropriate vessel at the starting point of the voyage. Patrons can move the vessel one space along the route for each point earned. Points can be earned for completing the activities in the General Guidelines, and for:

1. Reading a novel related to the sea theme and completing a Sea Fiction Book Review Form.
2. Reading a novel not related to the sea theme and completing a Fiction Book Review Form.
3. Reading nonfiction book related to the sea theme and completing a Sea Nonfiction Book Review Form.
4. Reading a nonfiction book not related to the sea theme and completing a Nonfiction Book Review Form.

Program Forms

1. Sea Fiction Book Review Form
Title:
Author:
Publisher and date:
Brief summary of plot:
Where did the story take place?
How important was the setting to the plot of the book?
2. Fiction Book Review Form
Title:
Author:
Publisher and date:
Brief summary of plot:
I would rate this book: "A triumphant voyage," "A successful journey," "Smooth sailing," "Lost at sea," "Bailed out after sending an SOS."
3. Sea Nonfiction Book Review Form
Title:
Author:
Publisher and date:
Brief description of information:
What was the most interesting part of the book and why?
Would you recommend this book to a friend? Why or why not?
4. Nonfiction Book Review Form
Title:
Author:
Publisher and date:
Brief description of information:
I would rate this book: "A first class oceanliner," "Ship shape," "A seaworthy vessel," "This ship has sprung a few leaks," "A shipwreck."

Program Activities

1. High Seas Cinema. Entertain teens with a movie that takes place on a ship or submarine, such as *The Hunt for Red October.*

2. Ship Shape Crafts. Set up a variety of activities involving sea vessels. Teens can choose to build model ships, tie ships' knots, learn semaphore or Morse code, make ships' flags, etc. Invite people who are experts in these areas to host the activities.

3. Sea Songs. Gather recordings of sea chantey to play for a group of teens. You can pass out copies of the verses so that everybody can sing along. If possible, invite a folk singer to perform some traditional songs.

4. Treasure Hunt. In the past, many pirates and privateers roamed the seas in search of treasure. Organize a treasure hunt in and around the library for your young adults. Teens can search the online or card catalog, reference sources, the stacks, and other areas to track down clues that are hidden in books, displays, and vertical files. You may want to put teens in groups and give each one a different set of clues to follow, each leading to the "treasure."

5. Food from the Sea. Teach teens some simple seafood recipes, such as salmon croquettes or seafood salad, at a special cooking activity. You can also discuss the nutritional value of fish and ask patrons to contribute their favorite seafood recipes for a cookbook.

6. Sea Smarts. Contestants can prove their knowledge of the sea by participating in a theme-related game show program. Topics can include Seafaring Stories, Sea Sports, Great Sea Explorers, Tragedies at Sea, Sea Vessels, and Name That Sea. For fun, you may want to have players spin a mock ship's wheel to determine which category of question they must answer.

7. Sea Scenes. Set aside an area in which teens can create an ocean exhibit. Encourage patrons to draw pictures and craft models of plant and animal life, a coral reef, sea vents and underwater volcanoes, the shoreline, a shipwreck on the ocean floor and other scenes. This can be an ongoing project throughout the duration of the unit.

8. Mysteries at Sea. Provide several books, stories and articles about unexplained phenomena pertaining to the oceans and seas, such as the Bermuda Triangle, ghost ships and superstitions. Teens can discuss these topics or conduct a debate in which they cite documentation to prove or disprove one of these mysteries.

9. Seaworthy Work. Conduct a job fair to introduce teens to careers related to the sea, such as work in navigation, marine biology, boat/submarine engineering and construction, underwater exploration, the fishing industry, oceanology, the navy and coast guard. Provide information about these and other jobs, and a list of colleges that offer training in related areas.

10. Ahoy, Mates! Young adults can come to a costume party wearing sailor uniforms, pirate costumes, and other seaworthy outfits from the past or present (even ocean animals, if they like!). Play songs with a sea or water theme, serve seafood such as tuna sandwiches, and decorate the room appropriately.

Curriculum Tie-Ins

1. English Literature and Composition. There are many myths and legends pertaining to the sea and oceans. Students can read mythology about Greek, Roman or Norse sea gods, folklore about mermaids and sea monsters, or the legend of Atlantis. Ask students to write their own stories based on the sea lore they have read.

2. Science. Students can learn about ocean tides, waves and currents, and discuss how the oceans affect the weather. You may also want to present units on ship/submarine technology, navigation, marine life, or environmental concerns about the seas and oceans.

3. History/Geography. Have students locate the oceans and some major seas on a world map. They can also trace the routes of several ocean explorers and mark the locations of famous ship wrecks and other disasters at sea. Students may enjoy creating a relief map of the ocean floor.

4. Math. Distances on the seas are measured in knots rather than miles or meters. Have students solve distance problems in knots. You can also devise problems involving water pressure or echo sounding.

Activity Sheet Ideas

1. Word search or crossword puzzles of: a) sea plants and animals, b) names of seas, or c) parts of a ship.

2. Word scrambles or cryptograms of: a) quotes about the sea, b) verses from sea chanteys, or c) names of famous sea and pirate captains.

3. Matching activities: match a) theme-related books to their authors, b) characters in sea myths and legends to their countries of origin, or c) seafaring expressions to their meanings.

Suggested Resources

Reference and Nonfiction

Aebi, Tania, and Brennan, Bernadette. *Maiden Voyage*. Simon & Schuster, 1989.

Ballard, Robert D., and Archbold, Rick. *The Discovery of the Titanic*. Warner, 1987.

Banister, Keith, and Campbell, Andrew. *The Encyclopedia of Aquatic Life*. Facts on File, 1986.

Brett, Bernard. *The Fighting Ship*. Oxford University Press, 1988.

Brosse, Jacques. *Great Voyages of Discovery: Circumnavigators and Scientists*. Stanley Hochman, 1985.

Callahan, Steven. *Adrift: Seventy-Six Days Lost at Sea*. Ballantine, 1986.

Cousteau, Jacques, and Dumas, Frederic. *The Silent World*. Lyons & Burford, 1987.

Erickson, Jon. *The Mysterious Oceans*. TAB, 1988.

Gustafson, Charles. *How to Buy the Best Sailboat*. Hearst Marine, 1991.

Hackwell, W. John. *Diving to the Past: Recovering Ancient Wrecks*. Scribner, 1988.

Harrison, Dave. *Sports Illustrated Canoeing*. NAL, 1988.

Hays, David, and Hays, Daniel. *My Old Man and the Sea*. Algonquin, 1995.

Heitzmann, William Ray. *Opportunities in Marine and Maritime Careers*. VGM, 1988.

Kiley, Deborah Scaling, and Noonan, Meg. *Albatross: A True Story of a Woman's Survival at Sea*. Houghton, 1994.

Lord, Walter. *A Night to Remember*. Bantam, 1956.

Macaulay, David. *Ship*. Houghton, 1993.

Marrin, Albert. *The Sea Rovers: Pirates, Privateers, and Buccaneers*. Macmillan, 1984.

Martin, Colin, and Parker, Geoffrey. *The Spanish Armada*. Norton, 1988.

Miller, Helen Hill. *Captains from Devon: The Great Elizabethan Seafarers Who Won the Oceans for England*. Algonquin, 1985.

Pickford, Nigel. *The Atlas of Ship Wrecks and Treasure: The History, Location, and Treasures of Ships Lost at Sea*. Dorling Kindersley, 1994.

Richie, Robert. *Captain Kidd and the War Against the Pirates*. Harvard University Press, 1986.

Rousmaniere, John. *The Annapolis Book of Seamanship*. Simon & Schuster, 1989.

The Seafarers series. Time-Life.

Soper, Tony. *Oceans of Birds*. David & Charles, 1990.

Stein, Wendy. *Opposing Viewpoints: Atlantis*. Greenhaven, 1989.

Stonehouse, Bernard. *Sea Mammals of the World*. Penguin, 1985.

Thubron, Colin. *The Ancient Mariners*. Silver Burdett, 1981.

The Visual Dictionary of Ships and Sailing. Dorling Kindersley, 1991.

White, Rick. *Catamaran Racing: Solutions, Secrets, Speed*. Putnam, 1983.

Zadig, Ernest A. *The Complete Book of Boating*. Prentice, 1985.

Fiction

Avi. *The True Confessions of Charlotte Doyle*. Orchard, 1990.

_____. *Windcatcher*. Bradbury, 1991.

Beatty, Patricia, and Robbins, Phillip. *Eben Tyne, Powdermonkey*. Morrow, 1990.
Benchley, Peter. *Beast*. Random, 1991.
Boulle, Pierre. *The Whale of Victoria Cross*. Vanguard, 1983.
Bunting, Eve. *SOS Titanic*. Harcourt, 1996.
Campbell, Eric. *The Shark Callers*. Harcourt, 1994.
Clancy, Tom. *The Hunt for Red October*. Putnam, 1984.
Clarke, Arthur C. *The Ghost from the Grand Banks*. Bantam, 1990.
Cussler, Clive. *Raise the Titanic!* Pocket, 1990.
Dekkers, Midas. *Arctic Adventure*. Watts, 1987.
George, Jean Craighead. *Shark Beneath the Reef*. Harper, 1989.
Hunter, Mollie. *The Mermaid Summer*. Harper, 1988.
Iverson, Marc. *Persian Horse*. Orion, 1991.
Katz, Welwyn Wilton. *Whalesinger*. Macmillan, 1990.
Koller, Jackie French. *The Last Voyage of the Misty Day*. Atheneum, 1992.
Lisle, Janet Taylor. *The Lampfish of Twill*. Orchard, 1991.
Lisson, Deborah. *The Devil's Own*. Holiday, 1991.
Llewellyn, Sam. *Deadeye*. Summit, 1991.
_____. *Death Roll*. Simon & Schuster, 1990.
McKillip, Patricia. *The Changeling Sea*. Atheneum, 1988.
Melville, Herman. *Moby Dick*. Oxford University Press, 1988.
Norton, Andre. *Operation Time Search*. Ballantine, 1985.
O'Dell, Scott. *The Two Hundred Ninety*. Houghton, 1976.
Rand, Gloria. *Salty Dog*. Holt, 1989.
Shachtman, Tom. *Wavebender: A Story of Daniel au Fond*. Holt, 1989.
Strasser, Todd. *Beyond the Reef*. Delacorte, 1989.
_____. *The Diving Bell*. Scholastic, 1992.
Thiele, Colin. *Shadow Shark*. Harper, 1988.
Verne, Jules. *Twenty Thousand Leagues Under the Sea*. Airmont, 1964.

Periodicals

Oceans. Oceanic Society.
Sea Frontiers. International Oceanographic Foundation.
Seascape. Seascape Publications.
Underwater Naturalist. American Littoral Society.

Feature-Length Films

The Abyss. Fox, 1989. (PG-13)
The Hunt for Red October. Paramount, 1990. (PG)
Moby Dick. CBS/Fox, 1956.
A Night to Remember. Paramount, 1958.
The Poseidon Adventure. CBS/Fox, 1972. (PG)
Waterworld. MCA/Universal, 1995. (PG-13)

Computer Software

Coral Reef: The Vanishing Undersea World. Maxis, 1994.
High Seas Trader. Impressions Software, 1995.
Ocean Planet. Discovery Multimedia, 1995.
Oceans Below. Software Toolworks, 1994.
Sail Away! ScanRom Publications, 1995.
Stephen Biesty's Incredible Cross-Sections: Stowaway! Dorling Kindersley Multimedia, 1994.

41

Space Shots

The countdown is on at the library. If you are interested in stargazing, space exploration or rocketry, we have nonfiction books that will send you into orbit. The library also has many science fiction books, videos and soundtrack CDs for you to explore. Whether you harbor a secret ambition to become an astronaut, or you just like to read space westerns, check out these Space Shots at the library!

Display Ideas

Science fiction novels and videos set in outer space or on a spacecraft can be displayed with nonfiction books on space exploration, astronauts, rocketry, space technology, astronomy and other related areas. Add soundtrack music, posters and novelty items from space movies and television shows to the display.

Sponsorship for Prizes

1. Ask a bookstore to donate paperback copies of space exploration novels.
2. Ask a video rental store to donate certificates for free rentals of space movies.
3. Ask a toy or hobby store to donate models of space crafts.
4. Ask a local movie theater to donate movie posters or free passes for space movies.

Program Game

Draw a game board that contains several planets in a galaxy of your own creation. Draw spaces connecting the planets to each other. Starting from the designated Home Planet, patrons can move one space in any direction for each point earned. Each time a player lands on a planet, a dot can be placed on it. The goal of the game is to reach as many planets as possible. Points can be earned for completing the activities mentioned in the General Guidelines and for:

1. Reading a science fiction novel with a space exploration or rocketry theme, and completing a Space Fiction Book Review Form.

2. Reading a novel not related to the outer space theme, and completing a Fiction Book Review Form.

3. Reading a nonfiction book with a space exploration or rocketry theme and completing a Space Nonfiction Book Review Form.

4. Reading a nonfiction book not related to the outer space theme and completing a Nonfiction Book Review Form.

Program Forms

1. Space Fiction Book Review Form
Title:
Author:
Publisher and date:
Brief summary of plot:
What was your favorite part of the book and why?
Would you want to read more space fiction? Why or why not?

2. Fiction Book Review Form
Title:
Author:
Publisher and Date:
Brief summary of plot:
I would rate this book: "An awesome galaxy," "A blazing sun," "A habitable planet," "A lumpy asteroid," "A crater."

3. Space Nonfiction Book Review Form
Title:
Author:
Publisher and date:
Brief description of information:
What was the most interesting part of the book and why?
Would you like to read more on this subject? Why or why not?

4. Nonfiction Book Review Form
Title:
Author:
Publisher and date:
Brief description of information:
I would rate this book: "Discovered new worlds," "A successful moon landing," "Maintained an even orbit," "Countdown delayed indefinitely," "Blew up on the launch pad."

Program Activities

1. Rocket Flick. Entertain teens with a space movie such as *Apollo 13* or *The Right Stuff*.

2. NASA Patches. A special patch has been designed for every manned NASA space flight. Show young adults pictures of some of these clothing patches. Then provide art materials and let teens design a patch for an imaginary space mission. If you have access to a button-making machine or a laminator, you can use it to preserve these patch designs.

3. Stargazing. If there is an astronomy club in your area, arrange for patrons to go with the club one night to look at stars. Astronomers can point out various constellations and planets, talk about which heavenly bodies can be seen in the sky at different times of the year, demonstrate how to look through a telescope, and answer questions.

4. Space Books. Ask young adults to bring in their favorite science fiction novels that have space exploration themes, or in which much of the action takes place on a space ship. Readers can engage in a book discussion, and rate books in areas such as adventure, accuracy of scientific facts, realistic characters and events, creativity, satisfying ending, etc. Teens can compile a list of recommended space books, which can be printed and distributed to patrons.

5. **Space Crafts.** Set aside an area in which teens can construct a model space settlement. Let them use various scrap materials to create futuristic buildings, transport vehicles, highways, etc. They may want to build a space station and several space ships. This can be built during a one-day workshop, or have patrons add to it over a period of time.

6. **Space Cadets.** Teens with a knowledge of space information can participate in a trivia game show. Categories can include Rocket Scientist (rocketry terms), Other Worlds (planets, stars and galaxies), Blasts from the Past (history of space missions), Missionaries (astronauts), What Is It? (objects photographed in space), Lost in Space (failed or problem missions).

7. **Lunar Model.** Use a map of the moon as the basis for this activity. Teens can use clay or papier maché to recreate a model of the moon's surface. Craters, mountains, and other features should resemble those on the moon map. When the model is dry, teens can label the lunar features with the names given on the map. You may want to have teens work on two moon models (one for each face of the moon) if the models are lying on a flat surface.

8. **NASA Funding.** Should the United States government put more money into the space program, let funding continue at current levels, or reduce the space budget? Pose this question about NASA funding to teens and allow them to give their views. Participants in this debate should be able to back up their opinions with facts.

9. **Spaced-Out Jobs.** Present a program of career opportunities in space technology and exploration, such as jobs in astronomy, physics, nuclear technology, communications, computers, space photography and aeronautics. People are also needed to build and fly rockets, design and manufacture astronauts' clothing, create food to eat in space, staff the command center, analyze data, and more. Provide information on college majors in related fields and associations teens can write to for more information.

10. **Star Persons.** Sponsor an Out-of-This-World dance party at the library. Teens can come dressed as characters from space movies, TV shows, or novels. Play soundtrack music from these films and programs as well as space-themed tunes by popular recording artists.

Curriculum Tie-Ins

1. **English Literature/Composition.** Many science fiction stories, and even songs, have been written about what it is like to live in a rocket ship for several days. Read some fiction and nonfiction about life in space with the class. Then have students write a fictitious journal from the point of view of an astronaut who is on a 14-day space mission. Students can decide on the specialties of their astronauts and which type of space ship they are on.

2. **Science.** Show students several models and designs of NASA space crafts. Discuss rocket technology and engineering. Then divide students into groups and let them build rockets from store-bought kits. With supervision, allow students to launch their rockets outside.

3. **History/Geography.** Create a timeline of important events in astronomy and space exploration. List early astronomers who published theories about the universe, rocket scientists, and also important space missions, dates, astronauts and their countries. On a map of the world, locate where the astronomers lived and where space missions originated.

4. **Math.** Have students solve math equations based on the distances between planets, the gravity of various planets and moons, light years and space travel.

Activity Sheet Ideas

1. Word search or crossword puzzles of: a) space technology terms, b) names of man-made satellites, or c) names of planets, suns, or galaxies.

2. Word scrambles or cryptograms of: a) names of astronauts, b) space-related associations and research centers, or c) titles of books, movies, or TV shows about space exploration.

3. Matching activities: match a) rocketry terms (or anagrams) to their meanings, b) NASA astronauts to the rocket ships they manned, or c) names of flight crew positions to their job descriptions.

Suggested Resources

Reference and Nonfiction

Apfel, Necia H. *Space Station*. Watts, 1987.

Arnold, H.J.P., ed. *Man in Space: An Illustrated History of Spaceflight*. Smithmark, 1993.

Boyne, Walter J. *The Smithsonian Book of Flight for Young People*. Atheneum, 1988.

Camp, Carole Ann. *American Astronomers*. Enslow, 1996.

Clark, Phillip. *The Soviet Manned Space Program: An Illustrated History of the Men, the Missions, and the Spacecraft*. Salamander, 1988.

Crouch, Tom F.D. *The National Aeronautics and Space Administration*. Chelsea, 1990.

Donnelly, Judy, and Kramer, Sydelle. *Space Junk: Pollution Beyond the Earth*. Morrow, 1990.

Fisher, David E. *The Origin and Evolution of Our Own Particular Universe*. Macmillan, 1988.

Gibson, Bob. *The Astronomer's Sourcebook: The Complete Guide to Astronomical Publications, Planetariums, Organizations, Events, and More*. Woodbine, 1992.

Henbest, N. *The Night Sky*. EDC, 1993.

In Space. Time-Life Books, 1991.

Kelch, Joseph W. *Small Worlds: Exploring the 60 Moons of Our Solar System*. Messner, 1990.

Lampton, Christopher. *Supernova!* Watts, 1988.

Lemonick, Michael D. *The Light at the Edge of the Universe*. Princeton University, 1993.

Logsden, Tom. *Space, Inc.: Your Guide to Investing in Space Exploration*. Crown, 1988.

Long, Kim. *The Astronaut Training Book for Kids*. Lodestar, 1990.

Maples, Wallace R. *Opportunities in Aerospace Careers*. VGM, 1995.

Mayall, R. Newton, et al. *The Sky Observer's Guide*. Western, 1977.

Moeschl, Richard. *Exploring the Sky: Projects for Beginning Astronomers*. Chicago Review, 1992.

Murray, Bruce. *Journey into Space: The First Three Decades of Space Exploration*. Norton, 1989.

Raben, Richard, and Cohen, Hiyaguha. *Boldly Live as You've Never Lived Before: (Unauthorized and Unexpected) Life Lessons from Star Trek*. Morrow, 1995.

Ridpath, Ian. *Atlas of Stars and Planets*. Facts on File, 1993.

Sagan, Carl. *Pale Blue Dot: A Vision of the Human Future in Space*. Random, 1994.

Schick, Ron, and Van Haaften, Julie. *The View from Space: American Astronaut Photography, 1962-1972*. Crown, 1988.

Schulke, Flip, et al. *Your Future in Space: The U.S. Space Camp Training Program*. Crown, 1986.

Shipman, Harry L. *Humans in Space: 21st Century Frontiers*. Plenum, 1989.

Spangenburg, Ray, and Moser, Diane. *Living and Working in Space*. Facts on File, 1989.

Vbrova, Zuza. *Space and Astronomy*. Gloucester, 1989.

Vogt, Gregory L. *The Solar System: Facts and Exploration*. Twenty-First Century, 1995.
Wolfe, Tom. *The Right Stuff*. Farrar, 1983.

Fiction

Abels, Harriette. *Strangers on NMA-6*. Crestwood, 1979.
Adams, Douglas. *The Hitchhiker's Guide to the Galaxy*. Crown, 1980.
Allen, Roger MacBride. *Ambush at Corella: Book One of the Corellian Trilogy*. Bantam, 1995.
Anderson, Poul. *New America*. Tor, 1985.
Asimov, Isaac. *Nemesis*. Doubleday, 1989.
Barnes, John. *Orbital Resonance*. Tor, 1991.
Bisson, Terry. *Voyage to the Red Planet*. Morrow, 1990.
Bradbury, Ray. *The Martian Chronicles*. Doubleday, 1958.
Brunner, John. *A Maze of Stars*. Ballantine, 1991.
Clarke, Arthur C. *Rendezvous with Rama*. Ballantine, 1988.
Coppel, Alfred. *Glory's War*. Tor, 1995.
Crispin, A.C., and Marshall, Deborah A. *Serpent's Gift*. Ace, 1992.
Duane, Diane. *Spock's World*. Pocket, 1989.
Gilden, Mel. *The Planetoid of Amazement*. HarperCollins, 1991.
Heinlein, Robert A. *A Time for the Stars*. Macmillan, 1990.
Hoover, H.M. *Away Is a Strange Place to Be*. Dutton, 1990.
Lawrence, Louise. *Moonwind*. Harper, 1988.
Lewis, C.S. *Out of the Silent Planet*. Macmillan, 1968.
Lichtenberg, Jacqueline. *Dreamspy*. St. Martin's, 1989.
Longyear, Barry B. *The Homecoming*. Walker, 1989.
MacAvoy, R.A. *The Third Eagle: Lessons Along a Minor String*. Doubleday, 1989.
McCaffrey, Anne, and Nye, Jody Lynn. *The Death of Sleep*. Baen, 1990.
Norton, Andre. *Flight in Yiktor*. Tor, 1986.
Ore, Rebecca. *Being Alien*. Tor, 1989.
Pike, Christopher. *The Season of Passage*. Tor, 1992.
Pinkwater, Daniel. *The Snarkout Boys and the Avocado of Death*. 1982.
Riding, Julia. *Space Traders Unlimited*. Atheneum, 1987.
Scott, Melissa. *Mighty Good Road*. Baen, 1990.
Sleator, William. *Singularity*. Dutton, 1985.
Zelazny, Roger. *A Dark Traveling*. Avon, 1989.

(Also other series titles and science fiction works by these authors.)

Periodicals

Air and Space/Smithsonian. Smithsonian Associates.
Analog Science Fiction and Fact. Dell Magazines.
Astronomy. Kalmbach Publishing Co.
Griffith Observer. Griffith Observatory.
Sky and Telescope. Sky Publishing Co.
Spaceflight: The International Magazine of Space and Astronautics. G.V. Groves British Interplanetary Society.

Feature-Length Films

Apollo 13. MCA/Universal, 1995. (PG)
The Right Stuff. Warner, 1983. (PG)
Space Camp. Live Home Video, 1986. (PG)
Star Trek Generations. Paramount, 1994. (PG-13)
Star Wars. CBS/Fox, 1977. (PG)
2001: A Space Oddysey. MGM/UA, 1968. (PG)

Computer Software

Amazing Universe III. Hopkins Technology, 1995.
Americans in Space. Multicom Publishing, 1993.
Multimedia Space Explorer. Betacorp Technologies, 1995.
NASA Spaceviews Vol. I & II. Aztech New Media Corp., 1994.
Redshift. Maris Multimedia/Maxis, 1993.
Space Shuttle. Mindscape, 1993.
Voyage Through the Solar System. Compton's NewMedia, 1994.

42
Play to Win—Use the Library

Hello, sports fans, and welcome to the library, where every player is a winner. In the main arena, we have sports books and magazines—each one a knockout! On the field, you'll score big with fiction and nonfiction books of all types. Waiting in the bullpen are videos and CDs. Whatever your game is, we can help you make your goal. The ball is in your court now, so Play to Win—Use the Library!

Display Idea

Display a selection of nonfiction books about various sports and athletes, sports novels, magazines and videos. If a glassed-in showcase is available, you can fill it with sports memorabilia such as cards, action figures, baseballs, caps, etc. Hang posters of popular sports figures near the display.

Sponsorship for Prizes

1. Ask a local sports team, arena, or civic center to donate free passes to games.
2. Ask a sports apparel store to donate coupons for team logo sportswear or equipment.
3. Ask a sports memorabilia store to donate sports cards or other items.
4. Ask video stores to donate free rental certificates for sports videos.

Program Game

Use a replica of a quarter-mile track loop for the game. Position a runner figure at the starting line. The runner can advance along the track for every point earned, until the course has been completed. Points can be earned for completing the activities mentioned in the General Guidelines, and for:

1. Reading a sports novel and completing a Sports Fiction Book Review Form.
2. Reading a nonfiction sports book and completing a Sports Nonfiction Book Review Form.
3. Reading any fiction or nonfiction book not relating to sports and completing a Book Review Form.
4. Reading a sports magazine and completing a Sports Magazine Review Form.

Program Forms

1. Sports Fiction Book Review Form
Title:
Author:
Publisher and date:
Brief summary of plot:
I would rate this book: "A grand slam home run!," "An RBI," "A base hit," "A foul ball," "Struck out again."
2. Sports Nonfiction Book Review Form
Title:
Author:
Publisher and date:
Brief description of information:
What was the most interesting part of this book?
Would you recommend this book to other young adults? Why or why not?
3. Book Review Form
Title:
Author:
Publisher and date:
Brief summary of plot or information:
I would rate this book: "A gold medal," "A silver medal," "A bronze medal," "Didn't qualify for the finals," "Didn't even make the team."
4. Sports Magazine Review Form
Name of magazine:
Date of publication:
What kind of information is contained in this magazine?
What was the most interesting article and why?
To whom would this magazine appeal and why?

Program Activities

1. Sports Flick. Show a sports documentary, such as *Hoop Dreams*, a feature film with a sports theme, or a sports "blooper reel."

2. Memorabilia. Collecting autographs, ticket stubs, trading cards and other sports mementos is a popular hobby. Allow teens an opportunity to display their collections. Invite a long-time collector to talk about the value of some items, and give teens tips on what and how to collect.

3. Local Heroes. Invite athletes from a variety of sports to speak to teens. It may not be possible to get major league players, but minor league and college athletes may be willing to come to the library—especially if it is off-season for them. Create a panel of local sports heroes and let them answer teens' questions about their games, their lives and "going pro."

4. Go, Team, Go! Enlist some athletic members of the school or library staff and challenge teens to a game of softball, basketball, or another team sport. You can turn this into a fund-raising event for the library by asking patrons to pledge a certain amount of money for each point scored by their favorite team.

5. Gatorade Plus. Athletes should develop good eating habits. Present a brief talk on diet and nutrition. Then make some tasty, high-energy snacks. Teens can experiment with creating healthy juice drinks in a blender, yogurt-based snacks and other fun foods.

6. Sports Trivia. Two or more teams of young adults can compete in a game show that tests their knowledge of sports trivia. You may choose to limit your questions to a certain sport or sports, professional or college sports only, Olympic sports, or another area. Categories can include Olympic Champions, World Records, Sports Statistics, Superbowl (or other final game) Winners, Team Logos and Mascots, and Female Athletes.

7. Sportswear Chic. Put on a sportswear fashion show using teen volunteers as models. Ask a local sportswear store to provide workout apparel, team logo clothing, swimsuits, uniforms and other sports-related clothing. Play recordings of sports music, such as "Centerfield" by John Fogarty, while models show off these fashions.

8. Sports Talk. Hold a forum for young adults to express their opinions about sports issues. Teens can offer pro and con arguments on topics such as violence in sports, players going on strike, professional athletes' salaries, and athletes charging fans for their autographs. You may want to set time limits or have teens read short position papers to maintain order in the discussion, and take an opinion poll at the end of the program.

9. The Sporting Life. Showcase various sports careers in a special library program. In addition to professional athletes, coaches, trainers and managers, discuss job opportunities in sports journalism and broadcasting, marketing, clothing and equipment manufacturing and sales, sports medicine and physical therapy, and other related fields. If there is a sports arena or stadium nearby, invite a representative to talk to teens about gaining part-time employment there. Provide lists of colleges that offer sports-related majors and books on these subjects for teens to check out.

10. Team Spirit. Ask high school cheerleaders, majorettes and band members to lead a program for younger teens. Cheerleaders can teach middle-grade students some cheers, majorettes can demonstrate a few moves, and band members can talk about learning to march in formation. High schoolers can offer tips on making their squads, and can answer questions from their younger peers.

Curriculum Tie-Ins

1. English Literature/Composition. Tell students to read the sports pages and pick out the descriptive nouns, verbs and adjectives used by sports journalists. List these terms and phrases and discuss how effective they are in conveying the emotional impact of the sport. Then have students write an article describing an actual or fictitious sports event.

2. Science. Some athletes take anabolic steroids because they believe these drugs will make them more competitive. Discuss the different types of steroids that are found naturally in the human body, and contrast them with anabolic steroids. Have students research the chemical structures of various steroids and how they affect the body. Why are anabolic steroids dangerous?

3. History/Geography. Divide the class into groups and assign each one a different sport. Groups will trace the history of their sport, noting how, when and where it originated, highlights of its development, and where in the world the sport is popular today. On a map of the world, note where the summer and winter Olympic Games have been held. Then find the countries that sent teams to the most recent summer and winter Olympics.

4. Math. Create math problems based on different sports. For example: a) List the plays made by a football player during the course of a game, and have students figure out how many total yards he ran on the field; b) Given the number or hits, runs, strikeouts, etc. and the number of times at bat, figure out a baseball player's batting average and other statistics; c) Graph a sports team's win/loss record; d) Explain rules for scoring decathlon events, then describe the decathalon performances of five athletes and have students determine who won the gold medal.

Activity Sheet Ideas

1. Word search or crossword puzzles of: a) pro or college team names, b) sports terms, or c) sports equipment.

2. Word scrambles or cryptograms of: a) names of professional athletes, b) sports biographies or other best-selling sports books, or c) names of sports awards or important games.

3. Matching activities: match a) team names to their logos, mascots, arenas/stadiums, cities, or year(s) they won the final game/series, b) athletes to the year they won the Most Valuable Player (or other) award, or c) sports terms to their meanings and sports.

Suggested Resources

Reference and Nonfiction

Berger, Gilda. *Violence in Sports*. Watts, 1990.

Berlow, Lawrence H. *Sports Ethics*. ABC-CLIO, 1995.

Clark, Andy, et al. *Athletic Scholarships: Thousands of Grants and Over $400 Million for College-Bound Athletes*. Facts on File, 1994.

Diagram Group. *Rules of the Game: The Complete Illustrated Encyclopedia of All the Sports of the World*. St. Martin's, 1990.

Dragoo, Jason L. *Handbook of Sports Medicine*. Renaissance, 1993.

Dudley, William, ed. *Opposing Viewpoints: Sports in America*. Greenhaven, 1994.

Fulgaro, Elizabeth B., and Fulgaro, John M. *Free Sports Memorabilia: Where to Get It*. Betterway, 1992.

Funk, Gary. *A Balancing Act: Sports and Education*. Lerner, 1995.

Gardner, Robert. *Experimenting with Science in Sports*. Watts, 1993.

Gay, Kathlyn. *They Don't Wash Their Socks! Sports Superstitions*. Watts, 1990.

Heitzmann, William Ray. *Careers for Sports Nuts and Other Athletic Types*. VGM, 1991.

Hollander, Phyllis, and Hollander, Zander. *More Amazing But True Sports Stories*. Scholastic, 1990.

Jarrett, William S. **Timetables of Sports History** series. Facts on File, 1990.

Judson, Karen. *Sports and Money: It's a Sellout!* Enslow, 1995.

Knudson, R. R., and Swenson, May. *American Sports Poems*. Orchard, 1988.

Larson, Mark K., ed. *101 Sports Card Investments: Best Buys from $5 to $500*. Krause, 1993.

Nardo, Don. *Drugs and Sports*. Lucent, 1990.

Nelson, Cordner. *Careers in Pro Sports*. Rosen, 1990.

Numer, Hank. *Recruiting in Sports*. Watts, 1989.

_____. *Sports Scandals*. Watts, 1994.

Owens, Thomas. *Collecting Sports Autographs*. Bonus Books, 1989.

Palmatier, Robert A., and Ray, Harold Lloyd. *Sports Talk: A Dictionary of Sports Metaphors.* Greenwood, 1989.

Phillips, Louis, and Holmes, Burnham. *Yogi, Babe, and Magic: The Complete Book of Sports Nicknames.* Prentice, 1994.

Sanders, George R., et al. *The Sanders Price Guide to Sports Autographs.* Scott, 1993.

Sherman, Eric. *365 Amazing Days in Sports: A Day-by-Day Look at Sports History.* Little, 1990.

Smith, Nathan J., and Worthington-Roberts, Bonnie S. *Food for Sport.* Bull Publishing, 1989.

Stewart, Mark. *House of Cards: The Insider's Guide to Baseball Cards.* Crown, 1993.

Stine, Megan. *Family Sports Adventures: Exciting Sports-Filled Vacations for Parents and Kids to Share.* Little, 1991.

Taylor, John. *How to Get a Job in Sports: The Guide to Finding the Right Sports Career.* Collier, 1992.

Woolum, Janet. *Outstanding Women Athletes: Who They Are and How They Influenced Sports in America.* Oryx, 1992.

Fiction

Bennett, James. *The Squared Circle.* Scholastic, 1995.

Brooks, Bruce. *The Moves Make the Man.* Harper, 1984.

Carter, Peter. *Bury the Dead.* Farrar, 1987.

Crutcher, Chris. *The Crazy Horse Electric Game.* Greenwillow, 1987.

Deuker, Carl. *Heart of a Champion.* Joy Street, 12993.

———. *On the Devil's Court.* Avon, 1991.

Duder, Teresa. *In Lane Three, Alex Archer.* Houghton, 1989.

Dygard, Thomas J. *Game Plan.* Morrow, 1993.

Gallo, Donald R., ed. *Ultimate Sports: Short Stories by Outstanding Writers for Young Adults.* Delacorte, 1995.

Hermann, Spring. *Flip City.* Orchard, 1988.

Hughes, Dean. *End of the Race.* Atheneum, 1993.

Klass, David. *Wrestling with Honor.* Scholastic, 1990.

Koertge, Ronald. *Mariposa Blues.* Joy Street, 1991.

Lehrman, Robert. *Separations.* Viking, 1990.

Ley, Elizabeth. *Cold as Ice.* Morrow, 1988.

Lipsyte, Robert. *The Brave.* HarperCollins, 1991. (Also *The Chief.*)

MacLean, John. *When the Mountain Sings.* Houghton, 1992.

McCracken, Mark. *A Winning Position.* Dell, 1982.

Miklowitz, Gloria D. *Anything to Win.* Dell, 1989.

Murrow, Liza. *Twelve Days in August.* Holiday, 1993.

Myers, Walter Dean. *Slam!* Scholastic, 1996.

Norman, Rick. *Fielder's Choice.* August House, 1991.

O'Dell, Scott. *Black Star, Bright Dawn.* Houghton, 1988.

Paulsen, Gary. *The Voyage of the Frog.* Orchard, 1989.

Riddell, Ruth. *Ice Warrior.* Atheneum, 1992.

Savage, Deborah. *To Race a Dream.* Houghton, 1994.

Spinelli, Jerry. *There's a Girl in My Hammerlock.* Simon & Schuster, 1991.

Townsend, Tom. *Queen of the Wind.* Panda, 1989.

Voight, Cynthia. *The Runner.* Atheneum, 1985.

———. *Tell Me If the Lovers Are Losers.* Ballantine, 1983.

Periodicals

Inside Sports. Century Publishing Co.
The Olympian. United States Olympic Committee.
Sport. Sport Magazine Associates.
The Sporting News. Sporting News Publishing Co.
Sports Illustrated. Time, Inc.
Women's Sports and Fitness. Women's Sports Publications.

(Also magazines devoted to individual sports.)

Feature-Length Films

Eight Men Out. Orion, 1988. (PG)
The Great White Hope. CBS/Fox, 1970. (PG)
Hoop Dreams. New Line Home Video, 1994. (PG-13)
A League of Their Own. Columbia Tristar, 1992. (PG)
Lucas. CBS/Fox, 1986. (PG-13)
The Sports Blooper Awards. Marbowe, 1991.
Vision Quest. Warner, 1985. (R)

Computer Software

Gold Rush—Summer Olympics Game. Time-Warner Interactive, 1993.
Let's Play Soccer. Intellimedia Sports, 1994.
Manic Sports. MacroMedia, 1994.
NCAA Sports Video Almanac. Mindscape, 1995.
NFL Math. Sanctuary Woods, 1995.
Sports Illustrated CD-ROM Sports Almanac. Time-Warner Interactive, 1992.

43
Books Can Help You Survive

If you were stranded alone in the woods, could you survive? Could you start a fire, build a shelter, find and cook your food? At the library, you'll find many exciting stories about people who faced the elements, either by choice or happenstance, and survived. You can also pick up information about camping techniques, identifying edible wild plants, blazing a trail, and other outdoor skills. Whether you prefer to experience nature in the wild or in an easy chair, Books Can Help You Survive.

Display Idea

Set up a display of nonfiction books about camping and other outdoor activities, fiction about survival in the wilderness, related magazines, short story collections and videos. Place camping equipment, maps of national forests and local hiking trails, field guides on identifying flora and fauna, and labeled samples of local wildflowers in this area.

Sponsorship for Prizes

1. Ask a local, state, or national park in your area to donate free passes.
2. Ask a bookstore to donate fiction or nonfiction books about adventure or survival in the wilderness.
3. Ask a sporting equipment store to donate small items, such as mess kits, canteens, or camping manuals.
4. Ask a video rental store to donate free rental certificates for survival adventure movies.

Program Game

The game board is a picture of a mountain that has several ledges. Draw a trail that progresses up the mountainside to the summit. Patrons will earn a step along the trail for each point earned. Points can be earned for completing the activities mentioned in the General Guidelines, and for:

1. Reading a novel not related to the survival theme and completing a Fiction Book Review Form.
2. Reading a nonfiction book not related to the survival theme and completing a Nonfiction Book Review Form.
3. Reading a survival adventure novel, nonfiction book, or short story collection, and completing a Survival Book Review Form.

4. Reading an outdoor field manual or guide and completing an Outdoor Manual Review Form.

Program Forms

1. Fiction Book Review Form
Title:
Author:
Publisher and date:
Brief summary of plot:
I would rate this book: "A thrill-a-minute, action-packed adventure," "An amazing story," "It had some interesting moments," "It didn't excite me," "A bore."

2. Nonfiction Book Review Form
Title:
Author:
Publisher and date:
Brief description of information:
I would rate this book: "An incredible achievement," "It's one for the record books," "A noteworthy accomplishment," "It took a lot of stamina to get through this ordeal," "Bail out while you still can."

3. Survival Book Review Form
Title:
Author:
Publisher and date:
Brief summary of plot:
What was your opinion of this book?
Would you like to read more survival adventure books? Why or why not?

4. Outdoor Manual Review Form
Title:
Author:
Publisher and date:
Brief description of information:
When would the information in this guide be useful?
Do you think the information is this book is complete? Why or why not?

Program Activities

1. Big Screen Adventure. Show a feature film with an outdoor survival adventure theme, such as *The River Wild*.

2. Nature Crafts. Conduct a crafts workshop to show teens how to make items from woodland materials that would be useful for hunting and trapping game. Discuss what trees, plants, and other materials are best for fashioning bows and arrows, fishing poles and hooks, and baskets. You can also make whistles and other musical instruments out of reeds and wood scraps.

3. Good Sports. Invite an outdoor sports enthusiast, a representative of Outward Bound, or someone from a scouting organization to present a slide show or talk about some outdoor recreational activities, such as backpacking, mountaineering, or whitewater rafting.

4. Take a Hike. Take teens on a nature walk through a local park or woodland area. Bring along some field manuals to help you identify plants, trees and birds. Follow a marked trail or route mapped out by park officials. Discuss hiking and camping safety rules. Plan for patrons to carry food and utensils in backpacks and have a picnic in the woods. Be sure to clean up after yourselves.

5. Acorns for Lunch. In *My Side of the Mountain*, Sam creates many unusual meals from foods he has foraged in the woods. Gather a large supply of acorns and have teens follow Sam's instructions for cooking acorn pancakes. You may want to use another recipe in a book by Jean Craighead George or another naturalist, depending on what wild foods are available locally.

6. The Survival Instinct Show. This game show consists of two parts. Divide participants into teams of five. Each team should elect a spokesperson, but the entire group confers for the answers. In Part 1, the game show host poses true or false statements about survival, such as "Toadstools are safe to eat" or "You can start a fire by striking flint against steel." Each correct answer will earn that team 10 seconds to use in completing Part 2. In Part 2, one member of each team must attempt to find his or her way through an obstacle course or maze. The number of correct answers in Part 1 determines how long each person has. Award prizes to the team that successfully navigates the maze within the allotted time.

7. The Well-Equipped Camper. Ask a local sporting goods store or manufacturer to present a demonstration of outdoor sports equipment. The guest can give teens hands-on instruction on how to use a compass, pitch a tent, cast a fishing line, utilize mountain-climbing gear, roll up a sleeping bag, etc. He or she can also talk about the best type of equipment to use in different situations.

8. Survival Scenarios. Devote a session to discussing outdoor survival during emergency situations. Divide participants into teams of four. Randomly hand out slips of paper that describe where (in the Arizona desert, on a tropical island, in a pinewood forest, etc.) and when (during a summer heat wave, as a storm is brewing, in the fall, etc.) their team has been stranded. Each team must decide on six items (pocket knife, matches, string, etc.) they would need in order to survive for one week. Have each team share their answers with the group. Then present a list of twelve character types (math teacher, architect, track star, musician, etc.) and have each team choose four people that they think would have the best chance of surviving together in the previous scenario. Again, let each team explain their choices to the group.

9. Work Out. Sponsor a career day of outdoor occupations. Feature jobs in conservation, forestry, wildlife management, recreation, park or forest services, archeology, and ecology, as well as positions in organizations such as Outward Bound. Include nonfiction books and pamphlets about these careers, and list colleges that offer them as majors.

10. Choose An Adventure Game. Prepare a stack of index cards with a different adventure listed on each one. Sample adventures: take a trip to the moon, go bungee-jumping, take part in a dog-sledding race in the Arctic, etc. Divide teens into groups. Place the cards face down and have one player take the top card. He will have three minutes to act out (charades-style) the adventure. If the player's team guesses the adventure, a point is scored. The team with the most points, after everyone has had a turn, is the winner.

Curriculum Tie-Ins

1. English Literature/Composition. Have students read a fiction or nonfiction survival adventure story from a magazine. Then have them rewrite the story in the first person or from the perspective of another character in the story.

2. **Science.** Many wild plants, such as dandelion greens, hawthorn berries and cattail tubers, are edible. Have students make a list of foods that can be foraged in your area. Note which part(s) of each plant can be eaten. Determine which foods are natural sources of certain vitamins and minerals.

3. **History/Geography.** Look through the *Guinness Book of Records* or another reference source and list several adventurous explorers and their accomplishments, such as Admiral Byrd's trek to the South Pole. Have students create a timeline of these historical achievements, and locate on a map where they occurred. Have each student write a report on one of these explorers.

4. **Math.** Hikers and campers must be able to read a map. Give students a map of forest trails. Teach them how to use the legend to figure out distances between points along a trail and to determine which trail out of several is the shortest route to a specific destination. You can also give students a map of the United States, and have them locate a list of national parks and forests by noting their latitudes and longitudes.

Activity Sheet Ideas

1. Word search and crossword puzzles of: a) outdoor activities, b) occupations, or c) camping terms.

2. Word scrambles or cryptograms of: a) survival adventure films, b) recreational programs and organizations, c) or popular hiking, camping and climbing destinations.

3. Matching activities: match a) survival adventure books to their authors, b) real-life adventurers to their accomplishments, or c) outdoor recreational equipment to the activities for which they are used.

Suggested Resources

Reference and Nonfiction

Axcell, Claudia, et al. *Simple Foods for the Pack.* Sierra, 1986.

Boy Scouts of America. *The Boy Scout Handbook.* BSA, 1990.

Cook, Charles. *The Essential Guide to Wilderness Camping and Backpacking in the United States.* Kesend, 1994.

Elman, Robert. *The Hiker's Bible.* Doubleday, 1982.

George, Jean Craighead. *Acorn Pancakes, Dandelion Salad, and 38 Other Wild Recipes.* HarperCollins, 1995.

_____. *The Wild, Wild Cookbook: A Guide for Young Wild-Food Foragers.* Crowell, 1982.

Gerrard, Layne. *Rock Gear: Everybody's Guide to Rock Climbing Equipment.* Ten Speed, 1990.

Ghinsberg, Yossi. *Back from Tuichi: The Harrowing Life-and-Death Story of Survival in the Amazon Rainforest.* Random, 1993.

Gill, Paul G., Jr. *Simon & Schuster's Pocket Guide to Wilderness Medicine.* Simon & Schuster, 1991.

Greenwald, Michael. *Survivor.* Blue Horizons, 1989.

Hart, John. *Walking Softly in the Wilderness.* Sierra, 1984.

Kiley, Deborah Scaling, and Noonan, Meg. *Albatross: A True Story of a Woman's Survival at Sea.* Houghton, 1994.

Krakauer, Jon. *Eiger Dreams: Ventures Among Men and Mountains.* Lyons, 1990.

Long, John. *How to Rock Climb!* Chockstone, 1989.

McManners, Hugh. *The Backpackers Handbook*. Dorling Kindersley, 1995.

McMillon, Bill. *Wilderness U.: Opportunities for Outdoor Education in the U.S. and Abroad.* Chicago Review, 1992.

Miller, Louise. *Careers for Nature Lovers and Other Outdoor Types*. VGM, 1992.

Nature Craft. North Light, 1995.

Olsen, Larry Dean. *Outdoor Survival Skills*. Chicago Review, 1990.

Riviere, Bill. *The L.L. Bean Guide to the Outdoors*. Random, 1981.

Rowell, Galen. *Galen Rowell's Vision: The Art of Adventure Photography*. Sierra, 1993.

Sandi, Michael. *Sports Illustrated Backpacking*. NAL, 1989.

Simer, Peter, and Sullivan, John. *National Outdoor Leadership School's Wilderness Guide*. Simon & Schuster.

Simmons, James C. *The Big Book of Adventure Travel: 500 Great Escapes.* NAL, 1990.

Thomas, Dian. *Roughing It Easy*. Betterway, 1994.

Venning, Frank D. *Wildflowers of North America: A Guide to Field Identification*. Western, 1982. (Also other **Golden Field Guides.**)

Westmoreland, Preston, and Westmoreland, Nancy. *Stay Alive! A Guide to Survival in Mountainous Areas*. Westmoreland, 1993.

Fiction

Baillie, Allan. *Little Brother*. Viking, 1992.

Baird, Thomas. *Where Time Ends*. Harper, 1988.

Blackwood, Gary L. *The Dying Sun*. Atheneum, 1989.

Campbell, Eric. *The Place of Lions*. Harcourt, 1991.

Cole, Brock. *The Goats*. Farrar, 1987.

Cooney, Caroline B. *Flight #116 Is Down*. Scholastic, 1992.

Farmer, Nancy. *A Girl Named Disaster*. Orchard, 1996.

George, Jean Craighead. *Julie of the Wolves*. Harper & Row, 1974.

_____. *My Side of the Mountain*. Puffin, 1988. (Also *On the Far Side of the Mountain*.)

Halvorson, Marilyn. *Hold On, Geronimo*. Delacorte, 1988.

Hobbs, Will. *Downriver*. Macmillan, 1991.

Lasenby, Jack. *The Lake*. Oxford University Press, 1989.

McClung, Robert. *Hugh Glass, Mountain Man*. Morrow, 1990.

Macdonald, Caroline. *The Lake at the End of the World*. Dial, 1989.

McFann, Jane. *No Time for Rabbits*. Avon, 1991.

Masterton, David S. *Get Out of My Face*. Atheneum, 1991.

Mayne, William. *Low Tide*. Delacorte, 1993.

Mikaelsen, Ben. *Rescue Josh McGuire*. Hyperion, 1991.

Morey, Walt. *Death Walk*. Blue Heron, 1991.

Myers, Edward. *Climb or Die*. Hyperion, 1994.

Naylor, Phyllis Reynolds. *The Fear Place*. Atheneum, 1994.

O'Dell, Scott. *Island of the Blue Dolphins*. Houghton, 1990.

Palmer, David R. *Emergence*. Bantam, 1984.

Paulsen, Gary. *Hatchet*. Bradbury, 1987. (Also *The River* and *Brian's Winter*.)

Regan, Dian Curtis. *Game of Survival*. Avon, 1989.

Ruckman, Ivy. *No Way Out*. Crowell, 1988.

Taylor, Theodore. *The Cay*. Avon, 1970. (Also *Timothy of the Cay*.)

Thompson, Julian. *The Grounding of Group Six*. Avon, 1983.
Ure, Jean. *Plague*. Harcourt, 1991.
Wallace, Bill. *Danger in Quicksand Swamp*. Holiday, 1989.
White, Robb. *Deathwatch*. Dell, 1973.

Periodicals

Backpacker. Rodale Press, Inc.
Boy's Life. Boy Scouts of America.
Field and Stream. Times Mirror Magazines, Inc.
Outdoor Life. Times Mirror Magazines, Inc.
Sierra. Sierra Club.
Sports Afield. Hearst Corp.

Feature-Length Films

Cliffhanger. Columbia TriStar, 1993. (R)
Gold Diggers: The Secret of Bear Mountain. MCA/Universal, 1995. (PG-13)
Jeremiah Johnson. Warner, 1972. (PG)
The River Wild. MCA/Universal, 1994. (PG-13)
Shadow of the Wolf. Columbia Tristar, 1992. (PG-13)
Testament. Paramount, 1983. (PG)

Computer Software

Cliffhanger. Sony Electronic Publishing, 1993.
The Eyewitness Encyclopedia of Nature. Dorling Kindersley Multimedia, 1995.
Fodor's Interactive Sports and Adventure Vacations. Creative Multimedia Corp., 1995.
How Would You Survive As? Grolier Electronic Publishing, 1995.
North Polar Expedition. Virgin Interactive Entertainment, 1990.

44

Teen Scene

The teen years are a special time in your life. Young adults experience an array of good times, troubled times and changes. The library has books to help you celebrate the joys, cope with the rough spots, and understand what is happening to you and the world around you. You can also pick up some magazines written especially for teens, plus music and videos tailored to your interests. If you're into your second decade of life, come to the library and check out the Teen Scene.

Display Idea

Select fiction and nonfiction books that deal with a variety of adolescent concerns, such as self-esteem, peer and family relationships, health and sexuality issues, school, substance abuse, teen violence, fads, fashion, coming of age, etc. Add poetry and short stories written by and about teens, teen-oriented magazines, music and videos about teen experiences. Posters of teen idols and cartoons of teen observations can add some fun to the display.

Sponsorship for Prizes

1. Ask a bookstore to donate books about teen issues.
2. Ask a video store to donate free rental certificates for movies about teens.
3. Ask a magazine store to donate issues of teen-oriented magazines.
4. Ask a novelty store to donate posters, T-shirts, calendars, or other items that take a light-hearted look at the teen years.

Program Game

Draw a game board for "The Game of Teen Life," which starts at a teenager in his or her bedroom and ends at high school graduation. Spaces along a twisting path should pass through Home Sweet Home, School, the Mall, and popular teen hang-outs and landmarks. Some spaces can contain messages such as "Clean your room," "You aced the exam," or "Congratulations! You got rid of your braces." Patrons can advance one space for each point earned. Points can be earned for completing the activities mentioned in the General Guidelines, and for:

1. Reading a novel that explores a teenage concern and completing a Teen Fiction Book Review Form.
2. Reading a novel not related to the teen theme and completing a Fiction Book Review Form.

3. Reading a nonfiction book about a teen issue and completing a Teen Nonfiction Book Review Form.

4. Reading a nonfiction book not related to the teen theme and completing a Nonfiction Book Review Form.

Program Forms

1. Teen Fiction Book Review Form
Title:
Author:
Publisher and date:
Brief summary of plot:
What were some of the teen concerns dealt with in the story?
Do you think these issues were treated realistically? Why or why not?
2. Fiction Book Review Form
Title:
Author:
Publisher and date:
Brief summary of plot:
I would rate this book: "Rad," "Cool," "OK," "Bogus," "It bites."
3. Teen Nonfiction Book Review Form
Title:
Author:
Publisher and date:
Brief description of information:
What was the most interesting section of this book and why?
Would you recommend this book to a friend? Why or why not?
4. Nonfiction Book Review Form
Title:
Author:
Publisher and date:
Brief description of information:
I would rate this book: "Excellent," "Awesome," "It didn't make me want to heave," "It's not worthy," "The best book I ever read—NOT!"

Program Activities

1. Teen Screen. Teens can view a movie that features a teenage cast in a contemporary situation, such as *Clueless.*

2. Class Of... High school graduation is usually a high point in a person's life. Provide an art or craft opportunity for teens to celebrate their graduation classes. Supply materials for making T-shirts, buttons, banners, jewelry, ceramic tiles, or other memorabilia that can boast your patrons' graduation year(s) and school name(s), mascot(s), or logo(s).

3. Talk About It. Invite a guidance counselor, adolescent psychologist, or other expert in communicating with teens to hold a rap session with young adult patrons on issues that concern them. You may want to seek this person's advice or participation in other activities in conjunction with the Teen Scene program.

4. The Teen Age. Teens can submit original drawings, poetry, short stories, interviews, puzzles, "tips for teens," etc., that express their views on what it's like to be a contemporary teenager. They can edit and arrange these materials for a magazine that the library can publish and distribute to patrons.

5. Act It Out. Ask patrons to come up with several problem situations that young adults regularly face, such as arguing with parents over their choice of clothes or friends, peer pressures regarding cheating in school or underage drinking, etc. Teens can gather in small groups to role-play how they would handle a situation. Discuss each scene after it has been acted out. Would other teens have acted differently? How?

6. Teens On The Tube. Many sitcoms on TV are geared toward today's adolescents. Young adults can participate in a game show in which they must answer questions about the characters and plots of their favorite TV shows. Categories can include topics such as Who's Going with Whom? (current romances), Be True to Your School (name the school the characters attend), Cool Cars (what kind of car that character drives), Rocky Romances (who broke up with whom), Tough Luck (what's going wrong in a character's life), and My Hometown (where the show takes place). Choose five to ten currently popular shows to which teens relate, such as *Beverly Hills 90210*, to feature in this game.

7. Go In Style. Arrange for a clothing store that sells to teens to lend items for a fashion show. Young adults can volunteer to model casual, athletic, school, and formal clothes and accessories. You could also invite a hairdresser to style models' hair for the show.

8. Hot Topics. Devise a survey of issues that concern teens, and ask teen patrons to complete it. Be careful how you word controversial topics. Instead of asking, "Do you smoke pot?" say, "Do you think marijuana should be legalized?" Instead of "Have you ever considered suicide?" ask, "Do you know anyone who has considered or committed suicide?" Tabulate answers and discuss the results with your patrons. You may want to invite a teen counselor to help you devise the survey and moderate the discussion.

9. Get a Job. There are many places that employ teens during the summer or after school. Gather job applications from movie theaters, supermarkets, fast food restaurants, stores, sport venues, hotels, summer camps and other businesses that hire teens. Invite a job placement counselor to talk to teens. You can also inform teens of opportunities to volunteer their services in the community and the library.

10. Teens At the Top. Many people have become famous during their teen years. Post pictures of popular teens from the past and present on a bulletin board. Include famous teen actors, athletes, musicians, dancers, writers, inventors, adventurers, etc. Make a collage of these photos and number each one. Hold a contest in which patrons must try to identify as many of these famous teens as possible.

Curriculum Tie-Ins

1. English Literature/Composition. Have students read a novel of a contemporary teen's experiences, and another novel about life at some time in the past. For example, *Catcher in the Rye* may be compared to *Celine*. How are the lives and the feelings of these people similar? Is there such a thing as a "universal teenage experience"?

2. Science. Teach a health or physiology unit to help teens understand their changing bodies. This need not be a sex education unit, unless that is your intent. Other topics to discuss could include hormones, nutrition, voice changes, growth spurts and acne. You could also talk about the effects of smoking, drinking alcohol, using illegal drugs, or taking anabolic steroids.

3. History/Geography. Divide the class into small groups and assign each one a different decade in history. Each group must research what the teenagers of their decade were like. How did they dress? What music did they listen to? What did they do for entertainment? What books did they read? What problems did they have to cope with? What was school like? Students can look at old high school yearbooks, newspapers, magazines, and photographs of the times to gather information about teens in the United States and around the world.

4. Math. Give students several math problems featuring the numbers 13-19 to solve. You can also teach them math tricks and games involving these teen numbers.

Activity Sheet Ideas

1. Word search and crossword puzzles of: a) current teen slang expressions, b) famous teenagers, or c) teen activities.

2. Word scrambles and cryptograms of: a) movies aimed at teen audiences, b) brand-name products that appeal to teens, or c) music groups that teens like.

3. Matching activities: match a) popular teen expressions from the past to their meanings, b) authors of YA novels to their books, or c) characters in teen-oriented TV shows to the actors who play them.

Suggested Resources

Reference and Nonfiction

Arthur, Shirley. *Surviving Teen Pregnancy: Your Choices, Dreams and Decisions.* Morning Glory, 1991.

Atanasoff, Stevan E. *How to Survive as a Teen: When No One Understands.* Herald, 1989.

Ayer, Eleanor H. *Everything You Need to Know About Teen Marriage.* Rosen, 1990. (Also others in series.)

Benedict, Helen. *Safe, Strong and Streetwise.* Little, 1987.

Blake, Jeanne. *Risky Times: How to Be AIDS-Smart and Stay Healthy: A Guide for Teenagers.* Workman, 1990.

Blume, Judy. *Letters to Judy: What Your Kids Wish They Could Tell You.* Putnam, 1986.

Carlip, Hillary. *Girl Power: Young Women Speak Out!* Warner, 1995.

Carter, Carol. *Majoring in High School: Survival Tips for Students.* Farrar, 1995.

Coombs, H. Samm. *Teenage Survival Manual: How to Reach 20 in One Piece (and Enjoy Every Step of the Journey).* Discovery, 1989.

Edwards, Gabrielle. *Drugs on Your Streets.* Rosen, 1991.

Fenwick, Elizabeth, and Smith, Tony. *Adolescence: The Survival Guide for Parents and Teenagers.* Dorling Kindersley, 1994.

Gaines, Donna. *Teenage Wasteland: Suburbia's Dead End Kids.* Pantheon, 1991.

George, Nelson, ed. *Stop the Violence: Overcoming Self-Destruction.* Pantheon, 1990.

Gilbert, Sara. *Get Help: Solving the Problems in Your Life.* Morrow, 1989.

Hellmuth, Jerome. *Coping with Parents.* Rosen, 1985. (Also others in series.)

Hunter, LaToya. *The Diary of LaToya Hunter: My First Year in Junior High School.* Crown, 1992.

Hyde, Margaret O. *Kids in and Out of Trouble.* Cobblehill, 1995.

Hyde, Margaret O., and Forsyth, Elizabeth Held. *Suicide*. Wilson, 1995.

Johnson, Eric W. *Love and Sex and Growing Up*. Bantam, 1990.

Kaufman, Miriam. *Easy for You to Say*. Key Porter, 1995.

Kittredge, Mary. *Teens with AIDS Speak Out*. Messner, 1991.

Kolodny, Nancy J., et al. *Smart Choices*. Little, 1986.

Lang, Denise V. *But Everyone Else Looks So Sure of Themselves: A Guide to Surviving the Teen Years*. Shoe Tree, 1991.

Leahy, Michael. *Hard Lessons: Senior Year at Beverly Hills High School*. Little, 1988.

Levine, Mel. *Keeping a Head in School*. Educators, 1990.

Newton, David E. *Teen Violence: Out of Control*. Enslow, 1995.

Nourse, Alan E. *Sexually Transmitted Diseases*. Watts, 1992.

Packer, Alex J. *Bringing Up Parents: The Teenager's Handbook*. Free Spirit, 1992.

Resumes for High School Graduates. VGM, 1993.

Rosenberg, Ellen. *Growing Up Feeling Good: A Growing Up Handbook Especially for Kids*. Puffin, 1989.

Silverstein, Virginia, et al. *The Addictions Handbook*. Enslow, 1991.

Stavsky, Lois. *The Place I Call Home: Voices and Faces of Homeless Teens*. Shapolsky, 1990.

Straight Talk series. Facts on File.

Teenage Perspectives series. ABC-CLIO.

Wirths, Claudine G., and Bowman-Kruhm, Mary. *I Hate School: How to Hang in and When to Drop Out*. Crowell, 1987.

_____. *Where's My Other Sock? How to Get Organized and Drive Your Parents and Teachers Crazy*. Crowell, 1989.

Weston, Carol. *Girltalk about Guys*. Harper, 1988.

Zvirin, Stephanie. *The Best Years of Their Lives: A Resource Guide for Teenagers in Crisis*. ALA, 1992.

Fiction

Arrick, Fran. *What You Don't Know Can Kill You*. Bantam, 1992.

Asher, Sandy. *Out of Here: A Senior Class Yearbook*. Penguin, 1993.

Barr, Linda. *The Wrong Way Out*. Willowisp, 1990.

Barrett, Peter A., ed. *To Break the Silence: Thirteen Short Stories for Young Readers*. Dell, 1986.

Benard, Robert, ed. *Do You Like It Here?* Dell, 1989.

Bennett, James W. *I Can Hear the Mourning Dove*. Houghton, 1990.

Boyd, Candy Dawson. *Breadsticks and Blessing Places*. Macmillan, 1985.

Brooks, Jerome. *Naked in Winter*. Orchard, 1990.

Clarke, Judith. *Al Capsella and the Watchdogs*. Holt, 1990.

Cohen, Miriam. *Laura Leonora's First Amendment*. Lodestar, 1990.

Cole, Brock. *Celine*. Farrar, 1989.

Cooney, Caroline B. *Among Friends*. Bantam, 1987.

Cormier, Robert. *The Chocolate War*. Bantam, 1986.

Geller, Mark. *My Life in the Seventh Grade*. Harper, 1986.

Gold, Robert, ed. *Stepping Stones: Seventeen Stories of Growing Up*. Dell, 1981.

Head, Ann. *Mr. and Mrs. Bo Jo Jones*. NAL, 1973.

Hinton, S.E. *The Outsiders*. Dell, 1989.

Irwin, Hadley. *So Long at the Fair*. Macmillan, 1988.

Joose, Barbara A. *The Pitiful Life of Simon Schultz*. HarperCollins, 1991.

Kassem, Lou. *Middle School Blues*. Houghton, 1986.

Kaye, Geraldine. *Someone Else's Baby*. Hyperion, 1992.
Klein, Norma. *Just Friends*. Random, 1990.
_____. *No More Saturday Nights*. Knopf, 1988.
Landis, J.D. *Looks Aren't Everything*. Bantam, 1990.
Levit, Rose. *With Secrets to Keep*. Shoe Tree, 1991.
Levy, Marilyn. *Rumors and Whispers*. Fawcett, 1990.
Maguire, Jesse. *Nowhere High*. Ivy, 1990.
Park, Barbara. *My Mother Got Married (and Other Disasters)*. Knopf, 1989.
Posner, Richard. *Goodnight, Cinderella*. M. Evans, 1989.
Reynolds, Marilyn. *Beyond Dreams: True-to-Life Series from Hamilton High*. Morning Glory, 1995.
Roos, Stephen. *You'll Miss Me When I'm Gone*. Delacorte, 1988.
Ryan, Mary E. *The Trouble with Perfect*. Simon & Schuster, 1995.
Salinger, J.D. *The Catcher in the Rye*. Little, 1991.
Shoup, Barbara. *Wish You Were Here*. Hyperion, 1995.
Sieruta, Peter D. *Heartbeats: And Other Stories*. Harper, 1989.
Sommers, Beverly. *The Uncertainty Principle*. Fawcett, 1990.
Stoehr, Shelley. *Crosses*. Delacorte, 1991.
Thomas, Joyce Carol. *A Gathering of Flowers: Stories About Being Young in America*. Harper, 1990.
Townsend, Sue. *The Secret Diary of Adrian Mole, Aged 13³/₄*. Grove, 1986.
Willey, Margaret. *If Not for You*. Harper, 1988.
Zolotow, Charlotte, ed. *Early Sorrow: Ten Stories of Youth*. Harper, 1986.

Periodicals

High School Senior Magazine. High School Senior, Inc.
Scholastic Update. Scholastic, Inc. (Also other Scholastic titles.)
Seventeen. Triangle Communications.
Teen. Petersen Publishing Co.
Teen Generation. Teen Generation, Inc.
YM. Gruner & Jahr Publishing.

Feature-Length Films

Class Act. Warner, 1991. (PG-13)
Clueless. Paramount, 1995. (PG-13)
The Man in the Moon. MGM/UA, 1991. (PG-13)
Permanent Record. Paramount, 1988. (PG-13)
Renaissance Man. Touchstone, 1994. (PG-13)
Say Anything. CBS/Fox, 1989. (PG-13)
Sixteen Candles. MCA/Universal, 1984. (PG)

Computer Software

DISCovering Careers and Companies. Gale Research, semiannual.
Kids in History. MPI Multimedia, 1994.
Multimedia Dropout Prevention. Cambridge Educational, 1995.
Multimedia Study Skills. Cambridge Educational, 1995.
National Archive on Sexuality, Health and Adolescence. Knowledge Access International.
Peterson's College Database. Silver Platter Information, annual.
Score 800. Queue, 1992.

45
All the World's a Stage

Want to "play around"? Your library has just the thing for you—scripts of comedies, musicals, dramas and monologues, books on acting and stage production, theater trivia, Broadway cast albums, and videos of theater productions and plays that were made into movies. Some great young adult novels are set in the theater, too. Don't miss this cue to add some drama to your life. You'll find that All the World's a Stage at the library.

Display Idea

Set up a book display of plays, including one-acts, monologues, scene anthologies, contemporary and classical works. Add books about theater production, history, criticism and acting. Other materials that will appeal to teens are young adult novels that have a theater setting and drama periodicals for middle school and high school students. Dress up the display with posters advertising local or professional theater productions, playbills, and a replica of the masks of comedy and tragedy.

Sponsorship for Prizes

1. Ask a local community or school drama group to donate free passes to one of their productions.

2. Ask a novelty store to donate T-shirts, mugs, or other souvenir items marked with a theater theme or logo.

3. Ask a music store to donate certificates for original cast album recordings.

4. Ask a bookstore to donate paperback copies of plays, or of novels set in the theater.

Program Game

Make a game board that looks like a large auditorium. Players start at the back of the auditorium and advance one seat for each point earned until they reach the stage. Points can be earned for completing the activities mentioned in the General Guidelines, and for:

1. Reading a novel and completing a Fiction Book Review Form.

2. Reading a nonfiction book and completing a Nonfiction Book Review Form.

3. Reading a theater script or screenplay, or watching a live theatrical production, and completing a Play Review Form.

4. Researching some aspect of the theater in a periodical or reference source and completing a Theater Expert Form.

Program Forms

1. Fiction Book Review Form
Title:
Author:
Publisher and date:
Brief summary of plot:
I would rate this book: "A standing ovation!," "Take another curtain call," "Good, but won't win any Tony Awards," "Needs more rehearsing," "Even Shakespeare couldn't have saved this mess."

2. Nonfiction Book Review Form
Title:
Author:
Publisher and date:
Brief description of information:
I would rate this book: "Standing room only," "A solid box office hit," "Polite applause," "Needs a rewrite," "A flop."

3. Play Review Form
Title:
Author (book):
Music composer (if applicable):
Lyricist (if applicable):
Date seen (if applicable):
Type of play: Comedy, drama, musical, monologue, one act(s)
Brief summary of plot:
What was your opinion of this play?

4. Theater Expert Form
Aspect of theater you researched:
Name, author, date, and page numbers of source(s) used:
Brief summary of what you learned about this subject:

Program Activities

1. Readers' Theater. Teens can participate in a readers' theater group. Select an appropriate scene and let teens audition for parts. Allow them to rehearse several times before performing the piece for their peers.

2. Setting the Stage. If a local theater or school drama group is working on a play, perhaps you can arrange for your teen patrons to help build the set. The set designer can show participants lighting and other stage equipment. Teens can participate in building, masking, and painting flats, coloring and hanging lights, and other set construction tasks.

3. The Roar of the Greasepaint. Invite a make-up artist from a local theater group to conduct a workshop on stage make-up. Teens can volunteer to be made up, or practice applying different types of theater make-up on their peers.

4. Play Time. Take your patrons on a field trip to see a live play, or invite a theater group to perform at the library. Ask the group if they would allow your teen patrons to observe the actors as they put on their make-up, and watch the stage and house crews prepare for the show. After the performance, perhaps teens can discuss the production with the members of the theater group.

5. Warm-Ups. Actors usually prepare themselves for going on stage by practicing vocal and physical warm-up exercises. An acting coach can lead participants through a series of common ones, such as breathing techniques, loosening-up exercises and vocal exercises.

6. The Play's the Thing. Host a theater trivia game show. Teens can answer questions in categories such as Name That Broadway Tune, Theater Actors, Famous Directors, Musical Theater, Composer/Lyricist Teams, and Classic Plays.

7. The Clothes Make the Character. Many innovative costumes have been created for theater productions. Invite a costume designer to explain how he or she designs and constructs costumes. Perhaps he or she can show pictures or slides of unusual costumes, and bring in some items for teens to try on. Artistic teens may want to try their hand at drawing costumes for selected characters.

8. Improvisational Theater. Conduct an improv workshop with teens. Explain what improvisation is, and let patrons suggest character types or comic and dramatic situations for scenes. Then have teens act out these scenarios. You can also hand out simple props and let students work them into short skits.

9. Broadway Bound. Hold a career day that spotlights occupations in the theater, such as actor, playwright, director, choreographer, lighting or sound technician, producer, costume or set designer, props coordinator, musician, dancer, vocal coach, make-up artist, house or publicity manager and other related careers. Invite local residents who have theater experience to speak. Have available several nonfiction books on these topics for patrons to borrow, and a list of colleges that offer majors in these areas.

10. Brush Up Your Shakespeare. Many young adults are probably more familiar with the Bard than they realize. Gather some famous Shakespearean quotes and have teens identify the plays from which these lines came. Have several copies of Shakespeare's plays and related reference works available for teens to consult. You can also use this as a booktalking opportunity.

Curriculum Tie-Ins

1. English Literature/Composition. Teach students about plays as a form of literature. Have them read some popular, classic, and one-act plays to study their composition and other elements. Then have students read short stories and rewrite them as one-act plays.

2. Science. Use stage lighting as a starting point for a lesson on light waves and the color spectrum. Then discuss other forms of theater technology, such as computerized light boards, microphones and other sound equipment, and the pulley or hydraulic system for opening and closing the curtain.

3. History/Geography. Have students research theater forms throughout history and in different countries. Some questions to consider: What role did the church play in the history of theater? Who were the first actors? What are some theater superstitions? What is the history of women in the theater? What forms of theater exist today in different parts of the world?

4. Math. Set design and construction involves carpentry and precise measurements. A geometry unit can focus on the problems of building several movable sets for a play.

Activity Sheet Ideas

1. Word search or crossword puzzles of: a) terms relating to the format of a play, b) theater production, or c) theatrical occupations.

2. Word scrambles or cryptograms of: a) titles of plays, b) names of famous theater actors or production people, or c) famous quotes from plays.

3. Matching activities: match a) names of characters to the plays from which they came, b) musicals to the non-musical play, book, or movie on which they are based, or c) playwrights to their plays.

Suggested Resources

Reference and Nonfiction

Beard, Jocelyn, ed. *Monologues from Classic Plays, 486 B.C. to 1960 A.D.* Smith and Kraus, 1992.

Bernardi, Philip. *Improvisation Starters.* Betterway, 1992.

Bordman, Gerald Martin. *American Musical Theater: A Chronicle.* Oxford University Press, 1992.

Cassin-Scott, Jack. *Amateur Dramatics.* Cassel, 1992.

Freeman, Ron. *Makeup Art.* Watts, 1991.

Gallo, Donald R., ed. *Center Stage: One-Act Plays for Teenage Readers and Actors.* Harper, 1990.

Greenberg, Jan. *Theater Careers: A Comprehensive Guide to Non-Acting Careers in the Theater.* Holt, 1983.

Guernsey, Otis L., Jr., ed. *The Best Plays of 1995-1996.* Limelight Editions. (Also other years.)
_____. *Broadway Song & Story: Playwrights, Lyricists, Composers Discuss Their Hits.* Dodd, 1985.

Ingham, Rosemary, and Covey, Liz. *The Costume Designer's Handbook: A Complete Guide for Amateur and Professional Costume Designers.* Heinemann, 1992.

Ionazzi, Daniel A. *The Stage Management Handbook.* Betterway, 1992.

James, Thurston. *The Prop Builder's Molding and Casting Handbook.* Betterway, 1989.

Jankowski, Wanda. *The Best of Lighting Design.* PBC International, 1987.

Kehret, Peg. *Encore: More Winning Monologues for Young Actors.* Meriwether, 1988.

Lamb, Wendy, ed. *Ten Out of Ten: Ten Winning Plays Selected from the Young Playwrights Festival, 1982-1991, Produced by the Foundation of the Dramatists Guild.* Delacorte, 1992.

Latrobe, Kathy Howard, and Laughlin, Mildred. *Readers Theater for Young Adults.* Teacher Ideas, 1989.

Loxton, Howard. *Theater.* Steck-Vaughn, 1989.

Novelly, Maria C. *Theatre Games for Young Performers.* Meriwether, 1985.

Padol, Brian A., et al. *The Young Performer's Guide: How to Break into Show Business.* Betterway, 1990.

Pike, Frank, and Dunn, Thomas G. *The Playwright's Handbook.* NAL, 1985.

Ruby, Jennifer. **Costume Context** series. Trafalger.

Silver, Fred. *Auditioning for the Musical Theatre.* Newmarket, 1985.

Sitarz, Paula Gaj. *The Curtain Rises, Vol. II: A History of European Theater from the Eighteenth Century to the Present.* Betterway, 1993. (Also *The Curtain Rises, Vol. I.*)

Slaight, Craig, and Sharrar, Jack, eds. *Great Scenes for Young Actors from the Stage.* Smith and Kraus, 1991.

Straub, Cindie, and Straub, Matthew. *Mime: Basics for Beginners.* Plays, 1984.

Swinfield, Rosemarie. *Stage Makeup Step-by-Step.* Betterway, 1995.

Thurston, James. *The Theater Props Handbook: A Comprehensive Guide to Theater Props, Materials, and Construction.* Betterway, 1987.

Williamson, Walter. *Behind the Scenes: The Unseen People Who Make Theater Work*. Walker, 1987.
_____. *Early Stages: The Professional Theater and the Young Actor*. Walker, 1986.

Fiction

Blain, W. Edward. *Passion Play*. Putnam, 1990.
Brett, Simon. *Star Trap*. Warner, 1990.
Cameron, Eleanor. *The Private Worlds of Julie Redfern*. Dutton, 1988.
Coville, Bruce. *Fortune's Journey*. BridgeWater, 1995.
Covington, Dennis. *Lizard*. Delacorte, 1991.
Cross, Gillian. *The Dark Behind the Curtain*. Oxford University Press, 1984.
Daneman, Meredith. *Francie and the Boys*. Doubleday, 1989.
Deaver, Julie Reece. *Say Goodnight, Gracie*. Harper, 1988.
Geras, Adele. *Happy Endings*. Harcourt, 1991.
Gilmore, Kate. *Enter Three Witches*. Houghton, 1990.
_____. *Jason and the Bard*. Houghton, 1993.
Goldman, Katie. *In the Wings*. Dial, 1982.
Jones, Robin D. *No Shakespeare Allowed*. Atheneum, 1989.
Kerr, Katherine, and Greenberg, Martin, eds. *Weird Tales from Shakespeare*. DAW, 1994.
Kingman, Lee. *Break a Leg, Betsy, Maybe*. Morrow, 1993.
Lucas, Cynthia K. *Center Stage Summer*. Square One, 1988.
McDaniel, Lurlene. *Time to Let Go*. Bantam, 1991.
McNamara, Brooks. *The Merry Muldoons and the Brighteyes Affair*. Orchard, 1992.
Nixon, Joan Lowery. *The Weekend Was Murder*. Delacorte, 1992.
Paulsen, Gary. *The Boy Who Owned the School*. Orchard, 1990.
Sachs, Marilyn. *Circles*. Dutton, 1991.
Schwandt, Stephen. *Guilt Trip*. Atheneum, 1990.
Scoppettone, Sandra. *Trying Hard to Hear You*. Alyson, 1991.
Shreve, Susan. *The Gift of the Girl Who Couldn't Hear*. Morrow, 1991.
Singer, Marilyn. *The Course of True Love Never Did Run Smooth*. Harper, 1983.
Sonnenmark, Laura A. *Something's Rotten in the State of Maryland*. Scholastic, 1990.
Walker, Paul Robert. *The Method*. Harcourt, 1990.
Williams, Michael. *Crocodile Burning*. Lodestar, 1992.
Zindel, Paul. *David & Della: A Novel*. HarperCollins, 1993.

Periodicals

American Theatre. Theatre Communications Group.
Dramatics. Educational Theatre Association.
Musical Show. Tams-Whitmark Music Library, Inc.
Plays. Plays, Inc.
Theatre Crafts. Theatre Crafts Associates.
Variety. Variety, Inc.

Feature-Length Films

Author! Author! Fox, 1992. (PG)
The Band Wagon. MGM/UA, 1953.

Broadway Danny Rose. Vestron, 1984. (PG)
Noises Off. Touchstone, 1992. (PG-13)
The Producers. Columbia Tristar, 1968.
To Be or Not to Be. CBS/Fox, 1983. (PG)

Computer Software

Discovering Shakespeare. IVI Publishing, 1995.
Macbeth. Voyager Company.
Opening Night CD. MECC, 1995.
Virtual Variety Show. Scitron & Art.

46
Book Your Vacation at the Library

Imagine you have an opportunity to travel anywhere in the world. Where would you go? How would you get there? What places would you visit, what clothes would you wear, and what foods would you eat? The answers to these questions and more can be found in the travel section of your library. There are also magazines, fiction and videos to help you visualize your dream vacation. Whether you're an armchair traveler or an experienced globe-trotter, you'll have fun when you Book Your Vacation at the Library.

Display Idea

Surround an area with travel posters from around the world. Intersperse travel brochures, postcards, itineraries, airline and train tickets with nonfiction travel guides, foreign phrase books, books of advice to travelers and travel videos. Include novels with travel or vacation plots, related magazines, and clippings from newspaper travel sections.

Sponsorship for Prizes

1. Ask a video rental store to donate certificates for travel videos.
2. Ask a bookstore to donate travel guides.
3. Ask AAA or a travel agency to donate road maps to United States vacation spots, travel posters, and brochures.
4. Ask a drugstore to donate travel-size toiletry samples and disposable cameras.

Program Game

Use a world map for the game board. Mark your hometown with a star, and circle several travel destinations along the map. Connect these with a line that originates from the star, encircles the globe, and returns to the star. From the star, patrons will travel along this route, moving one destination for each point earned, until they return home. Points can be earned for completing the activities mentioned in the General Guidelines, and for:

1. Reading a novel that involves travel or a vacation, or that mentions some tourist spots, and completing a Travel Fiction Book Review Form.
2. Reading a novel not related to the travel/vacation theme and completing a Fiction Book Review Form.
3. Reading a nonfiction book not related to the travel/vacation theme and completing a Nonfiction Book Review Form.

4. Watching a travel documentary plus reading a nonfiction travel guide, magazine article, or brochure about the same destination, and completing a Travel Film and Article Comparison Form.

Program Forms

1. Travel Fiction Book Review Form
Title of novel:
Author:
Publisher and date:
Brief summary of plot:
What type of travel was mentioned in the book, and where did the main character go?
How important was this to the plot of the book?
2. Fiction Book Review Form
Title:
Author:
Publisher and date:
Brief summary of plot:
I would rate this book: "First class," "Had a great time," "Worth the trip," "About as exciting as losing your luggage," "This book goes absolutely nowhere."
3. Nonfiction Book Review Form
Title:
Author:
Publisher and date:
Brief description of information:
I would rate this book: "My best trip ever," "A choice destination," "It's a nice place to visit, but I wouldn't want to live there," "Cancel my reservations," "Hand me an air sickness bag."
4. Travel Film and Article Comparison Form
Name of film:
Year made:
Name of article:
Where it appeared and date:
Travel destination:
Which source had the best information and why?
What was the best travel tip, and in which source did you find it?

Program Activities

1. What They Did On Their Vacation. Show a feature film with a travel or vacation theme, such as *National Lampoon's European Vacation*.
2. Poster Puzzles. Ahead of time, mount some travel posters or maps of tourist attractions onto card stock. Hand out posters and scissors, and let teens cut them into jigsaw puzzles. Give them time to assemble their puzzles, and plastic bags in which to take them home afterwards.
3. Travel Smarts. Invite a travel agent to talk to patrons about travel tips. The agent can give pointers on making reservations, exchanging currency, best times to visit certain

places, what to pack, how to get a passport, local customs, tipping, best tours to take, choosing a resort, going through customs and other handy information.

4. Travel Games. Sponsor an indoor or outdoor game day. Invent some wacky activities in which teens can compete for prizes. A few examples: The Price Is Right (using foreign currency), the Maneuver-Your-Way-Through-the-Airport Obstacle Course, How Much Beach Equipment Can You Carry? How Much Stuff Can You Stuff Into a Suitcase? What Am I Eating? (guess main ingredients in foreign foods), and Find the Key That Will Unlock Your Hotel Room.

5. Food, Glorious Food. Each person should prepare a food dish from a different country to serve at an international buffet. Direct teens to the cookbook section and ask participants to provide a copy of the recipe they used so you can compile them into a cookbook of Foods from Around the World, which can be given to participants. You can also do this with regional dishes from places in the United States.

6. World Traveler Game. Host a game show with a travel theme. Teens can answer trivia questions about various foreign countries in categories such as Types of Currency, Capital Cities, Foreign Phrases, Famous Landmarks, Popular Tourist Attractions and Flags.

7. Photo Journey. Most people take lots of photos, slides, or videos when they travel. Invite a photographer to conduct a workshop on how to take great scenic photos. Teens can bring in their own photo and video equipment or try out some brought in by the photographer. Reserve a bulletin board for patrons to display pictures they take while on vacation.

8. Tourist Attractions. Present a multimedia slide show of popular vacation spots. Play music that corresponds to each place shown. Afterwards, discuss some interesting travel ideas.

9. The Traveling Life. Sponsor a career fair of travel-related jobs. Patrons can learn about various positions with a travel agency, airline, hotel or resort, travel magazine, tour book company, cruise ship, travel documentary company, and international bank, as well as jobs at popular tourist sites such as national forests and landmarks, theme and amusement parks, ballparks and stadiums, theaters and museums. Invite people who are employed in these fields to speak. Have related nonfiction books available for patrons to borrow, and supply a list of schools and colleges that offer training in the more specialized areas.

10. International Dance Party. Invite teens to wear costumes from different countries to the dance. Play music from other lands and teach patrons the steps to traditional dances.

Curriculum Tie-Ins

1. English Literature/Composition. Introduce students to classic travel titles, such as *Travels with Charlie*. Discuss what makes these books exciting to read. Let students view photos or video clips of vacation adventures such as whitewater rafting, or scenic vacations such as visiting the Taj Mahal. Then have them write first-person travelogues in which they describe their imaginary vacations to one of these places.

2. Science. Discuss some technology utilized by the travel industry, such as computerized ticketing, jet planes and cruise ships. Have students choose a topic and explain how advances in its technology make travel easier, more comfortable, safer, more convenient, or more efficient.

3. History/Geography. Assign each student a different country to profile. They can report about topics of interest to travelers, such as the country's geographical features, climate, language(s), people, customs, important cities, landmarks, food, tourist sites, government, economy, major holidays and festivals.

4. Math. Students can solve math problems based on computing the exchange rates for money in different countries, and on determining the hour in several time zones around the world.

Activity Sheet Ideas

1. Word search or crossword puzzles of: a) travel terms, b) related occupations, or c) vacation activities.

2. Word scrambles or cryptograms of: a) foreign phrases, b) festivals and celebrations around the world, or c) local fun spots to visit.

3. Matching activities: match a) popular tourist attractions to the country or state in which they are located, b) airlines to their country of origin, or c) traditional foods to their countries.

Suggested Resources

Reference and Nonfiction

Arnold, Thomas A. *The Adventure Guide to the Pacific Northwest.* Hunter, 1988.

Beasley, Conger, Jr., et al. *The Sierra Club Guide to the National Parks of the Desert Southwest.* Stewart, Tabori & Chang, 1984. (Also others in series.)

Bernstein, Joanne E. *Taking Off: Travel Tips for a Carefree Trip.* Harper, 1986.

Burgett, Gordon. *The Travel Writer's Guide.* Prima, 1991.

Carter, Frances. *Hawaii for Free: Hundreds of Free Things to Do in Hawaii.* Mustang, 1988.

Chaiet, Donna. *Staying Safe on Public Transportation.* Rosen, 1995. (Also *Staying Safe While Traveling.*)

Chatein, Bruce. *What Am I Doing Here?* Viking, 1989.

Cities of the World. 4 vols. Gale, 1997.

Crump, Donald J., ed. *America's Hidden Corners: Places Off the Beaten Path.* National Geographic, 1983. (Also others in series.)

Fodors... Europe's Great Cities. Fodor Travel Publications. 1990. (Also other Fodor's travel guides.)

Harvard Student Agencies. *Let's Go: The Budget Guide to Britain and Ireland.* St. Martin's. (Also other countries in series.)

Heyerdahl, Thor. *Kon-Tiki: Across the Pacific by Raft.* Pocket, 1987.

Hooper, Meredith. *Cleared for Take-Off: International Flight Beyond the Passenger Cabin.* Salem House, 1987.

Huff, Barbara A. *Welcome Aboard! Travelling on an Ocean Liner.* Clarion, 1987.

Jenkins, Peter. *Across China.* Morrow, 1986.

Lampton, Christopher. *Flying Safe?* Watts, 1986.

Lanting, Frans. *Okavango: Africa's Last Eden.* Chronicle, 1993.

McPhee, John A. *Coming into the Country.* Bantam, 1982.

Melchert, John S., ed. *Work, Study, Travel Abroad: The Whole World Handbook.* St. Martin's, 1988.

Milne, Robert. *Opportunities in Travel.* VGM, 1996.

Paradis, Adrian A. *Opportunities in Airline Careers.* VGM, 1996.

Patton, Phil. *Open Road: A Celebration of the American Highway.* Simon & Schuster, 1986.

Plawin, Paul. *Careers for Travel Buffs and Other Restless Types*. VGM, 1992.

Purcell, Ann, and Purcell, Carl. *A Guide to Travel Writing and Photography*. Writer's Digest, 1991.

Shaffer, Carolyn, and Fielder, Erica. *City Safaris*. Sierra, 1987.

Steinbeck, John. *Travels with Charlie*. Penguin, 1987.

Thubron, Colin. *The Lost Heart of Asia*. HarperPerennial, 1994.

Wiencek, Henry. *Virginia and the Capital Region*. Stewart, Tabori & Chang, 1989.

Fiction

Banks, Lynne Reid. *Melusine: A Mystery*. Harper, 1989.

Christie, Agatha. *Murder on the Orient Express*. Putnam, 1985.

Cook, Robin. *Sphinx*. NAL, 1983.

Creech, Sharon. *Walk Two Moons*. HarperCollins, 1994.

Cresswell, Helen. *Bagthorpes Abroad*. Macmillan, 1984.

Danziger, Paula. *Thames Doesn't Rhyme with James*. Putnam, 1994.

Hahn, Mary Downing. *The Spanish Kidnapping Disaster*. Clarion, 1991.

Hobbs, Will. *Changes in Latitude*. Atheneum, 1988.

Holt, Victoria. *The India Fan*. Doubleday, 1988.

Howe, Norma. *Shoot for the Moon*. Crown, 1992.

Johnston, Norma. *The Delphic Choice*. Four Winds, 1989.

_____. *Return to Morocco*. Macmillan, 1988.

Klass, Sheila Solomon. *Breakaway Run*. Dutton, 1985.

Lehrer, Jim. *Kick the Can*. Putnam, 1988.

L'Engle, Madeleine. *Troubling a Star*. Farrar, 1994.

Llewellyn, Caroline. *The Lady of the Labyrinth*. Scribner, 1990.

McBain, Ed. *Downtown*. Morrow, 1991.

McCrumb, Sharyn. *Missing Susan*. Ballantine, 1991.

MacLeod, Charlotte. *The Gladstone Bag*. Mysterious, 1989.

Merino, Jose Maria. *The Gold of Dreams*. Farrar, 1992.

Myers, Walter Dean. *Adventure in Granada*. Penguin, 1985.

_____. *Somewhere in the Darkness*. Scholastic, 1992.

Neville, Emily Cheney. *The China Year*. HarperCollins, 1991.

Paulsen, Gary. *The Car*. Harcourt, 1994.

Peck, Richard. *Those Summer Girls I Never Met*. Delacorte, 1988.

Roberts, Willo Davis. *What Could Go Wrong?* Atheneum, 1989.

Smith, Julie. *Tourist Trap*. Mysterious, 1986.

Stevenson, William. *The Bushbabies*. Peter Smith, 1984.

Wersba, Barbara. *The Best Place to Live Is the Ceiling*. Harper, 1990.

Periodicals

The Learning Traveler. Institute of International Education.

National Geographic Traveler. National Geographic Society.

Student Traveler. Student Traveler.

Travel-Holiday. Travel Magazine, Inc.

World Magazine. Hyde Park Publications.

Feature-Length Films

Death on the Nile. HBO, 1978. (PG)
Harry and Tonto. CBS/Fox, 1974. (PG)
If It's Tuesday, It Must Be Belgium. MGM/UA, 1969. (G)
Lost in America. Warner, 1985. (R)
National Lampoon's European Vacation. Warner, 1983. (PG-13)
Travels with My Aunt. MGM/UA, 1972. (PG)

Computer Software

AAA Trip Planner. Compton's NewMedia, 1994.
America Alive GUIDisc. CD Technology, annual. (Also *Europe Alive GUIDisc.*)
Famous Places. Jasmine Multimedia Publishing, 1992.
Key Action Traveler. SoftKey International, 1994.
Let's Go: 1993 Budget Guide to Europe. Compton's NewMedia, 1994.
Map 'N Go. Delorme Mapping Systems, 1994.

47

Teens on TV

Kids today watch a lot of TV, but how much do you really know about television? At the library, you can find books about TV production, the history of television, the TV industry, famous personalities, classic shows, novelizations and films based on TV shows, and more. You can also participate in activities that will let you express your opinions about TV shows and issues, learn more about television equipment, and maybe even appear on TV! So turn on the library for Teens on TV.

Display Idea

Choose nonfiction books about the history of television, TV production, popular TV shows and personalities, TV scripts and other related topics. Shelve these with novelizations of TV shows, fiction with TV in the plot, videos of classic TV shows and movies based on shows, and CDs of TV soundtrack music. Add copies of *TV Guide* and cable TV listings, posters of TV shows, and other props to enliven the display.

Sponsorship for Prizes

1. Ask a video rental store to donate free rental certificates for classic TV shows or movies based on TV shows.

2. Ask a novelty or department store to donate T-shirts, posters, or other novelty items with TV show images on them.

3. Ask a bookstore to donate TV-related fiction or nonfiction.

4. Ask a magazine store to donate issues of TV magazines.

Program Game

Duplicate a list of your local cable TV channels, including pay TV options, or get a list of various channels from *TV Guide*. For each point earned, highlight one channel on the list. Points can be earned for completing the activities mentioned in the General Guidelines, and for:

1. Reading a novel with a TV plot or a novelization of a TV show and completing a TV Fiction Book Review Form.

2. Reading a novel not related to the TV theme and completing a Fiction Book Review Form.

3. Reading a nonfiction book related to the TV theme and completing a TV Nonfiction Book Review Form.

4. Reading a nonfiction book not related to the TV theme and completing a Nonfiction Book Review Form.

Program Forms

1. TV Fiction Book Review Form
Title:
Author:
Publisher and date:
Brief summary of plot:
What was the best part of this book and why?
Would you recommend this book to a friend? Why or why not?
2. Fiction Book Review Form
Title
Author:
Publisher and date:
I would rate this book: "The best show ever," "Best in the current lineup," "An OK show," "One of the dumbest shows ever created," "They should have scrapped the pilot."
3. TV Nonfiction Book Review Form
Title:
Author:
Publisher and date:
Brief description of information:
What was the most interesting part of this book and why?
Would you like to read more books on this topic? Why or why not?
4. Nonfiction Book Review Form
Title:
Author:
Publisher and date:
Brief description of information:
I would rate this book: "An outstanding broadcast," "High-quality images," "Comes in clearly," "Reception fuzzy," "Nothing but static."

Program Activities

1. Big Screen TV. Let teens view a movie about the TV industry, such as *Quiz Show*.
2. The Rate Stuff. Devise a form for patrons to use to determine how much time they spend watching TV, and the shows that they watch. Ask teens to fill in the required information during one week as they watch their favorite shows. Then have some volunteers tabulate, print and distribute the results of the survey. Participants can then hold a discussion about their TV viewing habits.
3. Emmys. Teens can vote for their favorite TV shows and actors in categories similar to those used in the Emmy Awards. You can also add categories such as Best-Dressed Female and Coolest Teen Guy on TV, or "bad" awards, such as Stupidest Prime Time Character and Worst Cartoon Show.
4. Studio Tour. Arrange to take teens on a field trip to a local television studio. Have a station representative lead a tour and explain how a TV show is produced. Perhaps teens can sit in

the studio audience of a show that is being taped. If your library has access to a local TV station or closed-circuit TV, perhaps teens can have a chance to work with some of the equipment.

5. Pilot Projects. Divide teens into small groups and ask them to come up with an idea for a new TV show. They should decide on program format (sitcom, science fiction, soap opera, etc.), time length (hour or half-hour), when and where it takes place, intended audience, program concept, and a name for the show. They should also write descriptions of the main characters and a sample plot. They can suggest actors to play the roles, if they want. Each team can present its idea to the entire group. Or, write on slips of paper several types of TV program formats, settings and character types. Let each group choose a paper from each category. Teens should then create a program concept, title, and plot sample using this information.

6. TV Game Show. Conduct a TV trivia game show in which young adults can participate. Categories can include Classic TV Sitcoms, Saturday Morning Cartoons, Spy and Police Shows, TV Theme Songs, Game Shows, and Soap Opera Characters. If possible, videotape the show and let teens watch it on TV.

7. Future TV. Challenge patrons to think about what TV might be like in the future. What features and options would be available? How would it be accessed? What would TVs look like? Sponsor a future TV contest in which teens might submit a scale model or detailed drawing of their concepts of the ultimate television of the future. Each special feature must be explained on a separate sheet of paper. Display these creations and let patrons vote for their favorite design.

8. TV or Not TV. Many people have very strong opinions about television's influence on people—especially youngsters. Some arguments are that TV is full of sex and violence, that children who watch too much TV develop short attention spans, or that there is too much advertising on TV. Choose one controversial topic and invite people in the community to discuss the issue in a talk-show format in front of an audience. Or, ask teens to discuss a topic of their choice.

9. TV Guidance. Describe several television-related careers during this library program. Include jobs such as script-writer, director, producer, actor, production manager, art director, costume designer, set designer, composer, musician, news reporter, camera operator, sound or lighting technician, talk show host, technical director, announcer, talent agent, advertising sales person, cable TV installer, marketing representative, TV repair person and many more. List some colleges and technical schools that offer majors in these fields, and gather books about these topics for patrons to check out.

10. On the Air. Give teens an opportunity to produce their own TV news show. Select YAs to read local and world news, sports, weather, and entertainment news taken from short newspaper articles in the local papers or *USA Today*. Seat newscasters with their scripts behind a long table in a well-lit area and let them practice reading their news aloud. If the library does not own a camcorder, chances are that one of your patrons has one that you can borrow. Appoint one person to videotape the news show. Write down the sequence of speakers so the camera person will be able to focus on the correct reporter. After the program has been taped, everyone can watch it on TV. You can also have teens create their own commercials or short skits to videotape and watch.

Curriculum Tie-Ins

1. English Literature/Composition. Let students read several TV show scripts. Review the format used and remind the class that timing is very important; several minutes must be allowed for commercials. Then have students choose a current TV show and write a script for one episode, using the same format as the show uses.

2. Science. During a unit on electronics, explain how some pieces of television equipment (microphones, TV sets, etc.) work. If you have access to control room equipment, you can demonstrate how scenes are spliced together, sound is added, special effects are created, and titles (or credits) are made. You can also discuss how television signals are broadcast.

3. History/Geography. Students can trace the history of television. What are some important scientific experiments that led to the invention of television, and when and where did they occur? Discuss the rise of the major commercial networks. How have pay TV and recent technological advances changed the TV industry?

4. Math. The A.C. Nielsen Company rates the percentage of TV homes that are tuned to TV programs to determine which shows are the most popular. Explain to the class how the TV rating system works. Create several math problems that require students to draw up rating charts for some TV shows.

Activity Sheet Ideas

1. Word search or crossword puzzles of: a) types of television programs, b) TV production terms, or c) TV equipment.

2. Word scrambles or cryptograms of names of: a) popular TV shows, b) TV advertising jingles, or c) important historical events that were broadcast on TV.

3. Matching activities: match a) names of characters to their TV shows, b) current TV shows to their network affiliates, or c) actors to the TV roles they played.

Suggested Resources

Reference and Nonfiction

Bielak, Mark. *Television Production Today.* NTC, 1995.
Bishop, John. *Making It in Video.* McGraw, 1988.
Cader, Michael. *Saturday Night Live: The First Twenty Years.* Cader, 1994.
Castleman, Harry, and Podrazik, Walter. *Five-Hundred-Five Television Questions Your Friends Can't Answer.* Walker, 1983.
Chancellor, John, and Mears, Walter R. *The New News Business.* HarperPerennial, 1995.
Day, Nancy. *Sensational TV: Trash or Journalism?* Enslow, 1995.
Ellerbee, Linda. *Move On: Adventures in the Real World.* Putnam, 1991.
Fridel, Squire. *Acting in Television Commercials for Fun and Profit.* Harmony, 1987.
Genge, N.E. *The Unofficial X-Files Companion.* Crown, 1995.
Gitlin, Todd, ed. *Watching Television: A Pantheon Guide to Popular Culture.* Pantheon, 1987.
Goldberg, Robert, and Gerald, Jay. *Anchors: Brokaw, Jennings, and Rather and the Evening News.* Carol, 1990.
Herbert, Katherine Atwell. *Writing Scripts Hollywood Will Love: An Insider's Guide to Film and Television Scripts That Sell.* Allworth, 1994.
Hewitt, Don. *Minute by Minute.* Random, 1985.
Javna, John. *Cult TV: A Viewer's Guide to the Shows America Can't Live Without!* St. Martin's, 1985.

Jensen, Carl. *Censored: The News That Didn't Make the News—and Why: The 1994 Project Censored Yearbook.* Four Walls Eight Windows, 1994.

Kisseloff, Jeff. *The Box: An Oral History of Television 1920-61.* Viking, 1996.

Kronenwetter, Michael. *Free Press Vs. Fair Trial: Television and Other Media in the Courtroom.* Watts, 1986.

Leshay, Jeff. *How to Launch Your Career in TV News.* VGM, 1993.

MacDonald, J. Fred. *One Nation Under Television: The Rise and Decline of Network TV.* Pantheon, 1990.

Maltin, Leonard. *Leonard Maltin's TV Movies and Video Guide.* NAL, annual.

Markoe, Merrill, ed. *Late Night with David Letterman: The Book.* Random, 1985.

Montgomery, Kathryn C. *Target: Prime Time: Advocacy Groups and Entertainment.* Oxford University Press, 1989.

O'Nell, Michael J. *The Roar of the Crowd: How Television and People Power Are Changing the World.* Time, 1993.

Ritchie, L. Carol, ed. *My First Year in Television.* Walker, 1995. (Also *Please Stand By: A Prehistory of Television.*)

Sautter, Carl. *How to Sell Your Screenplay: The Real Rules of Film and Television.* New Chapter, 1992.

Shaw, Diana. *Gone Hollywood.* Little, 1988.

Verna, Tony, and Bode, William T. *Live TV: An Inside Look at Directing and Producing.* Focal, 1986.

Winn, Marie. *The Plug-In Drug: Television, Children, and the Family.* Penguin, 1985. (Also *Unplugging the Plug-In Drug.*)

Winship, Michael. *Television.* Random, 1988.

Fiction

Anderson, Mary. *Tune in Tomorrow.* Avon, 1985.

Andrews, Kristi. *Magic Time.* Bantam, 1987. (Also *Typecast.*)

Angell, Judie. *First the Good News.* Putnam, 1984.

_____. *Suds: A New Daytime Drama.* Bradbury, 1983.

Auch, Mary Jane. *Mom Is Dating Weird Wayne.* Holiday, 1988.

Cadnum, Michael. *Skyscape.* Carrol & Graf, 1994.

Clark, Mary Higgins. *I'll Be Seeing You.* Simon & Schuster, 1993.

Deaver, Julie Reece. *You Bet Your Life: A Novel.* HarperCollins, 1993.

Fraser, Antonia. *The Cavalier Case.* Bantam, 1991.

Goldsmith, Olivia. *Flavor of the Month.* Poseidon, 1993.

Hailey, Arthur. *The Evening News.* Doubleday, 1990.

Hamley, Dennis. *Blood Line.* Trafalgar, 1990.

Hauck, Charlie. *Artistic Differences.* Morrow, 1993.

Kaye, Marilyn. **Video High** series. Z*Fave Books.

Kerr, M.E. *I'll Love You When You're More Like Me.* Harper, 1977.

Kidd, Ronald. *Dunker.* Bantam, 1984.

Leroe, Ellen. *Confessions of a Teenage TV Addict.* Dutton, 1983.

Levinson, Nancy Smiler. *The Ruthie Green Show.* Lodestar, 1985.

McMurty, Ken. *Manhunt.* Bantam, 1992.

Martin, Ann M. *Just a Summer Romance.* Holiday, 1988.

Menick, Jim. *Lingo*. Carroll & Graf, 1991.
Miklowitz, Gloria D. *Love Story, Take Three*. Dell, 1987.
Nixon, Joan Lowery. *Encore*. Bantam, 1990.
Peck, Richard. *Representing Super Doll*. Dell, 1982.
Pfeffer, Susan Beth. *Prime Time*. Putnam, 1985.
Rosen, Richard. *Saturday Night Dead*. Viking, 1988.
Serling, Carol. *Adventures in the Twilight Zone*. DAW, 1995.
Shaw, Diana. *Gone Hollywood: A Carter Colborn Mystery*. Little, 1988.
Wolitzer, Meg. *This Is Your Life*. Crown, 1988.

Periodicals

Broadcasting and Cable. Cahners Publishing Co.
Daytime TV. Sterling's Magazines.
Emmy. Academy of Television Arts and Sciences.
Super Television. Miller Magazines, Inc.
TV Guide. Murdoch Magazines.

Feature-Length Films

Hero. Columbia Tristar, 1992. (PG-13)
King of Comedy. Columbia Tristar, 1982. (PG)
My Favorite Year. MGM/UA, 1982. (PG)
Network. MGM/UA, 1976. (R)
Soapdish. Paramount, 1991. (PG-13)
Tootsie. Columbia Tristar, 1982. (PG)
Quiz Show. Hollywood Pictures, 1994. (PG-13)
Wayne's World. Paramount, 1992. (PG-13)

Computer Software

Broadcast News. Primary Source Media, monthly.
Hullabaloo Volume One: Television's Classic Rock n' Roll Show. MPI Multimedia, 1994.
Nickelodeon Director's Lab. Viacom New Media, 1994.
Saturday Night Live 20th Anniversary Set. Game Tek, 1994.
Star Trek Omnipedia. Simon & Schuster/Prentice-Hall, 1995.

48

Power Up with Video Games

Do video games turn you on? Then you'll find lots of action at the library. Scroll down the nonfiction level to find books about video and computer game technology, game-playing tips and other fascinating reads. Follow a quest through fiction to find great novels. Boost your fun by selecting magazines, music, and movies to screen at home. The password for great times is L-I-B-R-A-R-Y. You will score big points when you Power Up with Video Games.

Display Idea

Set up a collection of nonfiction about the workings of video and computer games, plus books on how to play various games. Novels with virtual reality or video game plots, as well as related magazines, should be added to the display. Showcase some video game equipment, such as a controller and game cartridges, as well as trading cards and posters representing some popular games.

Sponsorship for Prizes

1. Ask a video rental store to donate coupons for free rentals of video games.

2. Ask a department or hobby store to donate discount coupons for video games and equipment.

3. Ask a bookstore to donate books on how to play video games.

4. Ask a magazine store to donate issues of video game magazines.

Program Game

Design the game board in style similar to the layout of a popular video game (see a video game magazine), or devise a layout of your own. Players will progress along the course, encountering bonuses and penalties, with points earned. Points can be earned for completing the activities mentioned in the General Guidelines, and for:

1. Reading a novel and completing a Fiction Book Review Form.

2. Reading a nonfiction book related to video or computer games and completing a Video Games Nonfiction Book Review Form.

3. Reading a nonfiction book not related to the video games theme and completing a Nonfiction Book Review Form.

4. Reading an issue of two different video or computer game magazines (such as *Nintendo Power* and *Gamepro*) and completing a Video Games Magazine Comparison Form.

Program Forms
1. Fiction Book Review Form
Title:
Author:
Publisher and date:
Brief summary of plot:
I would rate this book: "Incredible sound and graphics," "Realistic simulations," "OK animation," "Barely recognizable figures," "Static."
2. Video Games Nonfiction Book Review Form
Title:
Author:
Publisher and date:
Brief description of information:
What do you think is the most valuable information in the book and why?
Would you recommend this book to a friend? Why or why not?
3. Nonfiction Book Review Form
Title:
Author:
Publisher and date:
Brief description of information:
I would rate this book: "Awesome arcade action!" "Exciting game play," "Interesting moves," "Not very challenging," "For beginners only."
4. Video Games Magazine Comparison Form
Magazine #1 and date:
Magazine #2 and date:
How are these magazines similar?
How are they different?
Which do you prefer and why?

Program Activities

1. Big Screen Game. Show teens a movie with a plot that involves a computer or video game, such as *Tron* or *War Games*.

2. Game Gear. Patrons can bring in their own T-shirts and caps for a clothing craft workshop. Supply iron-on transfers of video game–related pictures, assorted letters, and crayons so teens can create their own designs. A staff member should operate the iron or pressing machine.

3. Create Your Own. If teens could create their own video games, what would they come up with? Organize kids into groups according to their interests to devise video games of strategy, role-playing, sports, etc. Supply long sheets of paper, pencils and markers so teens can draw out the game levels and characters and write out the game objective, how to score points, passwords and other information. Groups can share their ideas at the end of the program.

4. D&D RPG. RPGs (role-playing games) are a popular format for video games. Some people consider the RPG *Dungeons and Dragons* the predecessor to this type of video game. Host a *Dungeons and Dragons* party at the library. Teens can bring in their own books and join in the game.

5. Best Games. Allow teens to vote for their favorite video games in this players' poll. They can choose their overall favorite Gameboy game, arcade game, hand-held video game, video console game and computer game. Kids can also vote for several categories within these areas such as Best Graphics and Sound, Best Challenge, Best Play Control, Best Hero, Worst Villain, Best Sports Game, Best Educational Game, Best RPG, etc. Let teens devise the voting form, tabulate votes and name the winners.

6. Video Wiz. Teens can demonstrate their knowledge of video games in this game show program. Categories can include Hero or Villain? (Is the named character a good or bad guy?), Video Muzik (identify which game the audio clue comes from), What's the System? (tell which home system a game can be played on: Sega Genesis, Super NES, Turbo Grafix, etc.), Game Type (educational, simulation, strategy, sports, or RPG), Related Games (games that share characters), or Plots (identify the name of the game after hearing its plot summary). Players can spin a wheel to determine which category of question they will get. On this wheel you can include Game Play Spaces. If a player lands on one on these, he or she must play a hand-held video game and score a certain number of points within 60 seconds to gain bonus points.

7. Tournament. Choose a popular computer game to be the official contest game. Have patrons register to participate, and allow them to play some qualifying games to determine who will be the top finalists. Perhaps, on the day of the tournament finals, you can borrow an LCD monitor so an audience can watch the play. Award a prize to the computer game champion.

8. The Great Debate. Some people disapprove of video games, saying that they are too violent and a waste of time. Others argue that these games are educational and help to improve hand-eye coordination. Arrange for teens to stage a debate on this issue for their peers. Afterwards, patrons can discuss the points that were brought up.

9. This Is Your Video Life. Teens can explore occupations related to video and computer games during a special career day program. Provide information about jobs in computer technology, sales and marketing, magazine and book publishing, game rental, arcade management, game advisory, production of spin-off items, plus jobs in the entertainment industry (if movies and TV shows are based on games), etc. Make a list of colleges that offer computer programming majors to pass out to present future hackers.

10. Convention. Invite some video games experts, such as arcade owners or champion players, to share their tips at a video games convention. Set up booths for teens to exchange game-playing information; trade or sell second-hand games, equipment, video magazines and books; buy trading cards, pins, hats, and other souvenir items; etc. Ask a store that sells video games and equipment to lend some for teens to try out during this program.

Curriculum Tie-Ins

1. English Literature/Composition. Some video and computer games are based on books or movies. For example, *War in Middle Earth* is based on J.R.R. Tolkien's *Lord of the Rings* trilogy. Read a video game summary and the book on which it is based with the class, and discuss how the book was translated into the game. Then have students read a novel and write a paper describing how they would convert it into a video game.

2. Science. Discuss how computer games work, including the inner mechanisms of a computer. Introduce students to some programming basics and explain the binary code. If possible, create some simple computer games with the class.

3. History/Geography. Have the class trace the history of video and computer games. What were some of the first video games? Who invented them, and when? What were other landmark games and developments? Name some companies that pioneered video games and what happened to them. What companies are in the forefront of video game technology today, and where are they located? What is the future of video games?

4. Math. Provide the point system for a popular video game and have students solve math problems based on the action played on various levels of the game. They can add the points gained and subtract points lost, according to the action you describe.

Activity Sheet Ideas

1. Word search or crossword puzzles of: a) video and computer game terms, b) equipment, or c) game manufacturers.

2. Word scrambles or cryptograms of: a) popular games, b) characters, or c) game activities.

3. Matching activities: match a) characters to the games in which they appear, b) games to the system on which they are played, or c) the names of playing levels to their games.

Suggested Resources

Reference and Nonfiction

Barba, Rick. *Computer Adventure Games Secrets*. Prima, 1994.

Clark, James I. *Video Games*. Raintree, 1985.

Cotton, Bob, and Oliver, Richard. *The Cyberspace Lexicon: An Illustrated Dictionary of Terms From Multimedia to Virtual Reality*. Phaedron, 1994.

DeKeles, Jon C., ed. *Video Game Secrets: A Top Secret Guide to One Thousand Tips, Tricks and Codes*. DMS, 1990.

DeMaria, Rusel. *Sega CD Official Game Secrets*. Prima, 1994.

_____. *Super NES Games Secrets*. Prima, 1994.

DeNure, Dennis. *The Age of the Video Athlete*. Video Athlete, 1984.

Dewey, Patrick R. *Interactive Fiction and Adventure Games for Microcomputers: An Annotated Directory, 1988*. Meckler, 1987.

Dungeons & Dragons series. TSR, various editions.

Erlbach, Arlene. *Video Games*. Lerner, 1995.

Galloway, Bruce, ed. *Fantasy Wargaming*. Stein & Day, 1982.

Game Players Encyclopedia of Game Boy Games. GP.

Game Players Encyclopedia of Nintendo Games. GP.

Game Players Encyclopedia of Sega Genesis Games. GP.

Gygax, Gary. *Master of the Game*. Perigee, 1989.

_____. *Unearthed America: A Compendium of New Ideas and New Discoveries for AD&D Game Campaigns*. TSR, 1985.

Harris, Jack C. *Adventure Gaming*. Crestwood, 1993.

Herman, Leonard. *Phoenix: The Fall and Rise of Home Videogames*. Rolenta, 1994.

Krauss, Lawrence Maxwell. *The Physics of Star Trek*. Basic, 1995.

Kurzweil, Raymond. *The Age of Intelligent Machines*. MIT Press, 1990.

Larijani, L. Casey. *The Virtual Reality Primer*. McGraw, 1994.

Lavroff, Nic. *Behind the Scenes at Sega: The Making of a Video Game.* Prima, 1994.

Lockard, Nathan. *The Good, the Bad, and the Bogus: Nathan Lockard's Complete Guide to Video Games.* Adventure, 1994.

Loftus, Geoffrey R., and Loftus, Elizabeth F. *Mind at Play: The Psychology of Video Games.* Basic, 1983.

Pickover, Clifford A. *Mazes for the Mind: Computers and the Unexpected.* St. Martin's, 1992.

Praft, Vernon. *Thinking Machines: The Evolution of Artificial Intelligence.* Basil Blackwell, 1987.

Rovin, Jeff. *How to Win at Nintendo.* Various editions. St. Martin's Paperbacks.

Sandler, Corey. *Ultimate Unauthorized Nintendo Game Boy Strategies.* Bantam, 1990.

Schachtman, Tom, and Shelare, Harriet. *Video Power.* Holt, 1988.

Sheff, David. *Game Over: How Nintendo Zapped an American Industry, Captured Your Dollars, and Enslaved Your Children.* Random, 1993.

_____. *Video Games: A Guide for Savvy Parents.* Random, 1994.

Skurzynski, Gloria. *Know the Score: Video Games in Your High-Tech World.* Bradbury, 1994.

Slouka, Mark. *War of the Worlds: Cyberspace and the High-Tech Assault on Reality.* Basic, 1995.

Sullivan, George. *Screen Play: The Story of Video Games.* Warne, 1983.

Video Game Quest. DMS, 1990.

Fiction

Anthony, Piers. *Demons Don't Dream.* Tom Doherty, 1993.

Bova, Ben. *Death Dream.* Bantam, 1994.

Bowkett, Stephen. *Gameplayers.* Victor Gollancz, 1989.

Cadigan, Pat. *Synners.* Bantam, 1991.

Cooper, Susan. *The Boggart.* Macmillan, 1993.

Cross, Gillian. *New World.* Holiday, 1995.

_____. *A Map of Nowhere.* Holiday, 1989.

Dover, Joe. *Shadow in the Sand.* Berkley, 1986.

Friesner, Esther. *The Sherwood Game.* Baen, 1995.

Gibson, William. *Virtual Light.* Bantam, 1993.

Goldman, E.M. *The Night Room.* Viking, 1995.

Hawks, Robert. *The Richest Kid in the World.* Avon, 1992.

Jaffe, Rona. *Mazes and Monsters.* Delacorte, 1981.

Kritlow, William. *A Race Against Time.* Nelson, 1995.

Mace, Elisabeth. *Under Siege.* Orchard, 1990.

Manes, Stephen. *Video War.* Avon, 1983.

Norman, Roger. *Albion's Dream: A Novel of Terror.* Delacorte, 1992.

Rendal, Justine. *A Very Personal Computer.* HarperCollins, 1995.

Rubinstein, Gillian. *Skymaze.* Orchard, 1991.

_____. *Space Demons.* Dial, 1988.

Skurzynski, Gloria. *Cyberstorm.* Macmillan, 1995.

Sleator, William. *Interstellar Pig.* Dutton, 1984.

Thomson, Amy. *Virtual Girl.* Ace, 1993.

Velde, Vivian Vande. *User Unfriendly.* Harcourt, 1991.

Period icals

Computer Entertainer: The Newsletter. Computer Entertainer.
Computer Gaming World. Golden Empire Publications.
Gamepro. Infotainment World.
Nintendo Power. Nintendo of America.

Feature-Length Film

Brainstorm. MGM/UA, 1983. (PG)
The Double O Kid. Prism Entertainment, 1992. (PG-13)
Mazes and Monsters. Lorimar Home Video, 1982.
Street Fighter. MCA/Universal, 1994. (PG-13)
Tron. Walt Disney, 1982. (PG)
Wargames. CBS/Fox, 1983. (PG)

Computer Software

Best Windows Games. Digital Publishing Co., 1994.
Burn: Cycle. PMEP, 1994.
D/Generation. MacroMedia Europe, 1993.
Video Special Effects Volume 2. Jasmine Multimedia Publishing, 1992.
Virtual Reality. Meckler Media, 1995.
Virtual Variety Show. Scitron & Art.

49
You Can Make a Difference

Have you ever served on a committee, participated in a community project, collected for a charity, helped people in need, or volunteered your services for a worthwhile cause? Well, now is your chance to get involved. Read about what others have done to make the world a better place, and take part in projects sponsored by the library. You'll find that it feels good knowing You Can Make a Difference.

Display Idea

Display books about community service, what teenagers can do to help the planet, biographies of activists and other related nonfiction. Include theme-related fiction, and magazine and newspaper articles about volunteer projects and organizations. A list of local community service groups and photographs of their projects can accompany the display.

Sponsorship for Prizes

Note: Since the purpose of this program is to teach young adults the value of volunteering their time and energy to help others, they will not be receiving any prizes, other than the satisfaction of performing a good deed. Instead, you can ask businesses to sponsor this program by donating items that teens can give to people in need.

1. Ask a supermarket, department store, or bath shop to donate toiletry items.

2. Ask a craft store to donate materials for gift-making projects.

3. Ask a supermarket to donate pastry items for a bake sale, or canned and packaged foods to deliver to a soup kitchen.

4. Ask the local newspaper to donate ad space to publicize the various community service projects with which teens will be involved.

Program Game

Divide a sheet of paper into many small boxes. In each box, write the name of a local or national volunteer organization, charitable cause, environmental group, youth group, community or public service group, etc. For each point earned, patrons can highlight a box on the paper. Points can be earned for completing the activities mentioned in the General Guidelines, and for:

1. Reading a novel and completing a Fiction Book Review Form.

2. Reading a nonfiction book not related to the volunteer theme and completing a Nonfiction Book Review Form.

3. Reading a nonfiction book about volunteering, how teens can make a difference, or another related topic, and completing a Volunteer Nonfiction Book Review Form.

4. Reading a biography about an activist or someone who founded or worked for a volunteer organization and completing a Volunteer Biography Book Review Form.

Program Forms

1. Fiction Book Review Form
Title:
Author:
Publisher and date:
Brief summary of plot:
I would rate this book: "A boundless gift," "Gives generously," "Performs adequate service," "Stingy," "Has absolutely nothing to give."

2. Nonfiction Book Review Form
Title:
Author:
Publisher and date:
Brief description of information:
I would rate this book: "An important contribution," "A good, solid effort," "A help," "Didn't try very hard," "Never even bothered."

3. Volunteer Nonfiction Book Review Form
Title:
Author:
Publisher and date:
Brief description of information:
What was the most interesting part of this book and why?
Did the book make you want to become active in this cause? Why or why not?

4. Volunteer Biography Book Review Form
Title:
Author:
Publisher and date:
Person profiled in the book:
Brief description of information:
What was the most interesting part of the book and why?
Would you want to become active in this person's organization or cause? Why or why not?

Program Activities

1. Inspirational Film. Show a movie of what one or more people or organizations did to help a cause in which they believed. Or, show a video of a fund-raiser, such as Comic Relief.

2. 'Tis More Blessed to Give. Provide materials needed for teens to make gift items which would be given to seniors, children, or whoever is appropriate. Teens can help decide what to make and to whom it can be given. For example, they might make flower corsages to give to senior women on Mother's Day, sock puppets to give to children at Christmas time, etc. Or they can arrange gift baskets of donated food or toiletry items to give to needy families.

3. Senior Services. Let teenagers discuss what they can do to help senior citizens in the community. Make a list of chores, such as mowing the lawn, grocery shopping, walking the dog, getting library books, etc. Invite a person who works with seniors to speak to teens and to arrange for them to provide simple services.

4. Clean-Up Day. Provide garbage bags and supervise teens as they work to clean up litter from the area surrounding your school or library, or from another litter-prone location in your community.

5. Food Services. Teens can collect nonperishable foods to bring to a local food bank. You can also arrange a time for teen volunteers to work at a soup kitchen.

6. Charity Trivia. Select two teams of five trivia-savvy teens to compete in a fund-raising game show. Before the day of the game, each of the ten players must solicit pledges from family and friends, such as ten cents per team game point. Each team must also choose a charity to which they will donate all monies earned during the game. Make up categories for questions that are of interest to teens. Questions should be challenging but not too tricky, since you want both teams to rack up a lot of points so they will be able to donate a good amount of money to their charities.

7. Read-In. Sign up teens to read to young school children (grades K-3). Help YA volunteers choose appropriate books, and go over some storytelling techniques. Depending on your focus, you can also teach teens how to incorporate the use of puppets or flannel boards into their stories. Arrange to have children meet in the library or to bring teens to an elementary school on the day of the program.

8. Fund-Raising. Ask teens to choose one specific charity for which they would like to raise money, and then let them decide on the method of fund-raising. They may choose to hold a bake sale, car wash, rummage sale, or basketball game; collect returnable bottles; sell plants; etc. Offer guidance as needed so they can successfully carry out their plans.

9. Volunteer Careers. Spotlight some community service jobs, paid and unpaid. Include working for private and public organizations such as Habitat for Humanity, the Peace Corps, Big Brothers/Big Sisters, Boy or Girl Scouts, the March of Dimes and other health-related charities, Special Olympics, a homeless shelter, a soup kitchen, an environmental organization, etc. Provide a list a local community groups and skills such as food preparation, event organization, counseling, fund-raising, carpentry, public relations, etc., that may be helpful.

10. Library Aides. There are many ways for teens to volunteer in the library. They can put up bulletin board displays, prepare craft activities, help with the Children's Department summer reading program, etc. If your library plans to hold a book sale, ask teens to help with the preparations and on the day of the sale.

Curriculum Tie-Ins

1. English Literature/Composition. Good publicity is often the key to getting people involved in community service projects. Provide samples of PR news articles, flyers and letters written by several organizations. Discuss with the class which ones are the most effective and why. Then have students write their own PR pieces to publicize public service organizations or other worthwhile causes of their choice.

2. Science. Many charitable organizations devote their energies toward raising money for medical research. Have students make a list of some medical problems and the charities associated with them. Then let students research one medical problem. What are its symptoms? What facts are known about it? What do researchers still have to find out? What advances have already been made?

3. History/Geography. Students can choose a charity, an environmental organization, a community service group, a youth program, or another type of volunteer organization, and research its history. Who founded the group, when and why? Where is it headquartered? What are the group's goals, and what has it accomplished? Who supports the group, and how does it distribute donations?

4. Math. Have students look up statistical information about various charities and draw up charts and graphs of the amounts of money solicited, how it is distributed, etc.

Activity Sheet Ideas

1. Word search or crossword puzzles of: a) charitable causes, b) ways people can volunteer their services, or c) items that can be donated to the needy.

2. Word scramble or cryptograms of: a) community service organizations, b) environmental groups, or c) names of charities.

3. Matching activities: match a) notable people to the charity or service organization with which they are involved, b) organizations to their publicity slogans, or c) service groups and youth organizations to their picture logos.

Suggested Resources

Reference and Nonfiction

Anderson, Walter. *Read with Me.* Houghton, 1990.

Berger, Gilda. *USA for Africa: Rock Aid in the Eighties.* Watts, 1987.

Carroll, Andrew. *Volunteer USA.* Fawcett, 1991.

Casewit, Curtis W. *Summer Adventures.* Macmillan, 1994.

Caywood, Caroline A. *Youth Participation in School and Public Libraries: It Works.* ALA, 1995.

Connors, Tracy D., ed. *Volunteer Management Handbook.* Wiley, 1995.

Duper, Linda L. *160 Ways to Help the World: Community Service Projects for Young People.* Facts on File, 1996.

Ehberts, Marjorie, and Gisler, Margaret. *Careers for Good Samaritans and Other Humanitarian Types.* VGM, 1991.

Ellis, Susan J. *The Volunteer Recruitment Book.* Energize, 1994.

Fiffer, Steve, and Fiffer, Sharon. *Fifty Simple Ways to Help Your Community.* Doubleday, 1994.

Flanagan, Joan. *The Successful Volunteer Organization: Getting Started and Getting Results in Nonprofit, Charitable, Grass Roots, and Community Groups.* Contemporary, 1981.

Freedman, Marc. *The Kindness of Strangers: Adult Mentors, Urban Youth, and the New Voluntarism.* Jossey-Bass, 1993.

Garr, Robin. *Reinvesting in America: The Grassroots Movements That Are Feeding the Hungry, Housing the Homeless, and Putting Americans Back to Work.* Addison-Wesley, 1995.

Gilbert, Sara. *Lend a Hand: The How, Where, and Why of Volunteering.* Morrow, 1988.

Gurin, Maurice G. *What Volunteers Should Know for Successful Fund Raising.* Stein and Day, 1981.

Henderson, Kathy. *What Would We Do Without You? A Guide to Volunteer Activities for Kids.* Betterway, 1990.

Hollender, Jeffrey, and Catling, Linda. *How to Make the World a Better Place: 116 Ways You Can Make a Difference.* Norton, 1995.

Jampolsky, Gerald G. *One Person Can Make a Difference: Ordinary People Doing Extraordinary Things.* Bantam, 1990.

Lewis, Barbara A. *The Kid's Guide to Service Projects.* Free Spirit, 1995.

Logan, Suzanne. *Kids Can Help.* Perigee, 1992.

Luks, Allan. *The Healing Power of Doing Good: The Health and Spiritual Benefits of Helping Others.* Fawcett, 1992.

McMillon, Bill. *Volunteer Vacations: Short Term Adventures That Will Benefit You and Others.* Chicago Review, 1995.

Meltzer, Milton. *Who Cares? Millions Do....* Walker, 1994.

Paradis, Lex. *Careers for Caring People and Other Sensitive Types.* VGM, 1995.

Real People Working in Service Businesses. VGM, 1996.

Redmon, Coates. *Come As You Are: The Peace Corps Story.* Harcourt, 1986.

Salzman, Marian, and Reisgies, Theresa. *150 Ways Teens Can Make a Difference.* Peterson's Guides, 1991.

Volunteerism: The Directory of Organizations, Training, Programs, and Publications. Bowker, annual.

Wolfe, Joan. *Making Things Happen: How to Be an Effective Volunteer.* Island, 1991.

Wroblewski, Celeste J. *The Seven Rs of Volunteer Development: A YMCA Resource Kit.* Human Kinetics, 1994.

Wyant, Susan, and Brooks, Phyllis. *The Changing Role of Volunteerism.* United Hospital Fund, 1993.

Fiction

Banks, River. *Snow on the Carpet.* Magic Bullet, 1994.

Bond, Nancy. *The Best of Enemies.* Macmillan, 1978.

Colman, Hila. *Rich and Famous Like My Mom.* Crown, 1988.

Derby, Pat. *Visiting Miss Pierce.* Farrar, 1986.

Erdman, Marian W. *The Coming of Jan.* Erdman Associates, 1991.

Fleischman, Paul. *A Fate Totally Worse Than Death.* Candlewick, 1995.

Holl, Kristi. *Just Like a Real Family.* Atheneum, 1983.

Hopper, Nancy J. *The Interrupted Education of Huey B.* Dutton, 1991.

Kehret, Peg. *Cages.* Dutton, 1991.

McDaniel, Lurlene. *Now I Lay Me Down to Sleep.* Bantam, 1991.

McHargue, Georgess. *See You Later, Crocodile.* Delacorte, 1988.

MacLeod, Charlotte. *The Gladstone Bag.* Mysterious, 1989.

Major, Kevin. *Dear Bruce Springsteen.* Delacorte, 1988.

Meyer, Carolyn. *Because of Lissa.* Bantam, 1990.

_____. *Elliot and Win.* Macmillan, 1986.

_____. *The Two Faces of Adam.* Bantam, 1991.

Miklowitz, Gloria D. *Close to the Edge.* Delacorte, 1983.

Myers, Walter Dean. *Won't Know Till I Get There.* Viking, 1982.

Neufield, John. *Almost a Hero.* Atheneum, 1995.

Pfeffer, Susan Beth. *Thea at Sixteen.* Bantam, 1988.

Quin-Harkin, Janet. *One Step Too Far.* Ivy, 1989.

Raymond, Linda. *Rocking the Babies*. Viking, 1994.
Ryan, Mary C. *Frankie's Run*. Little, 1987.
Sauer, Jim. *Hank*. Delacorte, 1990.
Tamar, Erika. *The Truth About Kin O'Hara*. Atheneum, 1992.
Wojciechowski, Susan. *Patty Dillman of Hot Dog Fame*. Orchard, 1989.
Zindel, Paul. *A Begonia for Miss Applebaum*. Harper, 1989.

Periodicals

Care World Report. Care, Inc.
Monday Developments. Interaction.
National Service Newsletter. National Service Secretariat, Inc.
Peer Counselor Journal. Peer Resources.
Volunteering. National Volunteer Center.

Feature-Length Films

Best of Comic Relief '90. Rhino Home Video, 1990.
M.A.D.D.: Mothers Against Drunken Driving. MCA/Universal, 1983.
Major Barbara. Learning Corporation of America, 1941.
Samaritan: The Mitch Snyder Story. Fries Home Video, 1986.
The Slender Thread. Paramount, 1965.
Volunteers. HBO, 1985. (R)

Computer Software

American Heroes. PMEP.
Career Opportunities. Quanta Press, 1991.
Discovering Endangered Wildlife. Lyriq International Corp., 1995.
Earthquakes: Be Prepared. Cambrix Publishing, 1994.
Ecodisc CD-ROM. ESM, 1990.
Lifesaver 2.0. Media Design Interactive, 1991.

50
Do It, Write!

Of course, you go to the library to read. But did you know that the library is also a place where you can go to write? We have shelves of books and magazines to help you improve your writing skills and inspire you to generate your own great story ideas. Think about it: every book you read, song you hear, and movie you see had to be *written* first! Publishers and producers are always looking for talented authors, and the library can help you get started. So come in and let us help you to Do It, Write!

Display Idea

Set up a display of nonfiction books and magazines about writing, publishing and word processing, as well as novels with writing themes. Include books and short stories that have won writing awards such as the Newbery, Nebula, or Pulitzer. Display films, biographies and plays about writers, along with some basic writing supplies—paper, pens, a thesaurus, a wastepaper basket (with crumpled-up paper), a chart of proofreaders' marks, etc.

Sponsorship for Prizes

1. Ask a bookstore to donate books about writing, biographies of writers, or award-winning books.
2. Ask a stationery store to donate writing pads, blank books, pens and other writing supplies.
3. Ask a newsstand to donate magazines for writers.
4. Ask a computer store to donate discount coupons for word processing or home publishing software.

Program Game

Make up a game board for the Great American Novel Game. Start at "An author has an idea for a book" and continue with spaces that note the process of writing, submitting, editing and publishing a book. The last space can be "Rave reviews!" Patrons can advance one space along the game board for each point earned. Points can be earned for completing the activities mentioned in the General Guidelines, and for:
1. Reading a novel and completing a Fiction Book Review Form.
2. Reading a nonfiction book related to the writing theme and completing a Writing Nonfiction Book Review Form.

3. Reading a nonfiction book not related to the writing theme and completing a Nonfiction Book Review Form.

4. Reading a biographical article about a writer or a feature-length critic's review of a book and completing a Critic's Review Form.

Program Forms

1. Fiction Book Review Form
Title:
Author:
Publisher and date:
Brief summary of plot:
I would rate this book: "On my Best-of-the-Best list," "A Critic's Choice," "A good read," "A supplemental selection," "Avoid this book."

2. Writing Nonfiction Book Review Form
Title:
Author:
Publisher and date:
Brief description of information:
Name one interesting fact you learned from reading this book:
Do you think this book would be useful to you as a writer? Why or why not?

3. Nonfiction Book Review Form
Title:
Author:
Publisher and date:
Brief description of information:
I would rate this book: "Offer the author a big advance on his next book," "Order another print run," "Not bad, but don't rush to reprint," "Copies are collecting dust in the warehouse," "Destroy all unsold books."

4. Critic's Review Form
Name of article:
Author:
Source and date:
Brief summary of information:
Would you choose to read this book, or a book by this author, based on this article? Why or why not?

Program Activities

1. Writers on Stage and Screen. Plays such as *The Belle of Amherst* or *Tru* give insights into the lives of writers. Ask for teen volunteers to perform dramatic readings of excerpts from plays about writers or writing. Then show a movie about a writer, such as *Shadowlands*.

2. Fancy Writing. Supply pens and ink, and hold a workshop on calligraphy. Show teens different types of script and let them practice writing their names, lettering signs, copying famous quotes, making out invitations, etc.

3. **Author Visit.** Invite a writer to speak to teens about his or her work. Allow time for him or her to answer questions from the audience. Arrange to sell copies of the author's books, which he or she can autograph for patrons.

4. **Popular Books.** Ask young adult patrons to name a book they wish they had written and briefly tell why. Have them categorize books by genre. Publish this list of books and authors for patrons to take home.

5. **You Are What You Write.** Many people believe that a person's handwriting reveals something about his or her personality. Invite a handwriting analysis expert to explain basic writing characteristics and discuss handwriting samples. Prepare a bibliography of books on this subject for your patrons.

6. **The How to Write Right Game.** Divide patrons into teams. Ask questions as you would in a Spelling Bee format, eliminating people with incorrect answers until only one person is left. Questions can be about grammar rules, which homonym to use in a particular context, capitalization, punctuation, or any other facet of proper writing. Humorous examples, such as writing bloopers, make this game fun and illustrate how bad writing can sound foolish or result in unintended meanings. Stress that it is important to write correctly in order to communicate your message clearly.

7. **State-of-the-Art Writing.** Several computer software programs are available to writers. Invite a computer expert to discuss some programs that are currently on the market for word processing, designing graphics, publishing newsletters, writing resumes, etc.

8. **Publish What You Write.** Ask teens to write reviews, short stories, articles, puzzles and poems for a YA magazine to be published by the library. You may also want young adults to help select items for publication, edit, and plan the layout. Provide information on magazines that publish materials written by teens and encourage them to submit their work.

9. **The Writing Life.** Hold a career day to let young adults know about writing-related jobs, such as novelist, journalist, sports columnist, editor, publisher, writer's agent, indexer, proofreader, typesetter, printer, screenwriter, dramatist, sales representative, writing software developer, etc. Have information available on the different genres of writing, plus various writers' markets, including poetry, educational, children's, short story, magazine fiction and nonfiction, music, editorial, songwriting, business, technical, etc. Make a list of professional organizations, correspondence schools, and local courses offered to writers.

10. **Novel Costumes.** Invite teens to a costume party where they must dress as characters from their favorite novels. Encourage them to talk and act like their fictional counterparts. Then let partygoers try to guess each other's identities, and the books from which they came.

Curriculum Tie-Ins

1. **English Literature/Composition.** Have students choose a particular genre or style of writing and analyze its characteristic features. Who are some of the masters of that form of writing, and what makes them successful? Have students write a short fiction or nonfiction piece that incorporates those elements. Also, it is a good habit for students to keep journals and write daily entries.

2. **Science.** What technology is involved in publishing? Study machines that print newspapers, books and magazines. How are photos and color added? How are the pages of a book cut, gathered and bound? How is paper made?

3. **History/Geography.** Explore the history of writing. What were the first civilizations to create an alphabet, where did they live, and what language did they speak? Create a

timeline that includes the use of hieroglyphics, the development of various alphabets, the invention of paper and other writing surfaces, types of writing implements, modern writing technology, etc. Note where in the world these events occurred.

4. Math. Look at some New York Times Best Seller lists for fiction and nonfiction. Choose ten books when they first make the list. Follow these books each week, keeping a graph of their sales, until they fall off the list. How many copies of each book were sold? Over how many weeks? At approximately 10 percent royalties, how much money did the authors make on their books during this time?

Activity Sheet Ideas

1. Word search or crossword puzzles of: a) publishing terms, b) fiction genres or nonfiction categories, or c) occupations for writers.

2. Word scrambles or cryptograms of: a) famous writers, b) publishers, or c) magazine titles.

3. Matching activities: match a) award-winning books to their authors, awards, and years they won, b) authors to their book series, or c) writers' pseudonyms to their real names.

Suggested Resources

Reference and Nonfiction

Bauer, Marion Dane. *What's Your Story? A Young Person's Guide to Writing Fiction.* Clarion, 1992. (Also *A Writer's Story: from Life to Fiction.*)

Bough, L. Sue. *How to Write Term Papers and Reports.* NTC Business, 1992.

Bly, Bob. *Careers for Writers and Others Who Have a Way with Words.* VGM, 1995.

Carter, Robert A. *Opportunities in Book Publishing.* VGM, 1987.

Dear Author: Students Write About the Books That Changed Their Lives. Publishers Group West, 1995.

Everhart, Nancy. *How to Write a Term Paper.* Watts, 1995.

Faber, Doris, and Faber, Harold. *Great Lives: American Literature.* Atheneum, 1995.

Feehan, Patricia E., and Barron, Pamela Petrick, eds. *Writers on Writing for Young Adults: Exploring the Authors, the Genre, the Readers, the Issues, and the Critics of Young Adult Literature.* Omnigraphics, 1991.

Garvey, Mark, ed. *Writer's Market.* Writer's Digest, annual. (Also other Writer's Digest publications.)

Goldberg, Jan. *Careers in Journalism.* VGM, 1995.

Grant, Janet. *The Young Person's Guide to Becoming a Writer.* Free Spirit, 1995.

Harris, David. *The Art of Calligraphy: A Practical Guide to the Skills and Techniques.* DK, 1995.

Henderson, Kathy. *Market Guide for Young Writers.* Writer's Digest, 1996.

Janeczko, Paul B. *Poetry from A to Z: A Guide for Young Writers.* Bradbury, 1994.

Krull, Kathleen. *Lives of the Writers: Comedies, Tragedies (and What the Neighbors Thought).* Harcourt, 1994.

Kulpa, Kathryn, ed. *Something Like a Hero.* Merlyn's Pen, 1995.

Lederer, Richard, and Dowis, Richard. *The Write Way S.P.E.L.L. Guide to Real-Life Writing*. Pocket, 1995.

Lourie, Dick, et al. *Smart Like Me: High School-Age Writing from the Sixties to Now*. Hanging Loose, 1989.

Lydon, Michael. *Writing and Life*. University Press of New England, 1995.

Means, Beth, and Lindner, Lindy. *Everything You Needed to Learn About Writing in High School—But a) You Were in Love, b) You Have Forgotten, c) You Fell Asleep, d) They Didn't Tell You, e) All of the Above*. Libraries Unlimited, 1989.

Newlove, Donald. *Invented Voices: Inspired Dialogue for Writers and Readers*. Holt, 1993. (Also *Painted Paragraphs: Inspired Description for Writers and Readers*.)

Otfinoski, Stephen. *Putting It in Writing*. Scholastic, 1993.

Rhodes, Richard. *How to Write: Advice and Reflections*. Morrow, 1995.

Rice, Scott. *It was a Dark and Stormy Night: The Best (?) from the Bulwer-Lytton Contest*. Penguin, 1984.

Sears, Peter. *Gonna Bake Me a Poem: A Student Guide to Writing Poetry*. Scholastic, 1990.

Selditich, Dianne, ed. *My First Year as a Journalist*. Walker, 1995.

Stanek, Lou Willet. *Thinking Like a Writer*. Random, 1994.

Stillman, Peter R. *Write Away! A Friendly Guide for Teenage Writers*. Heineman, 1995.

Tebbel, John. *Opportunities in Newspaper Publishing*. VGM, 1989.

Willis, Meredith Sue. *Blazing Pencils: A Guide to Writing Fiction and Essays*. Teachers and Writers Collaborative, 1990.

Words of Love: A Collection of Winning Short Stories, Essays, and Poems by America's Young Writers. Seven Wolves, 1992.

Fiction

Bunin, Sherry. *Dear American Writers School*. Houghton, 1995.

Cameron, Eleanor. *The Private Worlds of Julia Redfern*. Dutton, 1988.

Christian, Mary Blount. *Growin' Pains*. Macmillan, 1985.

Cormier, Robert. *Fade*. Delacorte, 1988.

Cushman, Karen. *Catherine, Called Birdie*. Clarion, 1994.

Davis, Terry. *If Rock and Roll Were a Machine*. Delacorte, 1992.

Facklam, Margery. *The Trouble with Mothers*. Clarion, 1989.

Francis, Dick. *Longshot*. Putnam, 1990.

Grove, Vicki. *Good-bye, My Wishing Star*. Putnam, 1988.

Guy, Rosa. *The Ups and Downs of Carl Davis III*. Delacorte, 1989.

Haven, Susan. *Is It Them or Me?* Putnam, 1990.

Hesse, Karen. *Letters from Rifke*. Holt, 1992.

Hinton, S.E. *Taming the Star Runner*. Delacorte, 1988.

Koertge, Ronald. *The Harmony Arms*. Joy Street, 1992.

Lyons, Mary E. *Letters from a Slave Girl: The Story of Harriet Jacobs*. Scribner, 1992.

Malmgren, Dallin. *The Ninth Issue*. Doubleday, 1989.

Mazer, Harry, and Mazer, Norma Fox. *Bright Days, Stupid Nights*. Bantam, 1992.

Montgomery, Lucy Maud. *Emily of the New Moon*. Bantam, 1986.

Peters, Elizabeth. *Naked Once More*. Warner, 1989.

Pfeffer, Susan Beth. *Dear Dad, Love Laurie*. 1989.

Pike, Christopher. *Master of Murder*. Archway, 1992.

Pinkwater, Jill. *Buffalo Brenda*. Macmillan, 1989.
Riley, Judith Merkle. *A Vision of Light*. Delacorte, 1989.
Snyder, Zilpha Keatly. *Libby on Wednesday*. Delacorte, 1990.
Sonnenmark, Laura A. *Something's Rotten in the State of Maryland*. Scholastic, 1990.
Terris, Susan. *Author! Author!* Farrar, 1990.
Van Raven, Pieter. *The Great Man's Secret*. Scribner, 1989.
Westlake, Donald E. *Trust Me on This*. Mysterious, 1988.
Wood, Marcia. *The Search for Jim McGwynn*. Macmillan, 1989.
Zindel, Paul. *David and Della: A Novel*. HarperCollins, 1993.

Periodicals

Merlyn's Pen. Merlyn's Pen, Inc.
Quill and Scroll. University of Iowa, School of Journalism and Mass Communication.
The Writer. The Writer, Inc.
Writer's Digest. F & W Publications.
Writing. Curriculum Innovations.
Young Author's Magazine (YAM). Theraplan, Inc.

Feature-Length Films

Author! Author! CBS/Fox, 1982. (PG)
The Front. Columbia Tristar, 1976. (PG)
Romancing the Stone. CBS/Fox, 1984. (PG)
Shadowlands. HBO, 1994. (PG)
The Year of Living Dangerously. MGM/UA, 1982. (PG)

Computer Software

Junior DISCovering Authors. Gale Research, tri-annual.
Masterplots Fiction CD-ROM. Salem Press, 1994.
Microsoft Creative Writer. Microsoft, 1994.
Microsoft Publisher. Microsoft, 1994.
Student Writing Center. Learning Company, 1994.
You Be the Reporter. Educational Activities, 1994.

Bibliography

The following resources provide much useful information about the needs of young adults and many valuable suggestions for serving those needs.

Bridging the Gap: Young Adult Services in the library. Missouri Library Association, 1992.

Carnegie Council on Adolescent Development, Task Force on Youth Development and Community Programs. *A Matter of Time: Risk and Opportunities in the Nonschool Hours.* Carnegie Corporation, 1992.

Chelton, Mary K., and Rosinia, James M. *Bare Bones: Young Adult Services Tips for Public Library Generalists.* PLA and YALSA/ALA, 1993.

Directions for Library Service to Young Adults. YALSA/ALA, 1993.

Jones, Patrick. *Connecting Young Adults and Libraries: A How-to-Do-It Manual.* Neal-Schuman, 1992.

Lefstein, Leah M., and Lipsitz, Joan. *3:00 to 6:00 PM: Programs for Young Adolescents.* Center for Early Adolescence, University of North Carolina at Chapel Hill, 1986.

National Center for Education Statistics. *Services and Resources for Children and Young Adults in Public Libraries.* U.S. Department of Education, Office of Educational Research and Improvement, 1995.

VOYA (Voice of Youth Advocates). Magazine published quarterly by Scarecrow Press, Inc. (Metuchen, N.J.).

Weisner, Stan. *Information Is Empowering: Developing Public Library Services for Youth at Risk.* Bay Area Library and Information System (San Francisco), 1992.

Youth Participation in School and Public Libraries: It Works. YALSA/ALA, 1995.

Index